AF782820

NATO ASI Series

Advanced Science Institutes Series

A series presenting the results of activities sponsored by the NATO Science Committee, which aims at the dissemination of advanced scientific and technological knowledge, with a view to strengthening links between scientific communities.

The Series is published by an international board of publishers in conjunction with the NATO Scientific Affairs Division

A Life Sciences **B Physics**	Plenum Publishing Corporation London and New York
C Mathematical and Physical Sciences **D Behavioural and Social Sciences** **E Applied Sciences**	Kluwer Academic Publishers Dordrecht, Boston and London
F Computer and Systems Sciences **G Ecological Sciences** **H Cell Biology** **I Global Environmental Change**	Springer-Verlag Berlin Heidelberg New York London Paris Tokyo Hong Kong Barcelona Budapest

NATO-PCO DATABASE

The electronic index to the NATO ASI Series provides full bibliographical references (with keywords and/or abstracts) to more than 30000 contributions from international scientists published in all sections of the NATO ASI Series. Access to the NATO-PCO DATABASE compiled by the NATO Publication Coordination Office is possible in two ways:

- via online FILE 128 (NATO-PCO DATABASE) hosted by ESRIN, Via Galileo Galilei, I-00044 Frascati, Italy.
- via CD-ROM "NATO-PCO DATABASE" with user-friendly retrieval software in English, French and German (© WTV GmbH and DATAWARE Technologies Inc. 1989).

The CD-ROM can be ordered through any member of the Board of Publishers or through NATO-PCO, Overijse, Belgium.

Series F: Computer and Systems Sciences Vol. 91

The ASI Series Books Published as a Result of Activities of the Special Programme on ADVANCED EDUCATIONAL TECHNOLOGY

This book contains the proceedings of a NATO Advanced Research Workshop held within the activities of the NATO Special Programme on Advanced Educational Technology, running from 1988 to 1993 under the auspices of the NATO Science Committee.

The books published so far as a result of the activities of the Special Programme are:

Vol. F 67: Designing Hypermedia for Learning. Edited by D. H. Jonassen and H. Mandl. 1990.

Vol. F 76: Multimedia Interface Design in Education. Edited by A. D. N. Edwards and S. Holland. 1992.

Vol. F 78: Integrating Advanced Technology into Technology Education. Edited by M. Hacker, A. Gordon, and M. de Vries. 1991.

Vol. F 80: Intelligent Tutoring Systems for Foreign Language Learning. The Bridge to International Communication. Edited by M. L Swartz and M. Yazdani. 1992.

Vol. F 81: Cognitive Tools for Learning. Edited by P.A.M. Kommers, D.H. Jonassen, and J.T. Mayes. 1992.

Vol. F 84: Computer-Based Learning Environments and Problem Solving. Edited by E. De Corte, M. C. Linn, H. Mandl, and L. Verschaffel. 1992.

Vol. F 85: Adaptive Learning Environments. Foundations and Frontiers. Edited by M. Jones and P. H. Winne. 1992.

Vol. F 86: Intelligent Learning Environments and Knowledge Acquisition in Physics. Edited by A. Tiberghien and H. Mandl. 1992.

Vol. F 87: Cognitive Modelling and Interactive Environments in Language Learning. Edited by F. L. Engel, D. G. Bouwhuis, T. Bösser, and G. d'Ydewalle. 1992.

Vol. F 89: Mathematical Problem Solving and New Information Technologies. Edited by J. P. Ponte, J. F. Matos, J. M. Matos, and D. Fernandes. 1992.

Vol. F 90: Collaborative Learning Through Computer Conferencing. Edited by A. R. Kaye. 1992.

Vol. F 91: New Directions for Intelligent Tutoring Systems. Edited by E. Costa. 1992.

Vol. F 92: Hypermedia Courseware: Structures of Communication and Intelligent Help. Edited by A. Oliveira. 1992.

New Directions for Intelligent Tutoring Systems

Edited by

Ernesto Costa

Department of Electronic Engineering, University of Coimbra
P-3000 Coimbra, Portugal

Springer-Verlag
Berlin Heidelberg New York London Paris Tokyo
Hong Kong Barcelona Budapest
Published in cooperation with NATO Scientific Affairs Division

Proceedings of the NATO Advanced Research Workshop on New Directions for Intelligent Tutoring Systems, held in Sintra, Portugal, 6–10 October, 1990

CR Subject Classification (1991): I.2.0, K.3.1

ISBN-13: 978-3-642-77683-0 e-ISBN-13: 978-3-642-77681-6
DOI: 10.1007/978-3-642-77681-6

This work is subject to copyright. All rights are reserved, whether the whole or part of the material is concerned, specifically the rights of translation, reprinting, reuse of illustrations, recitation, broadcasting, reproduction on microfilms or in any other way, and storage in data banks. Duplication of this publication or parts thereof is permitted only under the provisions of the German Copyright Law of September 9, 1965, in its current version, and permission for use must always be obtained from Springer-Verlag. Violations are liable for prosecution under the German Copyright Law.

© Springer-Verlag Berlin Heidelberg 1992
Softcover reprint of the hardcover 1st edition 1992

45/3140 - 5 4 3 2 1 0 - Printed on acid-free paper

Preface

This book is a result of the NATO Advanced Research Workshop on New Directions for Intelligent Tutoring Systems, held in Sintra, Portugal, October 6–10, 1990. The main idea behind the workshop was to bring together scientists with different concerns about Intelligent Tutoring Systems (ITS) in order to discuss the positive and negative aspects of the current architecture paradigm (expert module, student module, instructional module, and interface module) and, eventually, propose some modifications or radical changes to it. This was a consequence of the increasing malaise felt currently by researchers in the area of artificial intelligence and education and in particular by those concerned with ITS. One symptom of this state of affairs is the fact that people have started talking about Intelligent Learning Environments (ILE) instead of ITS. To understand the reasons for this situation we promoted the discussion of questions like:

- To what extent do we need the technology of expert systems in ITS? Which other relevant AI techniques and methodologies are urgently needed?
- Is ITS a tool for knowledge communication or is it rather a belief system?
- How can the research already done on interactions among agents be utilized?
- Is it possible to find a formal theory to describe and solve the current problems with ITS?

The book contains the revised versions of the papers presented at the workshop. The new texts reflect the discussions that took place at the meeting. The book is divided into five parts reflecting the different backgrounds and interests of the participants. Each part is organized around a major theme which was observed from different points of view. Some papers display a formal orientation, others discuss some practical applications, while yet others combine the two aspects.

In Part 1 (Foundations), we put together all contributions that address generic aspects. Clancey presents a new theoretical view of human cognition which is the basis for the "situated learning" approach to instruction. Dillenbourg and Mendelsohn describe a new architecture based on the idea of levels and shifts of levels. Mántaras et al. describe a modular architecture that models metacontrol and uncertainty and speculate about its use for ITS. Self argues for a new discipline of "computational mathetics" which aims to unify at an abstract level the work done in the field of ITS. Winkels and Breuker describe another new architecture, based on the idea of functional decomposition.

In Part 2 (Student Modelling), we concentrate all contributions that specifically discuss student modelling. Cialdea proposes a formal method for describing the dynamics of the student modelling process based on a meta-level architecture. Costa and Urbano show the connections between machine learning and ITS and present an algorithm for student modelling based on an explanation-based learning technique. McCalla argues for one-to-one tutoring and considers different ways of dealing with the problem of student modelling in that context.

In Part 3 (ITS: Principles and Practices), we collect papers that discuss some general principles and practical experiments with ITS. Bierman et al. put forward some questions and give some answers to the problem of having a student model supported by cognitive principles in ITS. Verdejo shows the importance of discourse and natural language and its connection with instructional design. Vivet speculates about different contexts where an ITS could be integrated and discusses the consequences for the human teacher.

In Part 4 (Belief Systems), we concentrate the papers that use formalism related to belief revision. Cawsey shows how natural language dialogues can be responsible for students' misunderstanding and presents a solution based on a belief revision approach to the problems of modelling and repairing that situation. Martins proposes a formal theory for defining the structure and the dynamics of epistemic states. Wilks and Farwell present a project for second language teaching and show how the use of belief ascription techniques can be useful for the problem of modelling the participants in an ITS.

In Part 5 (Interaction Among Agents), we collect all papers dealing with aspects of interaction among agents. Baker sees the problem of communication between a learner and a teacher as a negotiation problem and describes KANT, a system that deals with generating tutorial interactions in ITS. Brazdil presents the technique of knowledge integration (of different theories of different agents) and shows how it can be used in ITS, particularly in noisy domains. Coelho identifies the hard problems resulting from knowledge communication among several agents and summarizes some work done in that area.

The grouping of the papers was not arbitrary, although it is clear that a paper in part X sometimes also discusses questions that are the central theme of another part Y. The reader is thus encouraged to go through all the papers in order to establish the implicit or explicit links between them. It is our belief that in this way a clear picture of what the issues are and of the possible solutions to the different problems of applying artificial intelligence to education can be constructed.

Acknowledgements

Organizing a workshop or editing a book is never a task one can do in isolation. So I would like to express my gratitude to several institutions and persons that helped me in making these events possible. First, to the members of the Scientific Committee (H. Coelho, W. Clancey, and J. Self) and to all participants. Their effort and enthusiasm before and during the meeting was fundamental for the success of the workshop. Second, to Caixa Geral de Depósitos, Fundação Luso-Americana para o Desenvolvimento, Instituto Nacional de Investigação Científica, and Junta Nacional de Investigação Científica. Without their complementary financial support it would have been impossible to bring together all these leading researchers in artificial intelligence and education. Third, to Professor Graça Martins of the Department of Computer Science of the Classical University of Lisbon who helped me when the support equipment followed "Murphy's law". Last but not least, to the secretarial staff, Olga Costa and Cristina Martins, who worked very hard and made my job much easier.

University of Coimbra
August 1992

Ernesto Costa

Table of Contents

4 Belief Systems

5 Interaction Among Agents

1 FOUNDATIONS

New Perspectives on Cognition and Instructional Technology

William J. Clancey
Institute for Research on Learning, 2550 Hanover Street, Palo Alto, CA 94304, USA

Abstract: Diverse perspectives from anthropology, philosophy, and linguistics lead us to view human knowledge as constructed moment-by-moment in interaction between people and their environment. The dynamics of human behavior is central, embracing all levels from *perception* (by which information is defined by the observer, not passively received), *interpretation* (by which representations are commented upon and thereby given meaning, not stored and retrieved from memory and simply "applied"), and *communication* (by which knowledge emerges through group interactions, not transmitted as predefined packets). This new conception leads us to view computer models in a new way.

Keywords: Cognitive modeling, Computer-aided instruction, Expert systems, Intelligent systems, Interactionalism, Knowledge-based tutoring, Learning, Social knowledge, Student models

Introduction

Over the past five years, diverse perspectives from anthropology [10, 11, 17], philosophy [8], and linguistics [13, 18, 19] have become increasingly central to cognitive science research, radically changing our understanding of human cognition. We are led to view human knowledge as something constructed moment-by-moment as an interaction between people and their environment, in order to cope with the situations at hand. Knowledge is not something stored and retrieved unchanged from memory and then simply "applied" [4, 6, 5, 9]. This new conception leads us to view computer models (e.g., "expert systems," "student models," and "intelligent tutoring systems") in a new way [14, 19]. In considering designs for learning environments in particular, we now pay special attention to how knowledge is constantly being created and given meaning through social interactions, as opposed to processes that take place exclusively inside of the heads of individuals. We consider the dynamics of human behavior to be central, embracing all levels from *perception* (by which information is defined by the observer, not passively received), *interpretation* (by which representations are commented upon and thereby given meaning, not retrieved and mechanically applied), and *communication* (by which knowledge emerges through group interactions, not transmitted as predefined packets of meaning). This paper introduces these ideas and considers the implications for how we use intelligent tutoring system technology.

What is learning?

We remain cognizant that, of course, it is individual people who articulate theories and act. However, what individuals say and do is not merely *conditioned* on what other people are saying and doing: Individual behaviors can only be described and understood as part of a larger whole, the goals and emergent activities of a social system. By analogy, the study of knowledge and learning is like thermodynamics, crucially built on an understanding of the properties of atoms and molecules, but fundamentally not about individuals in isolation. Rather, to understand what people believe and how they come to believe and do different things, we must broaden our perspective to describe the encompassing social system, the emergent effects of interactions, what people know about these effects, and how they seek to change them by their behaviors.

One way of summarizing this "interactional" point of view is that learning always involves adapting to the social and physical environment. In contrast, cognitive science has tended to view learning as something that takes place exclusively in the brain. But individual learning cannot be separated from the developing interactions of the group. How do people get their work done as a team and how does successful learning occur on the job? What *resources* does the environment make available as cues for structuring and supporting work [10, 17, 20]? Resources include reference materials, the physical layout of the office or shop floor, as well as team members with different specialities who provide direction and information.

We are particularly concerned about how computer models, no matter how realistic, artificially define the nature of a task by eliminating perceptual and problematic aspects of the actual setting [16]. In part, this awareness can help us develop more appropriate simulations (or justify choices that seemed arbitrary or a matter of opinion before, such as simulating sounds or simulating other agents). With the aim of promoting learning, we focus on the design of tools for accomplishing collaborative work, not isolated "tutoring systems" or even "consultation systems," which are often described in a decontextualized way, as if they could be understood or meaningfully used on any desk in any room.

To summarize some basic hypotheses that are radically changing our research on learning:

° **Representations**--what we say, write, draw, visualize--are constructed as *perceivable things*, they are not stored and retrieved in the brain. Human memory consists of the capacity to replay, organize, and recombine sequences of behavior (phrases) [1, 15]; this is *a memory of processes of perceiving and behaving*, not *descriptions* of how processes in the world or behavior routines appear to an observer [6]. Representations are constantly reinterpreted by new representations in an ongoing sequence of commentary. Their meaning is never fixed or definable [18].

° **Information** is created through individual perceptions that organize and reinterpret behavior and models of the world, as part of a larger process of interaction with the social and physical environment. Thus, the *cognitive* (individual statements and behaviors) is organized by the *social* (the dynamics of group activities and representations). Information is not given as objective pieces of data, but created by interaction of perceptual and external processes [12]. Information is not a sequence of words in a pipeline. To speak is to perceive is to represent is to generate knowledge [6, 9, 18]. This means that problems in the workplace, as well as theories for resolving them, are not supplied or predefined, but rather created anew in every situation by the participants in their interaction [16].

° **Learning** is how we describe and account for change in behavior. Strictly speaking it should not be viewed as acquiring some*thing*, so much as the development of a new routine, a capacity to interact more automatically in some setting. What is learned is not the description of the behavior, but a process for behaving. We must distinguish between our *"knowledge level" descriptions* as observers and the *internal mechanisms* that couple the individual to his or her environment. Knowledge-level descriptions are the province of the theoretician, accounting for behavior, they are not programs and data stored in the head of the subjects being studied [4]. Therefore, what is learned is not an observer's descriptions of how the performance will appear, but rather a capacity to move, look, and speak in a particular way in some situation.

What are computer tools?

These hypotheses have a dramatic effect on the design and use of computer tools. For example, we are less sanguine about developing an expert system and "transferring the knowledge" to a student. We are reconsidering how *theories* and *behaving* interact, that is, how talking about a situation, conceiving theories about it, and action are related. We do not by any means abandon the modeling methods of knowledge engineering and cognitive science [3, 7]. Rather, *we seek a radical reinterpretation of how knowledge-level models relate to human memory and perception.* We seek appropriate ways of using such models in the workplace in view of the dynamic, social nature of representation construction and reinterpretation. In essence, we move from viewing knowledge as something that can be fully captured and written in a "knowledge base," to accepting and working from the inherent and ongoing change in knowledge in every human perception and social interaction.

How can we design computer tools to enhance the everyday process by which people construct their own understanding of the task and the methods by which they organize their behavior? What assistance might facilitate sharing and reworking of conceptions? What recordkeeping by individuals would help a team develop its understanding of trends in the workplace over time? What mechanical aids would promote questioning, probing, and theory formation in the course of everyday work? How can computer controls be designed to facilitate their responsible use by people? *How can a program make people aware of its potential as a source of information and the weaknesses of its fixed design?* What features enable a team to customize a program to meet their changing goals and specific needs? How can a program help people detect inadequacies in their work and know what information they need to improve their understanding?

In summary, we reframe how intelligent tutoring system (ITS) technology (e.g., knowledge representations, student modeling, explanation) is used by viewing it in the context of computer tools for everyday work. As indicated here, all of the pieces in the puzzle--representations, information, learning--are themselves viewed in a new way. Perhaps the most central theoretical claim driving this new analysis is that knowledge is not stored in networks in the brain, but dynamically generated and reinterpreted in our words, drawings, images, in our ongoing social and physical interactions. Hence, we say that knowledge is situated; it is never in hand or describable apart from the setting in which the individual is interacting. Knowledge is not a thing, but a capacity to behave adaptively.

Reconsidering how ITS technology is used

How can we apply our revised theoretical perspective about the nature of knowledge and representations to the development of a new generation of computer tools? Specifically, we consider here how this conception changes our view of knowledge bases: They are not something to be delivered and memorized by a student, but are representations, created by social organizations and given meaning by the social and physical context. Both organization and context are not definable, and hence cannot be placed inside the knowledge base itself. Our changing perceptions of our social and physical setting change how we interpret a knowledge base, changing what the representations mean and hence their implications for our behavior. Rather than using an ITS program to deliver a predetermined, "finished" model to a student, we ask, *what kind of computer tools would facilitate the student's development of his own models?* We approach this question by considering failure analysis of computer models and how a knowledge base can be made into a "working document."

Glassbox Representations and Failure Analysis. Second generation expert system design (e.g., NEOMYCIN [7]) emphasizes that expert systems contain two kinds of models: a model of some domain system (e.g., a physical device) and a model of some reasoning process (e.g., a diagnostic or design procedure). Thus, kinds of knowledge are stated more abstractly, so they can be better explained, used for multiple purposes, and reused in the design of future programs. For example, "explanation-based learning" techniques enable a program to help users reason about and improve domain models.

Our new hypotheses about human knowledge suggest that explanation and "glass box" design is important because programs lack the flexibility of reinterpretation and reorganization of human perception. Indeed, the computer is "using representations" without giving them meaning. Any "interpretation" by the computer is grammatical. That is, it follows predefined relations between terms and predefined ways of organizing how data is processed. The inherent limitations of today's computer tools, relative to human perception and learning, place a primacy on exposing the computer's line of reasoning so people can be alerted about the limitations of the program's recommendations, and have a basis for improving them. To put this simply, a knowledge base *is just a model*. Models describe or simulate routine, stable interactions in the world. That is, models deal with patterns. Detecting when a model is inadequate and adapting it in subtle ways to the nuances of each new setting cannot be fully automatized by using models alone.

With the perspective that knowledge bases contain models, it is natural to *apply engineering approaches for describing the assumptions behind these models and formalizing the bounds of their applicability*. Recent research, such as in GUIDON-DEBUG, is considering means for integrating multiple representations, as leverage by which the program can detect weaknesses in its models and alert the user [2, 7]. GUIDON-DEBUG is a knowledge acquisition program in which the NEOMYCIN diagnostic expert system is enhanced by including explicit statements of what constitutes a good diagnosis. GUIDON-DEBUG then applies these constraints to evaluate NEOMYCIN's diagnoses and track them back to missing or incorrect facts in the domain model.

We might investigate how representations of strategy and representations of the setting that makes a strategy meaningful enable people to detect failures (in themselves, other people, or machines). Our new conception suggests that a strategy is not like a program that people "apply" by rote. Instead, a strategy is an observer's description of historical patterns in behavior. These patterns emerge from people interacting with each and their environment. They are not predefined plans that serve as instructions, but emergent, constantly adaptive routines and habits [6,17]. One role of strategic representations is to organize how we perceive new information for coping with failures; strategic talk (i.e., descriptions of what we typically do) directs our attention. We hypothesize that this *metacognitive knowledge*--representations of patterns in intelligent behavior as well as representations of the social and physical setting--is essential for expert system design (as glassboxes) that will promote human learning [2].

Notice that improvements to program design are coupled with the awareness of what cannot be incorporated in the program and remains the province of the people who interact with the program. Indeed, the role of glassbox and failure-sensitive designs is not merely to automate work, but to facilitate what only people can do.

The Working Knowledge Base. Knowledge acquisition is the process by which knowledge engineers construct expert systems. There are two basic concerns: interviewing experts and representation of knowledge. *We now realize that knowledge acquisition is a theory formation process, not a matter of simply writing down what has been preconceived and stored in the expert's brain.* In particular, we must make a distinction between an articulated, intellectual understanding of a task and the "activity-based knowledge," by which a person knows what to do when in a particular situation [20]. Such know-how cannot be reduced to theoretical knowing-that. This is similar to the previous observations that a strategy representation (knowing-that) is generated as an observation and is not the mechanism (knowing-how) by which behavior is generated.

For a strategic representation to change behavior, it must be external, out where it can be perceived as words, diagrams, gestures, etc. What can be said about a task and its environment is neither bounded nor definable from any given perspective. Models are inherently subjective and selective [18]. Thus, a knowledge base captures how people *talk* about a task environment from some perspective. Such concepts are useful for orienting and organizing work, but they do not constitute and cannot replace the adaptability of the human expert.

Knowledge acquisition is not delivering knowledge, so much as providing a tool for the community to collect and refine models of their work environment. Can we enhance their collaborative construction of better models and operating procedures by providing communication tools? In this way, we view the knowledge base as a working model, something never finished, always questioned and augmented through experience. Integral to this is a means of recording and indexing a case library--a record of what has happened in the past, which can be inspected and probed as theories are developed to cope with changing, difficult situations. Can we provide a means for annotating and sharing the detection of problems and the work-arounds people develop? A simple example of this is the use of e-mail bulletin boards. For example, Macintosh special interest groups allow programmers to ask for help and share tips without ever meeting the people they communicate with.

Consistent with our view of knowledge, *we don't view expert systems as a method of delivering what has been preconceived, but of promoting the means by which the team will construct its own models through their workplace interactions*. That is, our methods for knowledge acquisition should be integrated in the tools we provide for the workplace, which are tools for learning. This can be summarized as a variety of concerns:

Team orientation: An individual is not learning the subject matter so much as learning how to participate in a team's ongoing construction of what the subject matter is.

On-the-job learning: Work is inherently an activity of learning, not performing a predefined task, but constantly reinterpreting what is relevant and what constitutes good performance.

Assessment: Evaluation of learning is a natural activity of any community of practice, as people constantly form opinions about individual specialties and foibles, rather than something objective and imposed from outside.

Our theoretical perspective suggests that later reuse of a knowledge base can be enhanced by even informal annotations that record the history of the knowledge base's development and the rationale for design modifications. While they don't often reflect on this fact, knowledge engineers must reinterpret what happened in the past when they develop a new theory.

For example, a rule put in an expert system because of one case might need to be reinterpreted for a later case. Having a record of this first case could greatly change how the second case is interpreted. Thus, a knowledge base or any computer representation might be viewed in terms of accumulating layers of case experience and representation, in which we greatly benefit by being able to see through the entire past history, rather than just having a single layer with no annotations, which is the current case in most expert systems. Crucially, we can make these rationales available to the team on the workplace (or to the expert system itself) so the advantages and limitations of the computer system can be better understood.

What features for annotating and sharing experience in using a computer tool would *reflect back the team's performance,* so they became more aware of the quality of their work, knowing when to question what they are doing and have leads on how to change what they are doing? As an example, consider the disease taxonomy of NEOMYCIN. Our new perspective suggests that we view such medical knowledge not as a *product* to be delivered to a student, but as a model of a practice. In this respect, NEOMYCIN's disease taxonomy is greatly impoverished. Besides learning the various diseases and their relations, we would want the student to learn the following:

° Why do we taxonomize?
° What gets glossed? How do we know when this stereotypic view of physiological processes is misleading?
° Who knows this taxonomy; what is its origin?
° What is the nature of disagreements; how do they arise; how are they settled?
° How are taxonomies related to medical research? Are they becoming unnecessary as we develop better mechanistic models?
° What are good ways to keep a taxonomic perspective up-to-date?

By this view, knowledge is *knowing how to live* in a community, not static facts or procedures that *represent* what people do. We might say that we want a student to learn the *complement* of a conventional expert system knowledge base. Where did it come from? In what setting will it be useful? These matters can be represented, but the world and experience of the physicians (what they perceived and did in the past) cannot itself be put inside the machine. Becoming aware of this tension--an evolving dialectic between our environment and our representations--and skills for managing it are at the heart of *problem framing*, a step above and always outside what we have previously represented. This is much closer to what we want the student to learn and what we want our computer tools to support [16].

Learning Tools: Mediating conversations

The ideas of failure analysis and the working knowledge base emphasize that computers are tools that people use in a social setting. We can vividly illustrate this idea by considering two ways of viewing expert systems. In Figure 1, we show the traditional view of expert systems. The idea is that expertise is rare. Experts cannot always be present where their knowledge is needed. Therefore, the traditional view is to clone the expert by automating his reasoning in an expert system. The user (e.g., a medical intern or nurse) interacts with a computer program in which medical knowledge is formalized.

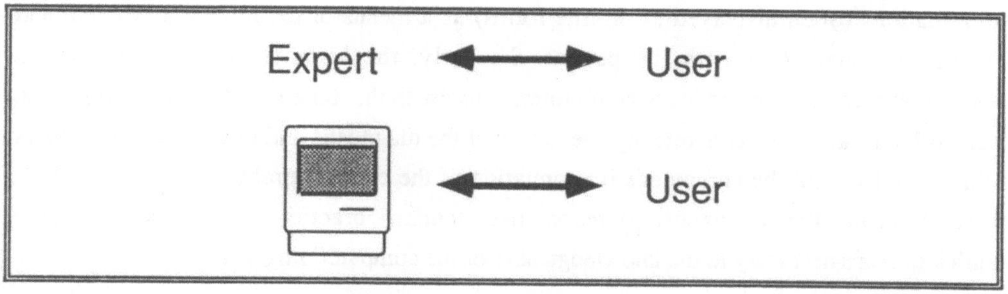

Figure 1. Traditional view of expert systems: Automate the role of the expert, replace the expert.

A more realistic view is that computer programs enable people to perform jobs they couldn't have done as well before. We are not replacing people so much as raising the level of competence of less-experienced workers (Figure 2). The idea is that the computer is a tool for mediating conversations [14, 19]. In this diagram, the user is a patient (more generally, a client). The service person is an intern or nurse. The expert still exists; he is available for consultation. But he is usually contacted only for difficult situations, those which can't be routinely handled, but require some customization of the standard procedures that have been formalized in the computer.

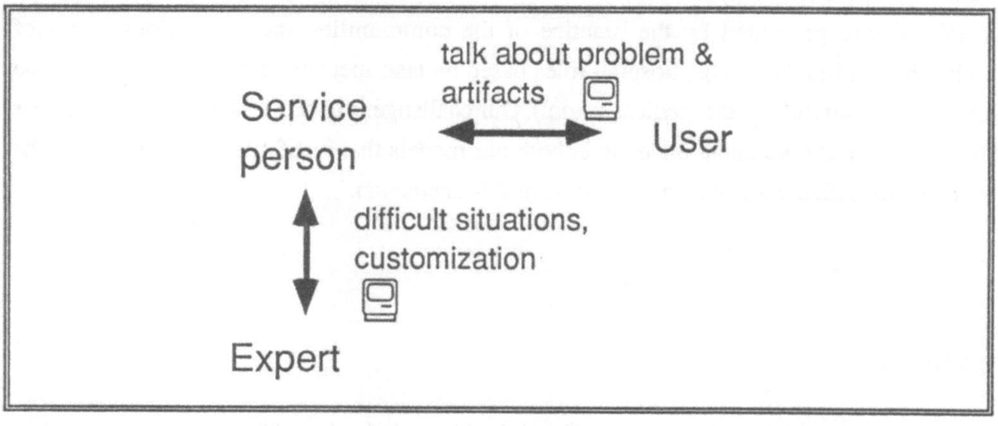

Figure 2. More realistic view of expert systems: Computer representations provide a medium for facilitating conversations.

Crucially, we view the computer tool not as doing anyone's job for them, but as a means for people to represent community practices and the theories that justify them, as well as the details of specific situations, and reflect upon them. The service person uses the computer representations (often displayed as on-line forms) as a means of organizing a problem and focusing her interaction with the patient. Similarly, the same representations form a conversation piece for the service person's interactions with the more senior, expert physicians. When problems arise, the concrete representation of the diagnostic and therapeutic procedures on-line, coupled with the computer's interpretation of the current problem, provides a well-grounded means for the expert to reconsider standard practices, and make whatever modifications are necessary to the knowledge base of the computer program.

In summary, it is more realistic and fruitful to view computer tools as enabling people to do their jobs more efficiently, to carry out new kinds of tasks. Indeed, *rather than removing people from the loop, properly designed job aids help people with different expertise and roles to work together more effectively.*

To be consistent with the theory of situated knowledge, such computer tools must be developed within their context of use. In the workplace environment the creation and reproduction of communities of practice, exemplified by apprenticeship in the hospital setting, are integral, and highly intentional, processes [11]. To paraphrase Lave and Wenger's analysis, the existence of a well-defined social institution, such as a hospital and medical school, facilitates the study of the relation between social and epistemological boundaries. On the one hand, the *institutional boundaries* are delineated by the social formation, including its structural and process organization and its competing constituencies. On the other hand, the *epistemological boundaries* are generated by the practice of the communities and the various forms of membership within them (e.g., hospital roles based on task specialization and seniority shape the topics and curricula of the medical school). Our challenge is to reflect the dynamic character of this social-epistemological dialectic in both our models that justify practice, as well as the tools that will facilitate the ongoing evolution of this interaction.

Conclusion

Our study of knowledge moves from stuffing it into knowledge bases, in which it is viewed as having a static character, to articulating how it arises in a social context and is given new form in every new situation. In parallel, our study of instructional programs moves from stuffing knowledge representations into the heads of students, to providing tools by which people can articulate their own theories. Crucially, these proposed computer tools are designed with the social context in mind by which representations are always being created, shared, recorded, and reinterpreted as people do their work. Programs to facilitate learning are no longer designed as one-dimensionally directed "from us to the students," but are instead designed with the historical, evolutionary, dynamic, and interactional character of knowledge in mind.

Simply put, tools for learning must be more like cameras and video-recorders than merely television screens or monitors. They must become a medium that prompts us to look out into the world in a new way, to make a statement, to adapt and reorganize what others have said, to present it to others, and then to reflect on what we have done. This dynamic view of knowledge provides an exciting, intuitively more balanced perspective for applying computer technology to education, but the work of realizing its potential has just begun.

Acknowledgements

Fitting the theory espoused here, most of the ideas in this paper emerged through my interactions with colleagues at the Institute for Research on Learning. I would particularly like to thank Penny Eckert and Jim Greeno, who co-authored a concept paper from which this paper is drawn. Discussions with Phil Agre, John Seely Brown, Brigitte Jordan, Jean Lave, Charlotte Linde, Jeremy Roschelle, Susan Stucky, and Etienne Wenger were equally influential.

References

1. Bartlett, F. C. *Remembering--A Study in Experimental and Social Psychology*. Cambridge: Cambridge University Press. (First published 1932) 1977

2. Clancey, W.J. The knowledge engineer as student: Metacognitive bases for asking good questions. In H. Mandl, & A. Lesgold (Eds.), *Learning Issues in Intelligent Tutoring Systems* New York: Springer-Verlag. 1988

3. Clancey, W.J. Viewing knowledge bases as qualitative models. *IEEE Expert* 4(2) 9-23, 1989

4. Clancey, W.J. The knowledge level reinterpreted: Modeling how systems interact. *Machine Learning* 4, 287-293. 1989

5. Clancey, W.J. Why today's computers don't learn the way people do. In P. Flasch and R. Meersman (Eds.), *Future Directions in Artificial Intelligence*. Amsterdam: Elsevier. pp. 53-62, 1991.

6. Clancey, W.J. The frame of reference problem in the design of intelligent machines. In K. vanLehn (Ed.), *Architectures for Intelligence: The Twenty-Second Carnegie Symposium on Cognition*. Hillsdale: Lawrence Erlbaum Associates. 1991

7. Clancey, W.J. Model Construction Operators. To appear in *Artificial Intelligence*. 1991

8. Dennett, D.C. Precis of "The Intentional Stance." *Behavioral and Brain Sciences* 12(3), 495-546. 1988

9. Greeno, J.G. *Situations, mental models, and generative knowledge.* In D. Klahr and K. Kotovsky (Eds.), *Complex Information Processing: The impact of H. A. Simon.* Hillsdale, NJ: Lawrence Erlbaum Associates. 1988

10. Lave, J. *Cognition in Practice.* Cambridge: Cambridge University Press. 1988

11. Lave J. and Wenger E. Situated Learning: Legitimate Peripheral Participation. Cambridge: Cambridge University Press, 1991.

12. Reeke, G.N. and Edelman, G.M. Real brains and artificial intelligence. *Daedalus,* **117** (1) Winter, "Artificial Intelligence," 1988

13. Rommetveit, R. Meaning, context, an control: Convergent trends and controversial issues in current social-scientific research on human cognition and communication. *Inquiry,* **30**:77-79. 1987

14. Roschelle, J. (1990). Designing for conversations. Paper presented at the AAAI Spring Symposium on Knowledge-Based Systems for Teaching and Learning Stanford, CA, USA, March

15. Rosenfield, I. *The Invention of Memory: A New View of the Brain.* New York: Basic Books. 1988

16. Schon, D..A. *Educating the Reflective Practitioner.* San Francisco: Jossey-Bass Publishers. 1987

17. Suchman, L.A. *Plans and Situated Actions: The Problem of Human-Machine Communication.* Cambridge: Cambridge Press. 1987

18. Tyler, S. *The Said and the Unsaid: Mind, Meaning, and Culture.* New York: Academic Press. 1978

19. Winograd, T. and Flores, F. *Understanding Computers and Cognition: A New Foundation for Design.* Norwood: Ablex. 1986

20. Zuboff, S. *In the Age of the Smart Machine: The Future of Work and Power.* New York: Basic Books. 1988

A Genetic Structure for the Interaction Space

Pierre Dillenbourg and Patrick Mendelsohn
TECFA, Faculté de Psychologie et des Sciences de l'Education, University of Geneva, Switzerland

Abstract: An intelligent learning environment (ILE) can be viewed as a space of interactions between rational agents. The task of the ILE designer is to analyse the structure of this interaction space. In this chapter, we propose to structure it as a sequence of hierarchically integrated sub-spaces. Each interaction sub-space associates a command language with a description language according to a simple chaining principle: the description language of each sub-space corresponds to the command language of the next sub-space. This structure instantiates the neo-Piagetian theory of R.Case, which takes into account both the qualitative changes that occur between two stages (or sub-spaces) with the quantitative change that happen within a stage. The quantitative changes result from the attempt to solve increasingly complex problems and lead to the saturation of the learner's working memory. It is then necessary to move to a new sub-space that provides the learner with operators for solving similar problems with a reduced cognitive load. The ability to use these new operators is based on the reflective activities triggered by the description language.

Keywords: Learning environment, Model of development, Reflection, Theory implementation.

Introduction: The Interaction Space

Designing an intelligent learning environment (ILE) consists in defining a set of interactions that may possibly happen between rational agents: the learner, the computer and any other participant. In this chapter, we call this set the *interaction space*. Considering an ILE as an interaction space fits with the current trend to pay less attention to the internal representations (the learner's and the computer's) and more attention to how agents actually interact together (see Clancey's contribution to this book).

The interaction space can be described in two ways: either as space of interactions, or as the interaction between two spaces, the representation space and the action space. We explore the later approach because it helps the designer to define the structure of the interaction space. The *representation space* is the set of displays (text and graphics) built by the computer. It is important to notice here that the term "representation" does not refer to the computer's internal representation nor to the learner's mental representation. It designates instead screen displays such as a ball hitting another ball or the trace of some problem solving path. The *action space* is the set of activities by which the learner can do something with these representations: can they only contemplate the representation or can they transform it, and, if so, in what way ?

The total interaction space is a set of [Action Space, Representation Space] pairs. Each of these pairs defines a microworld. In order to make learning efficient, the designer has to structure this set of microworlds. We chose the simplest structure: a linear sequence of microworlds. The educational value of this sequence is based on four properties :

- successive microworlds allow the learner to solve *increasingly complex problems* with a *constant cognitive load* (that only varies within a microworld);
- the sequence must reflect some *theory* of knowledge acquisition, in our case, the neo-Piagetian theory of *development* developed [7];
- the learner's move from one microworld to another results from their *metacognitive* activitie;
- the sequence is *transparent* , moving from one microworld to the next one is not hidden in the system but clearly visible at the interface.

This sequence of microworlds defines the core structure of an ILE. To be effective, it must be integrated with a rich learning environment, but here we will only analyze the core structure.

This chapter includes five sections. The first one describes the dimensions of interaction space. The theory of Robbie Case is briefly presented in the second section. In the third section, we present a framework that allows the designer to build a sequence of microworlds consistent with Case's theory. This framework includes two main concepts: the *pyramid metaphor* describes the *structure* of the microworld sequence and the *language shift mechanism* describes the *dynamics* of the sequence. In the fourth section, we outline how this sequence has been applied to the design of an ILE for acquiring basic skills in experimental psychology (MEMOLAB). The last section relates our intermediate framework to other theoretical positions.

The Interaction Space

Our study of the interaction space focuses on the dimensions of the representation space.

The Representation Space

The use of multiple representations in ILEs has been advocated by several designers. It is frequently seen as a solution to solve the incompatibility between the need for compiled and for articulated domain knowledge [23, 16]. A psychological justification has also been advanced to support the use of multiple representations in student modelling [18]. However, these statements concern internal representations (both the computer's and learner's), while this chapter is more concerned with external representations, i.e. the objects displayed on the screen. Our concern follows the work done by researchers such as [12, 13, 11] to provide multiple ways to represent a problem on the interface.

We view a representation space as the result of multiplying the designer's original representation by some *generic factors*. These factors define significative differences between representations. They determine the dimensions of the representation space.

The first generic factor was isolated [17] in his work on the Envisioning Machine (EM). Roschelle successively designed several representations for the same set of physical phenomena (particle movements). The first EM design focussed on the *epistemic fidelity* of the representation, i.e. the degree of consistency between the physical representation of some phenomena and the expert's mental representation of this phenomena [23]. However, mapping physical and mental representations is an inherently ambiguous interpretation process. Roschelle reports that the users of the early EM did not read representations as experts did. As [21] pointed out, attempts to build representations that avoid this inevitable ambiguity are vain. Therefore, representations must not be thought of as tools for eliminating uncertainty but as tools for managing uncertainty through communication. Later designs of EM focused on the ability of representations to support activities and dialogues that will lead to some shared understanding of the representation. Roschelle called this property *symbolic mediation*. However, epistemic fidelity remains an important issue : "*it is hard to imagine that the EM would be a better learning environment if its original design had not been based on high fidelity concerns*" [17]. The epistemic fidelity of some display and its ability to support clarifying dialogue are not exclusive properties. The goal is indeed to have both of them. Their partial incompatibility makes difficult to imagine a single representation that have both properties. But it can be by-passed if we think in terms of multiple representations, i.e. in terms of a representation space.

The second generic factor considers *what* is represented on the screen : *the objects to be learned or the learning subject herself.* In many microworlds, the screen displays some object that the user manipulates : a bowl hitting another bowl [20], a light connected to an electrical circuit [14], a line perpendicular to another line (e.g. in Cabri-geometry, Balacheff,1989), ... However, there is a growing interest in the possibility of representing the subject's solution process (e.g. how they solve an equation) in order to trigger reflective activities [4], as illustrated by the Geometry Tutor [2] or Algebraland [8]. Is the designer compelled to choose between representing the object or the subject ? Is she compelled to choose between the benefits of direct manipulation or the importance of metacognition. In some cases, a single representation can served both purposes, for instances, in TAPS II [9], where the structure of the representation of the given word problem determines indeed the solution process itself. An alternative consists in allocating the object and the subject to different areas of the representation space.

As third generic factor, we consider the role played by representations in the process of knowledge *transfer*, a process that has not receive in ITS research the attention it deserves. The ability to transfer knowledge from a source-problem to a target-problem implies two types of knowledge. One needs some compiled knowledge that has proved to be efficient with the source problem. One also needs some more abstract knowledge necessary to identify the target-problem as belonging to the same class as the source-problem and to adapt the source-solution to the target-problem. Research on second generation expert systems has emphasized the complementarity of these two types of knowledge [19]. Our point is that representations have to served two functions : to gather the context information necessary to solve a particular problem (off-loading the subject's working memory), and to detach the problem from the context-dependent features that make abstraction difficult. Once again, these conflicting requirements justify the necessity of designing a set of representations.

We cannot exhaustively enumerate the factors that generate the full representation space. Moreover, these factors are not independent. For instance, [3] reported experiments that establish a relationship between reflection (second factor) and transfer (third factor). Similarly, supporting reflection can be viewed as supporting the learner's dialogue (first factor) with themselves. In face of this complexity, the designer's challenge is to structure the representation space. The purpose of this chapter is precisely to propose a structure and a mechanism that allow the learner to move within the representation space.

Interactions between the Representation and the Action Spaces

The action space is the set of actions that the user is allowed to perform. The action space is partitioned into sub-spaces. An *action sub-space* is the set of actions that the learner is allowed to do at a particular stage of the learning process. For instance, the beginner may be allowed to enter their data as in a spreadsheet, while more advancved user may be allowed to specify quantities by moving the column tops in a histogram. All the actions necessary for entering data into a spreadsheet form an action sub-space, while the mouse actions on the histogram form another sub-space. Each sub-space is defined - as is often done in research on human-computer interaction - by a *command language*. The vocabulary of the command language represents the set of elementary actions that the learner can control. Syntactical rules determine how elementary actions can be regrouped into sequences and form complex behaviours.

Similarly, the representation space is partitioned into ***representation sub-spaces***. Each representation sub-space is defined by some ***description language***. For instance, you can represent a data set by a graph or a histogram. The rules for drawing a histogram constitute a description language. In the histogram sub-space, you will have many representations, one for each data set, each of them using the same description language. These analogous definitions of the action space and the representation space will allow us to specify the interaction between the two spaces in order to structure the interaction space.

We have so far presented the interaction space as a unstructured set of action-representation pairs. In order to order this set, we adapted the structure eloaborated by R. Case as a description of cognitive development from birth to adulthood. We will describe Case's theory and then explain how it fits with the design of an ILE.

Robbie Case's Theory of Cognitive Development

The key idea in Case's theory of intellectual activity and development [7] is what he calls the *executive control structure*. Problem solving across domains is viewed as the execution of a mental plan. This plan is defined as a sequence, or program of schema. There are two types of schema: *figurative schemata* represent states and *operative schemata* represent transformations. The mental plan is divided into three main sub-components :

(a) A representation of the "problem situation": this is the set of conditions relevant to the plan. The complexity of the representation will depend directly on the number of features a subject has to take simultaneously into account to solve the problem.

(b) The goals to be achieved defined as a set of new states, or "solution situation".

(c) The "problem solving process" to be used, stated as a set of operations that transform the problem situation into the solution situation.

These components are further analysed. Elements of the problem situation are mapped to elements in the solution situation, and both are mapped to transformations in the strategy set. The result is a well-defined formal structure that allows Case to associate specific tasks with problem solving processes in a rigourous way.

Case formulates his general theory with reference to developmental stages as they are identified in specific domains. One of the characteristics of his theory is that it relates quantitative changes within a stage to qualitative changes between stages: for example, an increase in the active unit capacity of working memory occurs within a stage, but helps to explain the transition to the next stage. Case distinguishes activities within a stage, i.e. *sub-stages*, by defining basic units of thought. Each new sub-stage within a stage is characterised by the subordination of a new basic unit to the executive control structure: the first sub-stage has two basic units, the second has three and the third has four. The complexity of subordination reached at the final sub-stage (in stage n) leads to the construction of a new basic unit at the next stage (stage n+1). The four-unit control structure of stage n is translated into a one-unit control structure at stage n+1. The last sub-stage of stage n can thus be considered as sub-stage zero of stage n+1. It is this formal process which Case calls "hierarchical integration".

An increase in "Short Term Storage Space" (STSS) permits the transition from one sub-stage to the next. STSS increases with age during development as a result of the maturation of the nervous system. It also increases during the learning of schemata as the result of an increase in the efficiency of the control structures: as the learner masters a task they free up short term memory to hold new objectives. The hierarchical integration of two control structures is thus dependent on the operational efficiency of their component schemata.

An Intermediate Framework

A computer based learning environment may reasonably be described as "intelligent" if its architecture and interface are designed according to the principles of some theory of human learning. Under this definition, traditional CAI is "intelligent" with respect to behaviorist learning theory, LOGO is "intelligent" with respect to Piaget's constructivist theory ... and the same applies to Anderson's LISP tutor with respect to his own ACT* theory. Engineering an ILE means implementing a learning theory. However, learning theories are rarely sufficiently operational. Moreover, there is no correspondence between the software engineering tools available to us and the language in which psychologists formulate our theories or models. As researchers, what should we do? Wait for the psychologists to develop their theories to the point where they are implementable using existing tools? Or wait for the programming language designers to develop some extraordinary new formalism that can capture the informal, verbal richness of psychological theory? Obviously not! Instead, we propose to build intermediary models that act as a bridge between the learning theories and the existing implementation languages. We will now present the intermediary framework we have built to translate Case's theory into system specifications.

We use the *pyramid metaphor* (Dillenbourg, to appear) to describe the core structure of the interaction space. The pyramid represents the concepts and procedures to be acquired by the learner, ranked bottom-up according to their level of abstraction and the type of object that the learner controls. Learning consists in moving up in the pyramid. Each level of the pyramid can be mapped to theoretical and engineering aspects :

- Each level corresponds to Case's concept of stage, i.e. the learner uses qualitatively different control structures.

- Each level corresponds to a microworld, i.e. it associates an action sub-space and a representation sub-space. This association is relevant if the description language (representation space) reifies some abstract features of the user's behaviour (action space), for instance by drawing a graphic picture of their problem solving strategy [4].

The pyramid metaphor includes an idea of hierarchy, i.e. that, in some interaction space, each level integrates its subordinated neighbour. At each level of the pyramid, the action sub-space uses a different command language. Similarly, each description sub-space uses a description language specific to its level. The integration between levels is encompassed in the relationship between the language used at successive levels : if a description language at some level L is used as a new command language at level L+1, then the concepts reified at level L must be explicitly used by the learner at level L+1. This is what we called the *language shift* mechanism [10] : when one offers as a new command language the previous description language, one compels the users to use in their solution process the concepts introduced in the description language. The structure of interaction space can then be described as a sequence of pairs [action sub-space, representation sub-space], a sequence in which the relationship between two successive pairs is described by the language shift mechanism.

Let's consider a simple example from algebra. At some level of the pyramid, one can show the learner with graphics that a good heuristic is to collect the X's on the same side of the equation. At the higher level, we can offer a new "regroup X" button in order to compel them to explicitly use this heuristic in their solution. A more complete example will be presented later.

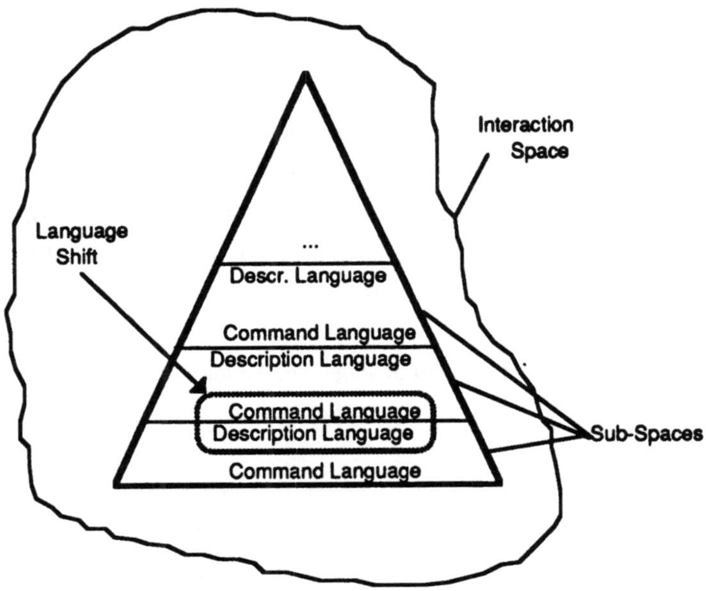

Figure 1 : The structure of the interaction space

The Design of MEMOLAB

The goal of MEMOLAB is to provide an Intelligent Learning Environment for acquiring basic skills in experimental psychology. The system provides the tools for designing, simulating, performing and analysing experiments on human memory. A user of the system is expected to work through the following cycle:

(a) Research the literature (in an on-line hypertext "Encyclopedia of Memory") and formulate an hypothesis to test, or select a challenge proposed by the system.

(b) Design an experiment to test the hypothesis. To do this they must select one or more experimental groups; define the experimental treatment procedure and target material; establish a performance measure and select a statistical model.

Example: *Two groups of 20 subjects each. Presentation of a list of 10 words for five minutes with subsequent recall. Group 1 is given a list of 10 semantically related words. Group 2 is given a list of 10 words that are not semantically related. The performance measure is the number of words correctly recalled. The statistical model is random assignment to groups,*

assumed normal distribution of scores within groups and the t-Test to establish a significant difference between the group mean scores.

(c) Conduct the experiment by using a simulation package included in MEMOLAB.

(d) Run the statistical analysis on the data collected and draw the appropriate conclusion.

The MEMOLAB pyramid has four levels reflecting the increasing *complexity of the experimental designs* required of the learner. Other necessary knowledge, such as statistics or the content of the experiments (human memory theory), has a special place in our model. Its acquisition is subordinated to the construction of plans in the same way that Case assumes any synthesis of two control structures is subordinated to one of them. Each level has its own command language, which means that the learner receives new tools for building experiments.

Level 1 Building an experiment involves assembling into a "workbench" a temporal sequence of discrete events. Each event has four components: a group of subjects, the target material, the task procedure and a performance measure.

Level 2 Building an experiment means making a first sequence of events. Then, for each experimental group, this sequence is duplicated and edited. The changes between sequences correspond to the concept of independent variable.

Level 3 An experiment is built in two steps. First, one creates a sequence with variable slots (e.g. group-X, word-list-Y). Then, one defines a table (a plan) that instantiate the sequence (e.g. that specifies the word-list-Y for each group-X).

Level 4 As in level 3, experiments are described by a sequence and a plan, but this plan is two-dimensional and therefore allows for the treatment of complex interaction of effects.

As presented in the intermediate framework, the concepts used in the next command language are first introduced as description language. Let's look for instance at the transition between the first and second levels. At level one, the learner puts on the workbench a set of independent events. The relationship between these events is implicit, it has to be reified in the description language to be used explicitly at the command language of second level. Therefore, we redisplay events as components of a sequence. The slots that have the same value in the events sequence (for instance those that concern the same group or the same list of words) are removed from the event frame and attached to the sequence frame. Then, after the language shift, the learners receive the new building block called "sequence". They can build a sequence, duplicate this sequence and obtain a new one by simply editing the sequence-specific slots.

The language shift reflects the qualitative difference that exists between Case's stages (i.e. our levels). The nice point in Case's theory is that it articulates qualitative and quantitative changes. Within each level of MEMOLAB, we define different levels of problems that match Case's concept of sub-stage. These problems appear in MEMOLAB as challenges proposed to the learner. At the outset of the level one, the system proposes challenges that can easily be met with the learner's available operators. For instance, a challenge is "*Prove it: People cannot remember 200 hundreds words after 2 minutes of reading*". Progressively, more complex challenges will be proposed. These increase the cognitive load of the experiment design. In the last sub-stage of level one, learners will have to solve challenges such as "*Prove it: Long words are easier to remember than short words*". This multiplies the number of events and relations between events that the learner must consider simultaneously. This complexity justifies the introduction of the level-2 command language. The new available operators (sequences) will allow the learner to solve similar problems with a reduced cognitive load and hence to tackle later more complex challenges (until the next language shift is necessary, and so forth).

The Complexity of Learning

Our framework can be linked to different theoretical perspectives. Gathering the support of multiple theoretical frameworks is very important because *an ILE must address learning in its full complexity*. For instance, an ILE must account for the importance of discovery, for the role of practice and for the effect of coaching, because all of them occur at some stage of any learning in the real world. We have concentrated so far on the relationship between our framework and Case's theory because it has been our main source of inspiration. However, we now briefly describe how the same framework can be used as an "object to think about" other approaches, the apprenticeship stream and the situated knowledge trend.

The *apprenticeship* idea is reified in the pyramid model by sharing control between the coach and the learner : when the learner is able to perform at some level, the tutor must take decisions that the learner is not able to take, i.e. it must assume higher floors of the pyramid. At each language shift, the learner will assume more control of his solution process and the coach's guidance will be reduced. The idea of "next level up" corresponds to the concept of *zone of proximal development* [22]. Moreover, [24] proposed a linguistic analysis of the *internalization* process that relates it to the language shift. He observed (in mother-child interactions) that the move from the inter-individual to the intra-individual plane was preceded by a language shift inside the inter-individual level: mothers replace a descriptive language by a language referring to objects according to their role in the problem solving strategy.

From [6] viewpoint, the language shift mechanism can be viewed as a process of inducing *interaction patterns*. An elementary interaction associates some sequence of user actions and the computer's description of this sequence. We showed that the meaning of the description language can result from inducing some relationship between the actions performed and their representation [10]. The interest of this approach is that it create a bridge between our model and current research on situated learning, where interaction patterns play a central role in learning [5].

Finally, the idea of automating complex control structure into new atomic operators seems very close to [1] idea of knowledge compilation. We must point out that the philosophy behind the language is quite different. Of course, some automatization of subskills is required in MEMOLAB to free the cognitive resources necessary to the language shift. However, the function of the description language is make explicit concepts that were implicitly used before. For instance, the creation of a difference between groups is reified at level one in order to be used explicitly for designing level 2 experiments. This focus on awareness is rather opposite to the idea of compilation and much closer to the Piagetian concept of "*reflected abstraction*" [15].

Conclusions

The behaviourist approach provides the designer with a methodology for content analysis, namely decomposition into very small pieces of knowledge. The constructivist approach has suggested a radically different approach : the learner is expected to explore complex problems. Unfortunately, unstructured learning environments often fail to cause learning. This chapter proposes an intermediate grain size for analysing the content to be taught. A learning environment could be viewed as a sequence of hierarchically integrated microworlds. This sequence of microworlds partially covers the representation space. The first microworld allows a novice to solve very simple problems. In successive microworlds, the learner is pushed to tackle more and more complex tasks, with more and more powerful operators. The use of these operators implies the internalization of the major concepts that constitute the expertise in the domain.

Each microworld is defined by the association of a description language and a command language. This association also specifies the relation between successive levels: the old description language becomes the new command language. This structure also encompass the mechanism by which learners are expected to move through the sequence. Moving becomes necessary because of the functional constraints of the problems to be solved (working memory load). It becomes possible because of the learner's reflective activities (triggered by the description language).

This empty structure of microworlds translates (a part of) Case's theory into a terminology that is relevant for the ILE designer. We therefore refer to this structure as an intermediary framework. This framework seems to be also useful for theoretical approaches. However, we did not investigate this issue deeply enough to make strong claim about the generalizability of our framework. Similarly, we have not assessed yet the generalizability of this framework to other learning environments.

References

1. Anderson J.R. (1983) *The Architecture of Cognition.* Harvard University Press. Cambridge.

2. Anderson J.R., Boyle C.F. and Yost G. (1985) The Geometry Tutor. *Proceedings of the Ninth International Joint Conference on Artificial Intelligence.* Los Angeles. Vol.1

3. Brown A. (1987) Metacognition, Executive Control, Self-Regulation and Other More Mysterious Mechanisms. in F.E. Weinert and R.H. Kluwe (Eds) *Metacognition, Motivation and Understanding.* Hillsdale, NJ: Lawrence Erlbaum, pp. 65 - 115.

4. Brown J.S. (1985) Process versus product : a perspective on tools for communal and informal electronic learning. *Journal of Educational Computing Research,* 1 (2)

5. Brown J.S. (1990) Toward a new epistemology for learning. in C. Frasson and G. Gauthier (Eds). *Intelligent tutoring systems at the Crossroad of AI and Education.* Norwood, NJ: Ablex.

6. Campbell R.L. and Bickhard M.H. (1986) *Knowing Levels and Developmental Stages.* Basel: Karger.

7. Case R. (1985) *Intellectual Development: from Birth to Adulthood.* New York: Academic Press.

8. Collins A and Brown J.S. (1988)The Computer as a Tool for Learning through Reflection, in H. Mandl and A. Lesgold (Eds), *Learning Issues for Intelligent Tutoring Systems.* New York: Springer-Verlag, pp. 1-18.

9. Derry S.J. (1990) Flexible Cognitive Tools for Problem Solving Instruction. Paper presented at the *AERA symposium, Computers as Cognitive Tools,* Boston, MA, April.

10. Dillenbourg P.(1992) The Language Shift : a mechanism for triggering metacognitive activities. In: Winne P. and Jones M. (Eds). *Adaptive Learning Environments.* NATO ASI Series F, Vol. 85. Berlin:. Springer-Verlag.

11. Fredericksen J.R. and White B.Y. (1988) Intelligent Learning Environments for Science Education, *Proceedings of ITS-88.* Montreal, pp. 250-257

12. LewBlanc M.D. (1988) Instructional Tools for Algebra Word Problems. *Proceedings of ITS-88.* Montreal, June 1-3, pp 238-242

13. McArthur D., Burdof C., Ormseth T. Robyn A., Stasz C. (1988) Multiple Representations of Mathematical Reasoning.*Proceedings of ITS-88*. Montreal, pp. 485-490

14. Palies O. (1988) Building a Student Model without a Bug Library.*Proceedings of the Summer University on Intelligent Tutoring Systems*, Le Mans, 26 Oct. - 3 Nov. 1988.

15. Piaget J. (1971) *Biology and Knowledge*. Chicago: University of Chicago Press.

16. Roschelle (1988) Sufficiency and Utility of Physics Problem Solving Processes. *Proceedings of ITS 88*. Montreal. June 1-3, pp. 132-139.

17. Roschelle J. (1990) Designing for Conversations. *Paper presented at the AAAI Syymposium on Knowledge-Based Environments for Learning and Teaching*, Stanford, CA, March 1990.

18. Self J.A. (1988) The Use of Beliefs Systems for Student Modelling. *Proceedings of the European Congress on Artificial Intelligence and Training*. Lille. Oct. 1988

19. Steels L (1990) Components of Expertise. *AI Magazine*, Vol .11 n 2, pp. 28 - 49

20. Stumpf. M, Opwis K. and Spadah. (1988) Knowledge acquisition in a microworld for elastic impact : the DiBi System. *Proceedings of the Summer University on Intelligent Tutoring Systems*, Le Mans, 26 Oct - 3 Nov. 1988.

21. Suchman L.A. (1987) *Plans and Situated Actions. The problem of human-machine communication*. Cambridge,UK: Cambridge University Press.

22. Vygotsky L.S. (1978), *Mind in Society. The Development of Higher Psychological Processes*. Edited by M. Cole, V. John-Steiner, S. Scribner and E. Souberman. Cambridge, MA: Harvard University Press.

23. Wenger E. (1987) *Artificial Intelligence and Tutoring Systems. Computational and Cognitive Approaches to the Communication of Knowledge*. Loas Altos, CA: Morgan Kaufmann

24. Wertsch J.V. (1985) Adult-Child Interaction as a Source of Self-Regulation in Children. *The growth of reflection in children*. Madison: Academic Press. pp. 69-97.

COLAPSES: A Modular Architecture and Language for Modelling Meta-Control and Uncertainty[1]

R. López de Mántaras, C. Sierra, J. Agustí
Centre d'Estudis Avançats de Blanes,Camí de Santa Bàrbara. 17300 Blanes, Girona, Spain.
e-mail: mantaras@ceab.es, sierra@ceab.es, agusti@ceab.es

Abstract: In this paper we present the management of uncertainty proposed in the COLAPSES language. Uncertainty is mainly a control parameter of the execution of a knowledge base. This language allows the possibility of defining local logics inside a hierarchic structure of modules containing rules. These local logics interact between them in a user defined fashion that gives to the uncertainty treatment a flexibility not found in other systems. The relation between control (meta-logic) and deduction (logic) is based on a reflexive architecture that uses introspection mechanisms to take decisions from the uncertainty in the facts. These features allow to mimic more closely human problem solving behaviour and particularly when uncertainty is present. We conjecture that this type of architecture may have implications for ITS because it allows to provide explanations involving control knowledge decisions.

Keywords: Meta-level architecture, Modularity, Uncertainty management.

Introduction

Most AI research on reasoning under uncertainty is concerned with global normative methods to propagate and combine certainty values and there is a controversial debate about which methods are most appropiate and why. Disagreement between the proponents of the different methods (Bayesians, Dempster-Shafer, fuzzy logicians) is about the meaning of uncertainty and having a formalism that produces rational conclusions with no claim to mimic human uncertainty management methods. In restricted domains where the uncertainty involved permits, for example, a direct interpretation in the probability theory sense and where the main decision of the expert system involves the computation of such uncertainty if appropiate data are available, then probability calculus would be the best independently of how humans solve problems in the same situation. However, the most interesting aspect of the expert systems research is to gain some insights of human problem solving strategies by trying to emulate them in programs. Although human problem solvers are almost always uncertain about the possible solution, they very often achieve their goals despite uncertainty by using methods to manage uncertainty that are particularized to the type of problem solving that they are performing at a given time. In fact, we believe that managing uncertainty consists in selecting actions that simultaneously achieve solutions and reduce their uncertainty. Since actions are selected not only for their domain effects but also for their effect on uncertainty, problem solving under

[1]Research partially supported by CICYT project SPES nº 880j382

uncertainty is more constrained that problem solving under total certainty as was also noticed by Cohen [2-3].

This view leads to consider uncertainty mainly as a control feature because it helps to constrain the focus of attention (i.e. which part of the problem to work next) and action selection (i.e. how to work on it). The problem solving strategies are implemented in the problem solver's control part. The knowledge engineers translate into control strategies the human problem solving strategies.

Problem solving strategies are a fundamental component of expertise and have to be acquired by first implementing a set of task-level primitives with which experts can describe their strategies. Uncertainty is, in our opinion, a task-level primitive that is used at the implementation level to descriminate alternative control decisions. Furthermore, when large expert systems emulate human problem solving strategies, the organization of their complex knowledge bases makes the propagation and combination of uncertainty a local, context dependent, process. In our opinion, such large domain expert systems draw their problem solving capabilities more from the power of their organizational and problem solving structures than from the particular uncertainty management formalism they use (different formalisms can be adjusted to give similar answers).

This paper discusses these ideas in the framework of COLAPSES a modular language based upon the MILORD language [4]. This expert systems building tool uses uncertainty as a control feature and performs local combination and propagation of uncertainty. A medical diagnosis application is used as example whose potential tutoring capabilities, to perform case studies by advanced medical students, are enhaced by the capability to provide justifications of the problem solving strategies selected at the control level.

Modularity and locality

A knowledge base is a large set of knowledge units that cover a domain of expertise and provide solutions to problems in that domain of expertise.

When faced with a particular case, human experts use only a subset of their knowledge for two reasons: adecuacy of the general knowledge -the theory- to the particular problem and availability and cost of data. For exemple, the suspicion of a bacterian disease will rule out all knowledge referring to virical diseases; and also a patient in coma will make useless all the knowledge units that need patient's answers.

The adequation of general knowledge to a particular problem is done at a certain level of granularity, for instance, the expert uses all the knowledge related to the diagnosis of a colon neoplasy or the knowledge related to the radiological analysis of a chest x-ray.
In particular the structuration of KB's is made in MILORD taking into account this granularity in the use of knowledge.

Each structural unit or theory (module from now on) will define an indivisible set of knowledge units (for example rules and predicates). The control will be responsible for the combination of the modules. The combinations will represent the particularization of general knowledge to the problem that is being solved. The control will determine which combinations are acceptable. For example, a module that determines the dosis of penicillin that has to be given to a patient must not be present in any acceptable combination for a patient allergic to penicillin.

The modularization of KB's leads to the concept of locality in the modules of a KB. It is possible to define the contents of a module independently of the definition of the rest of the modules. This possiblility, methodologicaly desirable, allows the use of different local logics and reasoning mechanisms adapted to the subtasks that the system is performing.

Modularity over MILORD: The COLAPSES language

The basic units of KB's written in our language, COLAPSES, are the modules. These may be hierarchically organized, and consist of an excapsulated set of import, export, rule, meta-rule and submodule declarations. The declaration of submodules in a module is what structures the hierarchy. The declaration of submodules does not differ from the declaration of modules. We shall briefly outline which is the meaning of the primitive components of a module. A complete definition of the language and its semantics can be found in [5].

Import: determines the non-deducible facts needed in the module to apply the rules. These facts are to be obtained from the user at run time.

Export: defines which facts deduced or imported inside a module are visible from the rest of the modules that include the modules as a submodule. The import, submodule declarations and export components define the interface of the module.

Rule: defines the deductive units that relate the import and the export components within a module.

Metarule: defines the meta-logical component of the module. Thus, the meta-rules of a module will control the execution of the rules in the module and the execution of the submodules in the hierarchy underneath the module.

The syntax of a module definition is as follows:

Module *modid = modexpr*

where *modid* stands for an identifier of the module and *modexpr* for the body of the definition made out of the components specified above. Let us look at an example of module definition.

```
Module Gram_esputum =
begin
        import Class, Morphology
        export Morphology, Esputum_ok
        deductive knowledge:
                Rules
                R001 if Class > 4 then Esputum_ok is sure
                ...
        end deductive
 end
```

There is also the possibility of defining generic modules that represent functional abstractions of several non generic modules.

Local Logics

It is clear that the experts use different approaches to the management of uncertainty depending on the task they are performing. Usually expert system building tools provide a fixed way of dealing with uncertainty proposing a unique and global method for representing and combining evidence. In the COLAPSES language it is possible to define different deduction procedures for each one of the modules. If from a methodological point of view a task is associated with a module then, a different logic can be used depending on the task. The definition of local logics is made by the next primitive in the COLAPSES language:

```
Inference systems
        Truth values = list of linguistic terms
        Renaming = morphisms between linguistic terms
        Connectives:
            Conjuction = function definition (or "AND" truth table)
            Disjunction = function definition (or "OR" truth table)
        Inference patterns:
        Modus ponens = function definition
```

This primitive is included as a component of the deductive knowledge of a module. Next, we shall explain each one of the components of the local logic definition.

Truth values. This component defines the set of linguistic terms that will be used in the logical valuation of facts, rules and meta-rules of the module where this logic is to be used. Different modules can have different sets of linguistic terms.

Renaming. Modules in a KB define a hierarchy of tasks. Each of the modules can have a different logic, so it is necessary to define a way of interconnecting these different logics. In MILORD this is done in a declarative way. Each module that contains several submodules has a set of morphism definitions that translate the valuations of predicates in the submodules to valuations in the logic of the module. Let us see an example

```
Module B =
 begin
     Module A =
      begin
          Import C
          Export P
          Deductive knowledge:
          Rules:
              R1 if C the conclude P is possible
          Inference system:
              Truth values = (false, possible, true)
          End deductive
      end
     Import D
     Export Q
     Deductive knowledge:
          Rules:
              R1 if A/P and D then conclude Q is quite_possible
          Inference system:
              Truth values = (impossible, moderately_possible,
                              quite_possible, sure)
              Renaming = A/false ==> impossible
                         A/possible ==> quite_possible
                         A/true ==> sure
     End deductive
 end
```

Notice in the above example that the predicate P exported by the submodule A of B which is used in the rule defined in B will be valuated with one of the three values: false, possible or true. To use this fact in the module B we need to change that value for a different one which is known by the logic defined in B. This is done via the renaming definition.

Connectives. This components defines the function that will be used in the deduction process associated with the module. Different multiple-valued functions can be defined depending on the task defined by the module or different truth tables can be used after their elicitation from the expert.

Inference patterns. This field defines the inference rules to be used along the deductive process. To date the only accepted pattern in COLAPSES in the modus ponens for which a propagating function can be defined.

Meta-reasoning by introspection using uncertainty

Having considered uncertainty as a logical component of the COLAPSES language, i.e. the semantics of formulae, the control of reasoning under the uncertainty must be considered as a meta-logic component. Thus the meta-inference over the uncertainty will determine which will the inference control be at the logic level. This meta-inference acts upon the logic component using mechanisms of introspection, this is, the same language represents the uncertainty of the propositions and provides mechanisms both to look at this uncertainty and to determine the control to be followed.

This meta-control is defined as a component of the modules, allowing a local meta-logic defintion. This control component acts over the deductive knowledge and over the submodule hierarchy. It determines which rules and submodules are useful for the current case. The mechanism of interaction between both components is a reflection mechanism: the deductive component reflects on the control component to know which will be the next strategic step, which submodule to execute next, or which rule to use next.

It is not a full reflection mechanism because we allow the meta-logic to see only the valuation of atomic formulae (facts) and the valuation of strategies (sets of modules that combined can lead the system to the solution of the problem), rules and meta-rules cannot be consulted by the meta-logic.

This general mechanism is used to drive the inference process in different directions; we are going to discuss some of them.

Evidence increasing

The current uncertainty of facts can be used to control the deduction steps in order to increase the evidence of a given hypothesis. So, for example, if we have an alcoholic patient showing a cavitation in the chest x-ray and there is low evidence for tuberculosis, then the Ziehl-Nielssen test to determine more clearly whether he has a tuberculosis should not be done. But if he also presents a risk factor for AIDS then we shall increase our evidence for tuberculosis and the test will be suggested. This is expressed as follows:

If tuberculosis > moderately_possible
then conclude Test Ziehl-Nielssen

If risk_factor_for_AIDS **then conclude** tuberculosis **is** possible

If Alcoholic **and** Cavitation
then tuberculosis **is** almost_impossible

It should be noticed that the first rule is a rule of the meta-logic component of the language whilst the others are rules at the logic level.

Strategy focusing

The uncertainty of facts can determine the set of hypothesis to be followed in the sequel. Example:

If the pneumonia is bacterial with certainty < quite_possible **and**
the pneumonia is atipical with certainty > possible
Then focus on
Mycoplasm, Virus, Clamidia, Tuberculosis, Nocardia, Criptococcus,
Pneumocistis-Carinii
with certainty quite possible

This example means that the modules to be used in order to find a solution to the current case are those indicated in the conclusion of the meta-rule and should be considered in the order specified there.

Strategies have a certainty degree attached to them. This is useful to differentiate the strategies generated by very specific data from those generated by general data. As an example consider the case of a patient with AIDS (a kind of immunodepression). If we know that the patient suffers from AIDS, a more specific strategy (and also more certain) can be generated. But if we just know that the patient has an immunodepression a less certain general strategy would be generated. Since we may have several candidate strategies simultaneously, combining different strategies is a matter of great importance in the control of the system. This is also achieved by looking at the uncertainty of the strategies, as shows the next example:

> **If** Strategy (X) **and** Strategy (Y) **and** Certainty (X) > Certainty (Y) **and**
> Goals (X) $\cap$ Goals (Y) $\neq \emptyset$
> **Then** Ockham (X,Y)

where Ockham (X,Y) is a combination of the strategies that gives priority to those modules found in the intersection of both strategies: (Goals (X) $\cap$ Goals (Y))

Knowledge adequation

As indicated at the begining of the paper a KB is a set knowledge units that have to be adapted to the current case. For example alcoholism is a useful concept when determining a bacterial pneumonia, but it is useless for non-bacterial diseases. Then, a possible use of the uncertainty of the fact bacterianicity is to decide about the use of a given concept in the whole KB, i.e. to adequate the general knowledge to the particular problem. Example:

> **If** no bacterian disease
> **then** do not use alcoholism in finding the solution

Solution acceptance

The degree of uncertainty of a fact can also be used to stop the execution of the system. For example

> **If** Pneumocistis-carinii **and** tuberculosis < possible **and** Criptococcus < possible
> **Then stop**

The control tasks we have discussed use uncertainty as a control parameter and are tasks of the meta-logic level. They are represented as a local meta-logic component of each module in what is called the control knowledge component of a module.

Metacontrol and locality

The structured definition of KB's helps not only in the definition of safe and maintainable KB's but also gives some new features that where impossible to achieve in the previous generation of systems. Among them the most important is the possibility of defining a local meta-logical component for each one of the modules.

The definition of strategies (ordered set of elementary steps to solve a problem) in the MILORD system was made globally. Only one strategy could be active at any moment. Presently, as many strategies as nodes in the modules graph structure can be active. This flexibility is linked with the fact that each module can have a different treatment of uncertainty. So, uncertainty plays a different role as a control feature depending on the association between module and logic.

Furthermore, given the fact that the system consists of a hierarchy of submodules the meta-logical components act ones upon the others in a pyramidal fashion. This allows us to have as many meta-logic levels as necessary in an application. Further research will be pursued along this line. A richer representation of the logic components in the meta-logic will also be investigated and sound semantics from the logic point of view will be defined. Finally, the potential for tutoring advanced medical students due to the higher explanation capabilities involving control knowledge will be evaluated.

Conclusions

The interesting aspect of building expert systems is to learn something about human problem solving strategies by trying to reproduce them in programs. Human problem solver's are uncertain in many situations and do not use a simple normative method to handle uncertainty. Instead they take advantage of a good organization in the problem solving task to obtain good solutions using qualitative approximations. This suggests to consider uncertainty as playing an important role at the control level by guiding the problem solving strategies. In order to illustrate these points, we have briefly described a modular architecture and language that extensively exploits uncertainty as a control feature and uses local context dependent combination and propagation uncertainty operators.

Bibliography

1. Agustí J., Sierra C., Sannella D. (1989): Adding generic modules to flat rule-based languages: a low cost approach, in *Methodologies for Intelligent Systems 4*, (Z. Ras, ed.), Elsevier Science Pub., pp. 43-51.

2. Cohen P.R., Day D., De lisio J., Greenberg M., Kjeldsen R., Suthers D., Berman P. (1987): Management of Uncertainty in Medicine, *International Journal of Approximate Reasoning* 1, pp. 103-116.

3. Cohen P.R. (1987): The Control of Reasoning Under Uncertainty: A Discussion of Some Programs, COINS Technical Report 87-81, University of Massachusetts at Amherst.

4. Godo L., López de Mántaras R., Sierra C., Verdaguer A., (1987): MILORD, the architecture and management of linguistically expressed uncertainty, *International Journal of Intelligent Systems*, 4:4, pp. 471-501.

5. Sierra C., Agustí J. (1990): COLAPSES: Syntax and Semantics, CEAB Research Report 90/8.

Computational Mathetics: The Missing Link in Intelligent Tutoring Systems Research?

John Self
Department of Computing, University of Lancaster, UK

Abstract: This chapter argues that an abstract, application-independent, psychologically-neutral level, which we call Computational Mathetics, is needed as a basis for Intelligent Tutoring Systems research. The aims and scope of Computational Mathetics are described by analogy with Computational Linguistics. Some preliminary examples of work within Computational Mathetics are outlined.

Keywords: Cognitive diagnosis, Instructional principles, Learner modelling, Viewpoints.

Introduction

According to the Shorter Oxford Dictionary, the word "mathetic" is an adjective meaning "pertaining to learning", from the Greek *manthanein*, 'to learn'. The noun "mathetics" is proposed to mean "the study of matters pertaining to learning", in rough analogy with "aesthetics" - the study of (matters pertaining to) art, from the Greek *aisthanesthai*, 'to perceive'; "linguistics" - the study of language; "robotics" - the study of robots; "cosmetics" - the study of the cosmos. To justify the neologism, mathetics should adopt a formal or theoretical approach to the study of learning, in contrast to the largely descriptive approaches offered in educational psychology.

"Computational Mathetics", then, is concerned with the computer-based study of learning. Like Computational Linguistics, Computational Mathetics should have a solid theoretical foundation and an orientation towards practical applications - in the case of the former, natural language front-ends, translation systems, etc; in the case of the latter, intelligent tutoring systems, computer-based learning environments, etc. Computational Mathetics is both analytic, being concerned with the development of computational formalisations of the processes of learning, and synthetic, being concerned with the design of computer-based systems to promote learning. So, Computational Mathetics is provisionally defined to be "the study of learning, and how it may be promoted, using the techniques, concepts and methodologies of computer science and artificial intelligence."

The Need for Computational Mathetics

Inventing an impressively pretentious term like Computational Mathetics is in itself no solution to any problem. But what is the problem we are addressing?

The field of research variously called Intelligent Tutoring Systems, AI and Education, AI in Education, Intelligent Educational Systems, Interactive Learning Environments, etc. is superficially flourishing but subficially in disarray. All the relevant conferences and journals attempt to impose some structure on the field by suggesting the various sub-fields in which papers may be written (for example, the Montreal ITS conference suggested 'learning environments', 'architecture and methodology', 'curriculum and knowledge representation', 'foundations', 'student modelling', 'design issues', 'practical use of ITS', and 'empirical studies'), but in practice authors and readers often cannot identify the sub-field to which a paper belongs. For example, most of the papers at the Montreal ITS conference could have been shuffled into a session of a different title and not looked out of place.

This matters because it leaves authors and readers (including referees) unsure of the standards and criteria that they are aiming for. For example, almost all the ECAI-90 ITS papers were rejected - a not unusual fate for ITS papers for any AI conference - but, more significantly, the referees' grounds for rejection were often radically different or even inconsistent. While one referee insists that a paper is totally unacceptable because no system has been implemented, another objects that a paper just describes yet another implemented system. In addition, a common referees' complaint was that authors did not seem to appreciate that techniques they described were in fact similar to those that other authors had previously described.

As a result, most papers in the field fall into one of the following categories:

(a) descriptions of partially implemented systems not susceptible to any kind of empirical evaluation (e.g. [7]);

(b) discussions of principles or 'slogans' which are so vague that they can be bandied back and forth forever (e.g. [14]);

(c) ridiculously ambitious research proposals which are quite incapable of implementation in the foreseeable future (e.g. [13]);

(d) empirical studies which do not reveal which aspects of designs are responsible for the success or failure of implemented systems (not guilty, m'lud).

The problem arises, I believe, because researchers have attempted to marry various associated methodologies within ITS research without identifying the stratum at which such research may make a significant, unique contribution. It is this stratum which Computational Mathetics is intended to identify.

Computational Linguistics and Computational Mathetics

In order to develop the content of Computational Mathetics we may first pursue the analogy with Computational Linguistics, mentioned above. There are some similarities in the processes of 'learning' and 'using language' (there is not one verb for this but several, e.g. 'writing', 'speaking'):

: They are 'universal' processes in that all normal individuals in all cultures develop some ability at the processes.

: There are universal principles that hold for language or for learning. In the case of language, the observation in 1786 by Sir William Jones (Chief Justice in Bengal) that modern languages "have sprung from some common source which, perhaps, no longer exists" was considered deeply insightful and is sometimes regarded as marking the birth of 'linguistics'. In the case of learning, the assumption of universal principles seems to have gone unremarked - but conversely if studies were carried out we might well find that cultures differ in their abilities at different learning processes.

: Although all individuals develop some ability in these processes, a deliberate educational effort can develop them further. In England, 'English language' is a core of the primary and secondary curriculum and courses such as 'study skills' are sometimes offered although more often teaching about 'learning' is distributed opportunistically around other courses.

: Both processes can be carried out individually or within groups: hence there are both cognitive and social aspects to consider.

: Both processes can be carried out by agents other than humans, for example, chimps, computers, etc.

But whereas Linguistics has been a recognised discipline for two centuries or more, there is no corresponding discipline for 'learning', and hence no noun filling the gap for which 'Mathetics' is proposed. To the extent that it exists today, Mathetics is contained within disciplines such as Education and Psychology. If Computational Mathetics were to exist, what would it look like?

Computational Linguistics fits within Linguistics as shown in Figure 1: it is one of a number of overlapping subdisciplines, with an established body of theory and techniques (e.g. [6]) which may be applied to build systems of various kinds.

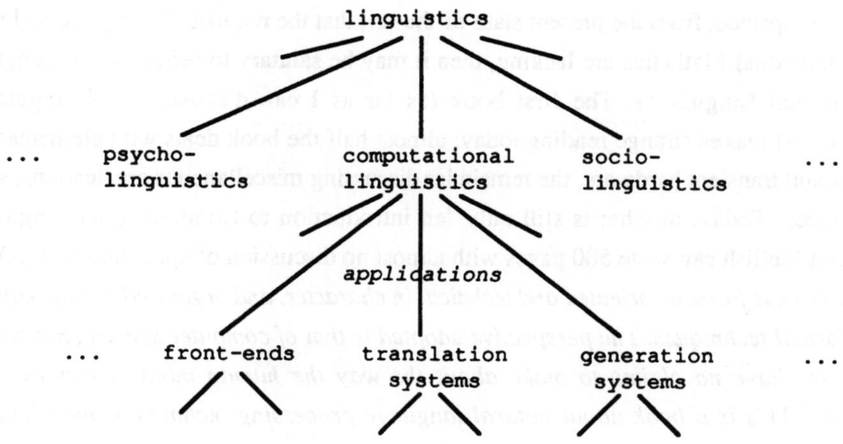

Figure1. The place of Computational Linguistics

By analogy, Computational Mathetics might fit as shown in Figure 2. It is not seriously suggested that the subjects of psychomathetics, sociomathetics, etc. be invented, but Computational Mathetics *is* proposed to provide an objective, systematic, explicit, computationally-oriented account of the various application areas. Most AI and Education research is concerned with the lower nodes of this tree - but as Wenger remarks, "in the long run, research on a precise definition of (learning and) teaching in computational terms is as important as engineering feats" [20].

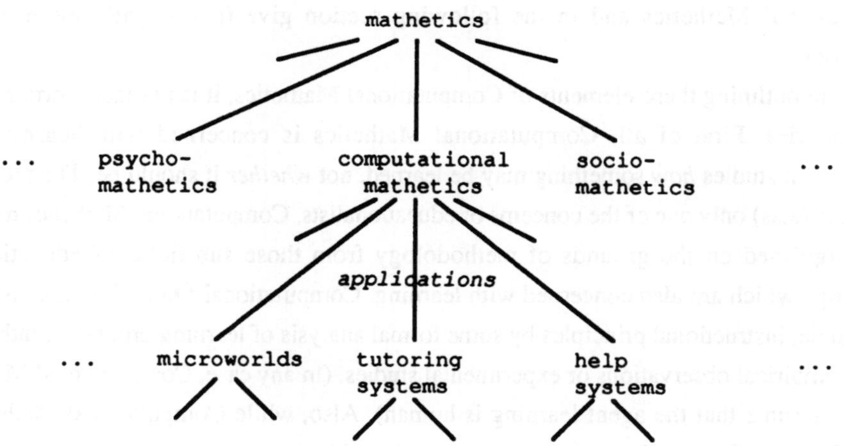

Figure 2. The place of Computational Mathetics

If it is suspected, from the present state-of-the-art, that the requisite 'theory and techniques' for Computational Mathetics are lacking, then it may be salutary to reflect on the progress of Computational Linguistics. The first book (as far as I can discover) on Computational Linguistics [8] makes strange reading today: almost half the book deals with elementary data structures and transient hardware, the remainder discussing miscellaneous applications, such as concordances. Today, in what is still only "an introduction to Computational Linguistics", Gazdar and Mellish can write 500 pages with almost no discussion of applications [6]. As they say, *"The book is formally oriented and technical in character, and organised, for the most part, around formal techniques. The perspective adopted is that of computer science, not cognitive science. We have no claims to make about the way the human mind processes natural language.... This is a book about natural language processing techniques, not about their application."* Is 'learning' so inherently more complex than 'language' that we cannot aspire to something similar for Computational Mathetics?

The Scope of Computational Mathetics

Some of the nascent elements of Computational Mathetics exist now in various sister disciplines. So far these elements have not been brought together to form an integrated, coherent area of study, and few of them have found direct application in computer-based learning system design. The formation of a field of Computational Mathetics might promote the synergetic development of these elements and, ultimately, to the principled implementation of computer-based learning systems. In this section we will just give an overview of the scope of Computational Mathetics and in the following section give four slightly more detailed illustrations.

Before outlining these elements of Computational Mathetics, it is perhaps worth marking its boundaries. First of all, Computational Mathetics is concerned with 'learning', not 'education': it studies *how* something may be learned, not *whether* it should be. The process of learning is (alas) only one of the concerns of educationalists. Computational Mathetics may also be distinguished on the grounds of methodology from those sub-fields of education and psychology which are also concerned with learning. Computational Mathetics aims to derive, for example, instructional principles by some formal analysis of learning processes, rather than through empirical observations or experimental studies. (In any case, Computational Mathetics does not assume that the agent learning is human). Also, while Computational Mathetics is intended to contribute to the design of computer-based learning systems, it does not provide a complete basis for successful such designs. It does not, for example, consider the properties of computer hardware in educational institutions and the socio-political problems of educational innovation - this is not to say that these issues are unimportant in the wider context but that they may usefully be divorced from the concerns of Computational Mathetics.

The elements of Computational Mathetics listed below represent only a preliminary survey of the field. In most cases, the elements do not yet exist in a sufficiently rigorous form to satisfy the aims of Computational Mathetics, and where they do they often are expressed in idiosyncratic notations. The hope is that identifying a field of Computational Mathetics will focus a programme of research and that, in due course, Computational Mathetics will become greater than the sum of its presently disparate elements.

The questions addressed within Computational Mathetics might be summarised under eight headings (although it is the approach rather than the topics themselves which makes Computational Mathetics distinctive):

The outcome of learning

Why do agents learn? Presumably to acquire knowledge which may be used to solve problems. Therefore we must consider the nature of knowledge, or rather, the natures of knowledge, since it comes in many forms. For Computational Mathetics, this is not just a philosophical exercise but involves a formal study of the properties of various kinds of computational knowledge representations, with a particular emphasis on transient knowledge structures rather than the final 'expertise' focussed on in much of AI. 'Knowledge' is really the intended, eventual outcome of learning: Computational Mathetics is about the processes of learning and at any intermediate stage, learners do not possess knowledge - rather they possess 'beliefs'. These beliefs might not have the desirable properties of knowledge - they may be untrue, inconsistent or incomplete. The computational representation of beliefs is accordingly more complex. Computational Mathetics will here look to work done on formalising knowledge and belief in philosophy and AI (possible worlds, situation semantics, etc.) and to educational philosophies of knowledge.

Learning from a knowledgeable agent

Much human learning is carried out by communicating with an agent (human teacher, textbook, intelligent tutoring system) which is assumed to have 'correct' knowledge of the domain of interest. Most ITSs are based on this 'knowledge communication' paradigm. In Computational Mathetics we aim to make precise the emerging standard techniques of ITS research, such as overlay models, differential models, model tracing, bug theories and mal-rules. In particular, we would aim to define the scope and limitations of the knowledge communication approach.

The "framework for learner modelling" discussed in section 5.1 is an illustration of a Computational Mathetics analysis of existing techniques abstracted from applications.

Learning from reasoning

Agents must possess some knowledge, or at least beliefs, before they acquire further knowledge. Sometimes learning occurs as an incidental or deliberate side-effect of using the knowledge already acquired in order to reason to solve a problem. For example, analogy and metaphor may provoke learning processes based on prior knowledge. Often, however, learners will have inadequate prior knowledge or they may make limited use of it (for example, by adopting an inappropriate viewpoint). To formalise these processes, in order to better understand the situations in which learning from reasoning may or may not be productive, we may look to AI research on problem-solving, analogical reasoning and explanation-based learning, and to various formalisations of the notion of a 'viewpoint' in belief logics and distributed AI (see section 5.3).

Learning from reflection

'Learning by doing' (as in 4.3 above) is a limited notion. Learning occurs less through the doing than through reflecting on what is done (either before, during or after the process). The importance of such metacognitive activities in enabling learning is being increasingly emphasised in educational philosophies. Moreover, it is seen that the acquisition of such metacognitive skills is an important outcome of learning. Work in AI has recently stressed the role of metaknowledge and has developed some formalisations of it, and there is related research on the definition of reflective computational architectures and of concepts such as introspection and self-awareness.

Learning through exploration and experimentation

Sometimes the learning environment provides more than just a context to solve problems in or to reflect on - it provides a world for the agent to explore and experiment with. The way in which such a world is presented to the learner is crucial. Perhaps recent work on interface models and ideas of direct manipulation can provide a basis. Also, we need to understand the way learners view the world, which will entail the development of research on naive science and qualitative reasoning, and of how learners form and refine hypotheses about the world. The somewhat amorphous idea of 'situated learning' (that learners should learn in context and that the context itself somehow embeds what has to be learned) may be made more precise. We might hope that this will lead to some integration of the simulation/microworld/ITS schools.

Learning through cognitive conflict

A prevailing view of learning is that it is provoked by a conflict between the agent's beliefs and some acquired evidence. This conflict may be deliberately created by some other agent, e.g. a teacher or ITS, or sought by the learner. Computational Mathetics needs therefore to consider formally how conflicts may be created, and their effects on a learner. This will involve some consideration of philosophical views of belief change and the application of AI work on reason maintenance.

Learning through interaction and dialogue

In most learning situations there are agents (teachers, other learners, computer systems) other than the learner. The interaction between these agents strongly affects the learning outcomes. In the simplest case, one teacher and one learner, we may aim to apply general dialogue principles, such as dialogue game theory, and theories of rational interaction based on agents' nested beliefs (i.e. beliefs about one another's beliefs). One aim might be to derive effective learning strategies formally (rather than through empirical observation or intuition). Different interactional styles, such as collaborative ones (advocated by some educationalists), may be defined precisely and their properties explored theoretically. Perhaps work in distributed AI and computer-supported collaborative work will be relevant. Computational Mathetics may develop some justification for the argument that knowledge is acquired through some kind of negotiative process, rather than absorbed from some knowledgeable agent. Maybe some precision can be given to the view that the products of learning are possessed not by an individual agent but by society as a whole.

Strategies for promoting learning

The outcome of these formal investigations into the nature of learning and how it may be promoted should be (apart from a deeper understanding of the process itself) a set of 'mathetic principles', that is, a set of formally-derived, precisely-stated principles for promoting learning. These principles should follow as corollaries of the analyses of learning. They should be more narrow, focussed and precise than the 'instructional strategies' of educationalists and therefore of greater applicability to the design and implementation of computer-based learning systems (the instructional strategies being notoriously difficult to apply as explicit algorithms rather than 'guiding principles'). This, of course, remains to be seen. The long-term aim (and it is clearly long-term since many of the elements of the programme sketched above exist only in rudimentary form and no doubt other unmentioned elements will also emerge) is that Computational Mathetics provides a formal, theoretical foundation for the design of computer-based learning systems in much the same way as aeronautics provides the foundation for aircraft design [16].

Four Illustrations of Computational Mathetics

In this section we will outline four preliminary studies which might be considered to be within the field of Computational Mathetics. At this stage, it is the methodology and objectives, rather than achievements, which are important.

A framework for learner modelling

The learner model is the central and yet most controversial component of intelligent tutoring systems. Part of the controversy derives from the observation that learner modelling research is "unabashedly psychological" [2]. If the learner modelling goal is taken to be to build a high-fidelity psychological model of a learner then of course cognitive psychologists will assert that it is unattainable and hence that ITS builders should manage without a learner model. However, a Computational Mathetics perspective emphasises the computational demands on learner models, that is, the functions they actually need to carry out within computer-based learning systems [15].

From this perspective, we can see that a large number of computational techniques for learner modelling have been described - which gives rise to a further controversy: which of these techniques is to be preferred? This is unanswerable without some basis for comparison, which is the role of Computational Mathetics - it should provide a precise, formal definition and description of the techniques from which their properties may be derived and assessed (rather as Computational Linguistics handles grammatical formalisms). In other words, the techniques are evaluated in terms of their computational properties not their psychological validity.

As a first step, we have devised a framework and a notation within which almost all present learner modelling techniques can be described [5] - see Figure 3.

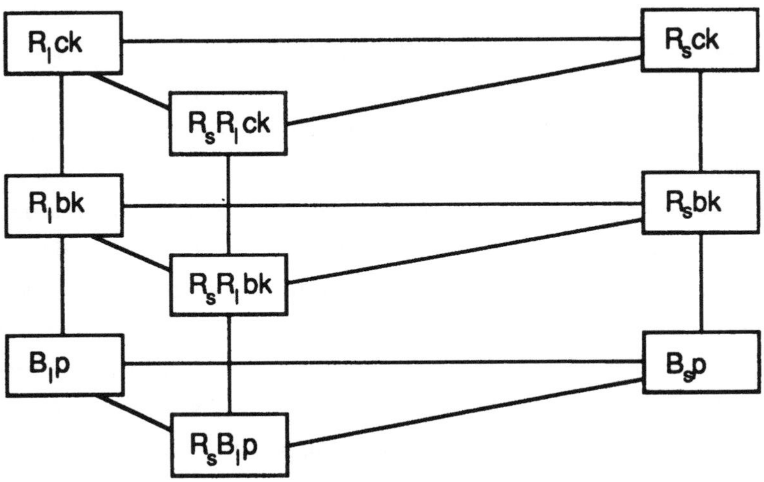

Figure 3. A framework for learner modelling

The framework is intended to provide an objective summary of computational techniques without any commitment to any underlying educational or psychological philosophy.

The meaning of the framework and the mapping of techniques onto it is fully described in [5]. Briefly, the basic framework (Figure 3) considers that learner modelling involves the system building a computational representation of the learner's representation of conceptual and behavioural knowledge (R_SR_lck and R_SR_lbk), given (usually) a representation of the learner's behaviour while solving some problem p (R_SB_lp) and the corresponding system representations (R_Sck, R_Sbk, and B_Sp). Like Gazdar and Mellish, we are making no cognitive science claims about the way the human mind works, merely providing (we hope) a fruitful way of describing existing techniques. In particular, the conceptual-behavioural distinction is not a psychological point but a computational one, and is related to discussions about deep and shallow knowledge, declarative and procedural knowledge, and ultimately to the fundamental computer science concepts of data and program.

In [5] we go on to map, one-by-one, existing techniques on to this framework. At the risk of incomprehensibility, I have combined some of these into one figure (Figure 4). While the framework does not yet provide a formal analysis of learner modelling, it does yield several potential benefits:

: It shows that existing techniques are often not in competition, as sometimes described, but address different aspects of the learner modelling problem.

: It begins to provide an analytic treatment of learner modelling viewed as a search process.

: It reveals where progress has and has not been made - for example, most learner modelling research is represented in the lower half of our framework, with little addressing the conceptual aspects.

: Like any notation, it provides a tool to think with (for example, a set of papers, superficially unrelated but all considered by their authors to be concerned with learning modelling, submitted to a workshop on language learning could be integrated within this framework [18]).

: It enables some progress to be made without interminable, imprecise discussions on deep philosophical, psychological and educational issues.

: It indicates how we might begin to describe other aspects of ITS design, such as didactics, which are also sorely in need of some precision.

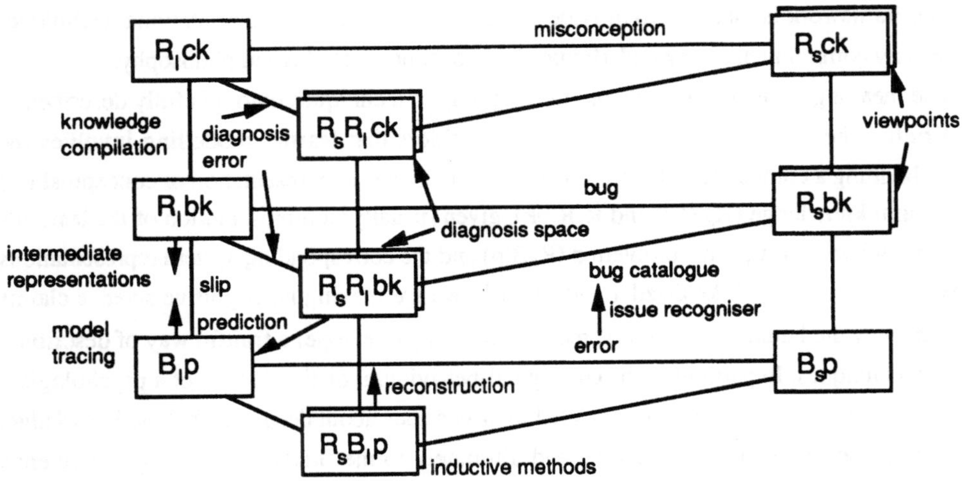

Figure 4. An embellished framework for learner modelling

Diagnosis

Diagnosis has been considered a prime objective of learner modelling - in fact, the term 'diagnosis' has the longest index entry in Wenger's definitive text on ITS [20]. And yet some researchers consider diagnosis to be unnecessary, arguing instead that a suitably reactive environment is what is needed. This seems to me to misconceive the purpose of diagnosis as being purely for remediation. Instead, diagnosis (in the sense of understanding the learner) can serve a number of pedagogical aims. The confusion is possible because of a lack of precision in the use of the term. Wenger, for example, makes no reference to the considerable body of AI research which attempts to develop computational formalisms for diagnosis.

For example, general theories of diagnosis from first principles, that is, by reasoning not dependent on domain-dependent heuristics representing compiled experience, have been developed (e.g. by Reiter [12]). The system (e.g. an electrical circuit, or a medical patient) to be diagnosed is described by means of a set SD of axioms defining the behaviour of the components of the system if they are not faulty, e.g.

$$\text{and-gate}(x) \ \& \ \sim\text{faulty}(x) \to \text{out}(x) = \text{in1}(x) \text{ and in2}(x)$$

i.e. if an and-gate is not faulty its output is the conjunction of its inputs. If all the components are not faulty the axioms determine the expected behaviour of the system, i.e.

$$\text{SD} \ \& \ \sim\text{faulty}(c_1) \ \& \ \sim\text{faulty}(c_2) \ \ldots \to \text{expected behaviour}$$

where c_1, c_2, .. are the components of the system. Diagnosis begins if the observed behaviour OBS differs from the expected behaviour.

Diagnosis involves retracting one or more assumptions that a component is not faulty to restore the consistency between expected and observed behaviour. Clearly we would tend to prefer a diagnosis which conjectures that some minimal set of components is faulty. Thus, a diagnosis D is a minimal set such that

$$\{c_1, c_2, ..\} \supseteq D \ \&$$

$$SD \cup OBS \cup \{faulty(c) \mid c \in D\} \cup \{\sim faulty(c) \mid c \in \{c_1, c_2, ..\} - D\}$$

is consistent. Re-expressing this in learner modelling terms, we might have a diagnosis D being a minimal set such that

$$\{p_1, p_2, ..\} \supseteq D \ \&$$

$$D_s \cup A_l \cup \{faulty(p) \mid p \in D\} \cup \{\sim faulty(p) \mid p \in \{p_1, p_2, ..\} - D\}$$

is consistent, where

$$D_s \ \& \sim faulty(p_1) \ \& \sim faulty(p_2) \ ... \ \text{->} \ A_s$$

where D_s is the system's domain knowledge, p_i are propositions or rules, A_l is the learner's answer, and A_s is the system's answer.

To determine a diagnosis we may systematically postulate that each component (proposition or rule) in turn is faulty, and then that each pair of components is faulty, and so on. Obviously, this method is too inefficient for systems with large numbers of components when a number of them may be faulty. A more efficient algorithm for computing diagnoses is given in [12]. In the learner modelling context, however, we may have little confidence in a diagnosis that postulated that several components were faulty, and hence a simple generate-and-test algorithm may be adequate. An application of Reiter's diagnosis procedure to learner modelling is described in [9].

In fact, a rather similar procedure to Reiter's had been proposed by Young and O'Shea [21] in their production system analysis of subtraction. The postulate faulty(c_1) effectively disables the definition of the component c_1 from SD: similarly, Young and O'Shea suggested that a system could diagnose many of a learner's subtraction mistakes by removing one or more rules from the system describing the component sub-procedures of a correct subtraction algorithm. Thus, the rules of their production system:

```
CM: processcolumn -> compare, finddiff, nextcolumn.
        B2a: S>M -> borrow.
              etc.
```

can be re-expressed as 'component axioms' in Prolog, e.g.

```
rule(cm):- not faulty(cm), processcolumn, compare, finddiff, nextcolumn.
rule(b2a):- not faulty(b2a), gr(S,M), borrow.
etc.
```

Running the rules (using an interpreter with the required conflict resolution strategies) with no assertions that a rule is faulty gives the expected (correct) output, because of Prolog's closed-world assumption. If we assert, for example, faulty(b2a), then the output is not as expected because rule(b2a) no longer fires.

Deleting a rule (for example, the one which decrements the preceding digit when borrowing) from a production system does sometimes produce output behaviour which corresponds to standard learners' mistakes. But sometimes it is known that when a component is faulty then it doesn't merely not work at all but it often works in some other predictable way. So in addition to deleting a rule by assuming it faulty we may add further rules which may correspond to the faulty behaviour (as suggested by Young and O'Shea). For example, we might add the rule:

```
rule(cm):- faulty(cm), processcolumn, finddiff, nextcolumn.
```

which says that a faulty version of the cm rule omits to carry out the compare operation (leading to the common mistake that 46 - 29 = 23). We could add a number of such rules to correspond to known faulty versions of the 'correct' rule.

The status of such faulty rules (or, more generally, beliefs) in the system needs to be carefully described. If f is such a rule, we cannot say that the system believes it to be true nor that the system can assume that the learner believes it. Rather, the system may believe that a typical hypothetical learner may believe it. In learner modelling, such faults are of course usually called *bugs* or *mal-rules* and a set of faults a *bug catalogue*.

We might now define a *fault-diagnosis* F to be a minimal set of paired terms $\{<p,f>\}$ such that

$$p \in \{p_1, p_2, ..\} \;\&$$
$$f \in \{f_1, f_2, ..\} \;\&$$
$$D_s \cup A_l \cup \{faulty(p_i) \;\&\; f_i \mid p_i \in D\} \cup$$
$$\{\sim faulty(p) \mid p \in \{p_1, p_2, ..\} - D\}$$

is consistent, where

$$D_s \;\&\; \sim faulty(p_1) \;\&\; \sim faulty(p_2) \; ... \; \text{->} \; A_s$$

that is, a fault-diagnosis is a minimal set such that if the description of a component p_i is replaced by that of an associated faulty component f_i, then the system may derive the learner's answer. It is conjectured that a fault-diagnosis (which describes *how* a component is faulty) provides more pedagogical leverage than a diagnosis (which says *that* a component is faulty). This conjecture has been the subject of recent debate (e.g. [19]).

Thus a diagnostic procedure might be as follows: first, attempt to derive A_l using D_s and D_l (where D_l is the learner's domain knowledge) - if this is successful, then the system may postulate that the learner believes those propositions used in the derivation; if it fails, then use a diagnosis procedure (such as Reiter's algorithm) to isolate missing or faulty components; then, for those components isolated, use a fault-diagnosis procedure to determine associated faults. An exhaustive fault-diagnosis procedure, in which each faulty component is systematically replaced by a member of the set of faults, is clearly not feasible in general. Instead, all ITSs which make use of a set of faults contain explicit pre-determined links between a component and its associated faults. Thus, identifying the faulty component leads directly to a small set of potential faults which can be exhaustively searched. In the case of the Lisp tutor's model tracing algorithm these steps are combined: the propositions (or rules) in the system's domain knowledge and in the bug catalogue are merged and this merged set is used to make predictions about the learner's next step.

Existing AI formalisms for diagnosis can be used to define some ITS approaches to cognitive diagnosis, which may help clarify their analytic properties. However, this is not simply a one-way process, which Computational Mathetics borrows formalisms from AI: the informal diagnostic procedures used in some ITSs seem to be much richer than those studied in AI. They do, for example, concern themselves much more with interactive diagnostic procedures. Formalising such techniques might lead to a sugnificant contribution to AI.

The notion of a 'viewpoint'

One of the outcomes of recent ITS research has been the conclusion that providing only a single correct domain representation to be communicated to a learner limits what ITSs may achieve. Often (for example, in physics and second language learning) learners have alternative and prior conceptualisations which need to be represented. Also, in some domains (for example, economics) there is no single correct representation but several competing theories - in such a domain, competence lies more in being able to adopt and reason within different theories than in being expert in any one of them. Consequently, it has been argued that ITSs need to represent such 'viewpoints' - for example, Wenger considers that "the topic seems ripe for more research" [20].

The case for representing viewpoints seems clear: what is needed now is not more philosophical discussion and psychological experimentation to clarify the notion of a viewpoint, but ways of making the notion computationally useful. As it happens, the concept of a 'viewpoint' appears under different guises throughout computer science: in software engineering, the term is used in recognition of the fact that a single top-down analysis is usually invalid and that systems need to be looked at according to the services used; in distributed processing, computational, engineering and enterprise viewpoints are technical terms denoting the standpoint from which the system is described; in database systems, different 'views' are represented; in artificial intelligence, the idea of viewpoints appears in distributed AI, belief systems, dialogue theories, cooperative problem-solving, and so on [17].

Of course, none of these views on viewpoints may meet the specific needs of Computational Mathetics. Nonetheless, there is a solid body of theory and techniques within computer science upon which we may build - in contrast to the opinion that the topic of viewpoints "has not yet been addressed by the field in principled ways" [20]. The position of the concept of a 'viewpoint' within Computational Mathetics may be rather like that of 'unification' within Computational Linguistics - a foundational concept within the field but one which in various forms is ubiquitous in computer science.

In general terms, a viewpoint is a set of beliefs which cohere in some way. With uni-agent viewpoints, the focus is on moving towards a viewpoint appropriate for a particular problem or in reconciling disparities between conflicting viewpoints. With multi-agent viewpoints, the emphasis is on the 'negotiative process' whereby agents with differing viewpoints may nonetheless work cooperatively or at least come to some agreement. Sometimes viewpoints are regarded as purely declarative structures; sometimes a procedural aspect is considered to be an integral part of a viewpoint. Within Computational Mathetics, the evolution of viewpoints will be as important as their representations and uses.

Nichols suggests that belief structures may be decomposed into viewpoints along several dimensions [11]. For example, macro-economics has at least the following dimensions and viewpoints:

: Theory - Keynesian, Monetarist, Marxist, ...

: Market - Labour market, Capital market, Foreign exchange market, ...

: International relation - Closed economy, Open economy, ...

These viewpoints may have sub-viewpoints which inherit the core beliefs from the parent viewpoint, and macro-economics is itself a viewpoint within economics, and so on. Reasoning then occurs within a 'current viewpoint' composed from these sub-viewpoints - for example, within a Keynesian Labour market macro-economic viewpoint. The development of computational compositional rules for viewpoints, while clearly part of the general knowledge representation enterprise, would be an activity within Computational Mathetics because it may be expected to lead to more powerful means of modelling learners and hence to support more insightful tutorial interactions.

The formalisation of tutoring principles

The tutoring component of ITSs is implemented in the absence of any formal educational theory from which tutoring principles may be derived. While it may be to misconceive the aims of educational research to hope that such a theory may be forthcoming from that field, nonetheless Computational Mathetics needs precise principles rather than ad-hoc algorithms.

One possibility is to attempt to derive such principles by empirical observation of human tutors, as Collins and Stevens [4] did for Socratic teaching. While these were intended to be "explicit rules needed to guide implementation of inquiry methods in ICAI systems", they were still stated in natural language rather than, say, formal logic and demand some careful interpretation before they can be implemented. Perhaps the main difficulty with the methodology is the large conceptual gap between observations and principles which has to be bridged by the theorisers. The principles are not direct generalisations of observed events but are derived from detailed (but implicit) hypotheses about the (unobservable) relationships between tutor and student belief systems.

Alternatively, rather than merely observing tutors, we could try to engage them in some knowledge acquisition process in which they attempt to make their tutoring strategies explicit. Our attempts in this direction have had mixed success [1]. Experienced teachers, at least in the domain we were concerned with (second language learning), have rich sets of examples which they draw on in certain situations but they cannot say precisely when and why. In addition, they are simply not used to carrying out the in-depth analysis of an individual learner's activities which ITS designers have in mind. The conclusion often drawn, that because human tutors do not appear to perform such analyses then ITSs need not either, is precisely wrong: ITSs should supplement and perhaps improve upon human tutoring, and the hypothesis (which ITS research is begin to support) is that detailed analyses of the kind ITSs aim for can lead to improved learning.

It may be possible to derive instructional principles from a different direction entirely, that is, by trying to write some axioms which characterise rational instructional interactions (as in attempts to derive a general 'theory of communication' [3]) and to reason with those. It must be emphasised at the outset that (as with learner modelling) the aim is not complete correctness, which is clearly unattainable: the aim is computational utility, explicitness and analysability (just as Computational Linguistics can proceed in the full knowledge that a complete correct grammar of a natural language is unattainable).

We might state as an axiom that if a teacher asserts a proposition p then p is true, the learner believes it, the teacher believes it, the learner believes the teacher believes it, and so on:

Asserts(t,p) -> p & B(l,p) & B(t,p) & B(l, B(t,p)) & ...

Of course, this is too simple (but not much simpler than that implicit in many implemented instructional strategies!): the question is, can we refine it sufficiently to be computationally useful? A similar rule is used in a system [10] to build a user model from a cooperative advisory dialogue:

B(u,expert(s)) & do(s,tell(s,u,p)) -> B(u,p)

i.e. "if the user u believes the system s to be an expert and s tells u the proposition p then u believes p". Kass provides thirteen such rules which are intended to formalise the nature of the dialogues he is interested in - here, for example, is the 'sufficiency rule':

coop-agent(u) & current-goal(s,g1) & subgoal(g2,g1) & ~do(u,g2)
-> ~B(u,current-goal(s,g1)) v ~B(u,subgoal(g2,g1)) v
B(u,can-do(s,g1)) v B(u,~can-do(u,g2))

i.e. "if the system knows that a certain action must be performed by a cooperative user to accomplish the current goal but the user fails to perform that action, then either the user doesn't know the current goal, he doesn't believe the action is relevant, he believes the system can achieve the current goal, or he believes he cannot perform the action." If this were to be used to support a tutorial dialogue, we can readily imagine how appropriate tutorial interventions might follow. In fact, Kass's system builds a "robust and detailed model of the user" carrying out a dialogue with an investment advisory system in order to enable the system to generate appropriate explanations.

Within Computational Mathetics, we try to provide similar rules to formalise instructional interactions. For example, the 'principles for Socratic tutoring' can be regarded not as the outcome of empirical studies but the result of reasoning based on representations of the participants' beliefs [16]. Here, for example, are some possible axioms:

Ask(t,q) & Contains(q,term) & B(l,p) & Contains(p,term) -> Aware(l,p)

i.e. "if the teacher asks a question about a term and the learner implicitly believes a proposition p about that term, then he becomes aware of that proposition (i.e. it becomes part of the beliefs with which he reasons)."

Aware(l,P) & ~Implies(P,q) & Asserts(l,q) & Aware(t,r) & Implies(P&r,q)
-> Poss(Aware(l,r))

i.e. "if the learner is aware of a set of propositions P which do not imply q and yet he asserts q and the teacher is aware of a proposition r which if added to P enables q to be derived, then perhaps the learner is also aware of r."

Aware(l,P) & Implies(P,q) & Implies(P,~q) -> Will-refine(l,P)

i.e. "if the learner is aware of a set of propositions which imply both q and ~q then he will refine the set P" (in some manner akin to reason maintenance systems).

Aware(l,P) & Implies(P,r) & Aware(t,q) & Implies(P&q,~r) -> Ask(t,q)

i.e. "if the learner is aware of a set of propositions which imply r and the teacher is aware of a proposition q which if added to P enables ~r to be derived, then ask the question q."

The details of the rules are not important here, nor is the fact that we will never be able to make them 'correct': the point is that they *can* be specified and that they could form a formal basis for supporting mathetic interactions. These axioms are not themselves primitive but ultimately derive from deeper interactional principles: to the extent that these can be specified we can move towards a true theory of learning and teaching.

Conclusions

This paper suggests that a theoretical level, which we have called Computational Mathetics, is needed for carrying out research on, and supporting implementations of, intelligent computer-based learning systems. Computational Mathetics is based upon the techniques, concepts and methodologies of computer science and artificial intelligence. It supplements the educational, philosophical and psychological considerations which pass for theory in 'AI and education' research today and to which implementers, because of the complexity of their task and the consequent apparent arbitrariness of their designs, have been overly subservient. There is a substantial body of computer science and AI which can be adopted and extended to form the basis of the field of Computational Mathetics.

The analogy with Computational Linguistics was pursued to indicate the status and role of Computational Mathetics. Just as Computational Linguistics forms the theoretical and technical foundation for implementations of linguistic systems, so Computational Mathetics forms the theoretical and technical foundation for implementations of mathetic (i.e. learning and teaching) systems. The historical accident that there is no discipline of Mathetics does not remove our need for a subject of Computational Mathetics!

We gave a preliminary survey of the scope of Computational Mathetics, indicating those areas of computer science and AI from which we would expect to draw. We then gave four slightly more detailed, but still very sketchy, illustrations of the kinds of work which Computational Mathetics encompasses. At this stage, the methodology and how it compares and contrasts with alternatives is the issue.

References

1. Chanier, T., Pengelly, M., Self, J.A. and Twidale, M.B. (1990). Experiments on knowledge acquisition for learner modelling, to be presented at *Delta and Beyond Conference*, The Hague, Netherlands.

2. Clancey, W.J. (1986). Qualitative student models, *Annual Review of Computer Science*, 1, 381-450.

3. Cohen, P.R. and Levesque, H.J. (1990). Intention is choice with commitment, *Artificial Intelligence*, 42, 213-261.

4. Collins, A. and Stevens, A. (1982). Goals and strategies of enquiry teachers, in R. Glaser (ed.), *Advances in Instructional Psychology* 2, Hillsdale, N.J.: New Jersey.

5. Dillenbourg, P. and Self, J.A. (1990). A framework for learner modelling, Technical Report AI-49, Department of Computing, Lancaster University.

6. Gazdar, G. and Mellish, C. (1989). *Natural Language Processing in Lisp: an Introduction to Computational Linguistics*, Reading, Mass.: Addison-Wesley.

7. Gilmore, D.J. and Self, J.A. (1988). The application of machine learning to intelligent tutoring systems, in J.A. Self (ed.), *Artificial Intelligence and Human Learning*, London: Chapman and Hall.

8. Hays, D.G. (1967). *Introduction to Computational Linguistics*, New York: Elsevier.

9. Huang, X., McCalla, G., Greer, J. and Neuhold, E. (1991). Revising deductive knowledge and stereotypical knowledge in a student model, in *User Modeling and User-Adapted Interaction*, 1: 87-115, 1991.

10. Kass, R. (1990). Building a user model implicitly from a cooperative advisory dialog, *Proceedings of the Second International Workshop on User Modelling*, Hawaii.

11. Nichols, D. (1990). A viewpoint-based approach to student and domain modelling in intelligent tutoring systems, internal report, Department of Computing, Lancaster University.

12. Reiter, R. (1987). A theory of diagnosis from first principles, *Artificial Intelligence*, 32, 57-96.

13. Self, J.A. (1985). A perspective on intelligent computer-assisted learning, *Journal of Computer-Assisted Learning*, 1, 159-166.

14. Self, J.A. (1988a). Bypassing the intractable problem of student modelling, *Proceedings of Intelligent Tutoring Systems Conference*, Montreal, pp. 18-24, C. Frasson (ed.), Univ. Montreal.

15. Self, J.A. (1988b). Student models - what use are they?, in P. Ercoli and R. Lewis (eds.), *Artificial Intelligence Tools in Education*, Amsterdam: North-Holand.

16. Self, J.A. (1990a). Theoretical foundations for intelligent tutoring systems, *Journal of Artificial Intelligence in Education*, 1, 4, 3-14.

17. Self, J.A. (1990b). Computational viewpoints, Technical Report AI-44, Department of Computing, Lancaster University.

18. Self, J.A. (1992). Unravelling the learner model mystery, in F. L. Engel, D.G. Bouwhuis, T. Bösser, G. d'Ydewalle (Eds.), *Cognitive Modelling and Interactive Environments in Language Learning*. NATO ASI Series F, vol. 87., Berlin: Springer-Verlag.

19. Sleeman, D.H., Kelly, A.E., Martinak, R., Ward, R.D. and Moore, J.L. (1989). Studies of diagnosis and remediation with high school algebra students, *Cognitive Science*, 13, 551-568.

20. Wenger, E. (1987). *Artificial Intelligence and Tutoring Systems: Computational and Cognitive Approaches to the Communication of Knowledge*, Los Altos: Morgan Kaufmann.

21. Young, R.M. and O'Shea, T. (1981). Errors in children's subtraction, *Cognitive Science*, 5, 153-177.

What's in an ITS? A Functional Decomposition

Radboud Winkels and Joost Breuker
University of Amsterdam, Department of Computer Science & Law, Kloveniersburgwal 72, 1012 CZ Amsterdam, the Netherlands (email: winkels@uvalri.UUCP)

Abstract: The status of the research in the area of Intelligent Tutoring Systems (ITS) has become ambiguous. The history of ITS research is rich, and especially in the 70s it was fundamental AI research, but now it is more and more applied AI. This means that many of the modern AI techniques are lacking. From [34] it is difficult to distil a unifying conception of ITS research. Literature of the 80s is descriptive rather than technical or theoretical. There are almost no attempts towards unification or formalization; on the contrary, there seems to be more confusion about what an ITS is about and what it is made of. In this paper we try to answer this last question by presenting, what we think the functional decomposition of ITS should look like, and we contrast it with the traditional "3-expert" framework that emerges from literature.

Keywords: Functional decomposition, Intelligent Tutoring Systems, Process control.

Introduction

The status of **Intelligent Tutoring Systems** (ITS) research within the AI community has become rather ambiguous. ITS research has a rich history, especially in the 70s when ITSs were used as test bed and source of inspiration for new AI conceptions and techniques. People like Carbonell, Collins, Brown, deKleer, and research institutes like BBN and Xerox Parc are connected to that period. The basis for qualitative reasoning was laid in SOPHIE-III [10, 18].

That situation has changed now. Developing an ITS is seen more as applied AI than as fundamental AI. People consider them to be a special kind of "expert systems" and - as with that branch of applied AI - ties with more fundamental AI research are cut. This means that many of the current ITSs are lacking AI techniques where they would be useful or necessary[1].

A second possible cause of this change of the status of ITS research is that the gap between conventional *Computer Assisted Instruction* (CAI) and ITSs has considerably narrowed. This has many good sides [8], but it also influenced the development of very hybrid ITSs that contain completely spelled out components in stead of generic ones; too much "compiled-out" knowledge and hardly any "deep", qualitative domain models. For practical purposes this may be justified, but in the longer run it is undesirable from a scientific and technical viewpoint.

A third factor that may contribute to the fact that theory formation and deepening was somewhat lacking the last decennium, is the more general question of what methods of education are effective and desirable, and specifically what role the computer can play in education.

---

[1] First of all one can think of the area of Knowledge Representation, but also of more practical techniques like "truth maintenance" and "meta-level reasoning".

This is indeed an old and general, even paradigmatic issue, but it has immediate repercussions on research. The LOGO-debate barely silenced and discovery worlds are in the picture now, or the role of an intelligent coach in such a world - i.e. an ITS - leads to the elimination of the very heart of an ITS[2]: a deep model of a system in the world [16] that represents the subject matter, is being replaced by general learning principles in order for the ITS to "discover" the underlying structure of the domain itself by observing the student. The ITS as student in stead of teacher [19]. Apart from the question whether such an endeavour is functionally plausible and technically feasible, this means that there is less attention for a technical and formal deepening of the ITS paradigm for the simple reason that it is no longer fashionable [44].

The jump from test bed to application happened too quickly for ITSs. [34] give a reasonably complete overview of the research in the 70s, and many will find it difficult to distil a unifying conception from that collection. In the 80s people have tried to do so, but the results are more discursive than technically and theoretically profound and coherent [35, 27, 32, 3]. [33] mentions the more or less pre-scientific character of ITS research. There is no agreed upon theory about learning and teaching from which the functionality and architecture of an ITS could be deduced and against which a working system could be tested. There are hardly any attempts at formalization; rather there is confusion about the components of an ITS, about what it is made of and how it works. It is this confusion we seek to resolve in this paper.

The question *What's in a...?* is of importance, not just to get a good separation of theoretical problems, but particularly because when such a decomposition adheres to the principles of maximal cohesion and decoupling, modules of one ITS can be used in another ("reusable code"). The components appear to implement general functions. In a sense, reusable code provides evidence for generality [44].

To avoid misunderstandings: ITSs do not stand for general functions in education. Nearly all ITSs are *coaches* [3] that are aimed at correcting and expanding the application of knowledge in a particular domain [20. There are few ITSs that are meant to actually teach that initial knowledge. To put it simply: an ITS is used to look over the shoulder of a student working on mathematical problems, but it does not teach the principles of algebra. Books for instance, may be more efficient for that purpose.

The traditional paradigm

If there is any agreement in the field of ITS, it is the idea that an ITS consists of a number of *experts*. Mostly three [25, 15], sometimes four when an "interaction expert" is added [37, 35]. These three or four specialists are (see also figure 1):

---

[2] Or should we use the word "lobotomy"?

[3] With coaching we mean a global function: Support while practicing a task. That is the typical job of a coach, so there is a clear functional overlap, but not a structural one, yet.

1. A **Domain expert** that knows about the subject matter.
2. A **Student expert** that tries to model the knowledge and problems of the student, based on general theories of learning and/or learning problems of the particular domain.
3. A **Teaching or Didactic expert** that knows how knowledge should be transferred or communicated in the educational process.
4. Finally, some people distinguish an **Interaction expert**. This is a specialist in the field of effective communication and therefore can be seen as an extension of previous experts, in particular the Didactic expert.

One can find such somewhat anthropomorphic decompositions in a branch of AI, where **agents** (actors, experts) communicate to perform certain tasks. In *distributed AI* people have developed important ideas and formalisms [4, , 21], and the metaphor of cooperating agents can be used for ITSs, but not in the way explained above. Figure 1a gives the way these agents are supposed to cooperate: independent and exchanging information.

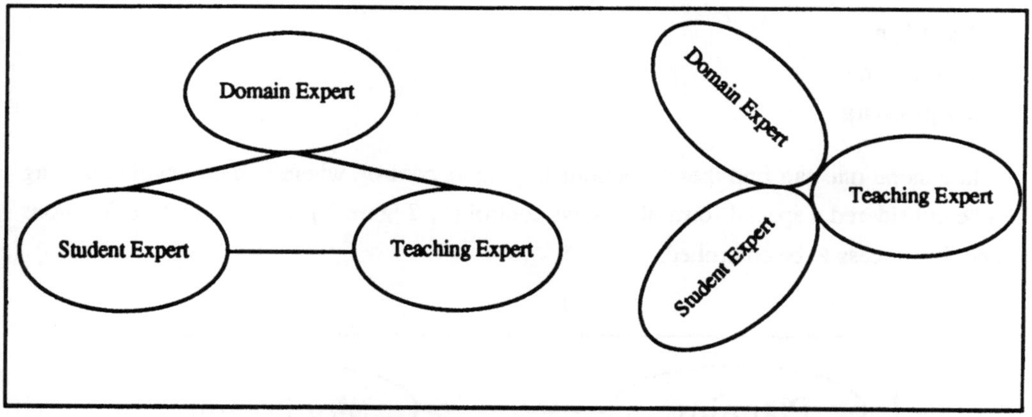

Figure 1: (a) The three experts as they are usually depicted, (b) as their knowledge/functions overlap

In reality, the independence is not there. If we look at the *knowledge* that each expert needs, there is a huge overlap. The most obvious one is that between domain expert and student expert. When trying to establish whether the student made an error and what causes the error, both experts use the same knowledge base, but different "interpreters" of it. It is no coincidence that all detailed student models are so called **overlay** models [12][4]. The Didactic experts uses the same knowledge too. The ordering of topics, i.e. the curriculum, is based on this knowledge plus abstractions of it (meta-knowledge).

---

[4] There is nothing wrong with that: it is the best approximation of the student's knowledge. It is wrong in principle (e.g. Ohlsson, 1988), but the only correct way would be to "look straight in the student's mind".

Besides the overlap in knowledge ("data"), there is a confusion of functions. The student expert for instance is responsible for detecting errors, for finding their cause, and for maintaining the student model, while the domain expert is involved in the first task as well, and the didactic expert in the last. This violates all principles of distributed AI and of good design. The cause of this confusion is a view of ITS in terms of "persons" in stead of functions (roles); perhaps the metaphor is too anthropomorphic after all.

A new metaphor: Coaching as process control

Another view on coaching is based on control functions in problem solving and distribution of tasks, or in AI terms: **meta-level reasoning** and **cooperation**.

[36] distinguish three functions in commercial preparation of wine:

- **Planning**
- **Monitoring**
- **Diagnosing**

In general one can find these functions in process control, whereby meta-level reasoning can be considered a special form of process control [6]. Figure 2 presents the three functions round the process to be controlled.

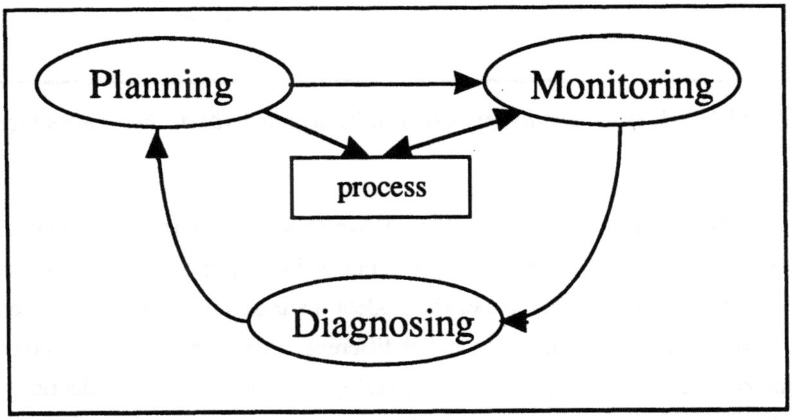

Figure 2: The three functions of process control

The process or task is goal directed, i.e. the execution is based on the planning of a series of actions. Whether the planning is dynamic, or whether it has been done at an earlier stage and a skeletal plan is retrieved, is not of immediate importance, neither whether it happens in top-down or bottom-up fashion. The plan is executed and this execution is being monitored. Monitoring means: results are being compared with expected outcomes. If there is a discrepancy that cannot be corrected right away (negative feedback), a diagnostic process is started in order to find the cause(s) and apply suitable remedies. These remedials will have to be planned as well, so a new cycle is entered. If a local cause and/or remedy cannot be found, a new plan for the original goal will have to be generated. This may imply the undoing of some actions (cf. non-monotonic reasoning).

Planning, monitoring and diagnosing in ITS

Characteristic of coaching is that tasks are performed by both the student and the coach [7, 23]. The role of the coach is not only based on its knowledge of the domain, but especially on its meta-knowledge of the problem solving process. Both student and coach monitor and diagnose this process. Both perform these activities almost simultaneously: the synchronization is mainly controlled by the monitoring function. This explains why "critiquing" [28] and "coaching" are alike. The functions are the same, the level of domain knowledge and meta-knowledge differs. In critiquing the participants are colleagues who compare each others lines of reasoning and conclusions; the levels of knowledge can be considered equal. In coaching these levels are not equal, most of the time.

The **planning** function is usually fixed in an ITS. Such a fixed problem solving strategy in an educational setting takes the form of an advisable course of action, or methods and techniques. In other cases, the student is expected to find a method himself, most of the time based on features of the problem. Whatever the solution, an ITS needs an explicit strategy. The meta-level of a (second generation) expert system is very suitable for that purpose. Identifying problem solving strategies is a great problem; it is the major part of the so called "knowledge acquisition bottle-neck" [7]. Planning such strategies dynamically is currently too difficult for ITSs.

The **monitoring** function is the trait d'union between coach and student. Therefore the coach has to have access to (intermediate) results of the student. This can be achieved through observation [20] or through communication (see below). The coach compares these results to a norm. In traditional CAI these norms are fixed, but in ITS they are generated by a component that simulates the normative problem solving behaviour: an "expert"[5].

---

[5] This is not however just an ordinary expert system (see: Winkels & Breuker, 1990). One of the requirements of such an expert model is that different layers and types of knowledge are well separated (Clancey, 1983).

The **diagnostic** function in problem solving is best illustrated when a student asks for specific information or knowledge. He has himself established what knowledge is missing for successful completion of his task. In most cases however, it will be difficult for a student to decide whether and why something went wrong. The coach is then expected to take the initiative. The diagnostic function is essential in ITSs. Although a lot of literature exists on diagnostic tasks, this is only of marginal importance. Diagnosing malfunctions in artefacts, or even the human body, appears to be simpler than diagnosing errors in a course of action (strategy) or knowledge. The number of things that can go wrong within an artefact is only a subset of what can go wrong with the knowledge about that artefact. On the other hand, the type of defects in artefacts are very heterogeneous, while we still hypothesize only two types of defects in knowledge about a domain: *lacks of knowledge* and *misconceptions* [42]. In most ITSs these last ones are represented as bug catalogs. A generic approach to the diagnosis of misconceptions is very difficult and strongly domain dependent. Even for very basic arithmetic skills this was hardly feasible [10]. Despite the fact that the diagnostic function in ITS is often hybrid and incompletely realised, they are quite useful in educational settings. Human coaches do often not perform better. They too have to deal with few facts and many hypotheses, not to mention their lack of time for dealing with this task.

In summary: the triangle of functions that govern the problem solving process, as depicted in figure 2, are performed by both the student and the coach. In an ITS these functions can be implemented partly generic, partly enumerative and fixed. This triangle of functions gives a completely different view on what the triad of experts are meant to represent in figure 1.

So far we talked about problem solving, and we mentioned few typical didactic functions, at best that a coach (ITS) is probably better at solving a problem and diagnosing what can go wrong in the process. In terms of the traditional framework, the domain expert fell apart in a planner (or: strategy) and part of the monitor. The student expert partly corresponds to the diagnostic function; other parts concern the maintenance of a student model, a supportive function for monitoring, diagnostic and communicative functions (see section: Communication Level). Where did the didactic expert go? This one too we will find scattered about, as we will show below.

Three levels

So far we have only concerned ourselves with the problem solving process, or rather the control of it, not the execution itself. That is situated at a lower level of abstraction: the domain-level in terms of reflexive architectures. We will not discuss the underlying domain level here

[26]. The level of the problem solving process we will call the *Task level.* Input to this level is a task or problem, but where do these tasks come from?

Curriculum level

In education, these tasks come from a *Curriculum level*, where we can distinguish the same triad of functions we found at the task level. The educational goals[6] are **planned** at the Curriculum level, i.e. the order in which domain concepts and training tasks are presented is decided. **Monitoring** consists of evaluating (testing) the results, and when these are not according to expectations, this may lead to for instance "remedial teaching" or an adjustment of the educational goals.

The relation between the curriculum level and the task level is mainly one of aggregation. This relation means that *learning* has to take place: simply put as a combination of the structure of concepts (insight) and increasing complexity of tasks (skill).

In almost all ITSs, as well as in CAI programs, the educational structure of the domain is explicitly represented. The best known example of an ITS with special didactic relations between domain concepts is WUSOR and its "genetic graphs" [24]. The didactic relations, e.g. specialisation and analogy, are meant to facilitate learning: new knowledge is presented when it is closely linked to existing knowledge. Attempts at the dynamic planning of educational goals are seen as modern developments in ITS [35]. [29] describes a Blackboard Instructional Planner that is mainly concerned with adjusting educational plans based on a diagnosis of accumulated student results. The current prototype only works relatively local, it does not plan and maintain an entire curriculum; neither is clear how domain dependent it is. If we want to build shells for ITS, such planners will have to be domain independent, based on learning principles like the relations in genetic graphs.

In the EUROHELP project we developed a shell for Intelligent Help Systems (IHSs)[7]. IHSs offer users of computer applications passive and active help. They can answer questions the user asks (passive side), but also "look over the shoulder" of the user when he is working and can intervene when necessary or appropriate (active side). In this, and many others, respect, an IHS has the same functionality and architecture as an ITS. Part of the EUROHELP shell is a Didactic Goal Generator (DGG) that generates curricula for all possible domains, i.e. computer applications [38, 39]. The DGG constructs genetic graph like structures by an exhaustive comparison of all domain concepts (commands, objects) and inferring didactic relations from their attribute descriptions. Of course this bottom-up procedure is very

[6] Actually, the term "goals" is somewhat incomplete. They are trajectories through the subject matter that lead to the ultimate goals.

[7] EUROHELP was partly funded by the European Community as an ESPRIT project, under contract P280. It ran for five years from 1985 and encompassed a total of 100 person years. Partners were: Axion (Denmark), ICL, University of Leeds (UK), Courseware Europe, University of Amsterdam (the Netherlands). See Breuker (1990) for a full description of the project.

inefficient, but it happens off-line, and a subset of all didactic goals is chosen for a particular user at a particular time.

The planning of educational goals is a typical function of the "teaching expert" from the traditional triad of figure 1. It is only a small part however of what we think "teaching" is about when we think of the interaction between a student and a teacher. In coaching, such interactions occur when the task performance of the student indicates that such is necessary or desirable. "Transferring" information to the student - e.g. what went wrong, what caused it and what the correct way is - requires communication.

Communication level

At the *communication level* we can again distinguish the triad of functions: Planning, monitoring and diagnosing. Both student and coach perform these functions, but the synchronization is different from the task level (see above). Here it happens through **initiative** [7, 22]. Figure 3 presents an overview of the three layers.

It is a recent notion that communication implies the planning of speech acts at the pragmatic level (discourse planning). Literature on the subject is growing: [2], Allen (1987). It may sound like forcing an open door now, but it took quite a long time before "teaching" activities were seen as normal speech acts, i.e. that teaching interactions are plain communication actions. People spent a lot of time looking for specific educational strategies that should form the basis for ITS (notably Ohlsson, 1988), but these do not differ a great deal from discourse strategies in general. Perhaps it is better to state that we use a rather stereotypical subset of ordinary discourse plans in educational settings [38]. The topics are stereotypical, the control of initiative is, and so are the goals (explanation, correction, instruction, etc.). Therefore we recently see a number of people in the ITS field working on *didactic discourse planning* [13, 19, 31, 40, 46].

In contrast to the one between the curriculum layer and the task layer, the relation between the task layer and the communication layer is one of embedding, not of aggregation. Communication is a sub-task, a means for transferring information necessary for the cooperation at the task level. In fact, the communication layer has the same object/meta level structure as the task level. Analogous to the execution of the problem solving process through inferences at the domain level, the communication per se is carried out by transforming speech acts into expressions via some kind of medium. In coaching activities however, communication plays a minor role in cooperation[8].

The communication layer represents the main part of the traditional "teaching expert". At the same time it is clear why the fourth expert - the interaction expert - was always dangling

[8] In ITS in general, imparting insight (declarative knowledge) plays a minor role. An exception is WHY (Collins, 1983). In this case there is no typical task layer, but a direct relation between the curriculum and the communication layer, as one can see from the structure of the Socratic Dialogue in WHY.

about or not mentioned at all: it is difficult to separate it from the teaching expert. The difference is only clear at the curriculum level.

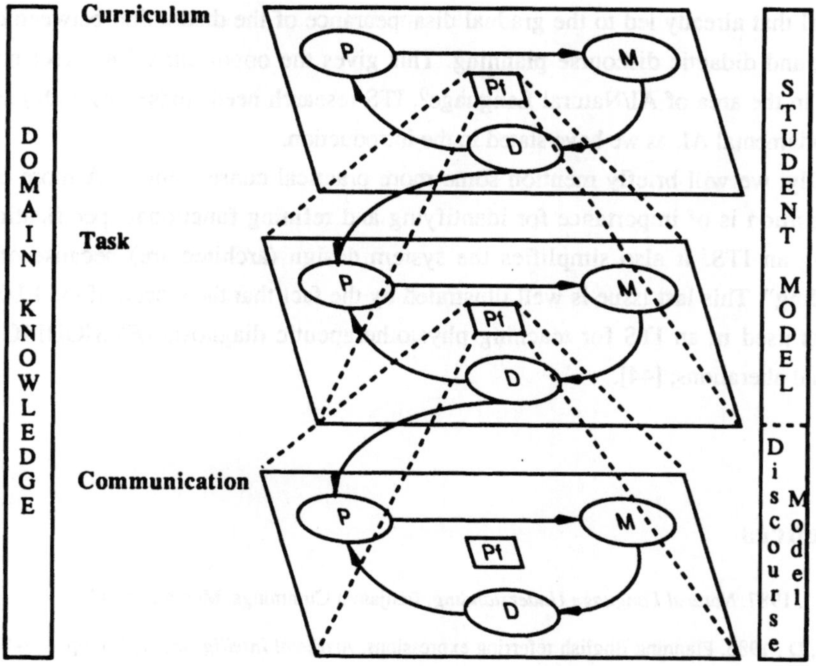

Figure 3: Three levels of process control in an ITS. Every level has three functions: P (planning), M (monitoring) and D (diagnosing), around Pf (performance)

What is the point?

In this paper we cannot specify the role of the two major knowledge or data structures in an ITS: the Domain Representation and the User or Student Model, as depicted in figure 3. Neither can we present an elaborated example of a typical ITS architecture and point out the relation between (sub)function and module [39].

It may have theoretical value that our decomposition of ITSs appears to be sounder, but what are the consequences?

First some consequences for research. Because we can point to a functional overlap with distributed AI, and in particular distributed problem solving [4], it is much easier to exchange insights and techniques than the one suggested by viewing ITSs as a somewhat awkward configuration of experts(ystems). Also the separation of control of, and the actual solving of problems, provides a link to second generation expert systems and especially research in the area of reflexive systems. The specification and elaboration of these control functions is currently one of the most important theoretical, but also practical developments in ITS research.

On a more detailed level, we can point to an overlap between teaching and communication in general that already led to the gradual disappearance of the distinction between discourse planning and didactic discourse planning. This gives the opportunity for direct input from research in the area of AI/Natural Language[9]. ITS research needs these ties with general and more fundamental AI, as we have stated in the introduction.

Finally, we will briefly mention some more practical consequences. A more consistent decomposition is of importance for identifying and refining functional specifications when designing an ITS. It also simplifies the system design (architecture) because of a better "decoupling". This last issue is well illustrated by the fact that the Coach of the EUROHELP shell was used in an ITS for teaching physiotherapeutic diagnosis (FYSIODISC) without substantial alterations; [44].

References

1. Allen, J., 1987. *Natural Language Understanding*. Benjamin Cummings, Menlo Park, CA.

2. Appelt, D., 1985. Planning English referring expressions. *Artificial Intelligence, 15(3)*, pp. 143-178.

3. Bierman, D., Breuker, J.A. & Sandberg, J.A.C.(eds). *Proceedings of the 4th International Conference on AI and Education*. IOS, Amsterdam.

4. Bond, A.H. & Gasser, L., 1988. *Readings in Distributed Artificial Intelligence*. Morgan Kaufman, San Mateo, CA.

5. Breuker, J.A. & deGreef, P., 1989. MODALITEIT, analyse van systeem-gebruiker cooperatie. In: L. Siklossy and R. R. Bakker (eds). *Proceedings van de NAIC-89*, pp. 169-178. Academic Service, Schoonhoven, NL.

6. Breuker, J.A. & Wielinga, B.J., 1987. Use of models in the interpretation of verbal data. In: A.L. Kidd (ed).*Knowledge Acquisition for Expert Systems, a practical handbook*. Plenum Press, New York.

7. Breuker, J.A. & Wielinga, B.J., 1989. Model Driven Knowledge Acquisition. In: P. Guida and G. Tasso (eds). *Topics in the Design of Expert Systems*, pp. 265-296, North Holland, Amsterdam.

8. Breuker, J.A., 1981. Intelligent and rather intelligent CAI. In: *Proceedings of the ADCIS-81*, Atlanta, GA, 1981. ADCIS.

9. Breuker, J.A., 1990 (ed). *EUROHELP: Developing Intelligent Help Systems*. EC, Copenhagen, 1990.

10. Brown, J.S., Burton, R.R. & deKleer, J., 1982. Pedagogical, Natural Language and Knowledge Engineering Techniques in Sophie I, II and III. In: D. Sleeman & J.S. Brown (eds). *Intelligent Tutoring Systems*, Academic Press, New York, N.Y.

11. Burton, R.R. & Brown, J.S., 1982. An investigation of computer coaching for informal learning activities. In D. Sleeman & J.S. Brown (eds). *Intelligent Tutoring Systems*. Academic Press, New York, N.Y..

[9] For other media this does not hold to the same extent, because the influence of AI is less; that of Cognitive Science in general is greater. Traditional CAI by the way, always had stronger ties with multi-media research than ITS and AI in general.

12. Carr, B. & Goldstein, I.P., 1977. *Overlays: A theory of modelling for computer-aided instruction*. Technical Report AI Memo 406, AI Lab. MIT.

13. Cawsey, A., 1989. The Structure of Tutorial Discourse. In: D. Bierman, J.A. Breuker & J.A.C. Sandberg (eds). *Proceedings of the 4th International Conference on AI and Education*, pp. 47-53, IOS, Amsterdam.

14. Clancey, W.J., 1983. The Epistemology of a Rule Based System - a Framework for Explanation. *Artificial Intelligence, 20*, pp. 215-251.

15. Clancey, W.J., 1986. *The Science and Engineering of Qualitative Models*. Technical report, Stanford Knowledge Systems Laboratory, Palo Alto, CA.

16. Clancey, W.J., 1987. *The Knowledge Engineer as Student : Metacognitive Bases for Asking Good Questions*. Working Paper KSL 87-12, Knowledge Systems Laboratory, Palo Alto, CA.

17. Collins, A.M. & Stevens, A.L., 1983. A Cognitive Theory of Interactive Teaching. In C.M. Reigeluth (ed). *Instructional Design Theories and Models: an Overview*. Lawrence Erlbaum, Hillsdale, NJ.

18. deKleer, J., 1990. Qualitative Physics: a personal view. In: D.S. Weld & J. de Kleer (eds). *Qualitative Reasoning about Physical Systems*. Morgan Kaufman, San Mateo, CA.

19. Elsom-Cook, M., 1989. *Dialogue and teaching styles*. Technical Report 62, CITE, Open University, Milton Keynes, GB.

20. Fischer, G., Brown, J.S.& Burton, R.R., 1978. Aspects of a theory of simplification, debugging, and coaching. In: *Proceedings of the Second Annual Conference of the Canadian Society for Computational Studies of Intelligence*, pp. 106-109, Toronto.

21. Gasser, L. & Huhns, M.N., 1989 (eds). *Distributed Artificial Intelligence, volume II*. Morgan Kaufman; Pitman, London, 1989.

22. Greef, P. de, Breuker, J.A. & Jong, T. de, 1988. *Modality: An Analysis of Functions, User Control and Communication in Knowledge-Based Systems*. ESPRIT Project P1098 Deliverable D6 (task A4), University of Amsterdam, 1988.

23. Greef, P. de, Schreiber, G. & Wielemaker, J., 1988b. StatCons: een case study in gestructureerde kennisacquisitie. In: *Proceedings NAIC-88*, pp. 72-80. Sociaal-wetenschappelijke Informatica, University of Amsterdam, April 1988.

24. Goldstein, I.P., 1979. The Genetic Graph: a Representation for the Evolution of Procedural Knowledge. *International Journal of Man-Machine Studies, 11*, pp. 51-77.

25. Hartley, J.R., 1973. The Design and Evaluation of an Adaptive Teaching System. *International Journal of Man-Machine Studies, 5*, pp. 421-436.

26. Maes, P. & Nardi, D., 1988 (eds). *Meta-Level Architectures and Reflection*, North Holland, Amsterdam.

27. Mandl, H. & Lesgold, A., 1988 (eds). *Learning Issues for Intelligent Tutoring Systems*. Springer Verlag, New York.

28. Miller, P.L., 1984]. A Crtitiquing Approach to Expert Computer Advice: ATTENDING. Pitman, London.

29. Murray, W., 1989. Control for Intelligent Tutoring Systems: a Blackboard Based Dynamic Instructional Planner. In: D. Bierman, J.A. Breuker & J.A.C. Sandberg (eds). *Proceedings of the 4th International Conference on AI and Education*, pp. 150-168, IOS, Amsterdam.

30. Ohlsson, S., 1988. Some principles of Intelligent Tutoring. *Instructional Science*, 1988.

31. Petrie-Brown, A., 1989. Intelligent Tutorial Dialogue: The structure of an interaction. In: D. Bierman, J.A. Breuker & J.A.C. Sandberg (eds). *Proceedings of the 4th International Conference on AI and Education*, pp. 195-201, IOS, Amsterdam.

32. Polson, M.C. & Richardson, J.J., 1988 (eds). *Foundations of Intelligent Tutoring Systems*. Lawrence Erlbaum Associates, Hillsdale, NJ.

33. Self, J., 1989. The case for formalising student models. In: D. Bierman, J.A. Breuker & J.A.C. Sandberg (eds). *Proceedings of the 4th International Conference on AI and Education*, pp. 314-322, IOS, Amsterdam.

34. Sleeman, D. & Brown, J.S., 1982 (eds). *Intelligent Tutoring Systems*. Academic Press, London.

35. Wenger, E., 1987. *Artificial Intelligence and Tutoring Systems: Computational and Cognitive Aproaches to the Communication of Knowledge*. Morgan Kaufman, Los Altos, CA.

36. Wielinga, B. & Breuker, J.A., 1984. Interpretation of verbal data for knowledge acquisition. In: T. O'Shea (ed). *Advances in Artificial Intelligence*, pp. 41-50, Elsevier Science Publishers, Amsterdam.

37. Wielinga, B.J., 1985. Kennisgebaseerde systemen ten behoeve van het onderwijs. In: J. Heene & T. Plomp (eds). *Onderwijs en informatietechnologie*. SVO, Den Haag, NL.

38. Winkels, R.G.F. & Breuker, J.A., 1990. Discourse Planning in Intelligent Help Systems. In: C. Frasson & G. Gauthier (eds). *Intelligent Tutoring Systems: At the Crossroads of Artificial Intelligence and Education*, pp. 124-139, Ablex Publishing Corp., New Jersey.

39. Winkels, R.G.F. & Breuker, J.A., 1990. Het modelleren van expertise voor onderwijsdoeleinden. In: H.J. van den Herik & N.J.I. Mars (eds). *Proceedings of the 3rd Dutch AI Conference, NAIC'90*, pp. 269-277, Maastricht, NL.

40. Winkels, R.G.F., 1988. The International Conference on Intelligent Tutoring Systems. *AI Communications*, *1*, pp. 30-33.

41. Winkels, R.G.F., 1990. A New Framework for Describing and Designing Intelligent Tutoring Systems. In: V. Marík, O. Stepánková & Z. Zdráhal (eds). *AI in Higher Education. Lecture Notes in Artificial Intelligence*, vol. 451, pp. 230-243, Springer-Verlag, Berlin.

42. Winkels, R.G.F., Sandberg, J.A.C. & Breuker, J.A. (1986). *Coaching Strategies and Tactics of IHSs*. ESPRIT Project P280 Deliverable 2.2.2, University of Amsterdam.

43. Winkels, R.G.F., Breuker, J.A. & Sandberg, J.A.C. (1988). Didactic Discourse in Intelligent Help Systems. In: *Proceedings of the International Conference on Intelligent Tutoring Systems*, Montreal.

44. Winkels, R.G.F., Achthoven, W. & Gennip, A. van (1989). Methodology and Modularity in ITS Design. In: D. Bierman, J.A. Breuker & J.A.C. Sandberg (eds). *Proceedings of the 4th International Conference on AI and Education*, pp. 314-322, IOS, Amsterdam.

45. Winkels, R.G.F., Sandberg, J.A.C. & Breuker, J.A. (1990). The Coach. In: J.A. Breuker (ed). *EUROHELP: Developing Intelligent Help Systems*, pp. 119-146. EC, Copenhagen.

46. Wolz, U., 1989. Tutoring that responds to user questions and provides enrichment. In: D. Bierman, J.A. Breuker & J.A.C. Sandberg (eds). *Proceedings of the 4th International Conference on AI and Education*, pp. 330-337, IOS, Amsterdam.

2 STUDENT MODELLING

Meta-Reasoning and Student Modelling

Marta Cialdea
Dipartimento di Informatica e Sistemistica, Università di Roma "La Sapienza", via Salaria 113, I-00198 Roma.
CUD - Consorzio per l'Università a Distanza, via G. Marconi 32, I-87030 Rende (CS), Italy.

Abstract: The student modelling process in Intelligent Educational Systems is the process of inferring a model of the student's knowledge by analysing his or her behaviour. When the student's behaviour is the result of a reasoning activity, the task of building a student model involves the system's reasoning about another agent's knowledge and reasoning (meta-reasoning). In this work we propose a method to describe the student modelling process and give a clear and explicit account of the assumptions which can be made on the student's reasoning activities. The approach is based on a meta-level architecture, where the domain specific knowledge of the student and the expert are represented at the object level, and the meta-reasoning principles are described in a first order logical theory at the meta-level. The abstraction work needed to formulate the basic principles informing the student model activity of some existing educational systems, in a neat and uniform way, has naturally brought some new insights and proposals.

Keywords: Diagnosis, Intelligent Educational Systems, Meta-reasoning, Student Modelling.

Introduction

Most papers on Intelligent Educational Systems (IES) contain long lists of "desiderata" that such systems should meet and problems that have to be faced while building them. However, research on IES still lacks a theoretical basis and systematization of the principles and guidelines to adopt in the conception of an IES. The engineering approach of "learning by doing" (let's construct IESs in order to learn something more about their nature) should be accompanied by a reordering of the basic ideas and concepts that come out from the empirical work, from existing approaches and also from a cognitive basis.

This work is a contribution in that direction. We propose a methodology which should help to make it explicit and clarify the nature of some principles usually adopted in the construction of IESs.

The work focuses on the diagnostic and student modelling problem in IESs. It proposes a first-order language for the systematic description of the assumptions that can be made about the student's reasoning activity, so that the diagnostic part of any particular tutoring system (in some class) can be configured as a logical theory, where the principles it is based upon appear clearly and explicitly. The work presented here is in progress and the approach is open to refinements, in order to experiment different and more complex diagnostic techniques.

Our proposal originates from the study of knowledge representation problems which require the ability to reason about knowledge and reasoning. In fact, the student model can be interpreted in terms of a knowledge base, which is updated after an analysis of the student's responses. If the domain knowledge of a tutoring system can be represented in first order logic, the student modelling component of such a system can be viewed as a set of first order logical theories connected in a meta-level architecture. This view follows after the ideas discussed in [2, 3], where a meta-level approach based on first order logic is proposed for reasoning about knowledge and reasoning. If we adopt their terminology, in the interaction with an IES, there are two agents: the teacher and the student. The first one is a computer program which reasons about the other agent's knowledge and therefore needs a representation of what he knows to be known to the other agent. Given this analogy, we proposed to explore the advantages which can be obtained by a meta-reasoning approach in the diagnostic process of IESs.

Basically, two approaches are available for reasoning about knowledge and reasoning: meta-level architectures and modal logics. Here we rely on the former mainly for ease of implementation and ease of integration with the other components of an IES. A detailed discussion on the merits and deficiencies of the two approaches to knowledge about knowledge and reasoning can be found for example in [3].

A meta-level architecture normally consists of an *object-theory* and a theory describing it, called *meta-theory*. In the case of a tutoring system, more than a single object theory have to be considered, since we require the system to reason about *expert* and *student* reasoning, in order to figure out how both correct and wrong answers can be achieved.

The analysis of the student's responses, performed by considering both the correct reasoning expected from the expert and the reasoning which justifies the answer given by the student, is described in the meta-theory. As a result of meta-reasoning a student model is obtained, which may be both incorrect and incomplete, with respect to the expert knowledge.

It is important for an IES not only to discover the reasons for students' mistakes, but also to justify the beliefs of the student when a correct answer is obtained from him and to determine which piece of knowledge the student is missing in case he is not able to provide an answer at all. Therefore, particular attention will be paid to the representation of what the student does not know.

The proposed approach has not only a methodological value, but also a practical counterpart. Due to the clarity and compactness of the description of the diagnostic principles, the language can be used as a high level specification language, permitting easy modification and adaptation to different object domains. Moreover, by means of programming languages based on first order logic, specifications can rapidly be translated into prototype systems, that can help to test the validity of the specifications themselves.

In the following sections we shall describe the object level components of the theory, i.e. the structure that the meta-theory is intended to describe, and then concentrate on the formulation of meta-level statements that could rule the diagnostic reasoning of a tutorial system.

The object level structures

This section contains an abstract description of the object-level structures representing what the system knows about the teaching domain and the student's learning status. Such structures are what the meta-theory reasons about.

The kind of systems we intend to describe are those which, according to the classification proposed by VanLehn [11], have a *bug library student model* over *declarative knowledge* (in particular, we assume that the teaching domain can be formalized in first order logic), when only the final result of the student's reasoning (or intermediate but non atomic steps) is available to the diagnostic program. So, the diagnostic cycle of the tutoring systems we have in mind can be thought as roughly consisting of the following steps:

1) a problem is presented to the student, who gives the system his solution (possibly a "I don't know" answer);
2) the system formulates a hypothesis about the reasons for that answer, i.e. it points out a set of basic assumptions that supports the student's conclusion;
3) the student model is updated accordingly.

The diagnostic phase may of course be followed by teaching actions, influenced by the student model and possibly modifying it, but we shall be concerned only with the use and update of the student model in the course of the diagnosis.

As already mentioned, we assume that any statement about the teaching domain is represented as a first order formula. Such a simplification is made only for methodological reasons and it does not impose an a priori restriction to the approach. For example, domain knowledge can itself be organized into meta-levels, where heuristic principles and reasoning strategies are represented at the higher levels, following [12, 13]; or else, the cumbersome logical expression of some operations on object level objects can be avoided by using semantic attachment methods [14].

According to the above assumption, the object level language is a first order language containing constants, predicates and functions denoting corresponding types of objects in the teaching domain. The expert knowledge and the student's beliefs can thus be represented by sets of first order formulas. A set of formulas will be called a *context*.

Corresponding to the Expert Module and the Student Model of IESs, in the object level structure there are two contexts: **E**, that contains exactly the formulas denoting correct statements about the teaching domain, and **S**, containing formulas believed by the student.

In a malrule approach, a "bug catalogue" is also considered: in the object level structure there is a context, **B**, containing formulas corresponding to the incorrect beliefs that could possibly be ascribed to a student. It plays the role of a database which the teacher consults when trying to explain a wrong answer given by the student.

Both during the diagnostic and teaching-remediation phase, the system has to access what the student knows and what he doesn't know. It must be remarked, however, that the system cannot be assumed to have complete knowledge about the student beliefs.[1] So if a formula α is not contained in **S**, the system cannot infer that the student does not believe α. It only means that the system does not know whether the student believes α or not. In other words, **S** contains what the system knows that the student believes. For this reason, we add a fourth component to the object level structure: context **U**, containing what the system knows that the student *does not know*. It may be considered part of the student model.[2]

It can be remarked that the same incompleteness situation may occur also in the case of the teaching domain, i.e. there may be object level statements that cannot be classified by the system either as correct or as incorrect. For example, this is often the case in natural language tutoring systems, where some sentences cannot be syntactically parsed, but are neither recognized as definitely wrong. We are not going to address such a problem in this work, although it seems to be tractable in the same style of the rest. So, we assume that the system knowledge about the teaching domain is complete.

Summarizing, the object level structure consists of four contexts, **E**, **B**, **S** and **U**, whose interpretation is the following:

if $\alpha \in$ **E**, then the system knows that α represents a correct statement;

if $\alpha \in$ **B**, then the system knows that α represents an incorrect statement;

if $\alpha \in$ **S**, then the system knows that the student believes α;

if $\alpha \in$ **U**, then the system knows that the student does not believe α.

---

[1] The system's knowledge may also be partially incorrect, in the sense that a previous hypothesis can reveal to be inconsistent with a new assertion of the student. This problem will not be touched upon within this work.

[2] Usually, existing IESs identify the student's ignorance with the systems's ignorance about the student. Mizoguchi [8, 9] recognizes the importance of the distinction, by use of four truth values for statements α about the object domain: *true* (the student knows α), *false* (the student knows $\neg\ \alpha$), *unknown* (the student does not know α), and *fail*, which is a meta-truth attribute, referring to the system's knowledge (the system cannot attribute any of the previous three values to α).

Of course, any particular tutoring system may lack some of the contexts. For example, overlay models [5] do not have **B**, and most systems do not have an explicit representation of what the student does not know (context **U**).

Obviously,

$$\mathbf{E} \cap \mathbf{B} = \varnothing.$$

It is reasonable to require also

$$\mathbf{S} \cap \mathbf{U} = \varnothing.$$

However, some contexts overlap. Precisely

$$\mathbf{S} \cup \mathbf{U} \cup \mathbf{E} \cup \mathbf{B}.$$

Within this framework we can give a precise characterization of the goal of diagnosis, intended, in a broad sense, as the enhancement of what the system knows about the student's learning state: it is the reduction of the difference between $\mathbf{S} \cup \mathbf{U}$ and $\mathbf{E} \cup \mathbf{B}$, thus progressively approaching the limit situation $\mathbf{S} \cup \mathbf{U} = \mathbf{E} \cup \mathbf{B}$, where, for each object level statement, the system can tell whether it is believed by the student or not (of course, we assume that the partition of $\mathbf{E} \cup \mathbf{B}$ in **S** and **U** is consistent with the student's behaviour).

Meta-theory

In the previous section we defined contexts as sets of formulas, explicitly containing all the formulas representing pertinent knowledge. Such a set theoretic characterization of contexts is better replaced by a proof theoretic one, where a context consists of a set of formulas (axioms) and a (possibly empty) set of logical inference rules. We stress that, for the sake of simplicity, we assume that the logic of a context lies completely in its inference rules, while its domain specific information is wholly captured by (the deductive closure of) the set of its axioms.

Contexts **E** and **S** can be considered as standard logical theories, in the sense that they contain correct inference rules (even if possibly incomplete). For the sake of generality, we do not make any assumption on the kind of logic in such contexts, even if, in actual implementations, it is not full first order logic (for example, **S** and **E** may be production systems or Horn clause theories). However we assume that the two contexts have the same logic. Even if such an assumption, that the student and the expert have the same reasoning capabilities, looks quite strong, it seems to be necessary in order for the system to be able to tell anything about the student's reasonings.

We do not make any assumption about the consistency of contexts: **B** is very likely to contain contradictory formulas. The same may happen to **S** - although its logic is correct - and **U**.

Context **B** has no logical rule at all: it is only a collection of incorrect statements about the object domain. We are not making any assumption about possible inference rules in context **U**; in fact, the concept of derivability in **U** will not be used at all. When there is no risk of confusion, the axioms of **B** and **U** will be simply called "statements".

In the rest of this section we focus on the meta-level component of the framework, where the diagnostic process is represented. What we shall describe does not consist actually of a single theory, but it is rather a language and a collection of formally stated principles; the adequacy of each of them for a particular system has to be established depending on the features of the teaching domain and the desired performances of the system. When a set of convenient principles has been singled out for a particular application, then they do constitute a meta-theory. In the following, the generic meta-theory will be called **MT**.

The meta-level language contains suitable constants, functions and predicates allowing the object level objects to be referred to. Among them, the following constants will be used, which refer to contexts: E, B, S, U denote respectively contexts **E, B, S, U**. Moreover, **MT** contains a functional symbol denoting union of contexts, so that $E \cup B$ denotes the context that is the union of **E** and **B** (a proof in **E** $\cup$ **B** consists of axioms in **E**, axioms in **B**, and formulas that can be derived from previous ones by means of inference rules in **E**).

Moreover, the meta-language contains constants denoting object level symbols, and functional symbols allowing the meta-level coding of object level complex formulas. If α is an object level formula, *'α'* denotes the representation of α at the meta-level, and *mknot('α')* the representation of the formula $\neg\, \alpha$. Similarly, if α and β are object level formulas, *mkand('α','β')* is the representation of the formula $\alpha \wedge \beta$. Finally, the language of **MT** contains a proof constructor, i.e. a functional symbol to represent object level proofs. The meta-level representation of a proof π will be denoted by *'π'*.

Answers given by the student are coded by the meta-level predicate *answers(φ,t)*, where *t* is either the constant *yes* or *dontknow*. We consider only two types of answers: "I don't know" and positive answers, since a question requiring a value as an answer, is turned into a relation instantiated with the answered value, and negative answers can be obtained by negating the question. So, we assume that the student is given the possibility to tell the system "I don't know", instead of being forced to give an answer which cannot have any meaningful explanation.

Link between object level contexts and meta-theory

In the following, **C** stands for any of the contexts **E, B, S, U, E ∪ B.** Similarly, *C* stands for any of the constants *E, B, S, U* or the term *E* ∪ *B* (*C* is a meta-meta-symbol!). The symbols α, β, γ, φ, π (possibly with subscripts) will be used as meta-level variables, when they are not quoted.

In order for **MT** to be a good meta-theory for the object-level contexts, the relation between a proof in context **C** and its conclusion has to be definable in **MT**, i.e. for any context **C**, there has to be a meta-level formula $proof_C(x,y)$ with two free variables such that for any proof **π** in **C** and formula **α**:

if **π** is a proof in **C** of the formula **α**, then **MT** $\vdash proof_C('\pi','\alpha')$, and

if **π** is not a proof in **C** of the formula **α**, then **MT** $\vdash \neg\ proof_C('\pi','\alpha')$.

So, $proof_C$ is the key meta-level predicate linking the object level contexts to the meta-theory: the intended meaning of $proof_C('\pi','\alpha')$ is that **π** is a proof of the formula **α** in context **C**. Note that this means that **α** is derivable by means of object level axioms and rules only, with no help of meta-reasoning.

Other object-level relations are assumed to be definable in **MT**. They will be progressively introduced in the sequel.

The nature of the diagnostic task

Besides the $proof_C$ predicate, representing results of deductions in object level contexts, **MT** contains the predicates $demo_C$, for any context **C**, representing the result of a meta-level reasoning. Different hypotheses on the student's way of reasoning can be expressed by means of the meta-level axioms defining the predicates $demo_C$, discussed below.

Considering the nature of the diagnostic task in IESs, two main cases can be distinguished:

1. The system has to discover the reasons why the student believes something (either correctly or not);
2. The system has to explain where the student's ignorance of some facts originates from.

In the first case the system has to deal with an abductive task: if the student believes **φ**, and $\pi_1,\ldots,\pi_n$ are all the possible (non-trivial) proofs of **φ** that can be constructed in **E ∪ B**, then only one of them has to be chosen. Let's say that π_j is the preferred one; if $\alpha_1,\ldots,\alpha_k$ are all the axioms of $\mathbf{E} \cup \mathbf{B}$ used in π_j, then it can be concluded that the student believes all of $\alpha_1,\ldots, \alpha_k$. Point 1 above will be called the abductive aspect of diagnosis.

The second case represents the dual situation. If the student does not believe φ, and if $\pi_1,\ldots, \pi_n$ are all the possible proofs of φ that can be constructed in $\mathbf{E} \cup \mathbf{B}$, then the system can reasonably conclude that the student is not able to construct any of them. In this case there is no abductive problem, being the system's task purely deductive. However, there is again a choice problem, at the level of the subsets of axioms used in the proofs: if $\alpha_1,\ldots, \alpha_k$ are all the axioms of $\mathbf{E} \cup \mathbf{B}$ used in π_j, for $1 \leq j \leq n$, then surely the student does not believe the conjunction $\alpha_1 \wedge \ldots \wedge \alpha_k$. But this does not mean that the student lacks all of $\alpha_1,\ldots, \alpha_k$, so an extra investigation should be performed in order to single out which of them the student actually does not know or possibly believes to be false. This second aspect of diagnosis will be called deductive.

Some preliminary definitions

The predicate $theorem_C$ is used as an abbreviation:

$$\forall \varphi\ (theorem_C(\varphi) \Leftrightarrow \exists \pi\ proof_C(\pi,\varphi))$$

Remark: it is not assumed that the predicate $theorem_C$ defines the sets of theorems of **C** (a generally non recursive set) in **MT**. Surely, as $proof_C$ defines the proof relation in context **C**, if φ is a theorem of **C**, then **MT** $\vdash$ $theorem_C('\varphi')$, but it may happen that φ is not a theorem of **C** and however not **MT** $\vdash \neg$ $theorem_C('\varphi')$.

The predicate $subconjunct(\alpha_o,\alpha)$ is defined so that it represents the relation holding between a subconjunct of a conjunction and the whole conjunction:

$$\begin{aligned}&\forall \alpha, \alpha_o\ (subconjunct(\alpha_o, \alpha) \Leftrightarrow \\ &\qquad \exists \beta, \gamma\ (\alpha = mkand(\beta, \gamma) \wedge \\ &\qquad\qquad (\alpha_o = \beta \vee \alpha_o = \gamma \vee subconjunct(\alpha_o, \beta) \vee subconjunct(\alpha_o, \gamma))))\end{aligned}$$

where the predicate = is syntactical identity. Note that, according to this definition, α is not a subconjunct of itself.

The predicate $derivable_C('\alpha','\varphi')$, defined below, is intended to represent the fact that α is a conjunction of axioms of **C** that entails φ in a non-trivial way, i.e. there exists a proof π of

φ in **C**, using exactly the axioms in α, and α is the minimal set of axioms from which φ can be derived in **C** and, finally, α is not contradictory (it does not entail everything). The consistency condition may seem a strong requirement in computational terms, because it is a generally non-decidable predicate. However, in actual systems, the proof procedure used at the object level usually guarantees both the consistency (it is impossible to derive everything from a contradiction) and the minimality requirements, so that there is no need to check for non-triviality of proofs.

In the definition of the predicate $derivable_C$ we assume that **MT** contains the following formulas:

1) $axiom_C(\alpha)$, that defines the set of axioms of **C**,
2) $axioms(\pi,\alpha)$, that defines the relation holding between a proof π and a formula $\alpha = \alpha_1 \wedge ... \wedge \alpha_k$, when $\alpha_1,..., \alpha_k$ are exactly the axioms used in π .

$$
\begin{aligned}
\forall \alpha, \varphi\ (&derivable_C(\alpha,\varphi) \Leftrightarrow \\
&\exists \pi\ (proof_C(\pi,\varphi) \wedge axioms(\pi,\alpha)) \\
&\wedge \neg \exists\ \alpha_o, \pi_o\ (subconjunct(\alpha_o, \alpha) \wedge proof_C(\pi_o,\varphi) \wedge axioms(\pi_o,\alpha_o)) \\
&\wedge \neg \forall \beta \exists\ \pi\ (proof_C(\pi,\beta) \wedge axioms(\pi,\alpha)))
\end{aligned}
$$

Meta-axioms for diagnosis

We shall discuss the axioms dealing with the deductive aspect first. Such axioms allow one to conclude that the student does not believe something, i.e. $demo_U(\alpha)$.

The first axiom states that if the student answered "I don't know" to a question φ, then he knows no way to derive either φ or the negation of φ. So, axiom **D1** (D stands for "Diagnosis") is:

$$
\begin{aligned}
\textbf{D1}\quad \forall \varphi, \alpha\ (&answers(\varphi,dontknow) \wedge \\
&(derivable_{E \cup B}(\alpha,\varphi) \vee derivable_{E \cup B}(\alpha,mknot(\varphi))) \\
&\rightarrow demo_U(\alpha))
\end{aligned}
$$

Note that α is a conjunction of axioms in **E** $\cup$ **B**, so axiom **D1** can lead to conclude that the student does not have a misconception. Even if such information is usually of no importance for the teaching and remediation activities, it can be useful when the student model is used during the diagnostic process itself. In fact, knowing that the student cannot have used a given misconception can help to reduce querying the student about her or his beliefs, when an incorrect answer has to be explained.

However, when the student answers "I don't know" to a question **φ**, usually the teacher would not be interested in examining all the possible misconceptions which could lead to prove **φ** (or its negation), but only in finding out the correct knowledge the student has shown to lack, so that a suitable teaching action can follow. In that case a simpler version of **D1** can be adopted:

D1' $\forall \varphi, \alpha\ (answers(\varphi, dontknow) \wedge (derivable_E(\alpha,\varphi) \vee derivable_E(\alpha, mknot(\varphi)))$
$\rightarrow demo_U(\alpha))$

The second axiom of the deductive aspect of diagnosis concludes that the student does not believe something from the fact that he believes something else. It states in fact that if the student believes **φ** to be true, then he does not know any way to derive the negation of **φ**. In other words, axiom **D2** states a minimal consistency hypothesis about the student's knowledge.

D2 $\forall \varphi, \alpha\ (answers(\varphi, yes) \wedge derivable_{E \cup B}(\alpha, mknot(\varphi)) \rightarrow demo_U(\alpha))$

The same remarks about **D1** apply to **D2** and a version **D2'** can be considered, when the axiom is to be used in case of incorrect (though defined) answers, to find out what correct knowledge the student has missed to consider that would lead him to discover that his answer is wrong.

D2' $\forall \varphi, \alpha\ (answers(\varphi, yes) \wedge derivable_E(\alpha, mknot(\varphi)) \rightarrow demo_U(\alpha))$

The problem of reducing the size of an unbelieved conjunction will be touched upon in Section 3.6.

Let's now face the issue of the abductive task of diagnosis, i.e. the formulation of axioms stating when a conclusion of the form $demo_S(\alpha)$ can be obtained.

Let us assume that the student admittedly believes **φ** to be true and that we already know how to perform abduction. If **α** is the conjunction of the axioms in **E ∪ B** that best explains **φ** (from which **φ** can be abduced), then the system can conclude that **α** must be in **S**:

D3 $\forall \varphi, \alpha\ (answers(\varphi, yes) \wedge explains(\alpha,\varphi) \rightarrow demo_S(\alpha))$

The hard task is the definition of the predicate *explains*: possibly there are different ways of proving φ, and the system cannot know *a priori* which of them actually corresponds to the student's reasoning. We shall describe an idealized situation first, where all the possible sets of assumptions (axioms of $E \cup B$) entailing φ are compared and the best of them is chosen.

Criteria for comparing two sets of axioms are difficult to be defined in general. They could include looking at which and how many of the hypotheses are contained in the student model, how recently they have been used, or, in the worst case, asking the student to provide some more information about his reasoning process.

We shall give here an example, showing how the following criteria can be encoded as axioms for the predicate *explains* :

- All sets of axioms containing a formula in U have to be rejected (if the system already knows that the student does not know something, than it can conclude that he cannot have used it in proving something else);
- Among the sets of axioms that do not contain any formula in U, identify as *good candidates* those which contain either the minimum number of formulas that are not axioms of S, or the minimum number of formulas that are not axioms of E, thus minimizing either the set of new knowledge that has to be ascribed to the student, or the number of mistakes he may have done (a set of axioms minimizing both may not exist). The hypothesis that the student always makes as few errors as possible is often made in the diagnostic process of IESs.
- If the set of good candidates is a singleton, then its only element is the best explication for the student's answer. Otherwise, an interaction with the student has to be performed, in order to test her or his beliefs about problematic axioms in good candidates; problematic axioms are those misconceptions that are not already in S. Here, the principle that the student makes as few mistakes as possible is adopted again, and correct axioms are not tested. ("Test" can consist of either just asking the student or proposing ad hoc exercises aiming at verifying whether the student believes a single problematic axiom, etc.)

So, *explains('α','φ')* must be derivable just when:

1) there is a non-trivial proof π of φ in $E \cup B$, such that α is the conjunction of all the axioms used in π;
2) α does not contain any formula in U;
3) compared with any other conjunction β of axioms of $E \cup B$ satisfying 1) and 2), α contains either a smaller number of formulas that are not axioms of S, or a smaller number of formulas that are not axioms of E ;
4) Either α is the single formula satisfying 1), 2), 3), or an interaction with the student confirms that he believes α .

In order to be able to express such conditions, we define some new predicates. If **α** is a conjunction of axioms in **E ∪ B**, then the formula $'\alpha_0' \in '\alpha'$ represents the fact that $\boldsymbol{\alpha_0}$ is one of such axioms (α is considered as the representation of a set of axioms). The intended meaning of the predicate *unknown('α')*, where **α** is assumed to be a conjunction of axioms of **E ∪ B**, is that some of them is known by the system to be unknown by the student (i.e. it is a statement in **U**).

$$\forall\alpha\ (unknown(\alpha) \Leftrightarrow \exists\alpha_0\ (\alpha_0 \in \alpha\ \wedge\ axiom_U(\alpha_0)))$$

It is worth noting that we have not defined *unknown(α)* simply as $theorem_U(\alpha)$, because we want its negation, ¬ *unknown('α')* to be a theorem of **MT** when no axiom in **α** is a statement in **U**. Now, by definition:

$$\forall\alpha\ (\neg\ unknown(\alpha) \Leftrightarrow \forall\alpha_0\ (\alpha_0 \in \alpha\ \rightarrow\ \neg\ axiom_U(\alpha_0))).$$

As the set of subconjuncts of **α** and the set of axioms of **U** are both finite, we can conclude not only that, for any **α**, if some axiom in **α** is a statement in **U** then

$$\mathbf{MT} \vdash unknown('\alpha')$$

but also that if no axiom in **α** is in **U** then

$$\mathbf{MT} \vdash \neg\ unknown('\alpha')$$

As remarked above, this cannot be generally assumed for the predicate $theorem_C(\alpha)$. In this case (and in the sequel), considering axioms of **C** instead of theorems is not a restriction, because the formula which they refer to is always assumed to be a conjunction of axioms of **E ∪ B**, and **S ∪ U y E ∪ B**.

In order to be able to define the property of being a good candidate, we assume that simple operations and functions on finite sets are representable in **MT**: the term *unknown-cardinality('α')* represents the number of axioms in **α** that are not in **S**. Similarly, the term *incorrect-cardinality(α)*, represents the number axioms in **α** that are not in **E** (i.e. the number of misconceptions in **α**).

The intended meaning of the predicate *less-unknown('α','β')* is that **α** has a number of axioms that are not in **S** smaller than **β**.

$$\forall\alpha,\beta\ (less\text{-}unknown(\alpha,\beta) \Leftrightarrow unknown\text{-}cardinality(\alpha) \leq unknown\text{-}cardinality(\beta))$$

In a similar way we define the predicate *less-incorrect*, holding between 'α' and 'β' when **α** has a number of axioms that are not in **E** smaller than **β**.

$$\forall\alpha,\beta\ (less\text{-}incorrect(\alpha,\beta) \Leftrightarrow incorrect\text{-}cardinality(\alpha) \leq incorrect\text{-}cardinality(\beta))$$

Remark: the relation represented by the disjunction *less-unknown*$(\alpha,\beta) \vee$ *less-incorrect*(α,β) is not antisymmetric: there may exist non equivalent α, β such that α has a smaller number of axioms that are not in **S** and yet β has a smaller number of axioms that are not in **E**. So, such a relation is not an order relation on the set of conjunctions of axioms of $\mathbf{E} \cup \mathbf{B}$.

In the following definition, *test-student*$('\alpha')$ is a formula representing the fact that a test on the student about his knowledge of α gives a positive result. So, *confirmed*$('\alpha')$ means that the student has confirmed all the problematic axioms in α (a problematic axiom is a misconception that is not in **S**).

$$\forall \alpha\ (\mathit{confirmed}(\alpha) \Leftrightarrow$$
$$\forall \alpha_0\ (\alpha_0 \in \alpha \rightarrow \mathit{axiom}_S(\alpha_0) \vee \mathit{axiom}_E(\alpha_0) \vee \mathit{test\text{-}student}(\alpha_0)))$$

The predicate *test-student* is very much like Prolog extra-logical predicates and it is assumed to be triggered only when necessary (in this case, only if $\mathit{axiom}_S(\alpha_0)$ and $\mathit{axiom}_E(\alpha_0)$ cannot be proved). Note that, in the definition above, it is not necessary to use the predicate $\mathit{theorem}_C$ instead of axiom_C, because α is a conjunction of axioms in $\mathbf{E} \cup \mathbf{B}$.

We can now define the property of being a good candidate:

$$\forall \alpha, \varphi\ (\mathit{good\text{-}candidate}(\alpha,\varphi) \Leftrightarrow$$
$$\mathit{derivable}_{E \cup B}(\alpha,\varphi)$$
$$\wedge \neg\ \mathit{unknown}(\alpha)$$
$$\wedge\ \forall \beta\ (\mathit{derivable}_{E \cup B}(\beta,\varphi) \wedge \neg\ \mathit{unknown}(\beta)$$
$$\rightarrow (\mathit{less\text{-}unknown}(\alpha,\beta) \vee \mathit{less\text{-}incorrect}(\alpha,\beta))))$$

Finally, axiom **E1** below states that if α is a good candidate as a possible explanation of φ, and either it is the single good candidate or testing the problematic axioms in α gives a positive result, then α explains φ.

E1 $$\forall \alpha, \varphi\ (\mathit{good\text{-}candidate}(\alpha,\varphi)$$
$$\wedge\ (\forall \beta\ (\mathit{good\text{-}candidate}(\beta,\varphi) \rightarrow \beta \equiv \alpha) \vee \mathit{confirmed}(\alpha))$$
$$\rightarrow \mathit{explains}(\alpha,\varphi))$$

Here, the formula $\beta \equiv \alpha$ defines the logical equivalence relation between conjunctions of object level axioms, i.e. $\beta \equiv \alpha$ iff β and α differ only in the order and associativity of subconjuncts (they represent the same set of axioms).

All this machinery can be too expensive from a computational point of view, specially when the object domain is such that many different proofs of a given statement can be constructed. So, we may happen to have to be content with less powerful versions of axiom **E1**, where no comparison between sets of axioms is made, but any of the possible proofs of the statement believed by the student is accepted, provided the system can verify its plausibility. In the following version, a set α of axioms is considered as a plausible explanation of φ if it satisfies conditions 1) and 2) given above, and:

5) an interaction with the student confirms that the student believes all the problematic axioms in α.

E1' $\forall \alpha, \varphi\ (derivable_{E \cup B}(\alpha,\varphi) \wedge \neg\ unknown(\alpha) \wedge confirmed(\alpha)$
$\rightarrow explains(\alpha,\beta))$

Most systems actually do not use the student model during diagnosis, but only to determine the teaching actions. In those cases, an even simpler version of axiom **E1** is adopted:

E1" $\forall \alpha, \varphi\ (derivable_{E \cup B}(\alpha,\varphi)$
$\wedge \forall \alpha_o\ (\alpha_o \in \alpha \rightarrow axiom_E(\alpha_o) \vee test\text{-}student(\alpha_o))$
$\rightarrow explains(\alpha,\beta))$

The above axioms can be used differently by different systems, according to the structure of the student model and to the style of repair interventions in the subject domain.

Some meta-theorems

The formal specification given above can help to understand the consequences of the assumptions made about the student's reasoning capabilities. In fact, some general theorems can be derived from the axioms for diagnosis. For example, the following theorem can be deduced from either **E1** or **E1'** (but not **E1"**) together with the definition of the predicates given in the previous subsection and assuming the definability of simple object-level relations in MT:

T1 $\forall \varphi, \alpha\ \ (derivable_S(\alpha,\varphi) \rightarrow explains(\alpha,\varphi))$

It states that if the student's answer is already derivable in **S**, then there is no reason to search for other explanations of it.

From either **E1** or **E1'** or **E1"**, together with some definitions and the assumption of the definability of simple object-level relations in **MT**, it can also be deduced that if there is a single correct set of axioms that entails the student's answer and that is not definitely unknown to the student, then the student has correctly derived the answer that way:

T2 $\forall \varphi, \alpha \; (\forall \beta \, (derivable_E (\beta,\varphi) \wedge \neg \, unknown(\beta)) \Leftrightarrow \beta \equiv \alpha) \rightarrow explains(\alpha,\varphi))$

So, while the three versions of **E1** apply independently of the correctness of the student's answer, if the student has given a correct answer, we can go a more straightforward way, under the hypothesis that the student always makes as few errors as possible.

Stronger versions of this statement can be assumed as axioms in the meta-theory, for example by dropping the control on what is unknown to the student:

E2 $\forall \varphi, \alpha \; (\forall \beta \, (derivable_E (\beta,\varphi) \Leftrightarrow \beta \equiv \alpha) \rightarrow explains(\alpha,\varphi))$

or even by making the strong hypothesis that there is always only one correct way of proving a given fact, hence dropping the uniqueness test:

E3 $\forall \varphi, \alpha \; (derivable_E (\alpha,\varphi) \rightarrow explains(\alpha,\varphi))$

The reduction of an unbelieved conjunction

The axioms presented in this section can help reducing the size of an unbelieved conjunction α. A first pass can be done by observing that if the system knows that the student believes one of the subconjuncts of α, than it can be concluded that he does not know the rest of them:

P1 $\forall \beta_1, \beta_2 \; (demo_U (mkand(\beta_1,\beta_2)) \wedge axiom_S (\beta_1) \rightarrow demo_U (\beta_2))$

The full exploitation of this axiom assumes the possibility of exchanging the order and associativity of the elements of a conjunction without affecting the $demo_C$ predicates:

$$\forall \alpha,\beta \; (demo_C (\alpha) \wedge \alpha \equiv \beta \rightarrow demo_C (\beta))$$

The second P-axiom (P stands for "pruning") states a minimality hypothesis: if a subconjunct of an unbelieved statement is already known to be unknown by the student, then the fact that he does not know the whole conjunction is already justified, and we can assume that the rest of the conjunction is not definitely unknown:

P2 $\forall \beta_1, \beta_2\ (demo_U\ (mkand(\beta_1,\beta_2\ ))\ \wedge\ axiom_U\ (\beta_1)\ \wedge \neg\ unknown(\beta_2)$
$\rightarrow\ \neg\ demo_U\ (\beta_2\ ))$

If interactive diagnosis is allowed, a further pruning of an unknown conjunction can be performed by testing the student:

P3 $\forall \beta\ (demo_U\ (\beta) \wedge\ \exists\ \beta_o\ (subconjunct(\beta_o,\beta\ ) \wedge unconfirmed(\beta_o))$
$\rightarrow\ demo_U\ (\beta_o\ ))$

where *unconfirmed* is defined by:

$$\forall \alpha\ (unconfirmed(\alpha) \Leftrightarrow \neg\ demo_S\ (\alpha\ ) \wedge \neg\ test\text{-}student(\alpha))$$

There is nothing more practical than a good theory

Leaving theoretical issues apart, this section is intended to explain what the formalization proposed above is good for, what is the advantage of writing down formulas instead of stating things in plain English and what is the reason for stating complex principles, which are in most cases out of concrete implementation possibilities. There are at least six good reasons supporting the usefulness of a formal approach to the problem of specifying general principles for student modelling in educational systems:

1. The use of a formal tool helps to recognize the consequences of the principles adopted and to apply them coherently.
2. The meta-language we have proposed can be used as a high specification language, when conceiving the student modelling features of a concrete system.

3. The high level specifications thus obtained can be directly implemented by use of programming languages based on logic; the prototypes constructed that way help to test the validity of the specifications and give the possibility to modify them rapidly, at low costs.
4. Even if computational limits impose drastic cuts to what can be done, it is important to have in mind what is the ideal situations we want to approximate.
5. The language proposed can be an instrument for a comparative study of existing systems.
6. An analytical study of the student modelling guidelines adopted in existing systems can lead to point out possible enhancements and enlargements of such principles.

In this section we are going to justify the first three claims above.

In order to check the validity and applicability of the concise axiomatization presented in the previous section, we have tested it against the fundamental diagnostic process of two existing IESs: SEDAF [1, 4] and LMS [10], by providing a straightforward translation of some meta-axioms into Prolog. We defined two versions of the program, embedding the domain specific knowledge and the student modelling process accomplished by SEDAF and LMS, respectively, and called them microSEDAF and microLMS. The micro-programs are implemented in LPA MacProlog™ 2.5 and run on an Apple Macintosh Computer. A description of an early version of the program, as well as some examples of interaction with the student, can be found [6, 7]. Here, we shall give only a brief description of MicroSEDAF.

SEDAF is a system that teaches students to graph mathematical functions by solving for the characteristics of the function (singular points, asymptotes, maxima, etc). It embeds an expert module consisting of a set of correct rules, and a student module consisting of a set of correct rules and malrules. MicroSEDAF reproduces the diagnostic activity of SEDAF, in particular the analysis of student responses in the identification of minimal points for a given function. It asks the student to give an answer for a given problem (allowing him to answer "I don't know"), reconstructs a proof leading to the solution given by the student and outputs the set of axioms used in such a proof, followed by the correct answer and its justification when it differs from the student's one.

MicroSEDAF uses the following axioms: **D1'**, **D2'**, **D3**, **E3** and an intermediate version between axioms **E1** and **E1'**, called **E1*** below:

E1* $\forall \alpha, \varphi\ (derivable_{E \cup B}(\alpha,\varphi)$

$\quad \wedge \forall \beta\ (derivable_{E \cup B}(\beta,\varphi) \rightarrow \neg\, less\text{-}incorrect(\beta,\alpha))$

$\quad \wedge \forall \alpha_o\ (\alpha_o \in \alpha \rightarrow axiom_E(\alpha_o) \vee test\text{-}student(\alpha_o))$

$\rightarrow explains(\alpha,\varphi))$

(The comparison among all possible set of axioms entailing the student's conclusion, in **E1***, is not performed literally, but the procedure for the generation of the best explanation of a given statement relies on the fact that proofs are generated in order of correctness - i.e. the axioms in **E** are used before statements in **B**.)

With this set of axioms, MicroSedaf actually performs better then "big" SEDAF itself. In fact, besides the fact that SEDAF does not allow the student to answer "I don't know" to a question and no diagnosis about what the student does not know is performed (i.e. SEDAF does not adopt axioms **D1'** and **D2'**), an incoherence in the applications of its diagnostic principles has been detected by the abstraction work: if the response given by the student is correct, "big" SEDAF assumes that it has been correctly derived and that the student knows all the facts and rules used in the deduction built by the expert module. But this principle is not recursively applied when reconstructing subproofs of correct statements used to reach a wrong conclusion. In other terms, SEDAF does not actually behave according to **E1***, but to the simpler statement:

$$\forall \alpha, \varphi\ (derivable_{E \cup B}(\alpha,\varphi) \wedge \forall \alpha_0\ (\alpha_0 \in \alpha \rightarrow test\text{-}student(\alpha_0)) \rightarrow explains(\alpha,\varphi))$$

A second limit in SEDAF diagnostic principles has come out from their formal reconstruction. SEDAF acts according to axiom **E3**:

E3 $\forall \varphi, \alpha\ (derivable_E(\alpha,\varphi) \rightarrow explains(\alpha,\varphi))$

But such an axiom assumes that there is always one single correct way of proving a correct statement. In SEDAF domain, this is exactly the case when proving positive statements, for example, that x is a minimal point for function f; but there may be different correct ways of proving that function f has no minimal points. In such cases, SEDAF (and MicroSEDAF) do not care to determine which is the proof that actually corresponds to the student's reasoning.

The fact that engineers can be helped in the conception of a system by a clear logical formulation of the principles to be followed must not surprise.

Concluding Remarks

In the previous section, the methodological advantages and practical payoffs emerging from a formal approach to student modelling have been pointed out. Here, we consider the sixth claim asserted before, i.e. that the analytical study and logical formulation of the principles informing meta-reasoning in the student modelling component of educational systems can lead to take into account something new.

A feeling of this fact comes out directly by comparing the simple meta-theory embedded in SEDAF with the complete axiomatization given in Section 3. More precisely, the abstraction work described in this paper has led to point out:

i) the information that can be extracted from "I don't know" answers and the possible uses of an explicit representation of what the system knows that the student does not know;

ii) the possible uses of the student model during the diagnostic process itself, in order to reduce querying the student as much as possible.

The present approach can be extended and refined in many directions. As a first example, different strategies for treating the set of malrules can be easily accommodated. For instance, instead of considering the union of the expert knowledge with the whole set of bugs, during the diagnostic process, it would be easy to organize misconceptions into subsets, possibly ordered according to a likelihood criterion.

Another improvement could involve a less rudimentary update of the student model after a diagnosis is made. Indeed, the last answer provided by the student may give information which is contradictory with that already stored in the student model. To this end different policies can be accommodated to establish a degree of confidence in the student misconceptions: frequency of occurrence, student typology, etc.

Another important question that could find an answer in this framework is how to treat the case where the student is allowed to have contradictory beliefs. And more: what happens if the student is allowed to have incomplete and possibly incorrect reasoning capabilities?

The last point to mention is the possibility to examine and describe principles for the tutor's reasoning about strategic knowledge in the same style. This analysis would require a new viewpoint and would surely lead to interesting results.

It is of great importance to deal with such issues in a uniform way, by exploiting both the theoretical and software engineering advantages of a meta-level abstract specification. The resulting system organization enjoys a clear separation of knowledge about the teaching domain and teaching techniques, thus leading to improved system performance.

Acknowledgements

Luigia Aiello and Daniele Nardi, besides providing much of the initial inspiration and contributing to the first version of this work in collaboration with James C. Spohrer, Alessandro Micarelli and myself [6, 7], have constantly supported me with precious advice and discussions. The research reported here has been carried on at CATTID of the University of Rome, within a cooperation with DIS and CUD.

References

1. Aiello, L., Carosio, M., Micarelli, A.: An Intelligent Tutoring System for the Study of Mathematical Functions. In: Proc. of the International Conference on Intelligent Tutoring Systems ITS-88. Montreal, Canada, 1988.

2. Aiello, L., Nardi, D., Schaerf, M.: Reasoning about Knowledge and Ignorance. In: Proc. of the Fifth Generation Computer Systems FGCS-88. Tokyo, Japan, 1988.

3. Aiello, L., Nardi, D., Schaerf, M.: Reasoning about Knowledge and Reasoning in a Meta-Level Architecture. University of Rome "La Sapienza", Technical Report DIS 30.88, 1988.

4. Aiello, L., Micarelli, A.: SEDAF: An Intelligent Educational System for Mathematics. Applied Artificial Intelligence - An International Journal, 4, 15-37 (1990).

5. Carr., B., Goldstein, I. P.: Overlays: a Theory of Modelling for Computer-Aided Instruction. MIT, Cambridge, Mass., AI Memo 406, 1977.

6. Cialdea, M., Micarelli, A., Nardi, D., Spohrer, J.C., Aiello, L.: A Rational Reconstruction of the Diagnostic Process in Intelligent Tutoring Systems. In: Proc. of Pacific Rim International Conference on Artificial Intelligence PRICAI '90. Nagoya, Japan, November 1990.

7. Cialdea, M., Micarelli, A., Nardi, D., Spohrer, J., Aiello, L.: Meta-level Reasoning for Diagnosis in ITS. University of Rome "La Sapienza", Technical Report DIS, 1990.

8. Mizoguchi, R., Ikeda, M., Kakusho, O.: An Innovative Framework for Intelligent Tutoring Systems". In: Artificial Intelligence Tools in Education (P. Ercoli and R. Lewis, eds.). Amsterdam: North-Holland 1988.

9. Mizoguchi, R., Ikeda, M.: A Generic Framework for ITS and its Evaluation. In: Proc. of the International Conference on Advanced Research on Computers in Education (ARCE-90). Tokyo, Japan, 1990.

10. Sleeman, D.H.: Assessing Competence in Basic Algebra. In: Intelligent Tutoring Systems (D.H. Sleeman, J. S. Brown, eds.), pp. 185-199. London: Academic Press 1982.

11. VanLehn, K.: Student Modeling. In: Foundations of Intelligent Tutoring Systems (M. C. Polson, J. J. Richardson, eds.), pp.55-78. Hillsdale, New Jersey: Lawrence Erlbaum 1988.

12. Vivet, M.: Reasoned Explanations need Reasoning on Reasoning and Reasoning on the Student. In: Artificial Intelligence Tools in Education (P. Ercoli, R. Lewis, eds.), pp. 121-128. Amsterdam: North-Holland 1988.

13. Vivet, M., Futtersack, M., Labat, J. M.: Metaconnaissance dans le tuteurs intelligents. In: Proc. of the International Conference on Intelligent Tutoring Systems ITS-88. Montreal, Canada, 1988.

14. Weyhrauch., R.W.: Prolegomena to a Theory of Mechanized Formal Reasoning. Artificial Intelligence 13, 133-170 (1980).

Machine Learning, Explanation-Based Learning and Intelligent Tutoring Systems[1]

Ernesto Costa and Paulo Urbano[2]
Laboratório de Informática e Sistemas, Quinta da Boavista, Lote 1, 1º, P-3000 Coimbra, Portugal

Abstract: We discuss the aplicability of machine learning techniques, in particular explanation-based techniques (EBL), to the development of tutoring systems. We propose a classification of machine learning systems based on the idea of knowledge level. We identify some of the drawbacks of EBL and put forward solutions for some of the problems encountered in this deductive learning technique. We finish by exploring the possible links between EBL and Intelligent Tutoring systems.

Keywords: Explanation-Based Learning, Imperfect Theories, Learning Systems, Machine Learning.

Introduction

Machine Learning (ML) is that area of Artificial Intelligence (AI) which is concerned with the development of computer programs which are able to construct new knowledge or to modify in a useful way "old" knowledge using some input information ([16])[3]. In the last years there has been an increasing interest in that area resulting in the appearance of several programs. In order to obtain further progress it is important that we are able to classify in a coherent way the (apparent?) diversity of approaches that had appeared in the litterature. In section 2, we will try do to so based on the notion on systems' levels introduced by [20][4].

In section 3, we will present in more detail the Explanation-Based Learning (EBL) technique and discuss some of its drawbacks putting forward solutions for some of the problems encountered in this deductive learning technique (section 4). We continue by exploring the possible links between EBL and Intelligent Tutoring Systems (section 5[5]) and conclude with some comments concerning future work (section 6).

---

[1] This work was partially financed by the EEC ESPRIT contract 2154 "Machine Learning Toolbox"

[2] Current address: Departamento de Informática , Faculdade de Ciências da Universidade de Lisboa, Av. 24 de Julho, 134, 7º, P-1200 Lisboa.

[3] This definition of ML has implicit a notion of learning which makes it indistinguishable from the notion of representation. This was criticized by [9] who propose to define learning as the interpretation of experience resulting in rational changes of a mental state or operation. This is not the place to pursue that discussion and we will not do it.

[4] In this classification we will be interested only in learning systems using symbolic methods. Subsymbolic approaches, like those based on neural networks, will not be considered.

[5] In [16], Michalsky and Kodratoff propose another multicriteria classification for learning processes. The criteria are the primary purpose of the learning method, the type of input information, the type of primary interface employed and the role of the learner's prior knowledge in the learning process. Again this is not a systemic view. An important aspect concerning the techniques is the fact that analogy is considered as a combination of induction ads deduction.

Classification of learning programs

Overview

(a) [2]

One of the first attempts to classify machine learning systems was made in a paper by Carbonell, Michalsky and Mitchell that appeared in volume 1 of "Machine Learning: an Artificial Intelligence approach". There three dimensions for classification were suggested:

- the application domain;
- the representation of knowledge or skill acquired by the learner;
- the underlying learning strategy.

The application domains are areas like chemistry, medical diagnosis, education, music, sequence prediction, and so on. The representations given by a system are decision trees, production rules, logical expressions, etc. Concerning the different learning strategies they propose a classification ordered by the amount of inference that the learning system must accomplish. Thus we have rote learning, learning from instruction, learning by analogy, learning from examples and learning by observation and discovery. Learning from examples could be further refined according to criteria like the source of examples (a teacher, the learner itself or the external environment), the type of examples (positive only, positive and negative) or the availability of the examples (all at once, incremental). Learning by observation and discovery can also be decomposed into passive observation and active experimentation if we take into account the degree of interaction between the system and the external environment.

(b) [14]

In the second volume of the mentioned series, Michalsky proposed two more dimensions for characterization of machine learning systems: research paradigms (where he made the distinction between symbolic and non-symbolic methods) and the learning orientation that concerns the scope and subject of study (searching for a general learning theory, searching for a computational model of human learning or task oriented studies). More important, Michalsky revises the learning strategies suggested in [2] proposing a new (more abstract) classification: rote learning, learning by deduction, learning by analogy and learning by induction. Analogy is viewed as being a combination of deduction and induction.

Again these types of learning were ordered by the amount of inference done by the learning system. This new proposal shows the appearance of deductive methods and the adoption of the type of reasoning as the main classification criterion. Each type of learning can be further refined. For instance, knowledge reformulation, knowledge compilation, formation of macro-operators, chunking, and so on, are distinct instantiations of the deductive paradigm.

Learning by examples and learning by observation and discovery become sub-classes of inductive learning.
This classification is used by Michalsky in other papers (see [15]).

(c) [1]
In the Encyclopedia of Artificial Intelligence Carbonell and Langley suggest that there are two main learning paradigms: numerical and symbolic. The last one can be decomposed, according to what they call categorial tasks or task domains, into learning by examples, learning search hierarchies, learning by observation and language acquisition. Each one of these classes can be refined according to different dimensions and pose some particular problems. For instance, systems that learn from examples can be characterized in relation with the direction of search (specialization/generalization), how search is controlled (depth/breadth), the type of the operators (data driven/model driven) or the way data is handled (one-shot/incremental). The problems that must be faced are the presence of noise, the fuzziness of the concepts or the representation bias.

(d) [3]
In the introduction to a special volume of the AI journal on Machine Learning Carbonell indicates the existence of four machine learning paradigms: inductive, analytic (including deductive and some forms of analogic learning), genetic and connectionist learning. As with other approaches some decompositions are presented. For example, in the analytic paradigm we can use the way instances are represented, the degree of generalization, learning from success or failure or an open or closed loop learning as a criterion for classification.

(e) [21]
Partridge and Paap discuss the possible definition of learning to decompose learning into two approaches: connectionist and symbolic. At a lower level they present other categories of learning:

- by adjustment of link weights
- by being told: new facts, rules, heuristics or if you are right/wrong
- by hill-climbing
- by generalization from examples
- by particularization
- by unlearning (!)

The discussion of this decomposition has a cognitive science flavor.

How to classify machine learning systems

Systems and levels

After presenting the most significant taxonomies and looking to the (apparent) diversity, it is time to think about them. Are they really different? Contradictory? Mutually inconsistent? Which one is the correct/best one? To answer these questions we must first clarify two points:

- what are we classifying: systems, algorithms, techniques, theories?
- at what descriptive level are we classifying these systems?

We think that our point of view concerning these two aspects will enable us to answer the above questions and say that some classifications are better than others.

First point: Learning Systems as functions

We are in fact interested in classifying learning systems. So, as any other systems they have three components:

- input
- output
- body (transforming the input into the corresponding output).

<u>Second point: different descriptive levels</u>

It is clear that the concrete learning systems implicitly reflect a learning theory and only work as the result of algorithms that implement a particular technique. So a learning system can be described at different levels ranging from the concrete ones to more abstract ones.

Systems levels [20]

In his presidential address to the members of the American Association for Artificial Intelligence Newell raised the point that a computer system (and other systems as well) can be described at different levels. For computer systems he devised the following hierarchical levels:

- device level
- circuit level
- logic circuit sublevel
- register transfer sublevel
- symbol level

Each level has several aspects, namely: a medium (i.e. what is to be processed), a system (which is the result of applying laws of composition to components) and laws of behavior (which determine how the system behavior depends on its structure). For example, the different aspects for a computer system at the register-transfer level are:

Aspects	Register-transfer level
systems	digital systems
medium	bit vectors
components	registers functional units
composition laws	transfer path
behavior laws	logical operations

According to Newell each level can either be defined autonomously or reduced to the level below.

Newell's main contribution was the introduction of a new level, called the knowledge level, placed above the symbol level and whose main characteristic is that it describes a system without any reference to implementation details. At the knowledge level, the system is the agent; the components are a set of goals, a set of actions and a body; the medium is knowledge; and the behavioral law is the principle of rationality that states that if an agent has knowledge that one of its actions will lead to one of its goals then it will select that action.
It would be interesting if we could apply these ideas to produce a coherent classification for machine learning systems.

In [7] an attempt was made to describe learning systems at the knowledge level. Dietterich took some well known systems like LEX, LEX2, MRS, AQ11 and ID3 and tried to analyze them using the idea of knowledge level. As an example lets look at LEX. Its goal is to print correct solutions to symbolic integration problems. Its knowledge is composed by the set of operators for doing symbolic integration. LEX works by solving several problems, trying to discover preconditions for applying the operators so that next time it tries to solve a problem it will perform better (i.e. faster). The problem is that this characteristic cannot be described at the knowledge level because the knowledge level ignores all questions of implementation. At the knowledge level, it is clear that the knowledge possessed by LEX does not increase in the sense that it will be able to solve the same class of problems (this is a consequence of what Dietterich called the knowledge closure axiom). There is learning at the "problem-solving" level but not at the knowledge level!

After analyzing the other systems the main conclusion of Dietterich was that there are two types of learning: learning that improves performance and learning that acquires new knowledge. The first type of learning gives rise to systems (like LEX and LEX2) that cannot be described at the knowledge level but only at the symbol level (i.e. with reference to implementation details). The other type applies to systems that exhibit knowledge level learning (KLL), i. e., that present a positive change in their knowledge during time. Nevertheless some of the systems presenting KLL cannot be (deductively) described at the knowledge level (this is the case for inductive programs like AQ11 and ID3 because the syntactic biases they use cannot be expressed as a set of logical axioms forming part of their background knowledge), while others (like MRS) can be. So, in conclusion, Dietterich proposed the existence of three machine learning systems:

- symbol level learning systems
- deductive knowledge level systems
- non-deductive knowledge level systems.

Good classifications

After the above discussion it is clear that the best classification is the one that has the two following properties:

- coherent, that is, it must classify all systems at the same level;
- complete, that is, it must refer to the three components (input, output and body) of a learning system.

Following the discussion so far we can present the different ways of characterizing learning systems.

Input	Body (Learning Strategy)	Output
Facts, Theories	Methods analogical dedutive indictive	Task Level kn. acquisition kn. base refinment
Type, Source noisy/not noisy positive/negative incremental, ...	Techniques EBL SBL discovery case-based	Problem Solving Level planning decision diagnosis
Structure vector of attr. predicate conj. horn clauses, ...		Structure decision trees rules characteristic descriptors

Fig. 1 - Levels for characterization of learning systems

Unfortunately there still remain some difficulties. For instance, if we follow the ideas of Dietterich we know that there are levels of description where coherence may not be possible. Is it possible to find another hierarchy of descriptive levels, adapted for machine learning systems, where this problem disappears? This is a problem to be solved in the future.

In any case the ideas expressed above will already enable us to make some comments concerning some of the classifications presented at the beginning of this section.

(a) [2]

This is a classification that may be classified as complete in the sense that the three dimensions of underlying learning strategy, representation of knowledge or skill acquired and application domains correspond respectively to the body, the output and the input of a system. Nevertheless, it is not coherent. In particular the learning strategies are not described at the same level (for example learning by analogy and learning from examples).

(b) [14]

The classification of learning strategies as deductive, inductive and analogic is a big improvement towards coherence.

(c) [1]

This classification seems to be very confusing. It puts together what is learned (search heuristics, grammars), with how it is learned (from examples, by observation).

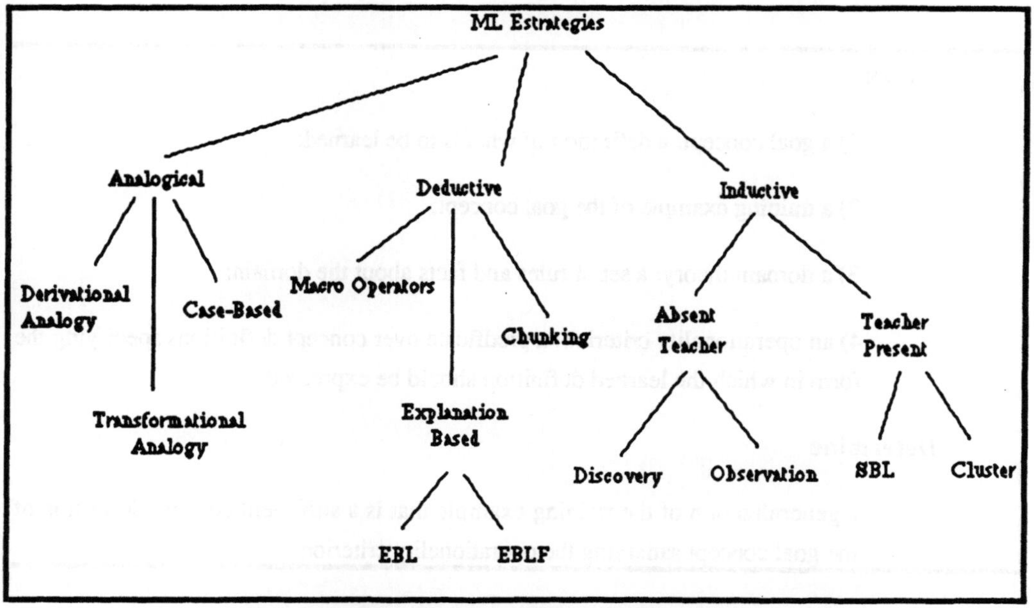

Fig. 2: Classification of learning strategies

Learning strategies

For the classification of learning strategies, we closely follow [14], to produce the taxonomy shown in the figure[5], EBL means explanation based learning, as usual, and EBLF means explanation based learning from failures. SBL has the usual meaning of similarity based learning. This seems to be the best classification we can propose, because it covers the most referenced learning strategies in a way we think coherent and useful.

How EBL works

Explanation-Based Learning (EBL) is a learning technique that works by creating an explanation about the compatibility between an example and a theory (background knowledge) and using that explanation for producing a more useful (or operational) concept definition ([6], [9], [17], [19])[6].

In more concrete terms the EBL methodology can be defined as follows:

Given

1) a goal concept: a definition of what is to be learned;

2) a training example of the goal concept;

3) a domain theory: a set of rules and facts about the domain;

4) an operationality criterion: a predficate over concept definitions specifying the form in which the learned definition should be expressed,

Determine

a generalization of the training example that is a sufficient concept definition of the goal concept satisfying the operationality criterion.

---

6 There are some different points of view concerning what EBL actually is. In our presentation we will follow [19].

Let us give an example. Suppose that we want to learn a system when it is safe to stack an object over another. In EBL terminology we have:

Given

goal concept:

safe-to-stack(x,y) <=> not (fragile(y)) or lighter(x,y)

training example:

on(obj1,obj2)
isa(obj1,box)
isa(obj2,endtable)
color(obj1,red)
color(obj2,blue)
volume(obj1, 1)
density(obj1, 0.1)
...

domain theory:

volume(p1,v1) and density(p1,d1) --> weight(p1, v1* d1)
weight(p1,w1) and weight(p2,w2) and less(w1,w2) -->
lighter(p1,p2)
isa(p1,endtable) --> weight(p1,5) [default]
less(0.1,5)
...

operationality criterion: the concept definition must be expressed in terms of the predicates used to describe the example or other selected, easily evaluated, predicates from the domain theory (like less).

Determine

a generalization of training example that is a sufficient concept definition for the goal concept and that satisfies the operationality criterion.

As we said in the beginning EBL is a two step process. First, using the theory we create an explanation showing why the training example is actually a positive example of the goal concept. In our case we will have the following proof structure:

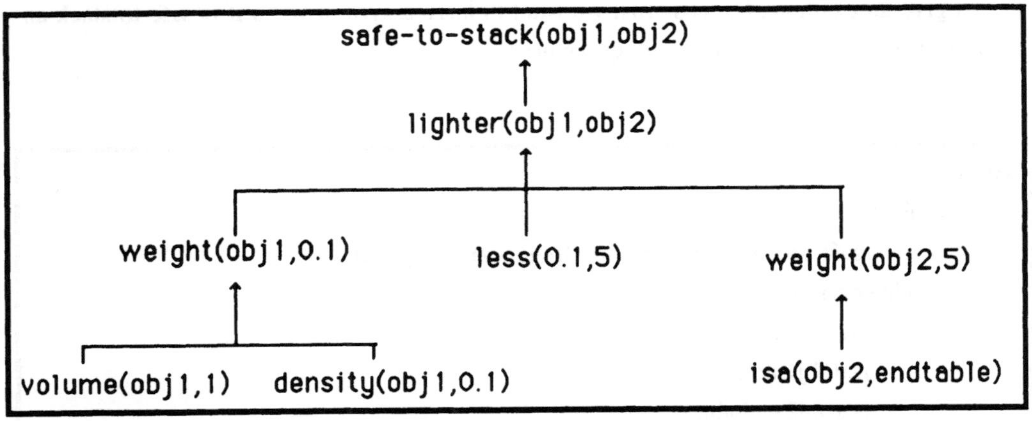

Fig. 3 - EBL proof

Notice how irrelevant information for the problem, like the color of the objects, disappears from the proof. Also the operationality criterion determines the leaves of the proof tree. This is important for the second step of EBL when, by a process of goal-regression, the explanation is generalized so as to produce a (new) sufficient operational concept definition. In the safe-to-stack example we will get:

volume(x,v1) and density(x,d1) and less(v1 * d1, 5)
and isa(y, endtable) --> safe-to-stack(x,y)

Extending EBL

Current issues in EBL

In recent years some authors have pointed out some problems with and limitations of EBL that seriously circumscribe the use of this technique ([6], [10], [17]). These have since become a matter of research. Here are some of those subjects:

- Formalization: the need of a domain independent definition for EBL.
- Explanation: what is its status? It is more than just a proof?
- Example: its role and number. Can we benefit by using more than a single positive example?
- Operationality: what are the consequences of considering the operational criterion as a context-sensitive concept?

- Domain: how to deal with theories which are imperfect, that is which are either incomplete (unable to prove all positive examples), inconsistent (able to prove and refute the same concept) or intractable (only usable with unlimited resources)?
- target concept: what to learn? Why not learn from failures?

There are already in the literature some (partial) answers for part of these problems. We will present our solution for the case of inconsistent theories.

The problem of inconsistencies

Lets have another look to the safe-to-stack example presented in section 3. If we now use the new operation rule to classify different instances of the concept we may have some odd behaviour. Consider for example the case:

Obj1: Volume=4, Density=1
endtable: Volume=2, Density=1

This is an incorrect example of the concept according with the initial theory. Nevertheless it will be accepted as a positive instance if we use the operational definition: our new rule will confirm that it is safe to stack the box2 on the endtable because the weight of Obj1 is 4 even though the weight of the endtable is less then the weight of that object!
Let us take a look to another case:

Obj1: Weight=14
endtable: Weight=24

Here we have the symmetric case: it is a positive example according to our primitive theory but will be rejected as such by the new learned rule.

The new (increased) theory is thus inconsistent! It is clear that if we use the starting theory instead of using the new operational rule the two examples will be correctly classified. So the questions to be answered are: a) where is the problem and b) how to solve it in such a way that we will keep and safely use the new operational rule.

The reason for that ill-functioning is the presence of default knowledge (assumptions) in the theory. As a consequence of this situation there are two different ways of computing the weight of an endtable, that is two different explanations, which are, in general, contradictory. So, when the weight is known and we want to keep consistency the system has to solve the resulting conflict between the two applicable rules. One possible solution is ordering the rules:

trying the default rules at the end. This approach can work well when we use the theory in the first time for learning the first operational rule because we only have to solve conflicts inside that theory. But the problem is how to order the different concept definitions in the new theory. Moreover, if the EBL algorithm is used incrementally (that is, using more than one example) new operational rules will be created. In our case if we use the (simplified) example:

Obj1: Volume=3, Density=2
Obj2: Volume= 4, Density= 13

the system will come with the following new operational definition:

```
safe_to_stack(X,Y) :- volume(X,Vx),
                      density(X,Dx),
                      Wx is Vx * Dx,
                      volume(Y,Vy),
                      ensity(Y,Dy),
                      Wy is Vx * Dx,
                      Wx < Wy.
```

Again, in what order we will use them in the future?[7] We need thus a solution to our problem that will guarantee that our theory will be both declaratively and procedurally consistent. The solution we propose consists in changing both the theory and the interpreter (the algorithm). The theory is changed so as to explicitly state what knowledge is assumed by default. This is done by introducing a new operator called "default/1". The interpreter is modified in such a way that the learned operational rules will explicitly mention the default knowledge that was used. For the example of section 2 the domain theory will have the fact

```
default ((weight(X,5) :- isa(X, endtable))
```

and the learned operational rule will be

```
safe_to_stack(X,Y) :- isa(X,box),
                      isa(Y,endtable),
                      volume(X,Vx),
                      density(X,Dx),
                      Wx is Vx * Dx,
                      not_known ((weight(Y,Wy))),
                      Wx < 5.
```

---

[7] Note that if we had a context sensitive notion of operationality we could have distinct operational rules for the same example. For instance, if weight is considered to be operational than the learned operational rule using the example above would be

```
safe_to_stack(X,Y) :- weight(X,Wx), weight(Y,Wy), Wx < Wy.
```

The literal not_known((weight(Y,Wy)) is introduced by the meta-interpreter to state that the weight of the endtable was not calculated[8].

In [12], Hirch proposes a different solution for that problem consisting in changing the theory so that we will have different predicate names for the predicates that admit default definitions. In our case, as there is only one default concerning the weight, we will have in the new theory weight1 and weight 2. The main inconveniences of that approach are:

a) the complexity of the theory will greatly increase while the understandability of the explanation will decrease;

b) the changed predicate cannot in an easy way be made operational;

c) the computational complexity will also be greater because some proofs will have to be done twice (unless we change the interpreter in a tricky way!).

These points are discussed in more detail in [23].

EBL and student modelling

The activity of learning can be viewed as a special case of interaction among rational agents. By rational we mean any agent that acts in a certain way if it believes that the execution of these actions will lead it to the achievement of its goals. Beliefs, plans and goals are thus important aspects for characterizing agents. In a tutoring situation we have only two agents: the teacher and the student. The teacher has the goal of assessing the student's competence on some subject. For that purpose he defines a plan to test that competence (the tutorial strategy) guided by his beliefs about the student (the student model). The student has a goal which is a problem externally defined by the teacher and is part of the teacher's plan. To solve the problem the student builds and executes his own plan using his beliefs (the interpretation of the question, the knowledge about the subject under discussion).

During the interaction between the tutor and the student the former is, in general, engaged in a process of discovery and revision of what it believes about the student beliefs, that is, he it is involved in the activity of dynamical definition of the student model. This is done implicitly from the problem (the goal) and the solution (the plan). In an earlier paper [4] we have shown the links between EBL and student modelling[9]. In fact the student modelling problem can be stated in EBL terms as:

---

[8] not_known will always be considered as operational. We admit that this solution goes against the idea that operational predicates must be more easily computable.

[9] Several other authors worked in applications of machine learning to tutoring systems, in particular with respect to the problem of student modelling [11], [13].

Given

goal concept: an unknown concept[10];

domain theory: the set of beliefs currently ascribed to the student by the tutor;

training instance: the pair question/answer;

operationality criterion: the explanation must be given using only predicates from the tutor theory or others given explicitly by the learner;

Determine

An operational explanation for the student´s answer (reflecting probably some small misconception).

In the cited paper we have applied the technique for the domain of history, more precisely French seventeenth century history. Nevertheless the technique is general and can be applied to other domains as well.

Another aspect of the problem is that the student model is not an amorphous set of beliefs but rather a set of sets of beliefs. Each of these sets can be viewed as a sub-agent (sub-theory). Moreover each sub-agent can be further decomposed into other sub sub-agents and so on[11]. This architecture for an rational agent as several aspects which are worth mentioning:

a) the agent is decomposed into a net of theories with the possibility for each theory to share with the others part of its knowledge;

b) each theory can be incomplete;

c) each theory can be internally inconsistent;

d) a group of theories can consistent when considered in isolation but inconsistent as a group.

This decomposition is compatible with the idea of the mind (of a rational agent) as a society ([8], [18]). It has several advantages[12]:

a) economy: as the result of the sharing of knowledge;

b) assumption based reasoning: as a solution to incomplete knowledge. At the moment this problem is overcome by means of an oracle;

c) multiple points of view[13]: the different ways an agent can perceive part of the reality can be used to detect misconceptions [4].

10 Contrasting with typical EBL, at the beginning we don´t have a concept definition to operationalize!

11 It is in theory possible to have recursive agents.

12 We would like to stress that we make no claim about the psychological validity of that approach.

13 See [23] for a detailed discussion on points of view.

With this view of tutoring as a special case of interaction between two rational agents and the idea of a mind as a collection of interrelated set of beliefs, the problem of student modelling isnothing more that the update of this collection as the result of the interaction. It is normally faced as a two step problem: first, identification of the sub-agent(s) responsible(s) for the learner´s behaviour; second, understanding of the student functioning. The big advantage of using EBL is that these two steps can be solved at the same time!

Conclusion

After several years of research in the domain of Intelligent Tutoring Systems, giving rise to the emergence of a common agreed architecture based on the existence of a domain module, a tutorial mode and a student module, it is our opinion that in order to improve and produce results this area need some rethinking. This can be achieved in different ways. One possible way is to look to other areas of AI and see if we can "import" some outcomes they are producing. Candidate areas are interaction among agents, dialogue systems, belief revision and machine learning. In this paper we concentrate on the last one and in particular in the technique known as Explanation-Based Learning. We weren't interested iwhether discussing if the explanations created by EBL have some psychological validity nor if the way EBL learns is rational [9][14]. We just try to show that it is possible to use EBL as an aid to the task of tutoring. We are aware that a lot of questions and problems still have to be solved, like the one of initially constructing the sub-theories.

Acknowledgements

We would like to thank Carlos Bento, José Luís Ferreira and Paulo Moura for many fruitful discussions.

References

1. J. Carbonell and P. Langley: Machine Learning, in Encyclopedia of Artificial Intelligence, S. Shapiro (Ed.), John Wiley and Sons, 1987.

2. J. Carbonell, R. Michalsky & T. Mitchell: An overview of Machine Learning, in Machine Learning : an Artificial Intelligence Approach, Vol. I, pp 3-23, R. Michalsky, J. Carbonell & T. Mitchell (Eds.), Tioga Publishing.

3. J. Carbonell: Introduction: paradigms for Machine Learning, *Artificial Intelligence* 40 (1989) 1-9.

[14] This statement does not mean that we think these are useless problems.

4. E. Costa, S. Duchénoy and Y. Kodratoff: A resolution based method for discovering students' misconceptions, in Artificial Intelligence and Human Learning: intelligent computer-aided instruction, J. Self (Ed.), Chapman and Hall, 1988.

5. G. DeJong: Some thoughts on the present and future of Explanation-Based Learning, Invited Talk, Proceedings of the European Conference on Artificial Intelligence ECCAI-88, Munich, 1988, 690-697.

6. G. DeJong and R. Mooney: Explanation-Based Learning: an alternative view, Machine Learning 1: 145-176, 1986.

7. T. Dietterich: Learning at the knowledge level, Machine Learning 1, (1986) 287-316.

8. J. Doyle: A society of mind, Proceedings of the IJCAI-83 Conference, 309-313, 1983.

9. J. Doyle: On rationality and learning, Technical Report, CMU-CS-88-122, 1988.

10. T. Elman: Explanation-Based Learning: a survey of programs and perspectives, ACM Computing Surveys, vol.21, nº2, June 1989.

11. D. Gilmore and J. Self, The application of machine learning to intelligent tutoring systems, in Artificial Intelligence and Human Learning: intelligent computer-aided instruction, J. Self(Ed.), Chapman and Hall, 1988.

12. H. Hirch: Explanation-Based Generalization in a logic-programming environment, Proceedings IJCAI-87, Milan, 1987.

13. P. Langley, S. Ohlsson and S. Sage: A Machine Learning approach to student modelling, CMU-RI-TR-84-7 Technical Report, Carnegie-Mellon University, Robotics Institute, 1984.

14. R. Michalsky: Understanding the nature of learning: issues and research directions, in Machine Learning : an Artificial Intelligence Approach, Vol. II, pp 3-25, R. Michalsky, J. Carbonell & T. Mitchell, Eds, Morgan Kaufmann.

15. R. Michalsky: Learning strategies and automated knowledge acquisition: an overview, in Computational Models of Learning, L. Bolc (Ed.), Springer-Verlag.

16. R. Michalsky and Y. Kodratoff: Research in machine Learning: recent progress, classification of methods and future directions, in Machine Learning: an artificial intelligence approach Volume III, Kodratoff and Michalsky (Eds.), Morgan Kaufman, 1990.

17. S. Minton, J. Carbonell, C. Knoblock, D. Kuokka, O. Etzioni and Y. Gil: Explanation-Based Learning: a problem solving perspective, Artificial Intelligence 40 (1989) 63-118.

18. M. Minsky: The society of mind, Simon and Schuster, New York, 1986.

19. T. Mitchell, R. Keller and S. Kedar-Cabelli: Explanation-Based Generalization: a unifying view, Machine Learning 1: 47-80, 1986.

20. A. Newell, The knowledge level: *Artificial Intelligence* **18**, (1982), 82-127.

21. D. Partridge and K. Paap: An introduction to learning, Artificial Intelligence Review **2**, (1988) 79-101.

22. J. Self, Computational viewpoints: AI-Report 44, Computing Department, University of Lancaster, March 1990.

23. P. Urbano and E. Costa: Explanation-Based Learning in the presence of default assumptions, Technical Report, Departamento de Engenharia Electrotécnica, Universidade de Coimbra, September 1990.

The Central Importance of Student Modelling to Intelligent Tutoring

Gordon I. McCalla
ARIES Laboratory, Department of Computational Sciencc, University of Saskatchewan, Saskatoon, Saskatchewan S7N 0W0 Canada

Abstract: Intelligent tutoring systems can be individualized if they are designed to take into account differences between students. The process of doing this is called student modelling. Unfortunately, student modelling is hard, and increasingly researchers are trying to avoid the need. The idea of one-on-one tutoring is taking a back seat to new ideas like collaborative learning, negotiated tutoring, guided discovery tutoring, and situated learning, as well as old ideas like discovery learning. In this paper I will argue two things:

- first, that the new approaches have, if anything, even more need for student modelling than does a one-on-one tutor; and
- second, that traditional idea of designing for individualized one-on-one interaction is still .

I will then consider various ways of tackling the "intractable" student modelling problem, and will conclude with some optimism for the future of student modelling and one-on-one tutoring.

Keywords: Cognitive modelling, Student modelling.

Introduction

Consider an excerpt from the famous "Who's on First" dialogue of Abbott and Costello:

S: I want to find out the names of the players on the St. Louis team.

T: Who's on first base, What's on second, I Don't Know is on third.

S: You know the players' names?

T: Yes.

S: Well, then who's playing first base?

T: Yes.

S: I mean the player's name on first base.

T: Who.

S: The guy on first base.

T: Who is on first.

S: Well, what are you asking me for?

If "S" is a student and "T" is a tutoring system, then we have here a classic case of a tutoring system that is not communicating successfully with the student. The tutoring system's perspectives as to what the student knows are completely off-base. The tutoring system assumes that it has been able to accurately convey to the student the names of the baseball players and their positions ("Who" is playing first base, "What" is playing second base, and "I Don't Know" is playing third base). Subsequent references made by the student are interpreted by the tutoring system in this context. In the parlance of intelligent tutoring systems, it is said that the tutoring system lacks an accurate *student model.*

Student modelling has been an active topic of research for many years. Since Self's seminal paper on student modelling [60], there have been many student modelling issues explored and many techniques developed. These are well surveyed in papers by Clancey [22] and VanLehn [68]. Recently, despite the plethora of work on student modelling, the need for student modelling has come into some dispute. In essence, there is a school of thought that suggests that student modelling is too difficult and not of enough utility in actual student-tutoring system interactions to warrant doing it.

In this paper I will maintain that no sensible interactions between a tutoring system and a student can happen without an accurate student model. The claim is made that no reasonable system meant to interact with a learner can possibly exist without at least generic knowledge of the learner's cognitive abilities, and that every such system can be vastly enhanced if individualized knowledge can be maintained about each student during that student's interaction with the system. In short, I will argue that having an accurate student model is of critical importance to any intelligent tutoring system. Failure to maintain an accurate student model will, in fact, invite interactions such as happened in "Who's on First".

The paper starts with a discussion of the different types of student modelling, with emphasis on the distinction between external and internal student modelling. Next, the motivation for doing student modelling is discussed, in particular illustrating how student modelling can enhance individualization and why individualization is important to instruction. Then, various objections to student modelling are raised and arguments are presented as to why these objections are not as serious as they may at first seem. Nevertheless, these objections carry enough weight that some consideration is given to various alternative paradigms for instruction in which the need for student modelling may be not as critical as it is in standard one-on-one tutors. Unfortunately, the conclusion drawn is that student modelling is necessary in all of these paradigms. The paper thus concludes with a brief overview of some techniques which have been developed which will help to overcome the difficult problems involved in student modelling.

What's in a Student Model?

Student modelling is the process of taking into account student cognition in the design of an intelligent tutoring system (ITS).[1] There are two types of student modelling: external and internal (see [51]). External modelling consists of inferring cognitive processes of typical students and designing the system with this in mind. In internal student modelling there is an explicit model of the cognitive processes carried out by students that is represented inside the system and that is available for consultation by the system. Each of these will now be considered in turn.

The goal of external student modelling is to make a system that takes into account actual cognitive processing of learners. The many successful discovery environments that exist (e.g. Logo [56], the Alternate Reality Kit [67], Boxer [26], etc.) are examples of systems that incorporate well designed external student modelling. In such systems, external student modelling affects the design of the interaction protocols, and is most evident in the interface presented to the student. It also has a role in initializing regular tutoring systems, setting up the "prior knowledge" which students are deemed to have. A strong claim of this paper is that no computing system that is meant to interact with human beings can effectively perform without external user modelling. This maxim applies to intelligent tutoring systems no differently from any computing system. The possible counter-claim that some "seat of the pants" designs work very well (e.g. the Xerox windowing environment) can itself be counteracted. The designers of any environment that works either do empirical testing prior or during the design of a system or have pre-compiled in their heads relevant knowledge about user-system interaction. Such people are able to put themselves into the shoes of various kinds of users, understanding their cognitive perspectives, and hence are able to design systems appropriate for these users. The relevant knowledge of user cognition is effectively already present in their minds.

The other kind of student modelling is internal student modelling where the goal is to allow the system itself to carry out cognitive modelling of the student. There are two types of internalized student model: generic and individualized. In a generic student model knowledge of general students is available to the ITS. A generic student model can be hard to distinguish from domain knowledge representation; the distinction is that generic student knowledge can be imbued with typical student misconceptions and the like. This is exactly the kind of student modelling discussed by Reiser et al [57] in their discussion of student modelling in the LISP Tutor.

In an individualized student model, knowledge about each particular student is available to the ITS. The ITS keeps track of what this particular student knows and doesn't know. This knowledge can include knowledge about the student's levels of awareness of various aspects of

---

1 I will use the term ITS in a broad sense to denote any computing system whose goal is to enhance student learning.

domain knowledge, but can also include knowledge of student goals, indications about motivational states of the student, and knowledge of misconceptions that the student holds. Of course, an ITS can never have perfect knowledge of a student---some sort of approximation is the best that can be expected.

There are several dimensions to individualized models. These are summarized in the "student modelling cube" shown in Figure 1:

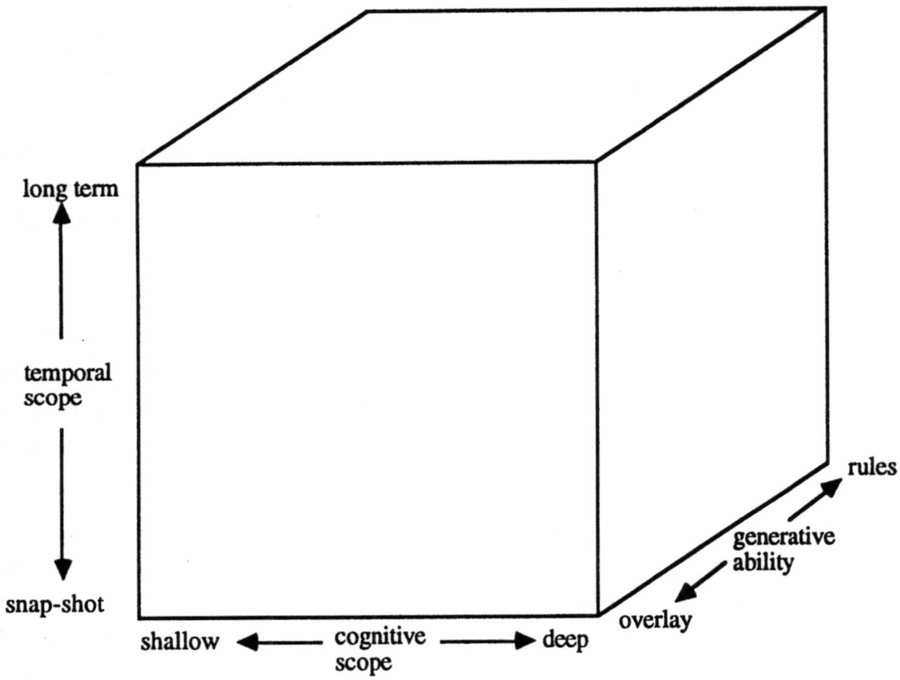

Figure 1: The student modelling cube [2]

The vertical dimension of this cube represents temporal scope: i.e. whether the student model records only a snap-shot of the student's current beliefs or whether it records longer-term trends showing evolving student behaviour. Some ITSs just do diagnosis and don't keep a longer term model (for example the SCENT-1 system [47] keeps track only of the current programming

[2] This figure was first created in a working group at the NATO-sponsored summer research institute held in Calgary in July of 1990.

strategy being employed by the student and has no role for longer term inferences about how that strategy may fit into an ongoing learning sequence being carried out by the student). Systems at the bottom end of this dimension avoid the problem of maintaining an ongoing student model, but also neglect important issues in how a student may be evolving his or her knowledge. Goldstein [34] shows how useful such "genetic" knowledge can be.

The horizontal dimension of the student modelling cube delineates cognitive scope: deep models vs shallow models. Some student modelling systems just model expertise of the domain. Others also include bugs. Still others are concerned with a student's reasoning and other deep cognitive abilities. Deep student models are concerned with issues such as mental modelling, etc.; shallow models with surface behaviour Traditional CAI systems [21] have shallow models, keeping track of student scores on various tests, but not being concerned with what these scores indicate about the deep cognitive activities of the student. In contrast, Bhuiyan [6] is concerned with analyzing how a student uses deep mental models in solving programming problems. QUEST [30] has deep student modelling, too, whereas SOPHIE [16] just looks at end result of student behaviour, not being concerned with the cognitive processes that led the student there. The BUGGY [15] subtraction tutor and the PROUST [37] programming tutor are somewhat in the middle ground: they deduce plans but not how they came about. The LISP Tutor [4] and Dinesh Gadwal's recent chess tutoring system UMRAO [32] try to account for step by step behaviour, and hence are deeper student modelling systems.

The third dimension of student modelling shown in Figure 1 is a dimension that is concerned with the generative ability of the tutoring system. Systems without any ability to generate their own understanding of the student are "overlay" systems, where the knowledge of the system about the student is overlaid upon a domain knowledge base. A generative system, on the other hand, is able to figure out what the student is doing by reasoning from first principles. This dimension captures the distinction between classification and simulation models discussed by Clancey [22]. Overlays have been castigated for encouraging the view that the student is a "subset" of the expert. This need not be the case. The subset view comes about when the generative ability dimension is confused with the cognitive scope dimension. When it is realized these two dimensions are different, then it becomes possible to have overlay models which overlay bugs, strategies, and other reasoning (e.g. SCENT3 [48] discusses student modelling in these more general terms). Generative models are hard to build even in the most trivial domains (e.g. in the BUGGY [15] project it took years of development to come up with the "first principles" Repair theory [17] of the kinds of processes students use in simple subtraction). A more significant criterion than generative ability might be coverage: the ability to cover a wide variety of student behaviour may be more crucial than reasoning from first principles.

It is important to realize that student models are at best imprecise. External modelling may neglect or not discover certain kinds of (rare) student cognitive behaviour. An internal model may not cover all possible knowledge and motivation states of a specific learner. A student model does not contain absolute truth, but represents an approximation of the beliefs, knowledge, and goals the student is deemed to have. Such incompleteness is not particularly problematical as long as it isn't too profound. Human teachers seldom have absolutely accurate perceptions of individual students. However, they still usefully employ their partial knowledge of student cognition to good effect, both generic knowledge of stereotypical students and particular knowledge of individual students whom they are tutoring.

Why Student Modelling?

The need for student modelling arises primarily as a by-product of the need for individualization and student control. Without detailed knowledge of what students actually do, it is impossible to allow the student any control and it is impossible to modify the system's behaviour to correspond to specific, individual needs of the student.

Is individualization good? Bloom's studies [9] have shown a "two sigma" effect of one-on-one (human) tutoring over traditional class room situations, i.e. students perform two standard deviations better with tutoring. On standardized tests, the average score of the individually tutored students would have placed in the 98th percentile of a control group taught using lectures alone. What appears to make the difference is the ability to provide feedback on an individual basis. Mastery learning with its emphasis on feedback and testing achieves a one sigma improvement in classroom settings. Bloom's paper attempts to find effective means short of one-on-one tutoring that teachers can use to approach the two sigma improvement. He doesn't once suggest intelligent tutoring systems as an economically viable solution to the problem of providing individualized one-on-one instruction for masses of students.

However, intelligent tutoring systems may be able to achieve the individualization that Bloom seeks, and hopefully the enhanced learning that follows. To do so requires student modelling. In particular student modelling, both external and internal, is needed to enhance:

- the tutoring system's fidelity to the real world of student-tutor interaction (i.e. it is useful to know what actually happens between a student and a tutoring system if the system is to be designed realistically);
- the ability of the system to communicate to an individual student in terms that will be relevant to the student's current state of knowledge;

- the system's understanding of an individual student's behaviour (i.e. to help the student overcome his or her problems it is critical to have some idea of what the student currently believes about the domain of instruction and why the student is behaving in a particular fashion);
- the pedagogic relevance of the system (i.e. to aid the student to learn what is appropriate to him/her at this point it is necessary to tailor instruction specifically to his/her state of mind); and
- the computational efficiency of the system (i.e. the student model can be used as a lens that allows the tutoring system to "see" and act upon only those things relevant to the particular student in a particular context, not all possible things that could be considered).

Objections to Student Modelling

Despite the obvious potential of student modelling to enhance the capabilities of an intelligent tutoring system, there is still a big debate in the ITS community about the usefulness of doing it. This debate stems in large part from the difficulty of doing it, especially of doing individualized internal student modelling. There are a number of arguments against doing student modelling; my counter-arguments follow each argument as it is raised:

- Student modelling can't be done in principle.
  Counter-argument: Humans seem to be able to do it, at least to some degree.

- Student modelling hasn't succeeded in ten or twenty years so it's time to give up.
  Counter-argument: Twenty years is a very short time in the history of science. Moreover, progress is being made, as section 6 will illustrate.

- Student modelling isn't necessary; e.g. coaches/teachers don't use it.
  Counter-argument: Coaches motivate on an individual basis, as do teachers. Even for computing systems, student modelling impacts systems that on the surface don't look like they have it, especially through the use of external modelling in the design of the system.

- Student modelling shouldn't be done---often refined to "diagnosis shouldn't be done". The analogy here is to medical diagnosis, where the next step after diagnosis is treatment to cure some disease, i.e. to remediate some bug. This is deemed by many to be a wrong-headed way to view student learning.

Counter-argument: It is not evil to diagnose; it is only evil to do bad things with the diagnosis. The AI term "diagnosis" merely means to make sense of behaviour, not necessarily to remediate in the traditional educational sense once that diagnosis is done.

- Even if student modelling can partially succeed, what good is it? A partial model may be worse than nothing; a little knowledge is a dangerous thing.
  Counter-argument: Even though we never have total knowledge of our fellow human beings, our partial models are still useful. We react differently to Aunt Maude than we do to our boss, despite having incomplete knowledge of both.

- Student modelling is a "level 16 problem"[3]; the real problems are at level 1, dealing with the context in which the system is to operate. This is "the situated perspective" (see [14]) in which the critical issues of context dominate relatively secondary issues such as student modelling.
  Counter-argument: The knowledge, social background, and goals of the student are crucial elements in the overall context. A truly situated system would need access to this kind of individualized knowledge of the student in order to respond intelligently and flexibly within the context of the student's needs. It is exactly those systems with little or no individualized knowledge that will be unresponsive to those aspects of the situation that change as the student changes.

- Student modelling is a superset of AI, and presupposes that all of AI has been solved. As argued in [45] a plethora of deep and interesting AI issues must be solved before student modelling can fully achieve its aims. In fact, it would seem that student modelling is, in some sense, AI-complete in that almost all the basic knowledge representation and reasoning problems must be solved before student modelling can be achieved.
  Counter-argument: This argument can be used against other areas of artificial intelligence, since many AI problems are "AI-complete". This objection is reminiscent of the objections by the Bloomfield school of linguistics in the 1930's [10] that performance issues could not be studied as part of linguistics, since to do so would require completely accurate scientific theories of the world. Of course, computational linguists now study the semantics and pragmatics of natural language using knowledge representation and reasoning schemes that can explicitly deal with incomplete knowledge. Similarly, although student modelling is difficult, we needn't solve all problems to make a start; partial models can be useful.

---

3 This term was used by Elliot Soloway at the NATO Advanced Studies Institute in Calgary in July 1990.

- Strong AI has failed, and student modelling is part of that idea.
  Counter-argument: Strong AI hasn't failed, and as Shute [65] shows particularly with respect to ITS there have been many successes by any standards (see below in section 5). Cercone and McCalla [19] argue explicitly that strong AI has chalked up many successes and there is no reason that it shouldn't continue to do so.

Abandoning One-on-One Tutoring

These objections to student modelling seem collectively damning enough that there has been a recent trend to try to do an end-run around the need to build the one-on-one tutoring systems in which the problem of student modelling seems to be especially acute. In particular, a number of alternative paradigms for student-system interaction have been proposed, motivated at least in part by the difficulty of doing student modelling. As in the previous section, I will present each of these alternative approaches along with my argument as to why the student modelling problem still exists for them:

- *collaborative learning* [54], where two students interact in a computer-supported learning environment.
  For the learning environment to influence the nature of the interaction, it is going to have to have models not just of one student, but of both students. Even if the system itself is not proactive, it must be carefully designed using external student modelling.

- *negotiated learning* [53], where student and system negotiate mutually acceptable learning goals.
  Unfortunately, negotiated learning implies the need for a student model to keep track of goals and mutual knowledge, if only to communicate. McCalla and Brecht [46] argue that the student modelling problem in a negotiated system is actually more critical than in normal one-on-one tutoring.

- *guided discovery* [28], where the tutoring system has a range of pedagogical options available to it, ranging from fully student-controlled discovery through fully tutor-controlled instruction. Since a range of tutoring options are available, guided discovery is a superset of one-on-one individualized tutoring with a clear cut need for student modelling.

- *discovery learning* [56], where the student explores on his or her own initiative an environment specially crafted to encourage learning in various domains.
  But, the LOGO experience has shown a clear need to have individual tutoring available to students in order to help them overcome various conceptual blockages and to get out of conceptual cul de sacs. An ideal discovery environment would thus have an intelligent one-on-one tutor available in the background to help out the student when necessary, and as with any one-on-one tutor, student modelling is of central importance to flexible, responsive behaviour. In any event, a discovery environment will be better if external student modelling has been done to find out how students actually interact with the system.

- *situated learning* [14], where a system is designed with central focus on the context in which the student is to use it.
  The argument is that the context is so incredibly complex, that it will completely dominate an individual human being, just as Simon's ant is controlled by its environment. The power is in the environment, not in the individual. Hence, student modelling, in fact cognitive modelling of any sort, is mostly irrelevant. Nevertheless, Simon's ant does react to its environment, and to determine how it reacts necessitates understanding how it processes signals from the environment. In the final analysis, which is easier to study: the complex environment, or the relatively simple cognitive agent in that environment? It seems to me that the very complexity of the environment is in fact strong support for the need to study how cognition makes sense of that environment, rather than to embark on a difficult exploration of the environment itself.

  The grain of truth in the situated argument is that cognitive modelling has often been based on very simple microworlds that bear no resemblance to the real world, and the methodologies developed in these microworlds cannot scale up. This is not an argument against cognitive modelling *per se*, but is rather an argument for more general cognitive theories that take the real world into account. Some theories (e.g. ACT* [2] and SOAR [38]) have been developed with just this kind of generality in mind, and are being explored in the context of intelligent tutoring [4], [70]), among other places.

  In any event, it is still too early to say exactly what the situated learning paradigm will turn out to be. Whatever shape situated learning systems ultimately take on, it would seem that they will have to be on a continuum between discovery environments and one-on-one tutoring, and thus like guided discovery environments will need to carry out some form of student modelling.

Thus, it seems that each of the proposed alternative approaches to one-on-one tutoring has a need for student modelling. Therefore, the desire to move away from one-on-one tutoring in order to avoid the student modelling problem would seem to be misplaced (although the alternative paradigms may be highly worthwhile pedagogically). Moreover, many one-on-one tutoring systems, using student modelling to a greater or lesser degree, have been very successful. Valerie Shute [65] discusses four systems (the LISP Tutor [4], Smithtown [66], Sherlock [40], and the Bridge Pascal ITS [11]), and shows that students using these tutoring systems learned much faster than classroom trained students. She suggests one of the main potential advantages of ITSs is to take students with different backgrounds and get them to the same place. To do this, of course, requires that student modelling be carried out. Thus, it would appear that abandoning the investigation of one-one-one tutors is premature. There have been many successes in the one-on-one tutoring paradigm and these successes should be built upon, not abandoned. This is not to say, of course, that the other interaction paradigms discussed above are not worth exploring as well.

The need for student modelling seems so pervasive, in fact, that it is hard to believe there is actually a debate about the issue. At some stage, either during design or during tutor-student interaction, every computer-based tutoring system will need to know what students actually do, i.e. will need external or internal student modelling. Given the central importance of student modelling, the focus must shift from trying to avoid student modelling by looking for some miracle end-run around the problem, to trying to achieve tractability. The next section looks at various techniques, some developed explicitly in ITS and others borrowed from elsewhere, that may prove useful in overcoming what Self calls the "intractable problem of student modelling" [62]. The section presents a variety of work, but tends to focus on work carried out in the ARIES Laboratory over the past few years where the issue of student modelling has been central in a number of projects.

Achieving Tractability

Enhancing External Student Modelling

Although the focus of section 6 will be on improving the tractability of internal student modelling, I would like to start with a very brief discussion of external student modelling. External student modelling can be enhanced through the application of numerous techniques from the social sciences. Diana Laurillard [39], for example, is experimenting with how phenomenography can be applied to the extraction of typical student behaviour patterns. According to Laurillard, phenomenography can achieve a fairly sophisticated map of student capabilities using as few as 20 students. Mildred Shaw and Brian Gaines have been applying personal construct theory to the problem of knowledge acquisition, and have constructed a knowledge acquisition shell called

KSSO [63] in which these ideas are incorporated. Although, at least to my knowledge, KSSO has not been used explicitly in a tutoring context, there would seem to be nothing preventing this.

Even if theories from the social sciences are not explicitly used, it is possible for computing technology to help in the external student modelling task. For example, Stefano Cerri and his group have constructed a knowledge acquisition system called Nobile [20] which is able to help the knowledge engineer extract student bugs. Nobile maintains a bug model to which it compares any new bug that the knowledge engineer can suggest exists. If the bug already exists, Nobile can tell the knowledge engineer; if not, it can integrate the new bug into its bug model. Systems like Nobile could be useful both in helping to manage the collection of information for external student modelling as well as in the creation of an internal student model. .

However the external student model is constructed, it must be validated. Mary Mark [42] has written an excellent survey outlining how techniques from psychology and elsewhere can be used to help in the various stages of evaluation of a tutoring system. In particular such techniques could be used to validate that the external student modelling has been done appropriately.

The ultimate goal of external student modelling would be to devise a predictive model so that not all of the external model would have to be discovered empirically. Brown and VanLehn [17] propose Repair theory with this goal in mind. Repair theory is based on making standard perturbations to various subtraction procedures that are already known. These perturbations result in a host of possible subtraction bugs, each essentially a prediction of Repair theory. The generation of these bugs from first principles has two advantages: first, the need for extensive empirical investigation is reduced, and second, the "cause" of the bug is explicit (i.e. the perturbation that created the bug is known). The disadvantage, however, is achieving accurate coverage of real bugs: there seems to be a trade-off between generating a multitude of spurious bugs versus leaving out important bugs. It is also difficult to envisage how Repair theory can be generalized to more complex domains. Nevertheless, the ultimate goal of external student modelling is to come up with a principled theory of student cognitive behaviour that can be used predictively.

Improving Internal Student Modelling

If external student modelling is difficult, internal student modelling is even harder. Certainly, it will never be possible to obtain a completely accurate description of a student's current state of mind, nor will it be possible to track with complete accuracy changes to this state of mind. Nevertheless, it is possible to do various things that will help to achieve at least an approximation to the student's current state of mind. In this section a number of suggestions are made about how the difficult internal student modelling problems can be tackled. Some of these suggestions arise from research in which I have been involved; some have been pioneered by other researchers.

Constrain the Student

The most common way of figuring out what a student is up to is to constrain the student to making a limited range of responses to the tutoring system. Sometimes this approach can be dictatorial, as in the LISP Tutor [4], where students solving programming problems have each s-expression checked as it is entered. Any s-expression that does not conform to one expected by the LISP Tutor is automatically deemed to be incorrect, and the student is forced to change to a correct one. Effectively, the student's behaviour is constrained to following one of the limited number of models the system has. By so constraining the student, the LISP Tutor is able to track his or her progress accurately. Despite being dictatorial, this kind of tutoring has proven to be effective when adequate external student modelling has been done initially to ensure that the various models the system has reflect real models that students have or are to acquire.

Moreover, such model tracing need not be dictatorial, as is illustrated by Gadwal's UMRAO chess tutor [32]. In UMRAO a student is constrained to following a pre-ordained set of paths through a strategy graph as he or she solves bishop-pawn chess end game problems. The strategy graph represents the system's knowledge of correct and incorrect plans and subplans to solve the end game problem. In UMRAO, the variety of paths is large enough, and the number of options that the student has is small enough, that the student is not nearly as constrained as in the LISP Tutor. This allows for a more natural interaction in which often the student doesn't become aware of any constraints whatsoever.

Natural constraints perhaps reach their zenith in gaming environments such as WEST [18], where the student learns arithmetic as a by-product of playing the game "How the West Was Won". In such gaming environments, the student is completely constrained to following the rules of the game, and as a result the system is able to diagnose his or her behaviour much more readily than in some less constrained environment. Yet, the student can be so motivated by the fun of playing the game, he or she willingly accedes to the constraints, to the mutual benefit of both system and student.

Recently, there has been a growing interest in providing tools to the student that allow him or her to explicitly manipulate intermediate problem representations en route to a final solution of some problem. For example, Bierman et al [7] discuss the use of scratchpads that encourage students to express almost all problem solving stages as they solve problems (the initial test domain was thermodynamics). This seems to be a pedagogically sound idea, since students have concrete access to their problem solving activities, but it also is important to the student modelling system, since the system can gain first hand knowledge of student problem solving behaviour. Effectively, the student is constrained to provide information that is useful to the system in a way that is not intrusive to the student, and in fact is probably quite useful. Reiser has done a similar thing for LISP programming in his GIL system [58], Bhuiyan is working on how mental models of recursion can be made available to students in the LISP tutoring domain [6], Brown in the ALGEBRALAND system [13] allowed students to reify steps in their algebraic derivations, and Anderson et al in the Geometry tutor [3] experimented with intermediate representations in the domain of geometry.

Ask the Student

One way of finding out what students know, believe, or want is to ask them. For example, in the QUEST [30] system students use menus to explain their reasoning, and to explain why they are doing what they are doing. This is quite similar to the intermediate representation idea mentioned above in that students are forced to be aware of the choices they are making, a useful pedagogical activity. Of course, if the menus are designed inappropriately, their use can be intrusive to the student; and if the student misinterprets what is asked, the system misconstrue what the student is telling it. This suggests, once again, that sound external student modelling should inform the design of any student feedback system. The ultimate means of querying the student is in the student's own natural language, but this presupposes great progress in natural language understanding and dialogue modelling. Using semantic grammars (as in SOPHIE [16], for example) is a short term way of cobbling together a reasonably useful natural language interface, at least for technical domains with limited ambiguity and lots of terms that can act as "islands of certainty" in the intepretation.

An alternative to explicitly asking the student what he or she knows, believes, or desires, is to feed back the system's model of the student to the student for his or her reaction. This has been suggested by Self [62], and would seem to be a good one. Who better to correct any system misunderstandings about the student than the student him or herself? Unfortunately, this, too, is fraught with problems in any but the simplest domains. First, the student model is likely to be quite big, and much of it quite irrelevant to current goals. Thus, the system must prune it to suit a particular situation. Second, the student model will be in a notation that is inappropriate for verbalizing to the student, and will have to be translated into some more human-oriented notation. Third, and perhaps most important, students sometimes don't know what they know; it isn't clear that students themselves are always the best judges of every aspect of the system's model of them. Nevertheless, it would seem to be a good strategy to, directly or indirectly, reveal at least some aspects of the student model to the student as a check that the system is on the right track.

Constrain the Tutoring System

The tutoring system should not be expected to diagnose every aspect of student behaviour. In fact, it need only worry about those things that relate to the tutoring problem at hand. If the tutor is helping the student learn arithmetic, it is unlikely that the student's beliefs about amateur sport matter a great deal. More subtly, if the tutor has posed a problem for the student to solve, then any response the student gives can be interpreted in the limited context of the problem that has been posed. This drastically constrains the need for the tutoring system to look far afield in its interpretation of student behaviour. Moreover, if the tutoring system has a limited range of pedagogical options at any given stage, it need only diagnose student behaviour to the point where it can choose among these options. Self [62] has axiomatized this point as "don't diagnose what you can't treat".

One advantage a tutoring system has over a human tutor is that students don't expect it to be infallible or in fact very smart at all. In our culture at this time, computing machines are expected to be obtuse, unresponsive, and literal. People expect to have to massage any message they have for the computer into a fairly restricted, computer-oriented form (this may be changing with the hypermedia revolution). This suggests that the limited bandwidth of computers can be turned into an advantage: any demands by the tutoring system for specialized input on the part of the student will only be what is expected, any flexibility in the tutoring system's interactions with the student will be appreciated.

Don't Try to be Perfect

As discussed by Bierman et al [7], human teachers usually do not understand all the subtleties and complexities of student behaviour. Instead, they tend to make general categorizations augmented by localized information about particular situations. This suggests that the student model in an intelligent tutoring system need not be fully accurate in all respects. It may often suffice to understand student behaviour only in general terms in order to make appropriately individualized pedagogical decisions. It is not necessary for the student model to be perfect.

Ideally, the student modelling system should be able to provide an understanding of the student that is as detailed as necessary for the situation at hand, or, if this can't be done, as detailed as possible for the information available. This will require the student modelling system to be able to do two things: first, represent information at various levels of detail and, second, gracefully degrade in the absence of information. Unfortunately, graceful degradation is notoriously difficult to achieve in any diagnostic system. In our laboratory we have been experimenting with a granularity-based reasoning system whose aim is to allow both of the above goals to be achieved (see [35], [49]). Possible student cognitive models are categorized into granularity hierarchies such as those shown in Figures 2 and 3 (which is used to recognize student programming strategies as part of the SCENT LISP tutoring system).

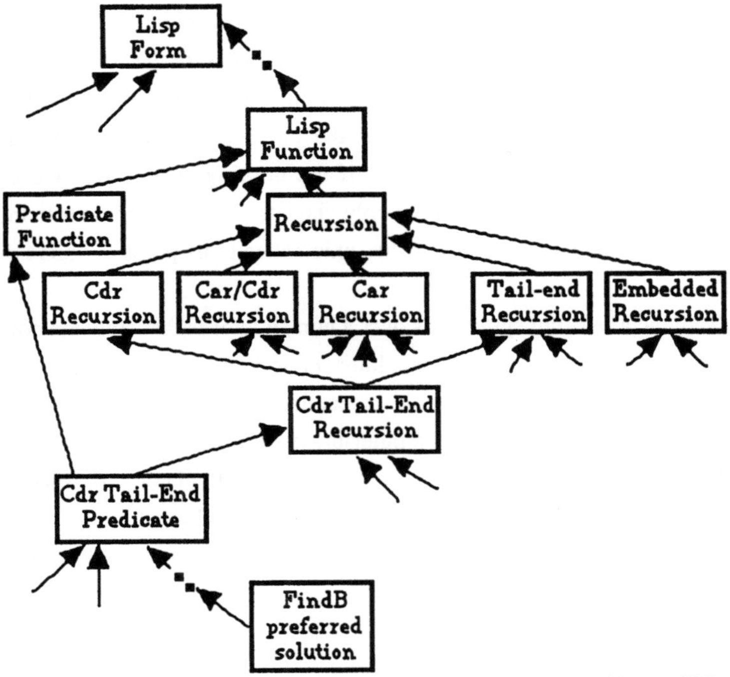

Figure 2: A fragment of the principal abstraction hierarchy (from [49])

In a granularity hierarchy, objects at the upper levels describe coarse-grained student cognitive perspectives, while objects lower down are more refined. For example in Figure 2 the upper levels represent general student programming strategies such as "recursive LISP strategy", while the lower levels represent specific student strategies such as "tail-end cdr recursion".

We have identified two orthogonal but interrelated granularity dimensions: abstraction and aggregation. The granularity hierarchy in Figure 2 represents the abstraction dimension. Beneath any object in this abstraction hierarchy can be an aggregation hierarchy describing at many levels of detail the various parts which make up that object. For example, the granularity hierarchy in Figure 3 represents the aggregation at many levels of detail of parts of the "cdr recursion" object in Figure 2. These two dimensions give our diagnostic system the required ability to represent information at various levels of detail.

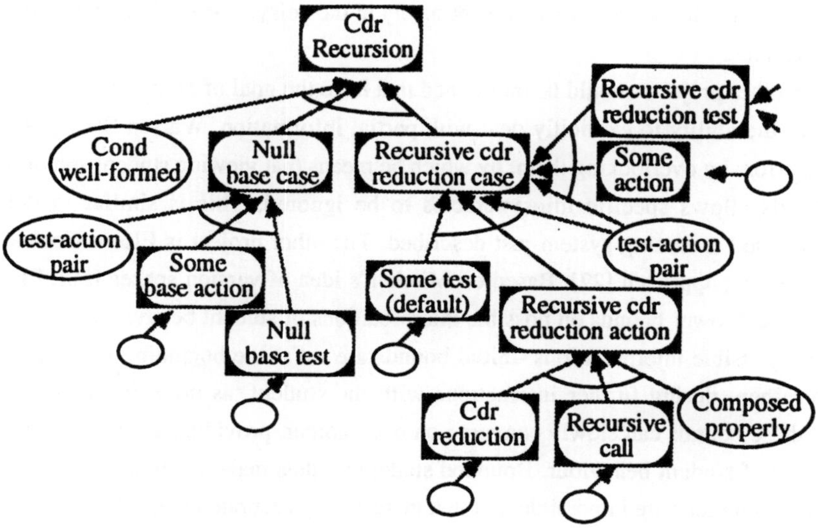

Figure 3: A Fragment of the Aggregation Hierarchy for Cdr Recursion (from [49])

The recognition system that uses these granularity hierarchies to diagnose student programming strategies can gracefully degrade if full recognition cannot be achieved. To see why, consider what happens when a student submits a LISP program as a possible solution to a preassigned task. The recognition system tries to recognize the stategy underlying the student's solution in as much detail as possible. Typically, all objects down to some level in the abstraction dimension can be completely recognized (i.e. their corresponding aggregation dimension can be fully elaborated). Beneath these fully recognized objects in the abstraction dimension are strategy objects which can only be partially recognized (i.e. some parts in their corresponding aggregation dimension can not be recognized). It is this combination of complete coarse-grained recognition and partial finer-grained recognition that provides the kind of graceful degradation desired in a student modelling system. Even if the information available does not allow a complete recognition of the student's programming strategy at a fine grain size, at least we have coarse-grained recognition. Moreover, the particular parts of the partially recognized finer-grained strategies that have not been recognized can form the basis of pedagogical decisions as to what kind of help to give the student (i.e. it may be these unrecognized parts that are the source of a student's misconceptions). Granularity-based reasoning thus holds great promise for providing a student modelling system with the capability to work nicely in the noisy, ill-specified real world of actual student behaviour.

Two other projects should be mentioned that have the goal of arming a student modelling system with the ability to explicitly deal with partial information. Warren Sack [59] proposes diagnosing errors by overlooking them, by which he means that viewing student solutions at more general levels allows specific idiosyncracies to be ignored. This is similar to the SCENT granularity-based reasoning system just described. The other project is Elsom-Cook's bounded student modelling approach [27]. Based on Mitchell's idea of version spaces [50], Elsom-Cook places upper and lower bounds on possible interpretations of student behaviour to help constrain the space of possible interpretations. Initial bounds are set at the beginning of the tutor-student interaction; then, during further interactions with the student, as more information becomes available, these bounds can slowly converge on one another, providing an increasingly accurate interpretation of student behaviour. Bounded student models make explicit the notion that fully accurate interpretations are impossible, but that increasingly accurate interpretations can be gained as time goes on. Unfortunately, in many domains there are likely to be some difficulties posed to the bounded student modelling idea by the vagaries of student behaviour, i.e. students do not always remain consistent over a range of interactions. Palthepu and Greer [55] are proposing the use of another machine learning technique, explanation-based reasoning, in helping to explain student behaviour at various levels of precision. VanLehn has carried out a number of experiments into how machine learning techniques can apply in intelligent tutoring (e.g. [69]). Costa [23] discusses how machine learning techniques, in particular explanation-based learning, apply to intelligent tutoring systems.

Whatever techniques are used to try to deal with the impossibility of depicting student behaviour with complete accuracy, it is important, as Self points out [62], that the student modelling system admit its fallibility to the student. Attempts to deceive the student into believing the tutoring system has perfect knowledge are likely to be easily detected by the student with a consequent decline in the student's faith in other aspects of the system. Moreover, admitting fallibility can set the stage for having the student behave co-operatively with the tutoring system, to work together with the system for their mutual benefit. That is, admitting up front that the system is not perfect may well encourage students to help the system to understand their problems so that the system can help them overcome these problems. It would be ideal if the student modelling system were to know what it didn't know, not only to explain to the student where it has doubts, but also so to keep it from making unwarranted assumptions in its own reasoning. This seems to be a very hard problem to solve, however.

Scavenge Ideas from Elsewhere

There are a plethora of techniques and concepts that have been developed in other areas besides intelligent tutoring systems that may prove useful in the student modelling endeavour. Scavenging ideas from other areas is a fruitful activity that has already been exploited in bounded student modelling, explanation-based reasoning, and various approaches to external student modelling.

The first place to look is elsewhere in artificial intelligence. The idea of a truth maintenance system is an intriguing one, explored from a number of perspectives by de Kleer [24], McAllester [44], Martins [43] and others. Truth maintenance could be adapted for use in maintaining the student model over time. In fact, Self [61] proposes doing just this, and Huang [36] has created an evolutionary belief revision system (EBRS, based on de Kleer's ATMS) specifically designed to track the evolutionary changes in a tutor's perspectives on a student's knowledge. Huang, in fact, has also borrowed ideas from the user modelling community. He has been able to show how stereotype hierarchies that are more sophisticated than those in systems like GUMS [31] can be used to encode default beliefs about different categories of students, and how these defaults can change drastically as knowledge about the student is seen to change using the EBRS. Systems like PROUST [37] have pioneered the adaptation of plan-recognition techniques (similar to those first proposed for understanding natural language dialogue by Allen and Perrault [1]) to the problem of recognizing student behaviour. Baril [5] shows how qualitative differential equations (expressed in the confluence notation of deKleer and Brown [25]) can be used for modelling the performance of physical devices can be used to model both correct and incorrect student models of such devices. In some sense these equations can be seen as representing the mental model level of a student's knowledge. Gilmore and Self [33], and as we have already seen Elsom-Cook [27], Costa [23], and Palthepu and Greer [55], have all applied machine learning techniques of various kinds to student modelling. The granularity-based reasoning system discussed in the previous section owes much to model-based computer vision techniques developed by Havens and Mackworth [41]. In short, artificial intelligence research offers a treasure house of techniques and ideas that can be used to enhance the capabilities of an internal student modelling system.

Education research can also prove a fruitful source of ideas. For example, Bloom [8] suggests that there are several levels at which a concept can be known. Brecht has adapted this idea to intelligent tutoring systems and posits in her PEPE instructional planning system [12] that students know things at three levels: fact, analysis, and synthesis. Brecht's instructional planner also has teaching functions that bear a remarkable resemblance to the learning functions proposed by educator Tom Shuell [64]. In the ARIES Laboratory, Permanand Mohan is exploring exactly how these learning functions can be interpreted computationally [52]. In education there are theories of how students process cues (e.g. Winne [71]), and doubtless theories of motivation and affect that could also prove to the useful. In fact, Winne is attempting to re-tool his theories for artificial intelligence applications [72].

Both education and cognitive science should prove to be a valuable source of empirical evidence about how students actually behave. This knowledge will, of course, be useful to external student modelling, but it can also be used to enhance the capabilities of the internal student modelling system. For example, Escott has shown that student programmers often use analogies to earlier programs in their creation of the initial solution to a new programming problem [29]. This observation could be deployed in an internal student modelling system to help it explain a specific student solution in terms of analogies to earlier solutions, and in particular, as Escott shows, to explain many errors as carrying out inappropriate analogies. Appropriate pedagogical advice could then be given to the student that would otherwise not have been available. This is just one example of the vast range of possibilities that open up for informed internal student modelling if the data collected in empirical studies can be re-interpreted computationally.

The Tractability of Student Modelling

In section 6 I have shown that the student modelling problem, both internal and external, is not as intractable as it might seem. Encouragingly, and, not coincidentally (in that I used many of his arguments), this is the same conclusion to which Self came in his landmark paper on intractability [62]. In the twenty years or so in which intelligent tutoring has been explored, and in the seventeen since student modelling was first proposed as a central problem, much progress has been made. The ultimate goal of a completely accurate student modelling system will never be reached; in fact, is probably impossible in principle. Nevertheless, through use of a multitude of techniques and approaches, borrowed and original, much can be done, and further progress can be expected to occur.

In earlier sections I argued that student modelling is essential to intelligent tutoring. The very definition of an intelligent tutoring system as intelligent and individualized is intimately tied to its student modelling capabilities. Without some sort of idea of what students do in general, an intelligent tutoring system cannot intelligently respond to them. Without some model of each specific student's idiosyncracies, the promise of individualization cannot be fulfilled.

Finally, I have argued that building one-on-one tutors is still a valid research activity. All of the problems that arise in one-on-one tutoring also crop up in other approaches, often in a more complex and virulent form. To hope to avoid these problems by avoiding the construction of one-on-one tutors is a vain hope. In fact, there is a strong argument that the cleanest and most straightforward way to study the basic problems of intelligent tutoring is through the construction of one-on-one tutors. All of the main problems that will confront any approach to tutoring come up in one-on-one tutoring, and yet the problems arise there in their purest form, uncluttered by other objectives. Because of this clarity, lessons learned in contructing one-on-one tutoring systems can be extended to other approaches more readily than lessons learned in a more complex environment. In a very real sense, I believe that one-on-one tutoring has the potential to be the "e-coli" or "drosophilia" of instructional systems.

As researchers pursue new paradigms for learning and instruction like collaborative learning, situated learning, discovery learning, negotiated learning, and guided discovery learning, let them be able to access a bedrock of solid ideas from one-on-one tutoring that can be used to enhance and inform the design of their new systems. Far from ignoring one-on-one tutoring this new research should learn from it. Far from stamping out the study of one-on-one tutoring, this new research should encourage further investigations. The bedrock should continue to be built; the properties of the "e-coli" or of the "drosophilia" should continue to be investigated, in particular the key problem of student modelling. No system of whatever stripe will be able to exist without it. In Elsom-Cook's immortal words: "the student model can run, but it can't hide!"[4]

Acknowledgements

I would like to thank all of my colleagues in the ARIES Laboratory for their many contributions to my research. In particular, Jim Greer, Srinivas Palthepu, Bryce Barrie, Paul Pospisil, Mary Mark, Randy Coulman, Xueming Huang, Mike Oliphant, and Luong Nguyen have contributed much to my perspectives on student modelling. I would also like to thank Ernesto Costa for inviting me to the New Directions in Intelligent Tutoring Systems workshop in Sintra, Portugal, where I first presented this paper, and to the many people there with whom I had stimulating discussions. NATO deserves a good deal of credit for sponsoring this and other Advanced Educational Technology workshops. Finally, I would like to acknowledge the ongoing financial support of Canada's Natural Sciences and Engineering Research Council for my research.

[4] A remark made at the NATO Advanced Studies Institute in Calgary in July 1990.

References

1. Allen, J.F. and Perrault, C.R.: Analyzing intention in dialogues, Artificial Intelligence, 15, 3, 143-178 (1980).

2. Anderson, J.R.: The architecture of cognition. Cambridge, Massachusetts: Harvard University Press 1983.

3. Anderson, J.R., Boyle, C.F., and Yost, G.: The geometry tutor. Proceedings of the Ninth International Joint Conference on Artificial Intelligence, pp. 1-7, Los Angeles, California 1985.

4. Anderson, J.R. and Reiser, B.J.: The LISP tutor. Byte, 10, 4, 159-175 (1985).

5. Baril, D.: Applying qualitative reasoning to student modelling in an intelligent tutoring system, M.Sc. Thesis, Department of Computational Science, University of Saskatchewan, Saskatoon, Canada forthcoming.

6. Bhuiyan, S.H., Greer, J.E., and McCalla, G.I.: Mental models of recursion and their use in the SCENT programming advisor. In: Knowledge-based computer systems (S. Ramani, R. Chandrasekar, K.S.R. Anjaneyulu, eds.), pp. 135-144. Bombay, India: Narosa 1989.

7. Biermann, D.J., Kamsteeg, P.A., and Sandberg, J.A.C.: Student models, scratchpads and simulation. In this volume.

8. Bloom, B.S.: Taxonomy of educational objectives, handbook I: cognitive domain. New York: David McKay 1956.

9. Bloom, B.S.: The 2-sigma problem: the search for methods of group instruction as effective as one-to-one tutoring. Educational Researcher, June/July, 4-16 (1984).

10. Bloomfield, L.: Language. New York: Holt Rinehart 1933.

11. Bonar, J.G. and Cunningham, R.: Bridge: tutoring the programming process. In: Intelligent tutoring systems: lessons learned (J. Psotka, L.D. Massey, S.A. Mutter, eds.), pp. 409-434, Hillsdale, New Jersey: Lawrence Erlbaum 1988.

12. Brecht, B.J.: Determining the focus of instruction: content planning for intelligent tutoring systems. (Ph.D. Thesis), TR 90-5, ARIES Laboratory, Department of Computational Science, U. of Saskatchewan, Saskatoon 1990.

13. Brown, J.S.: Process versus product: a perspective on tools for communal and informal electronic learning. Journal of Educational Computing Research, 1, 179-201 (1985).

14. Brown, J.S.: Toward a new epistemology for learning. In: Intelligent tutoring systems: at the crossroads of artificial intelligence and education (C. Frasson and G. Gauthier, eds.), pp. 266-282, New Jersey: Ablex 1990.

15. Brown, J.S. and Burton, R.R.: Diagnostic models for procedural bugs in basic mathematical skills. Cognitive Science, 2, 155-191 (1978).

16. Brown, J.S., Burton, R.R., and deKleer, J.: Pedagogical, natural language, and knowledge engineering techiques in SOPHIE I, II, and III. In: Intelligent tutoring systems (D.H. Sleeman and J.S. Brown, eds.). London: Academic Press 1982.

17. Brown, J.S. and VanLehn, K.: Repair theory: a generative theory of bugs in procedural skills. Cognitive Science, 2, 379-426 (1980).

18. Burton, R.R. and Brown, J.S.: An investigation of computer coaching for informal learning activities. In: Intelligent tutoring systems (D. Sleeman and J.S. Brown, eds.), pp. 79-98, New York: Academic Press 1982.

19. Cercone, N.J. and McCalla, G.I.: There is no magic wand, but then again there is no smoking gun either. Symposium on Artificial and Natural Intelligence, Knowledge-Based Computer Systems Conference, Bombay, India 1989.

20. Cerri, S.A., Cheli, E. and McIntyre, A.: "Nobile: user model acquisition in a natural laboratory", to appear in M. Jones and P. H. Winne (eds.), Foundations and Frontiers of Adaptative Learning Environments, Springer Varlag. In press.

21. Chambers, J.A. and Sprecher, J.W.: Computer assisted instruction: current trends and critical issues. Communications of the ACM, 23, 6, 332-242 (1980).

22. Clancey, W.J.: Qualitative student models. In: Annual reviews of computer science, volume 1 (J.F. Traub, ed.). pp. 381-450, Palo Alto, California: Annual Reviews Inc. 1986.

23. Costa, E.: Machine learning, explanation-based learning, and ITS. In this volume.

24. deKleer, J.: An assumption-based truth maintenance system. Artificial Intelligence, 28, 2, 127-162 (1986).

25. deKleer, J. and Brown, J.S.: A qualitative physics based on confluences. Artificial Intelligence, 24, (1-3), 7-83 (1984).

26. diSessa, A. and Abelson, H.: BOXER: a constructible computational medium. Communications of the ACM, 29, 9 (1986).

27. Elsom-Cook, M.T.: Guided discovery tutoring and bounded user modelling. In: Artificial intelligence and human learning: intelligent computer-aided instruction (J.Self, ed.), pp.165-178, London: Chapman and Hall 1988.

28. Elsom-Cook, M.T.(ed.): Guided discovery tutoring: a framework for ICAI research. London: Paul Chapman 1990.

29. Escott, J.A. and McCalla, G.I.: Problem solving by analogy: a source of errors in novice LISP programming. Proceedings of the Intelligent Tutoring Systems Conference, pp. 312-319, C. Frasson (Ed.) Univ. Montreal, Canada 1988.

30. Feurzeig, W. and Ritter, F.: Understanding reflective problem solving. In: Intelligent tutoring systems: lessons learned (J. Psotka, L.D. Massey, S.A. Mutter, eds.), pp. 435-450. Hillsdale, New Jersey: Lawrence Erlbaum 1988.

31. Finin, T. and Drager, D.: GUMS1: a general user modelling system, Proceedings of the Sixth Canadian Society for Computational Studies of Intelligence Conference, pp. 24-30, Montreal, Canada 1986.

32. Gadwal, D.: UMRAO: a chess endgame tutor. (M.Sc. Thesis), TR 90-4, ARIES Laboratory, Department of Computational Science, University of Saskatchewan, Saskatoon, Canada 1990.

33. Gilmore, D. and Self, J.A.: The application of machine learning to intelligent tutoring systems. In: Artificial intelligence and human learning: intelligent computer-aided instruction (J.Self, ed.), pp.179-196, London: Chapman and Hall 1988.

34. Goldstein, I.P.: The genetic graph: a representation for the evolution of procedural knowledge. In: Intelligent tutoring systems (D.H. Sleeman and J.S. Brown, eds.), pp. 51-77.. London: Academic Press 1982.

35. Greer, J.E. and McCalla, G.I.: A computational framework for granularity and its application to educational diagnosis. Proc. 11th International Joint Conference on Artificial Intelligence, pp. 477-482, Detroit , Michigan 1989.

36. Huang, X., McCalla, G.I., Neufeld, E., and Greer, J.E.: Revising deductive knowledge and stereotypical knowledge in a student model. User Modelling and User Adapted Interaction, , 1: 87-115, 1991.

37. Johnson, W.L. and Soloway, E.M.: PROUST: an automatic debugger for Pascal programs. Byte, 10, 4, 179-190 (1985).

38. Laird. J.E., Rosenbloom, P.S. & Newell, A.: Chunking in SOAR: the anatomy of a general learning mechanism. Machine Learning, 1, 11-46 (1986).

39. Laurillard, D.: Generative student models or knowledge-based teaching strategies? In Adaptative learning environments (Winne P.H. and Jones M.L. , eds.), NATO ASI Series F, Vol. 85. Berlin: Springer-Verlag 1992.

40. Lesgold, A.M., Bonar, J.G., Ivill, J.M., and Bowen, A.: An intelligent tutoring system for electronics troubleshooting: DC-circuit understanding. In: Knowing and learning: issues for the cognitive psychology of instruction (L.B. Resnick, ed.), New Jersey: Lawrence Erlbaum, 1987.

41. Mackworth, A.K. and Havens, W.S.: Structuring domain knowledge for visual perception. Proceedings of the Seventh International Joint Conference on Artificial Intelligence, pp. 625-627, Vancouver, Canada 1981.

42. Mark, M.: Evaluation of intelligent tutoring systems. TR 90-2, ARIES Laboratory, Department of Computational Science, University of Saskatchewan, Saskatoon, Canada 1990.

43. Martins, J.P.: Computational issues in belief revision, In this volume.

44. McAllester, D.A.: Truth maintenance, Proceedings of AAAI-90. pp. 1109-1115, Boston, Massachusetts, 1990.

45. McCalla, G.I.: Some issues for guided discovery tutoring research: granularity-based reasoning, student model maintenance, and pedagogical planning. TR 89-3, ARIES Laboratory, Department of Computational Science, University of Saskatchewan, Saskatoon, Canada (presented at the NATO Advanced Research Workshop on Guided Discovery Tutoring, Tuscany, Italy 1989).

46. McCalla, G.I. and Brecht, B.J.: Negotiated tutoring needs student modelling and instructional planning: arguments and experiences from the perspective of the SCENT project. In: R. Moyse and M. Elsom Cook (eds.), Knowledge Negotiation, Academic Press, London, 1992, pp. 41-68

47. McCalla, G.I., Bunt, R.B. and Harms, J.J.: The design of the SCENT automated advisor. Computational Intelligence, 2, 2, 76-92 (1986).

48. McCalla, G.I., Greer, J.E., and the SCENT Research Team: SCENT-3: an architecture for intelligent advising in problem-solving domains. In: Intelligent tutoring systems: at the crossroads of artificial intelligence and education (C. Frasson and G. Gauthier, eds.). pp. 140-161, New Jersey: Ablex 1990.

49. McCalla, G.I., Greer, J.E., Barrie, B., and Pospisil, P.: Granularity hierarchies. International Journal on Computers and Mathematics, special issue on Semantic Networks, 23, 2-5, February 1992, pp. 363-376..

50. Mitchell, T.M.: Generalization as search. Artificial Intelligence, 18, 203-226 (1981).

51. Moebus, C.: The relevance of computational models of knowledge acquisition for the design of helps in the problem solving monitor ABSYNT. Proceedings of the International Conference on Advanced Research on Computers in Education, pp. 57-64, Tokyo, Japan 1990.

52. Mohan, P.: Adapting instruction to the cognitive needs of learners in intelligent tutoring systems, M.Sc. Thesis Proposal, Department of Computational Science, University of Saskatchewan, Saskatoon, Canada 1990.

53. Moyse, R. and Elsom-Cook, M.(eds.), Knowledge Negotiation, Academic Press, London, 1992.

54. O'Malley, C. (ed.): Computer supported collaborative learning. NATO ASI Series F. Berlin: Springer-Verlag. In press.

55. Palthepu, S. and Greer, J.E.: The role of granularity in explanation-based generalisation. AAAI Workshop on Explanation, Boston, Massachusetts 1990. Private communication.

56. Papert, S.: Mindstorms: children, computers, and powerful ideas. New York: Basic Books 1980.

57. Reiser, B.J., Anderson, J.R., and Farrell, R.G.: Dynamic student modeling in an intelligent tutor for LISP programming. Proc. Ninth International Joint Conference on Artificial Intelligence, pp. 8 - 14, Los Angeles, California 1985.

58. Reiser, B.J., Friedmann, P., Kimberg, D.Y., Ranney, M.: Constructing explanations from problem solving rules to guide the planning of programs. Proc. International Conference on Intelligent Tutoring Systems (ITS '88), pp. 222-229, Montreal 1988.

59. Sack, W.: Finding errors by overlooking them. In: Intelligent tutoring systems: at the crossroads of artificial intelligence and education (C. Frasson and G. Gauthier, eds.), pp. 206-233, New Jersey: Ablex 1990.

60. Self, J.A.: Student models in computer-aided instruction. International Journal of Man-Machine Studies, 6, 261-276 (1974).

61. Self, J.A.: The use of belief systems for student modelling. First European Congress on Artificial Intelligence and Training, Lille, France, 1988.

62. Self, J.A.: Bypassing the intractable problem of student modelling. In: Intelligent tutoring systems: at the crossroads of artificial intelligence and education (C. Frasson and G. Gauthier, eds.), pp. 107-123, New Jersey: Ablex 1990.

63. Shaw, M.: Problems of validation in a knowledge acquisition system using multiple experts. Proceedings of the Second European Knowledge Acquisition Workshop, pp. 5.1-15, Bonn, Germany 1988.

64. Shuell, T.: Designing instructional computing systems for meaningful learning. In Adaptative learning environments (Winne P.H. and ones M.L. J, eds.), NATO ASI Series F, Vol. 85. Berlin: Springer-Verlag 1992.

65. Shute, V.: Rose garden promises of intelligent tutoring systems: blossom or thorn? Space Operations, Applications and Research Symposium, Albuquerque, New Mexico 1990.

66. Shute, V. and Glaser, R.: A large-scale evaluation of an intelligent discovery world: Smithtown. Interactive Learning Environments, 1, 51-77 (1990).

67. Smith, R.: The alternate reality kit: an animated environment for creating interactive simulations. Proc. IEEE Workshop on Visual Languages, pp. 99-106, Dallas 1986.

68. VanLehn, K.: Student modelling. In: Foundations of intelligent tutoring systems (M.C. Polson and J.J. Richardson, eds.), pp. 55-78, Hillsdale, New Jersey: Lawrence Erlbaum 1988.

69. VanLehn, K.: Learning one subprocedure per lesson, Artificial Intelligence, 31, 1, 1-40 (1987).

70. Ward, B.: ET-SOAR: an electrostatics tutor. Ph.D. Thesis, Department of Computer Science, Carnegie-Mellon University, Pittsburgh, Pennsylvania forthcoming, May, 1992.

71. Winne, P.H.: Theories of instruction and of intelligence for designing artificially intelligent tutoring systems. Educational Psychologist, 24, 3, 229-259 (1989).

72. Winne, P.H.: A framework for designing and interpreting interactions between learners and instructional computing systems. In: In Adaptative learning environments (P.H. Winne and M.L. Jones, eds.), NATO ASI Series F, Vol. 85. Berlin: Springer-Verlag 1992.

3 ITS: PRINCIPLES AND PRACTICES

Student Models, Scratch-Pads, and Simulation

Dick J. Bierman, Paul A. Kamsteeg & Jacobijn A. C. Sandberg
University of Amsterdam, The Netherlands

Abstract: The paper discusses the status of student models and it is proposed that in order to infer more subtle and complex student models from student's behaviour, an electronic scratch-pad or note-pad might be a valuable tool. A design methodology for these scratch-pads is explored. The method consists of a primary task analysis followed by a analysis of natural notes according to a scoring scheme based upon this task analysis. Special attention is given to notes that can not be classified. It is concluded that the task-analysis covers about 98% of the natural notes but that from the remaining 2% useful design criteria can be extracted. It is proposed that the point of view that for specific domains simulation can be seen as 'runnable' scratch-pads, might add futher design-criteria.

Keywords: intelligent tutoring, note-pad, scratch-pad, simulation, student model.

Introduction

There appears to be a general feeling of impasse in the field of ITS. Some claim that radically different architectures are needed [1], others try to reconcile the field with more open-ended learning environments [2, 3]. Special workshops are even organized (e.g. this volume). We suspect that one of the underlying reasons for this feeling is the implicit recognition that research on complete and truthful cognitive student models, one of the key-components in the traditional ITS architecture, has shown hardly any progress and that serious doubt exists whether this progress can be expected in the short term or is possible at all. One can even doubt that for practical purposes such a student model is necessary at all. This paper deals among other things explicitly with these doubts.

Student models: the emperor's clothes?

Computer generated student (user) models which are complete and truthful representations of the student's cognitive state are an illusion. It takes cognitive scientists weeks of work with one single subject and with tools not available to ITS, like the analysis of thinking aloud protocols, before they might be able to infer the cognitive processes underlying subjects' problem solving behaviour [4]. How could we ever expect the computer to perform this task in real time, given the restricted bandwidth of the man machine communication channel [5] and without interfering with the teaching process (e.g. by questioning the student about his cognitive state)?

Even if we had an ideal student model, we wouldn't know how to choose proper teaching actions based upon the model. There are simply no theories of learning which are strong enough to infer the relation between the subtle aspects of such a student model and optimal teaching action [6].

Recent surveys on student models [e.g. 7] generally discriminate between overlay, differential and perturbation models. However, these surveys fail to indicate that each of these models are around since the early days of the field. Overlay and differential models are acknowledged to be essentially incorrect because they assume the knowledge of the student to be a subset of the expert's knowledge.
Also there is serious doubt whether the use of perturbation models does increase the effectiveness of teaching. For instance it is highly questionable that teaching based upon correction of diagnosed malrules is better than teaching without explicit diagnosis of these malrules. Sleeman [8] compared Malrule Based Reteaching with Remedial Reteaching. Although in his study no difference was found, Sleeman, after emphasizing the effect of direct feedback (which is a feature appearing in traditional CAI systems and ITS alike), concludes *......the subfield of ITS should not conclude that the task of building an ITS is impossible but it should conclude that the task is harder than the field initially thought ... because ... The target knowledge structures are generally far more subtle and more complex than the simple models used in current ITSs.....*
Apparently Sleeman still believes that, given better student models and better learning theories, it should be possible to get better teaching than teaching that is not based upon a detailed student model.

This belief might be based upon the assumption that human tutors, who perform better than ITS's equipped with a malrule based student model [9], do maintain more subtle student models. But an analysis of thinking aloud protocols of human tutors suggests that, on the contrary, they *hardly* maintain a specific student model, their representation of the student seems to consist of a global classification augmented with a number of very localized diagnoses [10]. The reason that they outperform ITS possibly has to do with the non-verbal affective components of teaching rather than with the complexity of the student model. For instance, human tutors might more easily observe the amount of confidence that a student displays while solving a problem. Student's answers given with confidence should be treated differently than answers given hesitatingly. Similarly, students might become bored or angry without the ITS noticing it.

So should we forget about increasing the complexity and subtlety of student models when it comes to developing an ITS?

Before answering this question it should be noted that while research indicates that human tutors do not invest much in building a model of their student, the educational practice is that students with evident learning problems are singled out for further diagnosis in special institutes which spend much effort to localize the source of the problems. It might be that deep diagnosis is useful for this and maybe other special subgroups. In our view the answer to the question on the use of student models furthermore depends on the goal of the ITS.
If the goal is to produce a practical educational environment for a normal student population in a cost effective way the answer seems to be: forget about detailed cognitive student models, at least for the time being, and focus on global classification of the student in a number of subgroups. This prototype matching not only is the behaviour of real human tutors, but it also appears to be the most successful way to model users of non educational systems [11]. These latter models do not pretend cognitive validity but they appear to be useful for the task at hand. We might label them "useful models".
If the goal is to get clear insight in individual learning we feel that the development of more subtle and complex cognitive student models is necessary. In contrast with Sleeman we strongly doubt if computerized intelligent educational environments equipped with this type of subtle and complex cognitive student models will significantly increase teaching results compared to traditional (less intelligent) systems which use rough classification, and proper localized diagnosis and adaptive feed-back.

Although in principle it is possible to think of models that might represent more subtle and complex cognitive structures, there remains the practical problem in diagnosing these subtle and complex structures. This bandwidth problem, which is most evident in the context of cognitively valid student models, is also present if one only wants to have proper localized diagnosis in the context of LITS (less intelligent tutoring systems). So even outside of the research setting we have to face this problem. It is this problem which is addressed by the use of scratch-pads.

Scratch-pads

Relation to educational environments

One of the ways to get around the problem of inadequate student models is to assume that students themselves know best what teaching they need, and just supply them with an environment in which they have the opportunity to explore the information that they are

supposed to acquire. These discovery environments are assumed to have the positive side effect that the knowledge, once acquired, would be remembered better and possibly transferred more easily to other domains. It appears, however, that these assumptions have hardly any empirical support. Although one can sympathize with the uneasy feeling which might arise from the asymmetric model of a teacher who knows and transfers knowledge to a student who does not know, it should also be realized that the relation between parent and child has similar asymmetries. Asymmetry does not necessarily result in authoritarian behaviour: inequality in knowledge level does not preclude negotiation.
Combination of ITS's with a discovery environment should not be a strategy to hide and escape the underlying problem of inadequate student models. The environment might very well *look* like one that gives the student 'complete freedom' but, like Rousseau [as cited in 2] , we feel that this freedom should actually be completely under control of the teacher. In that case the problem of the inadequate student models just returns, because it should be decided on the basis of this student model at what moment what constraint should be put upon the apparent freedom of the student.

Interestingly, the combination of ITS with discovery environments results in a shift of focus from the internal representations of the ITS (and the related discussion on architectures) to an emphasis on the man-machine interface (and the related discussion to visual representations). Elsom-Cook [2] states for instance: *..An issue which has rarely been considered in tutoring systems is that of the interface the student actually sees... ...it is no longer reasonable to build a system and 'tack an interface on' afterwards. The interface is in many ways the keystone of the design process....*

Theoretical background

The importance of the man-machine interface for ITS has been emphasized earlier [12, 13] in the context of increasing the bandwidth of the communication channel, to enable better diagnosis. This increase of bandwidth facilitates local diagnosis and classification of the student but might even enable more subtle and complex student models.
Diagnosing students can be seen as inferring internal cognitive structures from external behaviour. More observable external behaviour potentially might result in better diagnosis. Compared to human teachers, artificial teachers are inferior in this respect, because the computer is neither able to observe non-verbal behaviour nor, at present, to interpret verbal behaviour (within reasonable processing times). The central premise for the approach of using scratch-pads (and related tools) to increase the diagnostic power is, that observable acts of the student can be interpreted as externalizations of knowledge which is at that moment in 'working memory. This is the very same premise as for the use of thinking aloud protocol analysis as a

diagnostic tool [4]. In other words: the target knowledge of diagnosis, the internal cognitive structure[1], is only accessible via two intermediate information systems: the contents of working memory and the externalization thereof. The externalization, in the case of protocol analysis, is the verbalization of the contents of working memory.
The externalization task should be stimulated and be set-up in such a way that working memory contains the relevant information, and that the externalization task does not interfere with the main task. The task can be approached in two ways: model-driven or data-driven. Or, to put it simply, by asking questions or by monitoring.

Questioning

Asking questions is (should be) model-driven. The contents of the question should be chosen in such a way that exactly those parts of the cognitive information in which one is interested, are brought into working memory. This approach is most suitable in cases where the student is not involved in a complex task or in a procedure which might be disturbed by the question.
Also, the question should not *result* in a complex task for the student. Thus, questions appear most suitable if they concern simple conceptual or procedural knowledge during the expository phase of the education.

Monitoring

When the student has to integrate knowledge, e.g. in solving problems, questioning is too disturbing and data can only be acquired more passively, by monitoring. Monitoring is data-driven: while the student is performing the task the diagnostic tool tries to tap working memory for as much information as possible. The diagnostic tool should unobtrusively stimulate the student to externalize results of sub-tasks which, then, hopefully are interpretable [15]. Of course, one could partition the complex task into subtasks by repeatedly asking questions, but in that case diagnosis of the student's cognitive *control* structures, which are important to solve the problem at hand, is impossible because the questions themselves tend to lead the student in some direction.

To be useful as diagnostic aids outside the research setting, that is in actual education, computerized tools which stimulate the student to externalize the contents of working memory should be useful to the student him/herself. The design should be such that the student can use the external working memory tools in a simple and natural way. If a piece of paper is a simpler

---

[1] The discussion about the actual physical form of these structures and whether or not they are created in working memory or are activated from long term memory is not relevant. We simply assume that getting some insight in the (context dependent) actual cognitive state is useful to know in order to change the context into a direction which might promote learning.

alternative, the student is not going to use the electronic tools. For instance, unnecessary typing will frustrate the use of these tools; it should be easy to copy information to the scratch-pad. By having other tools which can perform non-relevant tasks (like calculators or formula evaluators) embedded in the scratch-pad environment, the student will hopefully experience the extended scratch-pad as alleviating his/her problem solving task and will use it. Of course the tools should only take over those subtasks that are not of interest for diagnosing the main task at hand. Typically, these subtasks are ones which may be assumed to be mastered, but are time-consuming and error-prone. An example of such a subtask might be 'calculating' in a domain of teaching of a more complex nature, e.g. thermodynamics.

Kinds of externalized working memory tools

Basically, 3 types of monitoring can be effectuated:

1. Monitoring an action *type* by noticing that a certain tool (e.g. a calculator) is being used.
2. Monitoring of intermediate results on a scratch-pad. A problem here is that, if the student does not jot down a particular intermediate result, it can not be inferred that the student didn't reach this result. Another problem is that if some form of automatic logbooking is implemented, the student will usually not enter intermediate results on the scratch-pad.
3. Monitoring that an intermediate result is used as input for a new action. If some intermediate result is used as input for a tool (e.g a calculator) this is easily recognizable. If the action itself is not recognizable, because there is no tool for it, the only thing that might be deduced is that the student used the result. This deduction might be made if the intermediate result was stored in a lookup table with one item visible at a time and the student looks up the particular item. This implementation of a part of the interface conflicts somewhat with the idea of a scratch-pad but it can be used in a research-setting.

   The *interpretation* of an act of inspection of an intermediate result by the student is of course rather fuzzy. It is by no means certain that after inspection of an intermediate result the student will actually use this result in his/her next action. In that respect it can be compared with the interpretation of eye-movement recording data.

Level of structure and abstraction

One aspect of external working memory tools is the amount of pre-structuring that is required to enable parsing of the student's actions. For instance, it might be preferable to represent domain objects on e.g. a scratch-pad in their canonical form rather than in concrete form (for instance:

'pointmass' instead of 'fat-man'), to allow for diagnosis of the student's capabilities of transforming the problem from its concrete to its symbolic form. However, forcing structure onto the scratch-pad decreases the amount of a student's expression possibilities and also might give implicit hints to the student. Simultaneously the technical problems of parsing the student's actions decrease. The major design decisions concern these kinds of trade-offs pertaining to the amount of pre-structuring and the level (or levels) of abstraction on which entities of the domain are represented. Structure generally shifts the task of the student from generating to selecting. Especially if it is unknown what the relevant cognitive structures are (like generally in a research setting) it seems advisable to have the scratch-pad as open-ended as possible so that the student can make any note he/she wants. If the design requires selection, then all viable (correct and wrong) alternatives should be available to the student to select from.

Research findings

Previous research

Formal research concerning the design and the use of electronic scratch-pads in the framework of diagnosis is not abundant.

However, in the context of problem solving some research has been done. The scratch-pad in this research was embedded in a thermodynamics coach as a separate window with a number of canonical objects from the domain of thermodynamics (like pistons and containers). These objects could be dragged on to the scratch-pad. In this way intermediate representations of the problem, which was presented in text on another window, could be built. It was shown that with a proper design of the scratch-pad (and the explicit exclusion of paper near the machine) the vast majority of procedural steps that the student takes during problem solving can be detected [12]. The amount of structure of the scratch-pad was rather large: the primitive elements were canonical objects in the domain, which had (invisible) hooks that allowed them to interconnect selectively to specific places on specific other canonical objects [13]. A parser was able to semantically interpret the drawings made by the student. Since the environment was intended to teach the procedures to solve problems rather than the domain knowledge in the domain of thermodynamics, emphasis in the diagnosis was on detection of (premature) solution steps. The diagnostic power for this procedural aspect of problem solving was greatly improved by the scratch-pad. Although the research only used problems in the domain of thermodynamics we feel that the results can be generalized to all domains where intermediate representations of a problem are required to solve it.

Present research goals

Present research is aimed at getting at a general design strategy for these scratch-pads, in different domains.

Method

As a first approach, it was decided to start with an analysis of natural notes. As new domain, the use of psycho-diagnostic skills was chosen. This domain was expected to be quite different from the domain of thermo-dynamics, but it might be typical for other domains where diagnosis is essential.
A traditional CAI program has been developed which presents students with case material (verbal report) from which the students have to infer a preliminary diagnosis and additional required tests. After the data for these additional tests are supplied the student has to select the final diagnosis. 32 students participated in the course while making notes on completely blank pieces of paper. The course had a log-book already built in so that the students could look up all raw data that had been presented.
To score the notes a scoring scheme was designed on the basis of an analysis of the task that the students performed (appendix I). Each utterance on their notes had to be be classified according to this scheme while simultaneously classifying the form in which the utterance appeared (Eg. free text, drawing, numbers, arrows etc). Utterances which could not be scored were the primary focus of our attention because they might represent a natural need which we did not anticipate.

Results

In total the notes on 72 problems were scored. On the average 27.7 notes (sd= 16.7) were written down. The number of notes was clearly dependent on the difficulty of the case (for the easy cases:20.9; for the difficult cases:39.7). Some students wrote down all raw data in some cases while in other cases they only wrote down the transformed and partially interpreted data. Mostly text was used (95%), even for data that subject's had been trained to analyze graphically. Raw data constituted 54% of the notes although the vast majority of these data could also be looked up from the computer. It appeared that having to perform actions (like selecting a menu-item in order to lookup these data) was considered to be less attractive than writing this info down. There might be two reasons for this preference. In the first place looking up the info through the computer would temporarily block the active window. Secondly after consultation of this info it would disappear again and the student might feel that he/she might need it again.

In total, 38 utterances (= 2% of all notes) were found which could not be scored. From these, a few concerned non relevant tasks like the use of the CAI-program and messages that the student intended to mail to the teacher. The remaining concerned tasks that were relevant but were not anticipated in the task analysis like the evaluation of the final diagnosis and the task of writing a response to the (hypothetical) doctor that had sent the patient. Further annotations were found which had to do with the certainty of intermediate conclusions or the severity or importance of the symptoms / conclusions. Finally control-notes were observed. These notes concern elements of the control structure that steers the diagnosis. For instance, there are rules which require a minimum number of indications before a certain conclusion can be reached. Students might write down (parts of) these rules. These can be seen as reminders. Other kinds of reminders-type notes are exclamation marks with scores, and mentioning important aspects in isolation.

Currently design consequences of these findings are considered. In the first place it seems that 'looked up' raw data should be easy to copy to a the permanent electronic scratch-pad window. Furthermore the annotations that students make concerning the results of certain sub-tasks suggest that, for each result which is jotted down on the electronic scratch-pad, it should be possible to put an electronic "sticky note" on it. The annotations dealing with the control-knowledge suggest that the students might need a look-up table where they can easily find this knowledge (and which would help the program to diagnose that the student is considering to use certain control knowledge). Also there appears to be a need for checking definitions and norms.

The results further show that the vast majority of utterances can be anticipated by doing a task-analysis. However this empirical approach does not provide us with specific *new* suggestions how to implement the scratch-pad. This will be the focus for subsequent research.

Simulation

If the student, while solving a problem, builds a (proper) description of the problem on the scratch-pad, this description could in principle be used in a simulation. For instance, if the student has to solve a problem in the domain of electricity - say Ohm's law applied to parallel and serial resistors - he/she might make a drawing of the circuit on the scratch-pad. If the problem at hand is to find the potential over one of the resistors, the student might want to check his/her answer by having the circuit model which was built in the process of problem solving actually simulate the simple laws of electricity. Thus there appears to be an intrinsic relation between the scratch-pad and simulation. Making a drawing of a problem-state is equivalent of building an experimental set-up. One could consider a simulation environment to be a 'runnable' scratch-pad.

Therefore one of the things to keep in mind in designing scratch-pads is whether the design is usable as a simulation environment. For simulations too the question of the abstraction level at which objects and their relations should be represented is relevant. E.g. in the electricity model the simulation could be very concrete with electrons running through wires. It can be argued that the level of abstraction should not be fixed but should adapt itself to the actual student model. (Adherents of the complete freedom approach would make different levels of abstraction accessible and let the student choose).

Running simulations in the domain of for instance electronics requires a model about how electronic components work. So, if a scratch-pad is designed in connection to electronic trouble-shooting and this scratch-pad has to be runnable the model should be implemented too. It appears rather problematic to formulate a proper model for the domain of psycho-diagnosis. Like electronic trouble shooting, psycho-diagnosis is a classification task which might be taught by showing a simulation of the 'mind-circuit'. Experts in the domain of psycho-diagnosis however do not agree on this 'circuit'. Therefore this approach of letting the possible simulation environment guide the scratch-pad design fails for this domain.

Conclusion

The call for a totally different approach to 'intelligent' tutoring systems in which the traditional decomposition in three modules (a diagnostic module, a tutoring module and an interface module), all centred around the student model, is discarded, becomes louder and louder. There might be many reasons for this. A central one is that current ITS's do not incorporate complex and subtle representations of student's cognitive state. There are several related issues, like the lack of specific theories of learning and the impoverished communication channel, which might justify giving up on student models at least for practical purposes. In this paper we described the underlying ideas and some initial results of a research program aimed at the enrichment of the communication channel in order to enable more detailed cognitive diagnosis. It obviously is still uncertain that even with a far better communication channel, far better student models and a far better theory of learning, ITS could live up to our original expectations. The present research, which focuses on the diagnostic value of electronic scratch-pad during problem solving, however promises also to offer a framework for the practical design of simulation environments. Future research on scratch-pad design for domains where simulation is relevant like electricity and heat theory is in preparation.

In expository teaching, generally preceding the teaching of problem solving within a domain, scratch-pads might look like grids upon which a semantic net can be built by the student. Major concepts, which they detect in the educational material presented to them, can be placed upon the scratch-pad and attributes can be filled in. Relations that they infer can be made explicit by connecting the relevant concepts. Such a scratch-pad should be quite helpful in tracing the cognitive development of the student. To our knowledge this approach hasn't been used yet.

References

1 Self, J.: Bypassing the intractable problem of student modelling, Proceedings of the 1988 Conference on Intelligent Tutoring Systems, Montreal, June 1988.

2 Elsom-Cook, M.: Guided discovery tutoring. In M. Elsom-Cook (Ed.) Guided Discovery Tutoring, Chapman , London, pp.14 (1990).

3 Bierman, D.J.:. 'Intelligent' simulation environments in education. Proc. of the 7th European Conference on Artificial Intelligence, Part II- pp. 84-90. Brighton, July 1986.

4 Ericson, K.A. & Simon, H.A.: Verbal reports as data. Psychological Review, 87, pp. 215-251.

5 Goldstein,I.P.: The Genetic Graph: a representation for the evolution of procedural knowledge. In D. Sleeman & J.S. Brown (Eds). Intelligent tutoring systems. Academic Press, New York, pp.51-77 (1982).

6 Ohlson, S. Some principles of intelligent tutoring. In R.Lawler & M. Yazdani (Eds.) AI and education: Learning environments and intelligent tutoring systems. Ablex Publishing, Norwood (1987).

7 Kass, The role of user modelling in ITS. Technical Report MS-CIS-86-58. Dept. of Computer and Information Science, Univ. of Pennsylvania, Philadelphia, PA (1987).

8 Sleeman,D., Kelly, A.E., Martinak, R., Ward, R.D., Moore, J.L.: Studies of diagnosis and remediation with high school algebra students. Cognitive Science, 13, pp. 551-568 (1989).

9 Anderson, J.R., Conrad, F.G. & Corbett, A.T.: Skill acquisition and the LISP Tutor. Cognitive Science, 13, 467-505 (1989).

10 Kamsteeg, P.A. & Bierman, D.J.: Teacher thinking, student thinking: Think aloud protocol analysis in tutoring systems research. In: Peter Goodyear (Ed.) Teaching Knowledge and Intelligent Tutoring. Palo Alto: Ablex Corporation, Norwood, NJ., 1989.

11 Nessen, E.: SC-UM: User modelling in the SINIX consultant. Applied Artificial Intelligence, 3, pp. 33-44(1989).

12 Bierman, D.J. & Anjewierden, A.A.: The use of a graphic scratch pad for students in 'Intelligent' CAI., Proc. of the 27th Conf. of the Association for the Development of Computer Based Instructional Systems, New Orleans, Feb. 1986, pp. 68-71 (1986).

13 Barnard, Y.F., Sandberg, J.A.C. & Erkens, G.: Interaction in intelligent tutoring systems. Journal of Structural Learning, 10, pp. 197-213 (1990).

A Framework for Instructional Planning and Discourse Modelling in Intelligent Tutoring Systems

M. Felisa Verdejo
Sección Inteligencia Artificial, Departamento de Lenguajes y Sistemas Informáticos, Universidad Politécnica de Cataluña, Pau Gargallo 5, 08028 Barcelona, Spain. e-mail: eafelisa @ ebrupc51.bitnet

Abstract: This paper focuses on automatic tutoring using mixed-initiative dialogues in natural language. Two main issues are addressed: instructional design, i.e. how to plan and carry out a teaching session and, tutorial dialogue where two participants communicate in natural language to perform the educational task. We consider the tutor and the student as agents cooperating in a learning process but having their own goals. Under this assumption, the tutor initially states an instructional goal and plans a strategy to attain it. This strategy is refined in a dynamic way, so that the student's interactions are always considered. A natural language interface has been implemented. The system understands student's utterances, in spanish, and builds the dialogue structure dynamically interchanging messages both with the student and the planner.

Keywords: Discourse modelling, Instructional planning, Intelligent tutoring systems, Natural language interface, Tutorial dialogue.

Introduction

Tutorial principles have received attention and been referred to by several authors. Only recently, however, explicit models offering adapative instruction have been considered.This paper focuses on automatic tutoring using mixed-initiative dialogues in natural language. Two main issues are addressed: instructional design, i.e. how to plan and carry out a teaching session and, tutorial dialogue where two participants communicate in natural language to perform the educational task.

We consider the tutor and the student as agents cooperating in a learning process but having their own goals. Under this assumption, the tutor initially states an instructional goal and plans a strategy to attain it. This strategy is refined in a dynamic way, so that the student 's interactions are always considered. For he tutor to react to the student's intentions, reasoning processes are needed either to confirm an expectation about the student's behaviour, and follow the current strategy accordingly, or to detect a conflict and solve it by planning an appropiate strategy.

Flexibility and adapatability to the student as well as independence of a particular teaching domain are important requirements in ITS design. To fulfill them within the above framework, we propose a generic tutor based on a dynamic instructional planner cooperating with a natural language interface.

Our choice of natural language merits some further comments. The difficulty to obtain and infer useful information in order to build a student model is widely recognised. Some current alternatives propose to enhance problem solving processes by providing the student with intermediate representations and appropiate graphic interfaces to state goals and plans explicitely while solving a problem. This approach helps the student to indicate in an explicit way the steps of the problem solving process, as well as to represent the work in progress. However in an interactive situation, the student also needs to communicate other things such as doubts as to what to do next, comments on his understanding of what is going on, or requests for further specific domain knowledge and, natural language seems a convenient way to communicate this information to the tutor.

We have explored a model for tutorial dialogues, specifying the basic units and their organisation. This structure takes into account the tutor and the student goals and it is related to, but separate from the instructional strategy i.e. there exists two different models, the pedagogic model managed by the planner and the dialogue managed by the interface.

A natural langague interface has been implemented. The system understands student's utterances,in spanish, and builds the dialogue structure dynamically interchanging messages both with the student and the planner.

The next two sections present an overview of the two components, the instructional planner and the interface. Section four discusses in more detail the dialogue model. A sample dialogue to illustrate the tutoring process is given in Section five, and Section six compares our system with other related works. Finally a summary is given and future directions outlined.

The instructional planner

An overview

A teaching dialogue is formed by a sequence of tutor-student 's interchanges, where the tutor plans and performs instructional actions and the student carries out a learning activity.

Tutoring can be broken down into types of activities/tasks, with different levels of abstraction, from the most general where a global strategy is decided ,to the more concrete where a particular action is generated and carried out. We find it useful to distinguish four major kinds of activities involving instructional goals called pedagogic, thematic, teaching and supervising.

At the highest level of abstraction, we consider the "pedagogic decision" where the main task is to establish a final objective and the global approach to attain it. Thus a teaching **session** is the result of the application of a set of strategies to reach a pedagogic goal. A typical example would consist of "a general review, an introduction of new concepts, a review of conflicting points, while another one might include the "introduction of new concepts", or " a brief review of the last session and an introduction of new concepts".

In particular two kinds of activities are related to the pedagogic decision:

* Choosing a combination of strategies to attain a pedagogic objective,
* Developing the strategies established in a dynamic way.

The refining of a pedagogic objective in terms of the subject matter, taking into account an individual student, is called a "thematic decision". For example a thematic goal is to "Determine the next element to be taught and how it can be presented to this student".

To solve these goals the planner interacts with other separate sources of knowledge concerning the subject-matter representation and the problem library, as well as the student model.

Once the subject to be taught has been decided, carriyng out the presentation and/or controlling the acquisition are the main tasks related to the "teaching activity", involving didactic, diagnostic and repairing tasks. For instance a teaching goal is "the student knows how to use concept X" and can be accomplished by applying the plan "explain concept X", and "verify by means of an exercise".

"Supervising" focuses on conflict detection and resolution among the different objectives of the tutor and the student. Every time an interaction from the student takes place a supervisor goal is created. If there are no conflicts, planned activity goes on, while in other cases conflict resolution plans will decide whether to consider a local change or to notify "pedagogic decison" that a strategical change is needed.

Each type of activity is encapsulated in one knowledge base, so the tutor module is made up of four components: pedagogic, thematic, teaching and supervising. Figure 1 shows the functional design of the instrucional module as well as its external relationships with other modules in order to configurate a complete tutoring system.

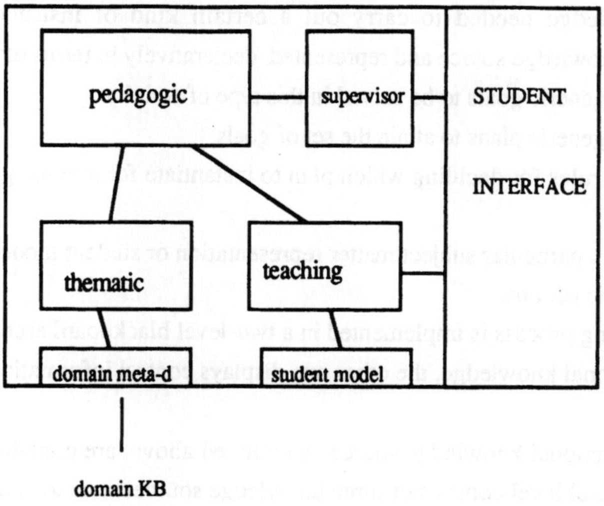

Figure 1: A functional view of the instructional component

From the architectural point of view, the instructional module is seen as a dynamic planner implemented by means of a two-level blackboard [5] separating tutoring knowledge from control.

The domain level contains the Instructional Knowledges Bases. **An instructional knowledge base** consists of a set of generic plans and selection rules, to solve a class of objectives of the same instructional class (pedagogic, thematic, teaching, or conflict resolution respectively).

A generic **objective** (OB) has different plans associated with it. Depending on the strategy, one of them will be selected in order to achieve an instantiated objective. A generic **plan** is made up of parametrised actions and subobjectives. The former can be described in declarative form (by rules) or procedural form. Subobjectives will be solved invoking the current Knowledge source or another one, depending on their type. A plan execution produces the raising of new objectives and the realization of elementary actions. The next section discusses the main features of the primitives provided by the instructional planner.

Basic components

A goal can be stated by the instructional planner at the beginning of the session or raised dynamically as the session is carried out to take into account the student's knowledge and intentions i.e. our instructional planner generates actions in a dynamic way.

The knowledge needed to carry out a certain kind of instructional activity is encapsulated in a knowledge source and represented declaratively in terms of:

- the set of generic goals to be solved in this type of activity
- the set of generic plans to attain the set of goals
- the set of rules for deciding which plan to instantiate for a given goal in a particular context.

Links with a particular subject matter representation or student model are set out in the form of a set of basic actions.

The planning process is implemented in a two-level blackboard architecture: one level represents instructional knowledge, the other one displays control information needed to carry out the process.

The instructional knowledge sources mentioned above, are contained in the domain level while the control level consists of three knowledge sources: one to activate an objective, another one to select a knowledge source for an objective and the third one to apply a selected knowledge source to solve a chosen objective. Further details about the control level are given in [5,6].

In this overview we focus on the domain level and in the next we elaborate on the definition of an instructional knowledge base.

Instructional Knowledge Base

The definition of an instructional knowledge base includes a structured description of the generic objectives involved for the type of instructional activity being modelled, the set of generic plans to be applied in order to achieve these objectives, and the set of rules to choose and activate a particular plan for a given goal. The external behaviour of a knowledge base is laid out in a set of preconditions and postconditions. Furthermore an instructional KB can receive and answer two types of messages:

"can you solve objective X?" - the answer is positive if this objective is an instance of one of the generic objectives defined in the KB and the KB preconditions are satisfied in the current context.

"solve objective X" - to respond to this message, rules and plans are activated in order to solve an instantianted objective.

Objectives

A generic goal is also described in a structured way, by specifying its type, name, the actor and the knowledge source to solve it.

We distinguish two actors: tutor and student. For a tutor we consider two main types of goals: strategic and common. Strategic objectives can be further divided into two sub-types; those which establish a global approach for a whole/part of a teaching session, and those which reconsider the current approach. Strategic objectives of the first subtype are always defined in the pedagogic KS, while those of the second appear in the supervisor KS.

The "decide teaching strategy" is an example of a strategic aim.The knowledge needed to attain this objective is contained in the pedagogic knowledge source, howewer its occurrences can be generated from the activity of other KS.

The meta-definition for a generic strategic objective is shown in the schema below:

IS_A: TUTOR
NAME: { an identifier}
DESCRIPTION: {a comment}
ACTOR: TUTOR
BELONGS_TO_KS: PEDAGOGIC_DECISION
TYPE_IS: STRATEGIC
ASSOCIATED RULES: {a set of selection rules}

Common objectives refine and develop a selected strategy. These are classified according to their content. Thematic goals, related to the subject-matter, are defined in the thematic knowledge source, teaching aims, subclassified as didactic, such as explaining or giving examples, diagnostic goals (debugging and repairing),.and those which assess the student such as controlling, or evaluating are included in the teaching and correction KS. The meta-definition for a common objective is as follows:

IS_A: TUTOR
NAME: { an identifier}
DESCRIPTION: {a commentary}
ACTOR: TUTOR
BELONGS_TO_KS:
TYPE_IS: COMMON
ASSOCIATED PLANS: {a set of instructional plans }
ASSOCIATED RULES: {a set of selection rules}

Instructional Plans

A common objective has different plans associated with it. Depending on the strategy one of them will be selected in order to achieve a particular goal. The following schema shows the meta-description of a generic plan .

{{ PLAN
IS_PART_OF: DOMAIN
IS_A+inv: CONDITIONAL_PLAN NON_ CONDITIONAL_PLAN
NAME:
OBJ_ASSOCIATED:
<type of objectives solved by this plan>
PLAN_DEVELOPMENT:
<composition of actions and/or subobjectives to solve an objective>
BELONGS_TO_KS:
<KS where the plan is included>
}}

The plan_development is expressed as a composition of actions and subobjectives. For a non conditional plan this composition is a sequence. A conditional plan can include alternative steps. During the running of the plan,once it has been instantiated, new objectives arise and/or elementary actions are carried out.

Subobjectives in a plan can be of different types, i.e. they will be solved by the current Knowledge Source or by the activation of a different one.

Below, is one of the plans included in the pedagogic KS to solve the common objective "initializing a session".

P-X1 Select a concept for explanation
P-X2 Remember
P- OB9 Decide whether or not to check

it is formed by three subobjectives, the first one "select a concept" is a kind of thematic objective, that has to be solved by a thematic plan involving actions operating on the subject-matter representation. The second one is a kind of didactic objective, which is attained by a series of instructional actions leading to an interaction with the student and the third one is a kind of strategic objective, to be activated once enough information about the student's state of knowledge is available.

Plans can state objectives recursively, as in the example below, where the strategic objective P-OB1 is broken down into three subobjectives, one of them being P-OB1 itself:

P-OB1: decide a guideline of the session and apply it

Plan-development:

P-OB8 Decide on a sequence of teaching strategies

P-OB2 Apply on the teaching strategies

P-OB1 Decide on a guideline of the session an apply it

Depending on the context, selection rules will instantiate either this plan or another one to solve the subobjective P-OB1.

Selection rules

As mentioned above, from the planning point of view, objectives can be considered of two main types: strategic and common.

Strategic objectives are solved by means of rules which decide either the strategy to be selected in a given context or the plan to solve a conflict.

A common objective can be solved by different plans, which are selected by a set of rules. A plan selection rule states for a class of common objectives and a set of conditions , the plan to apply.

The set of conditions and actions in a rule depends on the type of objective, and as we distinguish three main types, there are three subclasses of rules:

- rules for strategy selection
- rules for conflict resolution
- rules to select a plan to solve a goal under a stated strategy

Any rule considers, in the condition part, information about the type of instructional objective to be solved, the requirements of the student model, and some constraints on the current context of the session.

The context definition includes current and pending instructional objectives, focused objects belonging to the subject-matter, as well as other information described in the schema below:

{{ SESSION_CONTEXT
IS_PART_OF: DOMAIN
IS_COMPOSED_BY: I_ OBJECTIVES, CONFLICTS, OBJECTS
STARTING_TIME:
CURRENT_DATE_SESSION:
SESSION_NUMBER:
ESTIMATE_DURATION:

SPENT_TIME:
INTERVENTION_NUMBER:
CURRENT_STUDENT_OBJECTIVE:
<current student's objective >
}}

Strategy selection rules also take into account in the condition part, information about the last session and the estimated running time of the strategy application.

{{ STRATEGY_SELECTION_RULE
IS_A: RULE
CONDITION_PART:
<type of pedagogic objective>
<conditions about session context>
<conditions about student model>
<conditions about the last session >
<estimate duration of the strategy application>
ACTION_PART:
<strategy instance>
<modification of session context>
NAME:
<character string>
ASSOCIATED_OBJECTIVE:
<objective type in the condition rule>
BELONGS_TO_KS:
<KS instance where it appears>
}}

The following rule is an example of strategy selection, stating that if we want to start a session with a student, in the medium range, the last session has ended with the introduction of a new item to learn, and the time elapsed between both sessions is under a certain limit, then the strategy to start is "a concept review".

RSP06:	If	OBJ_TYPE = P-OB07	AND
		Testimate < Tintroduction	AND
		SESSION_NUMBER ≠ 1	AND
		ΔTbetween_sessions < ΔTmax	AND
		Student_TYPE = MEDIUM	AND
		Last_session_end = "Concept interruption"	

Then STRATEGY = "Concept review"
Testimate = Testimate + TIME(STRATEGY)

In the condition part rules for conflict resolution also consider the current student objectives.

On the other hand rules to select a plan specify under which strategy they can be applied, and their meta-description is the following one:

{{ PLAN_SELECTION_RULE
IS_A: RULE
CONDITION_RULE:
<condition about objective >
<condition about session context>
<condition about current strategy>
ACTION_RULE:
<plan instance>
<objective tree modification>
<session context modification>
NAME:
<character string>
ASSOCIATED_OBJECTIVES:
<objective type of the condition>
BELONGS_TO_KS:
<KS where it appears>
}}

For instance for the thematic objective "(TD-OB1) Select the list of objects to be taught", some of the plans are:

TD-P01: (TD-EA1): Get concepts from last session
(TD-EA2): DETAIL_LEVEL = Remember, FORM = Formal definition

TD-P03: (TD-EA5): Get first concept not known by the student
(TD-EA6): Establish detail-level and presentation form with the student's model

and examples of some rules to select them :

RSPTD03: If OBJ_TYPE = TD-OB1 AND
STRATEGY = "Brief session review"
Then Apply TD-P01

RSPTD04: If OBJ_TYPE = TD-OB1 AND
STRATEGY = "Introduce new concepts"
Then apply TD-P03

Figure 2 shows the conceptual primitives related to the instructional planner, student objectives are commented on next section.

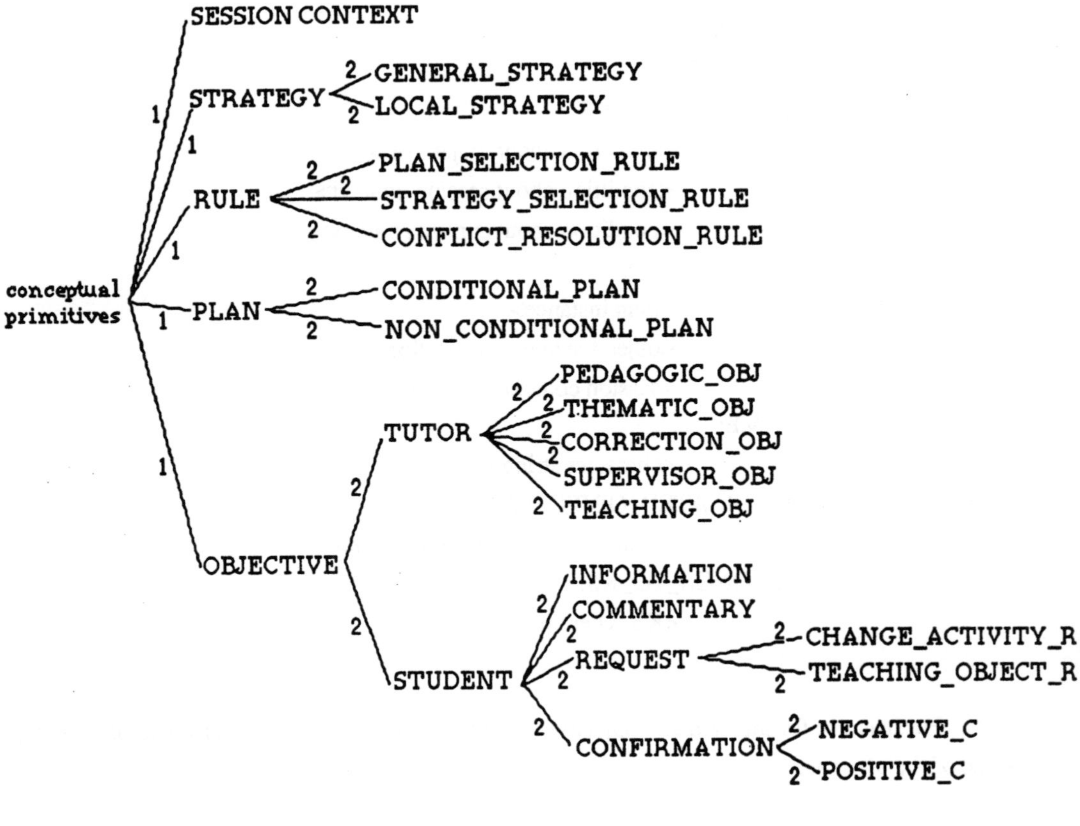

Figure 2: Conceptual primitives of the instructional planner

The interface

To provide knowledge in a problem-solving scenario, following a mixed-initiative dialogue, a tutor has to decide the sequence of instructional phases taking into account the student's intentions. In order to interact in a reasonable and cooperative way, the system must recognize what goals the student wants to achieve at each point of the dialogue. In order to carry out the communication process, student NL-utterances have to be interpreted in their context. Thus, understanding involves not only syntactic and semantic processes but also dialogue modelling.

Current theories of discourse structure try to define basic units and their interconnection, to represent a dialogue and provide mechanisms for the contextual processing of utterances. In particular Grosz [7] proposes an abstract model where the intentional structure of the participants and the focus of attention are considered. Taking into account these ideas, our aim is to define a framework for tutorial dialogue i.e. on the one hand to outline a catalogue of student and tutor communicative acts and how they form regular patterns, on the other hand to explain how these acts and patterns are related to the learner objectives and the tutor instructional goals and strategies.

Written dialogues corresponding to a teaching session consist of interrelated sentences, reflecting the underlined pedagogical strategy; each dialogue can be divided into segments stating the linguistic expressions produced by the student and the tutor to communicate a particular instructional goal. We call each segment an exchange.

For instance the three first lines in figure three form a simple exchange for "introduction", in this case corresponding to three interventions: a tutor presentation, followed by a tutor question and a student answer. However exchanges can be more complicated as is the case of the fragment between 5 and 6, corresponding to the instructional goal " introduction of a new concept". Here we find a pattern of three exchanges: a first exchange to agree on the next activity, then a presentation of a concept definition, and finally an exchange to confirm the understanding of the current explanation.

The intervention is the basic unit of the dialogue structure. An intervention is a message conveyed by the student or the tutor. It corresponds usually to a tutor or student sentence, however some times it includes either only a part or more than one nl-utterance.

The content of a student message is analysed and represented by the Interface on different linguistic levels: superficial, morphological, syntactic, logic, conceptual and illocutive. From this information and the structure of the dialogue, the intentions/objectives of the student can be inferred and provided to the tutor.

The interface operates in close cooperation with the tutor module; communication between them is conveyed through messages containing relevant information about the participants intentions for each intervention and the current state of the instruction task.

Next we will describe briefly the organization of the parsing process and in section four we will focus on the tutorial dialogue structure.

In our approach, the representation of an nl-sentence follows a stratified model; however, parsing is a cooperative process between the different morphologic, syntactic, semantic and pragmatic Knowledge Sources.

1-----
T Hello, this is Capra,
T what is your name ?
S Student 1

2-----
T Last day you learned about arithmetic expressions
T Have you any questions?
S No, I understand them

3-----
T Do you want to solve an exercise ?
S Yes

4-----
T Specify the following one
S {Right solution}
T O.K. your answer is right

5-----
T Now we are going to study how to specify functions appearing in the Output
5.1----
T Any questions before proceeding?
S No,
S let us go on
5.2 ----
T A function declaration...
T Is it clear ?
S I understand
5.3 ----
T The name of the function...
The domain...
The range...
The definition...
5.4 ----
T Do you have any questions?
S It's O.K,
S I understand how to define a function

6-----
T Well, let us now solve an exercise
T Specify ....

Figure 3: A fragment of a dialogue

These KS generate partial interpretations, interrupt each other, ask for information from other components, etc.

In order to describe and implement different parsing strategies, our system is based on the use of a multilevel **Blackboard Architecture.** Objects are placed at their corresponding level. When a blackboard is modified, its associated Knowledge Sources are activated. KS associated to a specific Blackboard can only manipulate objects attached to this blackboard. Other Knowledge Sources handle communication between levels; these KS are assigned to a blackboard but will include information at other levels.

The procedural contents of a KS can be **Rules, Packets of Rules** and **Procedures.** Rules are simply condition-action pairs. Rule packets are set of rules grouped for methodological purposes. Procedures are the action components of rules.

Control Strategy

At each descriptive level of the blackboard, at any moment, there will be a collection of concepts, already built into the parsing process, called **Realizations,** and another collection of virtual concepts, objects we wait for, called **Expectations.** The core of the parsing process consists of obtaining some new realizations satisfying current expectations. Realizations and Expectations are created at different levels. So, morphological Analysis creates **Morphological Interpretations**; syntactical analysis, **Syntactical Interpretations**; semantic interpretation **Logical Forms** and conceptual elements: either **Concepts** or **Conceptual Networks.** We implement all these objects in a frame-like formalism. Our system manages each level in three main ways: Refining expectations in simpler ones that, perhaps, will be satisfied. Composing realizations in order to obtain new ones. Matching realizations and expectations in order to determine if any of the former can be satisfied by any of the latter. If all three ways fail new expectations are created at another level.

The interface is embedded in a interface-generator system [10], providing access to Knowledge acquisition at the different levels. The morphological and syntactic components include a large dictionary and a Spanish grammar. For tutoring applications, the semantic component has been defined, taking into account the experimental material collected (140 hours of interactive teaching) from the Capra project, an ITS for teaching introductory programming. Portabilitiy has been considered one of the key issues in designing the interface, for instance the semantic taxonomy for verbs contain three groups: the first one related to the communication process (to say, tell..), the second one to the instructional task (to explain, make clear...) and the third one about the particular subject-domain, in this case including verbs such as to specify, program....A change of teaching domain will only require modifying this class, using the semantic acquisition facilities.

The dialogue model

Our natural language dialogue component is based on three data structures: the **dialogue structure**, to represent the organization of interactions between the participants in the conversation, the **intentional structure**, to represent their intentions explicitely and the **attentional structure**, where topics of the dialogue are related in a structured way.

The dialogue structure

The dialogue structure is a model of the comunication process. This structure is dynamically built up by the interface and is represented in a tree form.The root of the tree is **tutorial session**. A session takes place between three participants: the tutor, the interface and the student, and it consists of a set of related **thematic dialogues.** Dialogues are units of communication characterized by a specific topic, each of them involving a set of **tutorial interchanges.** A dialogue is then composed of one or more **interchanges**. There is a descriptor tying each dialogue to the attentional structure.

An interchange has an **objective** which must be filled. Objectives are inferred from simple or complex illocutionary acts performed by the speakers. An interchange points to the intentional structure where information about its goal, level of attainment and its evolution is represented. Interchanges are also tied to elements of the attentional structure.

In order to satisfy the goal of an Interchange some new interchanges or speakers interventions can be created. Session, dialogues and interchanges define internal nodes of the tutorial discourse tree structure

The intervention is the elementary component of the dialogue structure corresponding to leaves in the dialogue tree, representing each one of the messages uttered by the participants.

An intervention is produced in a specific time, a message sent by a speaker to a hearer. The content of the student's messages is represented by the interface at different levels: superficial, morphological, syntactical, logical, conceptual and illocutive.

Further information about aspects of dialogue management not discussed in this paper can be found in [4,10] .

The attentional structure

The attentional structure is used as a search-space in the resolution of some types of references. In our system, definite reference, direct and anaphoric, and, specially, pronominal and elliptical reference [3] use the attentional structure.

References appear frequently in tutorial dialogues, the student sentence between 2 and 3 in the fragment of the teaching session shown in figure three is a simple example.

In our system, the attentional structure is mainly conceptual. The syntactic structures saved (in a simplified fashion) are those related to the last user intervention and those corresponding to interventions of the current Interchange. For the rest we keep only some syntactic features, like gender and number which are incorporated into the conceptual objects associated to the semantic interpretation. Initially, every explicitly mentioned or inferred concept appearing during the conversation will belong to the attentional structure.

There are two ways to access the attentional structure: the **theme**, tied to a dialogue unit, and the **focus**, related to an interchange. Conceptual **objects** as well as inferred (not explicitly mentioned) **instances** are introduced in the theme. Explicitly mentioned instances are placed in the focus. Our focus mechanism is not limited to a single object, as usual, but to a collection of them. In some cases, as in pronominal reference, a distinguished object is needed. This is handled by the **center**. The center indicates, at any moment, the object of the focus which constitutes the main subject of the Intervention.

The intentional structure

Each dialogue node has an overall **purpose** corresponding to the **instructional strategy** that underlies the tutorial discourse. A dialogue is made up of a set of interchanges, each of them contributing to achieving a dialogue.

An interchange always has an associated **objective**: one of the **instrucional goals** generated by the instructional strategy. Examples of associated goals for the interchanges in the dialogue shown in figure three are:

Identification
Recall last learned concept
Propose problem-solving activity
Introduce a new concept

Interchanges are composed either of interchanges or interventions. Thus, relations between interchange goals are of two kinds: contribute to, and is a prerequisite of. An instructional goal is prerequisite for the rest of goals belonging to the same level. An instructional goal can contribute to a more abstract when it is related to a segment embedded in another interchange. For instance utterances between 5.2 to 5.3 in figure 3 form an interchange with the associated objective *Introduce subpart of a concept,* contributing to the main objective *Introduce a concept.*

Each intervention has an individual objective. An intervention contributes to the objective of the interchange where the intervention is embedded. In general there is not a finite list of speakers' intentions however, for tutorial secenarios, a range of intentions for each type of participant can be considered.

The following are some of the types of student intentions illustrated with an example:
Intend that the tutor perform the explanation of a concept

Could you tell me what is the polar representation ?

Intend that the tutor perform a continuation or change of activity

let us go on

Intend that the tutor know about the student 's learning state,

in general terms

I remember now

or in specific terms

I understand how to define a function

Intend that the tutor provide some help

I don't know how to proceed now to decide if is it an even number

Student's intentions are inferred by the contextual component of the interface. The interpretation process takes into account the kind of illocutive action being parsed, as well as knowledge from the dialogue structures.

An example

An excerpt of a dialogue is commented below. It correspond to an intermediate teaching session to learn about function specification. The general strategy underlining the dialogue, selected by the pedagogic component, is in this case "refresh, introduce new concept and finish".

T and S, identify tutor and student utterances respectively, sentences in cursive show relevant steps of the tutor (T) planning activity and the interface (I) interpretation of the student utterances in terms of goals.

T Carry out a teaching session , is broken down in two subgoasls: identify user and decide a strategy, the first one is attempted

...Identify user and load his model

T 0 Hello, this is Capra, what is your name ?
A 0 Student 1

....

T ... then , the second goal is solved by the rules selecting a strategy , the current instructional strategy becames "Refresh, Introduce new concepts, finish"
Apply Refresh strategy starts to be refined, generating the sequence of subgoals to be further attempted: determine concept, recall, verify with exercise.
....Determine with the student model the last concept learned,
......recall, in turn is decomposed on five subgoals

......Select a message S for concept C, Form= formal definition,
Exp=remember
...... Send message for concept

T1 Last day you learned about arithmetic expressions

T .....send message for confirmation

T2 Have you any questions?

....

T ....Interpret student answer
this is a kind of goal belonging to the supervisor, it waits for the interface message in order to either confirm its expectations, here a positive or negative answer, or not, in that last case a conflict goal would be inserted.

S1 No, I understand them

I the interface sends a message to the tutor: the student confirms a negative answer and informs positively about its understanding of arithmetic expressions

......

T no conflict is detected and next objective is attempted:
.....Update student model
the goals generated by the recall goal are now satisfied and next one is:

.....Propose an exercise, further refined into: send message and interpret student answer
....Send message to propose an exercise

T3 Do you want to solve an exercise ?
S 2 Yes

......

T
.....Interpret student answer-

I confirmation of activity

......

T
....Select problem P for concept C, level =3
.....Send problem P to the student

T4 Specify the following one........

S 3 {Right solution}

......

T
.....Evaluate student solution
.....Acknowledge

T5 O.K. your answer is right

.....End of refresh strategy

The structure of the dialogue built up by the interface up to this point is partly shown in figure 4. The dialogue node has two interchanges, one of them with the related tutor objective *identification* and the other one with the related instructional tutor goal *refresh*. The second interchange is composed of two exchanges with the related goals *recall* and *verify* respectively, both contributing to *refresh* and *recall* being the prerequisite for *verification*. It is worth noting that the instructional strategy underlines the dialogue structure but it is not the same, for instance the refinement of refresh includes three instructional goals, namely *determine concept, recall* and *verify*. However, the first one does not involve any student interaction, thus it is not relevant for the communication process, and as a result does not appear related to any node of the dialogue structure.

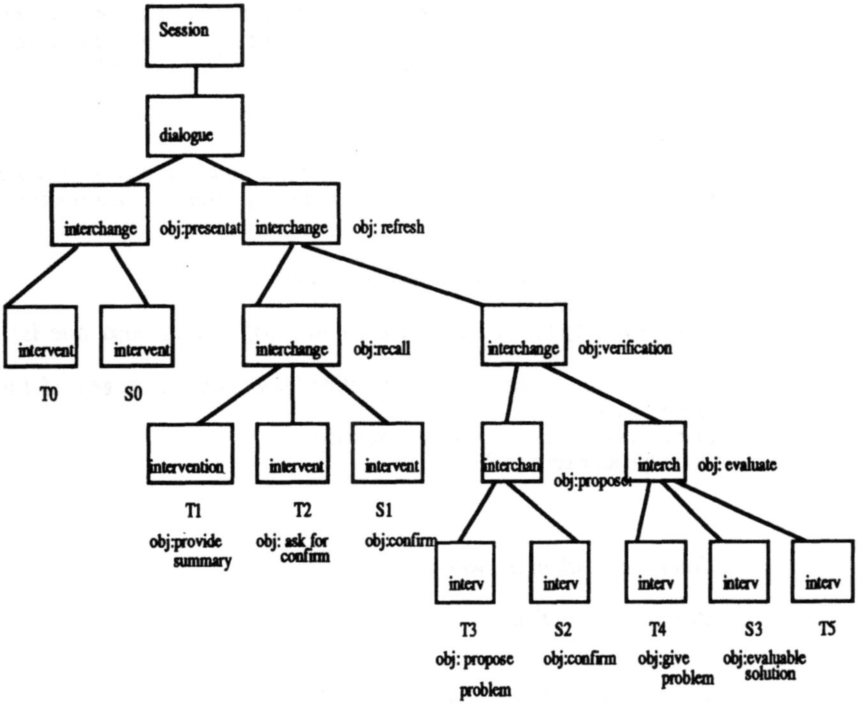

Figure 4: The dialogue structure until utterance T5

At this point of the dialogue the tutor carries out the second part of the strategy, *Introduce new concepts,* applying a plan composed of two subgoals: decide what to teach next and how to do it.

The thematic objective is solved taking into account subject matter description and student knowledge, the next concept is obtained and its profile is evaluated (from the information provided by the domain representation). Function specification is a complex concept, a strategy including an *explanation* of main subconcepts and *verification with exercises* is decided on. Starting with a general definition of "function declaration", the explanation goal is carried out from this point to S6. The second main subgoal *verification making exercise* starts in T15.

......
T
..... *Introduce new concepts*
..... *Select Nc next concept of C, Evaluate profile for Nc*
..... *Select a presentation strategy for concept Nc (Explanation and confirmation of Nc, with subconcepts Definition Verification of Nc)*
.....*Explanation with subconcepts of NC,*
..... *Select message for Nc, form= formal definition,exp= presentation*
..... *Send message*
T6 Now we are going to study how to specify functions appearing in the Output
....
T .....*Confirm activity*
T7 Any questions before proceeding?
T ...*Interpret student answer*

S4 No, go on

I ......*confirmation of activity*

....
T ...*Def. of subconcepts of Nc 1*
.....*Select message for concept Nc 1, level= formal definition, exp=detailed*
T8 A function declaration...
....
T ..... *Acknowledge*
T9 Is it clear ?
....
T ..... *Interpret student answer*
S5 I understand

I *The student Informs positively*
......
T ..... *Update student model*

..... *Select subparts for NC 1*
..... *Select message for Nc1.1s1, level= formal definition ,exp= standard*
..... *Send message*
T10 The name of the function
.....
T .... *Select message for Nc1.1s2, level= formal definition ,exp= standard*
..... *Send message*
T 11 The domain
.....
T ..... *Select message for Nc .1s3, level= formal definition ,exp= standard*
..... *Send message*
T 12 The range
.....
T ..... *End of def of subconcepts of Nc 1.*
..... *Select message for Nc 1.2, level= definition*
T 13 The definition
.....
T ..... *Acknowledge*
T 14 Do you have any questions?
.....
T ... *Interpret student answer*
S 6 O.K, I understand how to define a function

I *the student informs positively about his understanding of the concept being learned*

......

T ..... *Update student model*

..... *End of explanation for Nc1*

..... *Verification of Nc1*

T15 Well, let us now practise with an exercise

.....

T .... *Select a problem for Nc1, level = 2*

.... *Send text*

given....

T .... *Interpret student answer*

S8 Can you give me an example of logic expression, I can't remember well.

I *the student requests for an example of logic expression and provides further information to justify this request.*

....

T .....*here the tutor expects an answer to the proposed problem, and he receives a request* *then a goal to represent this conflict is inserted.*

From the interface perspective, the student intervention corresponding to S8 cannot be inserted under the current interchange; the situation is shown in figure 5.

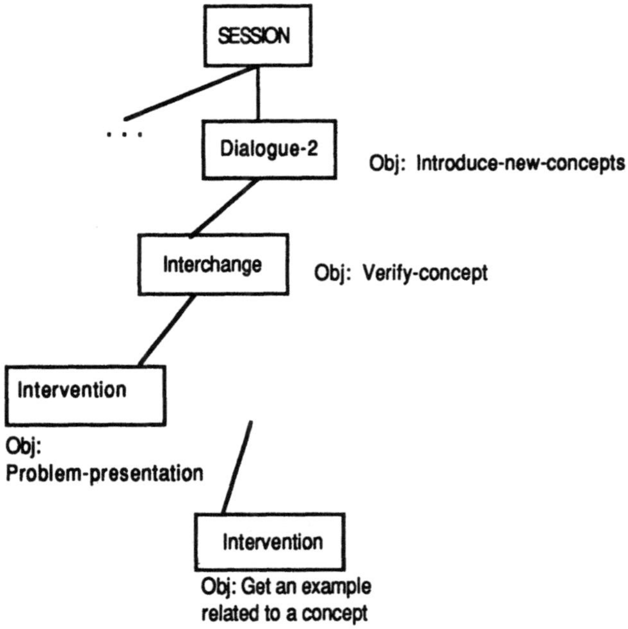

Figure 5: The student intervention corresponding to A8

T17 O.K, logic expressions are used for...here is an example...

Here conflict resolution rules decide on how to respond to the student request and a goal to apply the local strategy "to provide complementary information" is inserted dynamically. This goal is further refined and finally T17 is generated. The dialogue structure reflects the change, a new interchange has been created, in a bottom-up way, to respond to the student, and its request is inserted under this new node. The updated dialogue structure is given in figure 6.

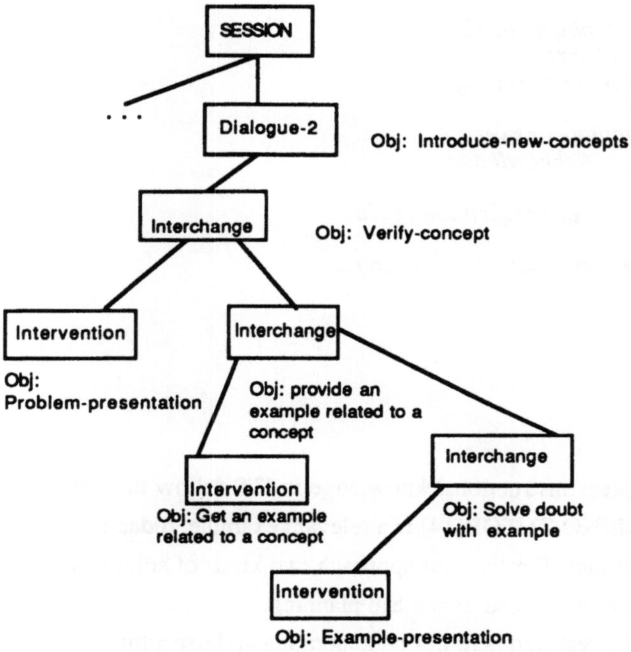

Figure 6: The new interchange to respond to the student request

The rest of the dialogue corresponds to the development of the strategy "verification by problem resolution".

First of all a problem is proposed, the student writes a buggy solution and the tutor provides some hint together with an indication to try it again

T18 try to do the exercise now .
S9 {buggy answer}
.... *Evaluate answer*
.... *Repair*
.... *Hint*
T19 You have some little problems. Remember that the type of arguments has to be indicated
.... *repeat problem*
T20 Try again

S10{right answer}
.... *Evaluate answer*
.... *Acknowledge*
T21 O.K. now it is right
.... *Update student model*

Another problem is proposed, the student gives a right answer, and then the strategy verifying is accomplished. T25 is the indication to continue the teaching session with the learning of a new concept.

.... *Select a problem, level = 2*
.... *Send text*
T22 Solve the following one: given....
S11{right answer}
.... *Evaluate answer*
.... *Acknowledge*
T23 O.K.
..... *End of Verification of Nc*

T24 Let us now introduce a new concept...

Related work

Techniques to express instructional knowledge in ITS follow three main streams: transition graphs, of which MENO-TUTOR[14] is a relevant example, didactic rules, as in GUIDON[2] and planning techniques. For this last approach two kinds of solutions have been considered, the classical Strips-like [9] , and dynamical planning.

The research presented here lies on generating and executing an instructional plan in an interleaved way, using skeletal plans. An analogous solution was developed at the same time by [8]. This trend is being pursued now in diverse on-going projects [11] based on different architectures.

Natural language dialogue management is an active area in computational linguistics. However concerning ITS interfaces only few attempts to use natural language are reported in the literature. Most of the current systems focus on the "what to say" i.e. the generation of knowledge to be communicated to the student [1,12,13,15]. Student input is usually handled by menus or intermediate formal languages.

Summary

We have presented a framework to represent instructional knowledge and carry out natural language tutorial dialogues.

We have developed our ideas under one main assumption: tutoring is a cooperative process, involving two intelligent agents. This viewpoint implies on the one hand a flexible tutorial control and on the other hand dialogue management including recognition of student's intentions. We have proposed to separate the NL- Discourse model from the Instructional one and we have identified their functional role for carrying out educational dialogues.

The instructional component is domain-independent and relies on a dynamical planning approach implemented by means of a blackboard architecture.

Our planner provides a set of generic objects in order to represent, in a declarative way, the knowledge involved in tutoring tasks: instructional knowledge source, strategy, goal, plan and selection rule. From a functional point of wiev four components are distinguished, encapsulating different kinds of instructional activities: pedagogic, thematic, teaching and supervising.

The interface handles communication in natural language. It includes a level for dialogue representation, so that the output of the parsing process provides an interpretation of the student's utterances.

Dialogue representation includes three structures, to reflect dialogue segmentation, participant's intentions and focus of attention.

Future developments fall into two main categories:

1. To develop a module to assist in eliciting tutoring knowledge, i.e. to provide interactive tools in order to a) inspect the instructional knowledge bases, b) define and include other goals, plans, rules or strategies, c) simulate plan execution in to figure out the import of the modifications.
2. To extend the capacity of the interface to carry out tutor explanations in natural language.

Acknowledgments

The research reported here was supported in part by the author's contract nº1381/82 with the CAYCIT, Spanish National Research Agency. Development of the tutor component and the natural language interface has been carried out by A. Díaz, I. Fernández and H. Rodriguez. Other contributions to the linguistic study for the system described have been made by: I. Castellón,T. Martí, M. Taulé. The equipment used was partly granted by Digital Equipment Corporation.

References

1. Cawsey, A.:The structure of tutorial discourse. Proc. of Artificial Intelligence and Education 1989, Amsterdam, pp. 47–53. IOS 1989.

2. Clancey,W.: Tutoring rules for guiding a case method dialogue. In Intelligent Tutoring Systems. D. Sleeman and J. Brown (eds.), pp. 201–225. Academic Press 1982.

3. Díaz, A., Rodriguez, H., Verdejo, M.F.: A mechanism for ellipsis resolution. Proc. of COLING 90, Helsinki (Finland), July 1990, pp. 452–454.

4. Díaz de Illarraza: Gestión de diálogos en lenguaje natural para un sistema de enseñanza inteligente. Tesis Doctoral. Universidad del País Vasco. 1990.

5. Fernández, I., Díaz, A., Verdejo, M.F.: A cooperative architecture for tutorial tasks. Proceedings of Expert Systems and their applications. 8th International Workshop, pp. 107–126 (Vol 2), Avignon 1988.

6. Fernández, I:Estrategias de enseñanza en un sistema inteligente de enseñanza asistida por ordenador. Tesis Doctoral. Universidad del País Vasco. 1989.

7. Grosz, B., Sidner, C.: Attention, intentions and the structure of discourse. Computational Linguistics Vol. 12, No. 3, 1986.

8. Murray, W: Control for intelligent tutoring systems: a blackboard-based dynamic instructional planner. Proc. of Artificial Intelligence and Education 1989, Amsterdam, pp. 150–168. IOS 1989.

9. Peachey, D., McCalla, G.: Using planning techniques in intelligent tutoring systems. International Journal on Man-Machine studies 24, pp. 77–98,1986.

10. Rodriguez, H: Guai, un generador de interfaces en lengua natural.Tesis doctoral Universidad Politécnica de Cataluña, Nov 1989.

11. Van Marcke, K.: GTE, a generic tutoring environment. Dida*Lab TR 89-19-03. May 1990

12. Winkels, R., Breuker, J., Sandberg, J.: Didactic discourse in intelligent help systems. Proceedings of the International Conference on Intelligent Tutoring Systems. pp. 279–285. Montréal 1988.

13. Wolz, U.:Tutoring that responds to user questions and provide enrichment. Proc. of Artificial Intelligence and Education 1989, Amsterdam, pp. 330–337. IOS 1989.

14. Woolf, B., McDonald, D.: Building a computer tutor: Design Issues. Computer IEEE, pp. 61–73 (Sept. 84)

15. Woolf, B. Murray,T.: A framework for representing tutorial discourse. Proc. of 10 IJCAI Conference, pp. 189–192. Milan 1987.

Uses of ITS: Which Role for the Teacher?

Martial Vivet
Laboratoire informatique, Université du Maine BP 535, F 72017 Le Mans Cedex, France, Tel: 33 4383 3211, fax: 33 4383 3366

Abstract: We examine here the role of the context around the learner when using an ITS facing the problem of integration of ITS in their context of uses. Questions are raised which impose constraints during the design of ITS themselves. For example, if a teacher is available near the learner, which role for this teacher? What about the knowledge the system has of this role? If there is a group of learners and few teachers, which representation of the available possibilities to help the learner? How to share teacher's time between different learners? What place for possibilities of experiments and hands-on work by learners in experimental sciences? How to take account of such possibilities? We describe some possible scenarios for use and explore some needs which are generally ignored when designing ITS.

Keywords: Didactical context, Intelligent Tutoring Systems, Pedagogical scenarios, Role of the teacher.

Introduction

The purpose is here to explore the possible uses of Intelligent Tutoring Systems (ITS). The study of the relative places for the teacher (if present!) and the learner underlines some needs which are generally not faced by the systems. Our hypothesis is that studying scenarios of uses for ITS can change the design of such systems. From the research point of view, facing the need for explicit representation of the help which can be provided by a teacher to a learner using an ITS is a way to work on elicitation and representation of pedagogical knowledge.

The first questions here are :

- Q1 : "Do we assume a student uses an ITS alone?" Or
- Q2 : "Is there a teacher available during, before, after use?"

According to the answers to such questions, we have to be precise about the possible roles of the teacher(s).

We try here to show how important is the need for study about the uses of ITS, pedagogical scenario for work with such tools, influence of the contexts around the learner.

The Dream ....

A possible dream consists in trying to write "automatic teachers"! The history of Computer Assisted Learning (CAL) shows us how prudent we must be, even if new techniques, tools, machines are now available.

1. If we assume the ITS can be used without any human help for the learner then we need very powerful possibilities in interaction management, dialogue control, student modeling, plan recognition...

Reaching high level of flexibility in dynamics during the sessions is still very hard. Will it be one day possible? Perhaps machine learning techniques can help ?

Our conviction is that this is perhaps only a dream and in any case, we need a long time to reach success.

2. We have to face this dream as a possible challenge because it is a way to move point of views on education, learning, teaching; We know that major progress on the earth has been achieved by trying to realize dreams: conquering the moon thirty years ago could have be seen like this! So, this dream is useful to go ahead and do progress in educational sciences, in cognitive psychology, in artificial intelligence.

3. Progress is also possible if we assume the learner is not alone when working with the ITS. "Not alone" means here that a human resource is available in real time for the learner, this resource being effectively present near the learner or being reachable by remote access.
If we do not assume such isolation of the learner while working with an ITS, then new questions arise:

– What about the role of the teacher(s), the tutor(s)?
– Is the teacher here only because the ITS is deemed to be fallible? In case of difficulty the system will delegate the management to the teacher.
– Which organisation around the ITS seen as an additional educational resource in a learning environment?

The ITS is here because it allows the construction of a specific learning situation, a situation designed and/or needed by the teacher. The ITS is thus a component of a didactical situation, and its use is a phase among others during a didactical sequence.

– Which scenario to play for effective work?

In each case, how does the teacher control the didactical situation and the results from the learning point of view? Is the ITS able to characterize in a pertinent pedagogical way a session or a part of a session with the learner?

Teacher(s) in the Scenario

The chosen way here is to explicit different scenarios for use of ITS to underline some needs and possible feedback on the design of such systems. We havė no claim for the moment about how complete is such a list of scenarios! The purpose is more in trying to open tracks for progress.

Each scenario can be described in terms of actors, conditions and possible contexts. Doing so helps the specification process and specific needs appear for each scenario. It becomes clear that in each case, we have to define precisely the relative places of the ITS and the teacher into the didactical system. We need to study carefully systems managing the relation [learner, teacher, knowledge] with a didactical systemic approach.

1- <u>scenario 1</u> :

ACTORS :

- one teacher + one learner

CONDITION, CONTEXT :

- the learner is lost in a session,
- the system is lost, unable to manage the interaction, misunderstanding what happens,...

NEED :

- the system must have the possibility
    - to know by itself that it is lost
    - to decide that a human being can do better

To do so, the system must include deeper knowledge for self-observation.

- the system may have knowledge about the kind of help the teacher can provide.

2- <u>scenario 2</u> :

The teacher's time is shared between set of co-learners who can work intensively while the teacher is busy with a co-learner;

A separate system is available per learner with no sharing of the sessions. At best, a network with E-mail between the workstations.

ACTORS :

- one teacher
- a group of learners

CONDITION, CONTEXT :

- a learner lost in a session,
- a system lost, misunderstanding what happens,...

NEED :

- once more, the system must have the possibility

  to know by itself that it is lost

  to decide that a human being can do better
- the system may have knowledge about the kind of help which can be provided.

Who have the best possibility to help ? Is it the teacher?, Is it a co-learner? Are they available to provide such a help?

- the system must know what the teacher is doing.

  Is it free now ?

  Is it busy for a long time?,...

We need here systems able to deliver didactical explanations, allowing the teacher to take the control of the didactical situation following what have been done. Is the system able to deliver summary of the didactical state? We need here didactical post-analysis of the interaction tracks.

- determination of how many students a tutor can help.

Pertinent at the economical and pedagogical points of view.

3- scenario 3 : Managment of a didactical sequence involving collectively one teacher and a set of learners.

The teacher's time is shared between a set of co-learners who can work intensively while the teacher is busy with a co-learner;

The system is written to share sessions between co-learners. Each co-learner can have access to the work done by the others.

ACTORS :

- one teacher + group of linked co-learners

CONDITION, CONTEXT :

- a learner lost in a session,
- system written to share sessions between co-learners

- system lost, unable to manage the dialogue, misunderstanding what happens for a learner,...

NEED :

- supervisor function to manage the work of the teacher and the co-learners

TIME management have to be studied carefully

- the system must have the possibility

to know by itself that it is lost

to decide that a human being can do better

- the system may have knowledge about the kind of help the co-learners or the teacher can provide. Determination of the student having the possibility to deliver advise : this can be time consuming for him (her) but from the pedagogical point of view, this can help him (her) because expliciting to others is a way to learn!

- study of pedagogical strategies based on "learning by explaining , expliciting" to a co-learner.

- determination of how many students a tutor can help.

- sharing of students models.

REMARKS :

i) this scenario can be derived by droping the teacher. The technical problems are more or less the same: managment by the ITS of a collectivity of learners.

ii) open possibilities in such cases :

It would be interesting to reach interactions like :

- "Compare your answer to this exercise with that by Hardy ..."

- "with Laurel, examine how you can ..."

4- <u>scenario 4 :</u> distance teaching...

ACTORS :

- group of learners, + teacher or group of teachers

CONDITION, CONTEXT :

- learners & teacher(s) linked via computer conferencing

- system lost , misunderstanding what happens,...

NEED :

- the system must have the possibility

to know by itself that it is lost

to decide a human being can do better

- the system may have knowledge about the kind of help the teacher(s) , the co-learner(s) can provide and when it can be provided

==> who in the network can answer at the best ?

It may be a co-learner, a teacher

==> need for representation of abilities, competences available

- Teachers representation ? sharing of student models....
- TIME management have to be studied carefully.

The context

The above observations show how it is important to take account of the human context when using ITS. Presence of people is not the only element in the context even if it is a major element to help in socialisation of knowledge. Other elements in the context can be important: for example, we have to wonder about the place of manipulations, hands-on when learning experimental sciences; "learning by doing" is important here and the systems have to allow such possibilities with effective physical devices. Working with screen simulations is not enough generally.

Rich contexts can help to develop creativity, discovery attitudes, inductive inferences. The work done around the design of learning environments and micro-worlds have to be merged with work done around ITS.

To enlarge the ideas developped at the beginning, let us list elements wich can be found in the context and which can be "known" by an ITS.

1- teacher(s)

The above part shows the importance for a system to know about the available teacher(s) in the environment of the learner(s).

The basic needs concern the representation of the kind of help which can be delivered and information to manage time.

2- co-learners

They can play a very important role for socialisation of knowledge, help in elicitation, formulation, formalisation

- relevant to re-enforce activity at the metacognitive levels
- need representation of co-learners (abilities, results, activity in order to manage time). This is pertinent for help during the sessions.

3- <u>experiments</u>

- When training learners with in experimental sciences like physics, chemistry, one of the major question is "which place for the manipulations?"

- We know that learning with physical devices differ from learning with only simulations and it could be interesting for an ITS to know about the possibility for the learner to do experiments.

So according to the answer to the question " is the work station for the learner into a laboratory or not?", the pedagogical strategies can be very different.

- Are the ITS to be reducted to only knowledge transmission ? Do we have to focus more on intelligent help ?

Open possibilities concern :

==> advising during manipulations [Courtois J. 88]

==> dialog to help in interpretation of data coming back from experiment;

From the interaction point of view, can we imagine loops like (explanation by the tutor -> determination of a relevant experiment -> manipulation by the learner -> interpretation of data coming from the hands-on ->)

- Need for :

- an appropriate representation of what can be done at the experimental point of view.

- "qualitative reasoning", qualitative physics in the usual AI sense to allow useful helps ?

4- <u>multimedia tools</u>

- description, explicit representation of knowledge available on the different medias.

- knowledge about the relevance of this media for specific learners

==> criteria to chose how to illustrate a given statement in a given didactical situation

- recovering of the control after browsing.

If we refer to "learning by browsing" :

==> how to manage time ? how to decide we can leave the learner browsing freely ? How to extract information (path followed in the base, item discovered, item which produced a cognitive conflict,...) from the work done like this?

==> how to check what have been learnt if the student works completely free ?

The Relative Places of the ITS and the Context

We examine here the relative places of the ITS in possible contexts of learning. Different schemes to organise learning resources for collective uses are possible.

A usual organisation is to put in a classroom only a teacher and a blackboard in front of a set of pupils. We know how effective and/or limited this can be. A second stage can be to have a blackboard ahead and experiments at the rear of the room. This allows some collective demonstrations or specific hands-on by few pupils. Possible rich scenarios can be reach by having these pupils explaining to others what they have done, etc. With ITS this can be similar and a possible scenario is to have a blackboard ahead and one ITS station at the rear, in a class room. This allows personal work for pupils at specific moments. The problem arises when generalising the possibilities to larger groups. For experiments, observations, the creation of specific rooms for practice is a usual way even if opening experimental possibilities can be done by access to an open museum. The first problem is here to have such access; The second one is in the organisation of the museum: possibilities for personal manipulations, individualised access to resources must be present. This is now well understood by most museum managers. We can also reach the concept of exploratorium as described by P. Dickson [Dickson 90]. Doing so, an ITS can be seen as a resource in an exploratorium. This can be interesting because a possible organisation is to share the time of differents pupils between several activities, some ones exploring the micro-world, other ones working on an ITS station to reinforce their knowledge to meet their needs about the space around them. So, the ITS is an additional resource, leaving the teacher more free to help in explorations. The presence of the teacher being interesting to help the ITS as pre-described in the scenarios 1-4. We so reach an integration of the ITS in the world where it is used. The balance of such activities inside the classroom and in the exploratorium is not very easy to manage. The classroom is used for synthesis periods, additional content transmissions,... The last step could be to have the class-room as a resource in the exploratorium. We thus get a learning space where children can share their time between hands-on, exploration, transmission and verification of knowledge with ITS, facing at some well defined moments a blackboard. The role of a teacher in such an environment is surely very different and need to be studied in itself!

Conclusion

Our problem is not for the moment to try to implement all theses ideas. But having them in mind can help us make progress in the field. The analysis of scenarios for use of ITS must have an influence on the design of them. This kind of analysis is necessary when designing ITS shells. We need to define architectures allowing to take account of a context. The work to be done to represent and exploit this context would be as difficult as that done for student modeling.

Another aspect could be interesting: representing the kind of help which can be provided by a teacher is a way to reinforce work on pedagogical knowledge: elicitation and representation of didactical knowledge and validation of such knowledge. Doing so, work in ITS appear as a possible laboratory for educational sciences. This could also be interesting to train teachers. A major challenge if we don't believe that it will be possible one day to replace teachers by systems!

References

1. Clancey W.J. (1983) The epistemology of a rule based expert system - a framework for explanations, Artificial Intelligence 20, 215-251.

2. Courtois J. (1988) SIAM: système intelligent pour l'apprentissage du diagnostic technique, Montréal-ITS88, pp. 327-333.

3. Dickson P. (1990) Environments for interactive learning: the computer exploratorium, private communication.

4. Genesereth (1982) The role of plans in intelligent teaching systems. In Intelligent tutoring systems, D. Sleeman, J.S. Brown (eds.), Academic Press, pp. 134-155.

5. Mandl H., Lesgold A.M. (eds) (1988) Learning issues for intelligent tutoring systems, Springer-Verlag, New York.

6. Nicaud J.F., Vivet M. (1988) Les tuteurs intelligents: réalisations et tendances de recherche, synthèse sur les tuteurs intelligents, revue Techniques et Science Informatiques -TSI, vol 7, n°1, Jan. 1988.

7. Nicolas P. (1989), Construction et vérification de figures géométriques dans le système MENTONIEZH, Thèse de l'Université de Rennes 1.

8. O'Shea T., Bornat R., Du Boulay B., Eisenstadt M., Page I. (1984) Tools for creating intelligent computer tutors. In: Human and artificial intelligence, Elithor, Banerjii (eds.), North-Holland.

9. Ohlsson S. (1986) Some principles of intelligent tutoring . Instructional Science 14, Elsevier, Amsterdam, pp. 293-326.

10. Papert S. (1980) Mindstorms: children, computers and powerful ideas, Basic Books, New York.

11. Py D. (1989), MENTONIEZH: an ITS in geometry, 4th international conference on AI & education, Amsterdam, pp. 202-209.

12. Ross P. (1988). Plan recognition for intelligent tutoring systems, Frascati, May 1987, Artificial Intelligence Tools in Education, P. Ercoli, R. Lewis (eds), pp. 29-38, North-Holland.

13. Self J. (1986). Artificial intelligence, Its potential in education and training, 5ième symposium canadien sur la technologie pédagogique, Ottawa, May 1986, pp. 69-77.

14. Self J. (1988a). Student Models : What Use Are They?, Frascati, May 1987, in Artificial intelligence tools in education, P. Ercoli, R. Lewis (eds.), North-Holland, pp. 73-86.

15. Self J . (1988b). Bypassing the intractable problem of student modelling, 4th Internatinal conference AI and Education, Amsterdam, May 1989.

16. Self J . (1989).The case of formalising student models (and ITS generally), ITS 88, Montreal, June 1988, pp. 18-24.

17. Sleeman D. and Brown J.S. (1982). Intelligent tutoring systems, Academic Press, London.

18. Vivet M. (1981), Apprentissage autonome, sur un usage de la technologie informatique dans l'éducation, Annexe du rapport SIMON, "Education et informatisation de la société", La documentation française.

19. Vivet M. (1987a). systèmes experts pour enseigner : méta-connaissances et explications, congrès CESTA : MARI-COGNITIVA 87, Paris, May 1987.

20. Vivet M. (1987b). Hierarchy of knowledges in an intelligent tutoring system; how to take account of the student, note interne CRIC, Presented during the European seminar on Intelligent Tutoring Systems, Tubingen, October 1987, pp. 25-31.

21. Vivet M. (1988a). Reasoned explanations need reasoning on reasoning and reasoning on the student,, Frascati, May 1987. Artificial intelligence tools in education, Paolo Ercoli, Robert Lewis (eds.), North-Holland (1988), pp. 121-128.

22. Vivet M., Futtersack M., Labat M. (1988b). Métaconnaissances dans les tuteurs intelligents. International Conference on Intelligent Tutoring Systems, Montréal, June 1988.

23. Vivet M. (1988c), Knowledge Based Tutors: Towards the design of a shell..., in International Journal for Educational Research and Instruction (IJERI), vol. 12, N°8, pp.839-850, 1988, Special issue edited by H. Mandl.

24. Vivet M. (1988d), la prise en compte du contexte avec les tuteurs intelligents, conférence invitée , Premier congrès européen "intelligence artificielle et formation", APPLICA 88, Lille, October 1988.

25. Vivet M., Carrière E., Delozanne E. (1988e), presentation of different aspects of AMALIA : a knowledge based system for mathematics, European summer university on intelligent tutoring systems, Le Mans, 1988, October 26 - November 2.

26. Vivet M. (1988f), Examination of two ways for research in advanced educational technology, Milton Keynes, OU, NATO Workshop on Advanced Educational Technolojy, November 11-12, 1988.

27. Vivet M. (1989), Which goal, which pedagogical attitudes with micro-robots in a class room ?, NATO Workshop on Advanced Educational Technology Student Development Of Physics Concepts: The Role Of Educational Technology, Pavia, Italy, October 1989.

28. Wenger E. (1987) , Artificial Intelligence and tutoring systems Computational and cognitive Approaches to the Communication of knowledge, Morgan Kaufmann.

29. Winans R.T., Whitaker E.T., Bonnel R.D. (1988), Theories of learning in computer-aided Instruction. Fifth International Conference on Technology and Education, Edinburgh, March 1988, pp. 86-89.

30. Yazdani (1986) . Intelligent tutoring systems survey, AI Review 1, pp. 43-52.

4 BELIEF SYSTEMS

A Belief Revision Model of Repair Sequences in Dialogue

Alison Cawsey
Department of Artificial Intelligence, University of Edinburgh, 80 South Bridge, Edinburgh, Scotland (ajc@aipna.ed.ac.uk)

Abstract: In any mixed-intiative dialogue it is important to be able to recognise and deal with problems and inconsistencies as they arise. For example, one participant may interpret an utterance in a way that was not intended. The other participant may be able to recognise this from the first participant's later utterance(s), and offer. a clarification. This type of misunderstanding and repair may occur frequently in tutorial and advisory dialogues, where, for example, one can not rely on users to be able to explicitly tell when they have misunderstood an utterance. This paper shows how a belief revision approach maybe used to model this, and related types of repair sequences in dialogue.

Keywords: Belief Revision, User Modelling, Dialogue, Repair, Miscommunication.

Introduction

Rather than presenting a general theory or approach to intelligent tutoring systems, this paper aims to illustrate some of the complexity of human communication by the detailed examination of a particular dialogue phenomena. We show how relatively formal AI techniques may be used to model this kind of dialogue, and so take one step further towards a computational account of human communication.

Understanding and developing formal models of how human dialogues work is arguably vital for the development of mixed initiative dialogue-based tutoring systems (e.g., [2,3,19]). In particular, in this type of dialogue it is important to be able to deal with both continually changing assumptions and apparent inconsistencies. These changing assumptions and inconsistencies may involve assumptions about the domain, assumptions about the user, and assumptions about each participant's interpretation of utterances in the discourse. We are therefore interested in how people resolve these inconsistencies, and deal with changing assumptions in a mixed initiative dialogue, and especially in the *repair* sequences which emerge as people deal with inconsistencies which become apparent in a dialogue.

This parer aims to show how a belief revision approach may be used to deal with these changing assumptions, and so provide the basis for a model of various dialogue phenomena. We will concentrate on how belief revision may be used as people attempt to resolve and clear up misunderstandings in the discourse, where the participant's interpretations of some utterance(s) have got out of step. This type of dialogue repair is vital for robust natural language dialogue systems, especially for tutorial and advisory systems, where misunderstandings are common.

The next section will introduce these repair sequences and discuss how they may be modelled using a belief revision approach. This will be followed by a brief discussion of belief revision, and two worked examples of how belief revision is used in dialogue repair.

Repair Sequences in Dialogue

Natural language is fundamentally ambiguous. Utterances may often only be understood in context, and misunderstandings frequently arise. One common cause of such misunderstandings is when one participant makes incorrect assumptions about the other's knowledge.

Where the problem is due to a lack of understanding, rather than a misunderstanding, this may result in an immediate clarification question (or *next turn repair initiator* [18]). However, sometimes misunderstandings are only recognised later in the discourse, when inconsistencies or lack of coherence[1] in the discourse become evident. This results in what have been termed third and fourth turn repairs [18,17].

Third turn repairs occur when one participant (say, A) says something, which is incorrectly interpreted by the other participant (B). B then says something which is inconsistent, or incoherent given A's intended interpretation, which causes A to change her assumptions about B's original interpretation and initiate a repair. The following example should illustrate this type of repair (taken from the author's own experience):

A: I think it's John's oral tomorrow.

B: Oh, he is going down to Cambridge?

A: No, I mean John Smith.

B: Oh, right.

Here, the second speaker (B) assumes that the first speaker is referring to John Levine - who is also just completing his PhD. The second utterance feflects that view (John Levine did his PhD at Cambridge, while John Smith - not is real name - did his at Edinburgh), and allows A to realise that her initial utterance was misunderstood. This leads to the clarification in the third utterance.

The examples illustrates how the assumption that the discourse is coherent allows each participant to use the other's utterances as evidence concerning the other's interpretation of their prior utterances. This is an important feature of discourse (developed by Clark & Schaefer [4] for example) which has been ignored in current work on user modelling in dialogue systems,

1 In this paper we will consider two utterances to be coherent if there are certain types of relationship between the two. In particular, we are in the relationships between speech act types (such as question-answer pairs, and other kinds of *adjacency pairs*), and relationships between the objects and events mentioned in the utterances.

where the tendency is to assume that the hearer (or user) will understand an utterance in the way the speaker (or system) intended (e.g., [11]). Clark and Schaefer develop a model of discourse *contributions*, which are the units of discourse whereby the participants arrive at the mutual understanding that some utterance was understood. Contributions have both a presentation and an acceptance phase, where the acceptance phase is the section of discourse in which the participants arrive at this mutual understanding that the presentation was understood. This type of discourse model seems to provide a better basis for user modelling than simply examining sequences of speech acts (or exchanges) alone, and is illustrated for a simpler variant of the above conversation in figure 1.

Fourth turn repairs occur when one participant realises, in a later turn, that their understanding of a prior utterance was correct, and indicates that they now understand it correctly. While third turn repairs tend to begin with "No, I mean..", fourth turn repairs tend to begin with "Oh, you mean" or just "Oh,.". In the following example (cited in [17,8]) B first interprets A's question as a presequence, indicating that A wanted to tell B who's going to the meeting (as in "Do you know who I saw the other day? It was")[2]. B therefore cooperatively

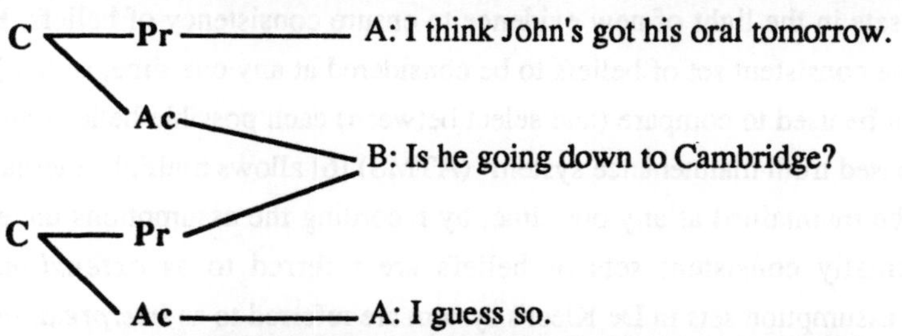

Figure 1: Discourse Contributions

asks A to tell him. On learning that A doesn't know who's going to the meeting, this forces B to re-interpret the original utterance as a request for information, and so tells A who he thinks is going:

A: Do you know who's going to the meeting?
B: Who?
A: I don't know.
B: Oh, probably Mrs Owen and...

In this example it is an inconsistency in the discourse which forces the re-interpretation. B's original interpretation was based on the assumption that A probably knew who was going, and does not make sense if she doesn't know.

---

2 Presequences are discussed by Levinson [14,ch6], for example.

Both these examples appear to involve belief revision. In third turn repair the first speaker revises her belief that the user will be able to interpret the given utterance in the intended way (which may in turn involve revising assumptions about the user's knowledge). In fourth turn repair the second speaker revises her belief concerning her interpretation of some prior utterance, prompted (in the above case) by an apparent inconsistency in beliefs about the first speaker. The basic mechanisms and organisation of repair sequences appears independent of the source of trouble [18]. However, in this paper we will only be concerned with the two types of trouble (or ambiguity) illustrated above-speech act and referential ambiguity.

Belief Revision and Cooperative Dialogues

So, what sort of belief revision model do we need to try and model these sorts of repair sequences? Truth (or reason) maintenance systems (e.g. [7,6]) show how a set of beliefs may be revised and made consistent given a new belief. Doyle's truth maintenance system [7] revises belief sets in the light of new evidence to ensure consistency of beliefs. However, he only allows one consistent set of beliefs to be considered at any one time, so his (and related) systems cannot be used to compare (and select between) each possible belief state. De Kleer's "assumption-based truth maintenance system" (ATMS) [6] allows multiple alternate consistent belief sets to be maintained at any one time, by recording the assumptions underlying these beliefs. Maximally consistent sets of beliefs are referred to as ***extensions*** while the characterising assumption sets in De Kleer's system are referred to as *interpretations*. This, and other truth maintenance systems are clearly described in [12], for example.

De Kleer's ATMS has been successfully used in, for example, plan recognition (e.g., Jones & Millington [10]), where given some initial steps in a plan there may be several alternate plans (or high level goals) consistent with these steps. As the user takes further steps in a plan, some of this partial plans may become dis-prefered, or inconsistent. The ATMS is a good tool for representing this alternate consistent contexts, and switching between them.

However, for belief revision an ATMS (or such) is insufficient. It must be possible to determine which is the preferred interpretation (or set of assumptions), so that there is some well-defined context to work within. Jones and Millington, for example, prefer interpretations with the fewest non-default assumptions.

One recent approach which deals with this issue of preferred interpretation and belief revision (given multiple consistent interpretations) is described by Galliers [9]. This model is developed as the basis for a theory of communication, and assumes that each assumption (in an interpretation) will have an associated *endorsement* [5]. These endorsements relate to the source of the assumptions (such as being told something first hand by a reliable person), and have some partial order defined among them, based on the reliability of the source. An ATMS is used to maintain the set of alternate interpretations, while belief revision (switching between interpretations) and a principle of minimal change. So, we prefer beliefs with well-supported assumptions, but prefer not to change our beliefs unless there is a good reason.

In order to explore certain ideas about belief revision in repair, a simple model of belief revision is used below. Like Galliers, we label all beliefs with their supporting assumptions, and give different types of endorsement to these assumptions. However, we do not maintain all possible extensions, merely revising the current belief set by the addition or removal of assumptions from the current context. Given an inconsistency in beliefs, the least endorsed assumption(s) which contribute to the problem are removed from the current context. This will result in a new set of valid beliefs, as these will depend on the assumptions in the current context.

Assumptions may be present for two reasons. They may be given as part of initial context, or they may be added because of the application of a plausible inference rule. For example, we could record in the initial context that the system assumes that the user knows that John hasn't submitted his PhD, or it might be derived by a *belief ascription* rule, which says that we assume that other agents hold the same beliefs we do unless their is some evidence that they do not. If it was derived by the latter (very weak) inference rule, we add that particular inference to the set of assumptions, with endorsement *belief ascription.* So the belief that the user knows that John hasn't submitted his PhD is now supported by both this assumption (the plausible inference) and by the system's belief that John hasn't submitted his PhD. If either one of these supporting assumptions are withdrawn the belief will no longer be valid.

The endorsements for assumptions initially held will normally be of the same sort as the endorsements for plausible inferences. For example, we might start initially with the assumption that the user knows that John hasn't submitted his PhD, with *belief ascription* as the endorsement. The initial premises and assumptions are those beliefs for which we are not concerned with how they were initially derived.

The current set of endorsements includes *belief ascription, plan inference* (supporting beliefs in the user's goals) and *belief transfer* (assuming that some communication has been successful). We also have un-named endorsement types *e1* and *e2* for cases in the example dialogues where it is unclear whère an assumption came from. A partial order is defined among these endorsements. The type of endorsements used are similar to Konolige and Pollack's plausible argument types [13], though they don't use these within a belief revision framework.

In the prototype system beliefs are represented as four argument predicates. The first argument is a unique identifier for that belief, the second the type of belief (assumption, premise, or inferred), the third the actual representation of that belief, and the last the support for that belief. The support may either be a type of endorsement (for assumptions), or a list of the identifiers of supporting assumptions (for inferred beliefs). In the examples below the second argument has been left out as non-essential.

Now, belief revision is important throughout cooperative dialogues. To see how the simple model above might be used in a normal conversation (not involving any kind of repair) consider the following example. Suppose B believes that John Levine hasn't submitted his PhD, that you can't have an oral until you submit your PhD, that A is honest and knows what she's talking about, and that "John" refers to John Levine. A then tells B that John has got his oral tomorrow. This is inconsistent with is current beliefs, so (in order to make them consistent) some belief must be abandoned - but which one? If any one of the above beliefs are abandoned the belief set will again become consistent. B may believe that A is lying, that she doesn't know what she's talking about, that "John" refers to someone else, that John Levine has in fact submitted his PhD and his having his oral, or that he's having his oral before submitting! The approach taken in this paper is to abandon the belief that is least well endorsed. In this example, B may have abandoned his assumption that John Levine hadn't submitted his PhD, because this was only a default assumption, based on the fact that he hadn't actually heard about him submitting. However, if this assumption was more strongly endorsed then our model might predict that B might say any of the following: "Which John?", "But he hasn't even submitted it yet." or "I don't believe you!"[3].

For examples like that above it is hard to be sure that belief revision is really taking place. However, in the third and fourth turn repair examples this is very obvious, as the participant's initial assumptions are revealed in their earlier utterances. The next section will therefore show how these types of repair may be modelled.

A Belief Revision Approach to Third and Fourth Turn Repair

In order to illustrate how a simple belief revision model may be used to model repair sequences, this section will give worked examples of the two repair sequences given in the second section.

Fourth Turn Repair

The example of fourth turn repair turns out to be fairly simple to model. A number of alternative interpretations of the initial speech act are possible, one of which is preferred because of a more strongly endorsed assumption. However, when that assumption is shown to be false, this causes the system to re-interpret that utterance:

---

[3] Note that similar reasoning is possible using default theories as Konolige's Hierarchical Auto-Epistemic Logic [1].

A: Do you know who's going to the meeting?

B: Who?

A: I don't know.

B: Oh, probably Mrs Owen and...

In the (implemented) example, the user inputs A's utterances in the form of surface level speech acts. The system's goal is to infer the user's intended indirect speech act and plan the appropriate response. Surface level acts are treated as premises ("certain" assumptions) - effectively we assume that the surface level utterance was mutually understood.

Rules for inferring possible indirect speech acts are based on Perrault and Allen's work [16]. It is treated as a plan inference problem, where the system first attempts to guess at a possible goal behind the surface speech act, then in responding to the user's question attempts to satisfy that derived goal, rather than the surface level act. For example, it might reason that a plausible reason for some agent asking whether someone knows something is because they want to know it. Using the indirect form minimises conflict in the case that the second agent does not know the answer.

Where we go beyond Perrault and Allen's approach is in recording the assumptions behind this interpretation, so that re-interpretation is possible if assumptions change. For example, in the above case (where some agent asks if the other knows something) the interpretation will depend on our assumptions about the speaker's prior knowledge, so we don't assume that someone wants to know something if we believe that they already know it. So, at each stage, the assumptions behind the various goals and beliefs are recorded. These will include assumptions about the user, as well as the assumptions that the various plausible inferences made are correct. Whenever belief revision takes place the interpretations of the past few utterances may easily be checked to see if they still appear to be valid, and if not the misunderstood utterance may be re-interpreted.

For the analysis below, three plan inference rules and four surface speech act definitions were required. These were similar to Perrault and Allen's, but allowed the derivation of the *pre-sequence* interpretation of the first utterance, where asking if the hearer knows something is interpreted as indicating that they want to tell the hearer, not that they want to know it.

Initially the system starts with the single assumption that the system believes that the user knows 'who's going', with endorsement *e1*. The user then enters a request that the system tell her whether it knows who's going[4].

Current Assumptions: [belief(b1, knowref(user, 'whos going')), e1]
Enter surface act:

[4] Typewriter font indicates system output, while *italics* indicate user input.

request(user, system, informif(system, user, knowref(system, 'who's going))).[5]

After the user's initial utterance the system uses the fact that it believes the user to already know who's going and uses the plan inference rules and speech act definitions to interpret the utterance as a pre-sequence indicating that the user wants the system to know who's going (b6). The system therefore (cooperatively) wants to know who's going (b7). These beliefs are given below, where the beliefs b2-b5 refer to the assumptions that the plan inference steps were correct (illustrated below by belief b4).

belief(b7, wants(system, informref(user, system, 'who's going'))), [b1, ..., b5])
belief(b6, wants(user, informref(user, system, 'whos going'))), [b1, ..., b5])
...
belief(b4, wants(user, knowif(user, knowref(system, 'whos going'))) ⇒
wants(user, knowref(system, 'whos going')), plan_inference)

Because the system now wants the user to tell it who's going, it request that the user inform it who's going (ie, asks who's going). This response involved using the speech act definitions and a set of planning rules to plan to achieve the system's goal.

System utterance: request(system, user,
informref(user, system, 'whos going'))

After the system's utterance (asking who's going) the user replies that they don't know who's going, using the representation below.

Enter surface act: *inform(user, system, not knowref(user, 'whos going')).*

However, the interpretation of this utterance results in the system believing that the user doesn't know who's going[6]. This conflicts with the belief b1 (the belief that the user does), so belief revision takes place. Now, the assumptions behind the former belief are relatively strongly endorsed. Effectively, we are assuming that the user, in saying that she didn't know, really meant the system to believe it (refered to as b9), and also wasn't trying to deceive the system (b10). There are therefore three alternative interpretations. These involve believing that you were mistaken about believing that the user knew who's going, that the user wants you to believe that she doesn't know - but she does really, or that the user may have said that she didn't know but didn't really mean you believe it. However, the least endorsed assumption

[5] This is the semantic form used for "Do you know who's going?", using the representation adopted by Perrault and Allen [16].

[6] This interpretation involves using plan inference to conclude that the user wants the system to know that she doesn't know who's going, then the system cooperative wanting to know that the user doesn't know who's going and adding this belief (with its supporting assumptions and plausible inferences) to the belief set.

behind the contradiction is the belief that the user knows who's going, so the first interpretation is the prefered one, and the assumption that the user knows who's going is removed from the current context.

Now, the interpretation of the first utterance as a pre-sequence is no longer valid in this new context. The system therefore attempts to re-interpret the first utterance (using plausible inferences b12-b15), and concludes that the user wanted to know who's going. The system therefore wants the user to know, and therefore tells the user, adding a marker ('Oh') to indicate that this is a re-interpretation. The important new beliefs are given below, along with the system output.

belief(b8, inform(user, system, not knowref(user, 'whos going')), [])
belief(b11, not knoeref(user, 'whos going'), [b8, b9, b10])
belief(b16, wants(user, informref(system, user, 'whos going')), [b8, ..., b15])
belief(b17, wants(system, informref(system, user, 'whos going'))), [b8, ..., b15])

System utterance: Oh,
System utterance: informref(system, user, 'whos going')

The main thing to get from this example is the idea that interpretations of utterances (as well as assumptions about the user) should not be seen to be fixed. They may be based on assumptions which change. In this example the interpretation of the utterance involved the derivation of the intended indirect speech act, while in the next example it involves the recognition of the intended referent. A general model of belief revision with endorsements may be used to explain these re-interpretations, using the same mechanism that changes in assumptions about the user or the world may be managed.

Third Turn Repair

This next example shows how the system can change its assumptions about the user's interpretation of a past utterance. This time the source of the ambiguity lies in the referent, rather than the speech act:

A: I think John's oral's tomorrow.
B: Oh, is he going down to Cambridge?
A: No, I mean John Smith.
B: Oh, right.

This example is important in illustrating the way that belief revision also applies to beliefs about the other participant's interpretation of past utterances, and how this interacts with beliefs about their knowledge. It won't be discussed in detail, but the important steps in the reasoning will be outlined.

Initially the system's preferred belief set includes the assumptions that the user knows that:

b1: If John Smith has his oral, then he won't be going to Cambridge.
b2: If John Levine has his oral, he will be going to Cambridge.
b3: John Levine hasn't submitted his PhD.
b4: If someone hasn't submitted their PhD they can't be having an oral.
b5 and b6: John Levine and John Smith are both called John.

These are represented below[7] .

Assumptions:

belief(b1, know(user,
    [has_oral(john_smith)] ⇒ not goes_to_cam(john_smith)), e2)
belief(b2, know(user,
    [has_oral(john_levine)] ⇒ goes_to_cam(john_levine)), e1)
belief(b3, know(user, not submitted_phd(john_levine)), e1)
belief(b4, know(user,
    [not submitted_phd(X)] ⇒ not has_oral(X))), e2)
belief(b5, know(user, name(john_levine, john)), e2)
belief(b6, know(user, name(john_smith, john)), e2)

The second belief is less well founded than the first - after all, B has never been to Cambridge so doesn't know about their PhD practices. The third especially is also weakly endorsed - A has no evidence that B knows whether or not John Levine has submitted his thesis, apart from knowing herself that he hasn't.

In the first utterance, the system chooses to refer to John Smith as John, as in the current context there is only one person mutually known called John who is in a position to be doing their oral. A more specific identifier of the person is therefore unnecessary. After this utterance the system assumes that the user heard and believe the utterance, correctly interpreted the referring expression, and therefore believes that John Smith has his oral. However, this belief is based on several assumptions, including the assumption that the user knows that John Levine hasn't submitted his PhD - if this wasn't the case then the user might have thought the

[7] Of course, these simple rules (especially b1 and b2) are more specific than those we would expect to actually be used in a general dialogue/reasoning system, but serve to illustrate the process of belief revision in dialogue given certain plausible domain specific inferences, as well as more general ones. We could represent the inference captured in b1 using a variety of more general inferences (such as the belief that people have their orals at the institution where they were registered for the research), but this would not contribute to what we are trying to model.

system meant John Levine. The system's utterance (in its simple semantic form) and the resultant system belief with its associate supporting assumptions is given below[8]:

System Utterance:

exists(X, name(X, 'John'), inform(system, user, [has_oral, X]))

New system belief:

belief(b8, know(user, has_oral(john_smith)), [b6, b3, b4, ...]).

However, after the user's utterance ('Is he going to Cambridge?') the system has a new belief - that the user wants to know if John Smith is going to Cambridge:

belief(b9, wants(user, knowif(user, [goes_to_cam, john-smith])), [b6, b3, b4, ...])

This belief is also supported by the assumptions b6, b3 and b4, as the referent for 'He' in "Is he going down to Cambridge" is based on assumptions about the user's interpretation of the referent in the previous utterance.

Now, using the plausible rule that people don't actively want things that are already true we can infer:

belief(b10, not knowif(user, goes_to_cam(john_smith)), [b6, b3, ...])

However, now we have a contradiction - B should have realised that if John Smith was having an oral then he couldn't possibly be going down to Cambridge, so would 'knowif' he was going. Belief revision is therefore necessary. It turns out that the preferred interpretation (according to the model of belief revision with endorsements used) involves dropping the two weakly endorsed assumptions b2 and b3. Given that the user doesn't know if John's going to Cambridge, the system will now infer that they interpreted 'John' to mean John Levine, and therefore offer the clarification in the third line. The current system may also attempt to address any apparent misconceptions inferred from the dialogue, and offer a cooperative response such as:

No, I mean -- exists(X, name(X, 'John Smith'),

inform(system, user, [has_oral, X]))

exists(Y, name(Y, 'John Levine'),

inform(system, user, not[submitted_phd, Y]))

---

8 The semantic form is mean to indicate that there is someone who is called John who has their oral, without comminting to a particular individual. This is all the information which could be obtained from the statement "John has his oral." without using the context to determine which individual is meant by 'John'.

or in English:

"No I mean John Smith. John Levine hasn't submitted his PhD yet."

This type of cooperative response is not possible in existing approaches (e.g. [13, 15]) which only consider the user's utterance(s), and not misconceptions and misunderstandings which become apparent through inconsistencies or incoherence between system and user utterances.

Now, this analysis is certainly not the only one possible. For example, it takes insufficient account of the fact that the discourse is likely to be coherent, as well as consistent, and that asking if John's going to Cambridge implies that it is deemed relevant to the current context. However, it shows how an inconsistency in a dialogue may prompt both a re-assessment of the user's interpretation of the system's past utterance, and also a revision of the system's model of the user's other beliefs. In this case the system concludes that the user doesn't know that you necessarily have Cambridge PhD orals in Cambridge, and doesn't know that John Levine hasn't yet submitted his PhD. Neither of these are obvious from the dialogue, and any simple approaches to user modelling in dialogue systems are likely to miss them.

It is unclear what should happen to the belief set after the clarification ("No, I mean John Smith"). The system should now believes John Smith to be having his oral - but should it still believe that the user doesn't know that John Levine hasn't submitted his PhD? Perhaps the user could only think of one John (John Levine) who was finishing his PhD, and on being told that he was having his oral revised his beliefs to believe that he had submitted his PhD, as discussed in section 3. Making these sorts of inferences seems to require treating the user model - as well as the user modelling/dialogue component - as a belief revision system.

Further Work

This research is still in its very early stages. Long term goals include modelling other aspects of cooperative dialogue using a belief revision approach[9]. However, in the immediate future certain extensions to the above work are envisaged.

First, the system must be extended to deal with the default assumption that the discourse is coherent. If it is found that two utterances are not (apparently) related this will prompt belief revision - but that revision may just involve removing the assumption that they are coherent.

Second, this overall framework should be able to support other types of repair, and be incorporated into a model of discourse contributions [4]. For example, if there are two alternate

[9] This work will be supported by a grant from ESRC/MRC/SERC, under the joint direction of Julia Galliers and Karen SparkJones, and based on the belief revision system described in [9].

(equally preferred) belief states this might prompt a clarification question to determine between them, while the user's backchannel utterances (yes, uhuh, etc.) may prompt various types of belief endorsement.

At the same time as developing a theoretical model of a dialogue repairs (based on belief revision) a small corpus of examples will be collected, concentrating on the third and fourth turn repairs discussed above. These will motivate the further research.

Conclusion: Belief Revision in Tutorial Dialogues

This paper has illustrated how a belief revision approach can explain some kinds of repair sequences in dialogue. These may involve re-interpreting a past utterance - or re-assessing how the user has interpreted a past utterance of the system. But what has that to do with tutorial dialogues?

The example of third turn repair shows how the system can use the user's utterance to show what sense the user has made of the system's utterance. This is important for user modelling in any dialogue system (including tutorial), as the assumption in previous work has tended to be that the user either will, or probably will understand the system's utterance as intended (e.g. [11, 2]). It also shows how apparent inconsistencies in the details of a dialogue may prompt subtle changes in the system's assumptions about the user's knowledge.

However, a belief revision approach can be used for more than modelling third and fourth turn repair sequences. This is just an illustration of one way belief revision occurs in cooperative dialogue. In different contexts, inconsistent beliefs may prompt changes in beliefs about the world, or changes in beliefs about the user, with no re-interpretation of the discourse. If the user is also treated as a belief revision system the system may plan to strategically revise these beliefs. These, and other aspects of belief revision in cooperative dialogues are the subject of ongoing research introduced in [0].

Now, this is long term research with many immediate problems to be overcome before it is of practical use in tutorial or advisory systems. However, we believe that it represents an important direction for research in these areas, giving us in the short term a greater understanding of human communication, and in the long term the prospect of robust and cooperative natural language dialogue systems (such as tutorial dialogue systems), able to deal with the miscommunications which inevitably arise.

Acknowledgements

This research is being carried out under a Science and Engineering Research Council post-doctoral fellowship. I would like to thank Jean Carletta, Julia Galliers and John Levine (who has now submitted his PhD!) for helpful comments on this work.

References

1. Appelt, D. and Konolige, K.: A practical non-monotonic theory for reasoning about speech acts. In: *Proceedings of the 26th Annual Meeting of the Association of Computational Linguistics*, pp. 170-178, 1988.

2. Cawsey, A.: The structure of tutorial discourse. In: *Proceedings of de Fourth International Conference on Artificial Intelligence and Education* (D. Bierman, J. Breuker, and J. Sandberg, eds.), pp. 47-53, 1989.

3. Clancey, W.: *Knowledge-Based Tutoring: the GUIDOM system*. Cambridge, MA: MIT Press, 1983.

4. Clark, H. and Schaefer, E.: Contributing to discourse. *Cognitive Science*, vol 13, pp. 259-295, 1989.

5. Cohen, P.: *Heuristic Reasoning About Uncertainty*. London: Pitman, 1985.

6. de Kleer, J.: An assumption based truth maintenance system. *Artificial Intelligence*, vol 28, pp. 127-190, 1986.

7. Doyle, J.: A truth maintenance system. *Artificial Intelligence*, vol 12, pp. 232-272, 1979.

8. Fox, B.: Interactional reconstruction in real-time language processing. *Cognitive Science*, vol 11, pp. 365-388, 1987.

9. Galliers, J. R.: *Belief Revision and a Theory Communication*. Technical Report 193, Cambridge University Computer Laboratory, 1990.

10. Jones, J. and Millington, M.: Modelling unix users with an assumption-based truth maintenance system: some preliminary findings. In: *Reason Maintenance Systems and Their Applications* (B. Smith and G. Kellerher, eds.), pp. 134-155, Ellis Horwood, 1988.

11. Kass, R. and Finin, T.: Rules for the implicit acquisition of knowledge about the user. In: *Proceedings of the National Conference on Artificial Intelligence*, pp. 295-300, 1987.

12. Kellerher, G. and Smith, B.: A brief introduction to reason maintenance systems. In: *Reason Maintenance Systems and Their Applications* (B. Smith and G. Kellerher, eds.), pp. 134-155, Ellis Horwood, 1988.

13. Konolige, K. and Pollack, M.: Ascribing plans to agents. In: *Proceedings of the 11th International Joint Conference on Artificial Intelligence*, 1989.

14. Levinson, S. L.: *Pragmatics*. Cambridge: Cambridge University Press, 1985.

15. McCoy, K. F.: Correcting object-related misconceptions: how should the system respond. In: *Proceedings of COLING 84*, pp. 444-447, 1984.

16. Perrault, C. R. and Allen, J.: Plan-based analysis of indirect speech acts. *Computational Linguistics*, vol 6, pp. 167-183, 1980.

17. Schegloff, E.: Pre-sequences and indirection: Applying speech act theory to ordinary conversation. *Journal of Pragmatics*, vol 12, pp. 55-62, 1988.

18. Schegloff, E., Jefferson, G. and Sacks, H.: The preference for self-correction in the organisation of repair in conversation. *Language*, vol 53, pp. 355-361, 1984.

19. Woolf, B. and McDonald, D.: Context-dependent transitions in discourse. *Proceedings of the National Conference on Artificial Intelligence*, pp. 355-361, 1984.

A Structure for Epistemic States

João Pavão Martins
Instituto Superior Técnico, Av. Rovisco Pais, 1000 Lisboa, Portugal

Abstract: In this paper, we investigate structure and the rules that should underlie a computer program that is capable of revising its beliefs or opinions. Such a program maintains a model of its environment, which is updated to reflect perceived changes in the environment. This model is stored in a knowledge base, and the program draws logical inferences from the information in the knowledge base. All the inferences drawn are added to the knowledge base.

Among the propositions in the knowledge base, there are some in which the program believes, and there may be others in which the program does not believe. Inputs from the outside world or reasoning carried out by the program may lead to the detection of contradictions, in which case the program has to revise its beliefs in order to get rid of the contradiction and to accommodate the new information.

Keywords: Belief revision, truth maintenance systems, reasoning

Introduction

In this paper, we investigate the structure and the rules that should underlie a computer program that is capable of revising its beliefs or opinions. Such a program is called a *Belief Revision System*, BRS for short. We assume that the BRS maintains a model of its environment, which is updated to reflect perceived changes in the environment. This model is stored in a knowledge base, a set of logical sentences, and the BRS draws logical inferences from the information in the knowledge base. All the inferences drawn are added to the knowledge base.

Among the propositions in the knowledge base, there are some in which the BRS believes, and there may be some others in which the BRS does not believe. Inputs from the outside world or reasoning carried out by the BRS may lead to the detection of contradictions, in which case the BRS has to revise its beliefs in order to get rid of the contradiction and to accommodate the new information. This change of beliefs should be preceded by a decision about what proposition is the culprit for the contradiction, its disbelief, and the subsequent disbelief of every proposition that depends on the selected culprit.

In our work, we take the word "belief" to denote *justified belief*: a proposition is believed by the BRS either because it was told so or because it depends on other believed propositions. When the BRS considers another set of beliefs, we say that *it changes its beliefs*.

There is a rich tradition in Artificial Intelligence related to the study of systems that maintain dependencies among propositions and are able to cope with the detection of contradictions, Truth Maintenance Systems [Martins 1990]. These systems, however, merely record dependencies as told by an outside system, the problem solver, and have no reasoning capabilities. In the philosophic literature, there is also work concerning the study of changing one's mind due to the occurrence of contradictions [Gärdenfors 1988, Gärdenfors and Makinson 1988, Harman 1986, Stalnaker 1984]. This work, however, is not concerned with the computer implementation of the theories developed and, furthermore, assumes logical omniscience, i.e., all the consequences of the premisses are known, which is unrealistic from a practical point of view.

The work reported in this paper pertains to both approaches by defining a model for maintaining belief states, for carrying out reasoning within these belief states, and for revising beliefs whenever contradictions are detected. [Gärdenfors 1988] proposes that the actual or possible cognitive state of an individual be characterized as an *epistemic state*. Epistemic states change under epistemic inputs. Gärdenfors makes no commitment concerning the content and structure of epistemic states, describing general properties that epistemic states verify assuming logical omniscience. In this paper we propose a structure for representing epistemic states (which we call *belief spaces*) and define how they change under epistemic inputs. Our main concern here is to present a model which can be implemented using a computer program, the BRS.

In the next section we describe the underlying inference mechanism for epistemic states, then we define belief spaces (corresponding to Gärdenfors' epistemic states) and finally we present the behavior of belief spaces under epistemic inputs, discussing what happens when a contradiction is detected.

SWM*

A program capable of changing its beliefs has to keep a record of where each proposition in the knowledge base came from - the *support* of the proposition. The support is used both during the identification of the possible culprits for a contradiction and in the process of changing the system's beliefs. In this section, we discuss a logic, SWM*,[1] that was developed to support BRS. The interesting aspect of supporting a BRS in SWM* is that the dependencies among

[1]After Shapiro, Wand, and Martins. The SWM* system is a sucessor to the SWM system [Martins and Shapiro 1983, 1988], which, in turn, is a sucessor to the system of [Shapiro and Wand 1976].

propositions are computed by the system itself rather than having to force the user (or an outside system) to do this, as in many existing systems.

SWM* is loosely based on relevance logic [Anderson and Belnap 1975]. The main features of relevance logic used in SWM* are the association of each wff with (1) a set containing all hypotheses (non-derived propositions) that were *really* used in its derivation (the origin set) and (2) the statement of the rules of inference taking origin sets into account, specifying what should be the origin set of the resulting wff.

Another important issue in systems capable of revising their beliefs consists in the recording of the conditions under which contradictions may occur. This is important, because once the BRS discovers that a given set is inconsistent, it may not want to consider it again, and even if it wants to consider it, it wants to keep in mind that it is dealing with an inconsistent set.

Knowledge states

A *knowledge state*, written [[KB, KIS]], is a pair contains a knowledge base (KB) and a set of known inconsistent sets (KIS). The *knowledge base* is a set of supported wffs (propositions, written as wffs, together with an indication of dependencies between that particular wff and other wffs in the knowledge base); the *known inconsistent sets* is a set containing those sets of wffs in the KB that are known to be inconsistent.[2]

A knowledge state is intended to represent the knowledge that we have at a particular moment: KB contains all the propositions that were received from the outside world up to that moment and the subset of their consequences that was derived so far; and KIS contains information about all the sets that have been discovered to be inconsistent. Since we do not consider logical omniscience, the knowledge base does not necessarily contain all the consequences that can be drawn from the propositions it contains. It may even happen that the knowledge base is inconsistent but that the inconsistency has not been discovered. Whenever new inconsistencies are detected, they are recorded in the known inconsistent sets.

The *knowledge base* is a set of supported wffs. Supported wffs are of the form $\langle A, \tau, \alpha \rangle$, where A is a wff with origin tag τ and origin set α. The pair (τ, α) is called the *support* of the supported wff $\langle A, \tau, \alpha \rangle$. The support of a supported wff is associated with a *particular*

[2] It is important to distinguish between a set *being* inconsistent and a set *being known to be* inconsistent. An inconsistent set is one from which a contradiction *can be* derived; a set known to be inconsistent is an inconsistent set from which a contradiction *has been* derived.

derivation of its wff. There are standard formation rules for wffs, and the language that they define is denoted by $\mathcal{L}$. The *origin tag* indicates how the supported wff was placed in the knowledge base (i.e., whether it was supplied by an outside system or was generated during deduction). It is an element of the set {*hyp, der, ext*}: *hyp* identifies hypotheses, *der* identifies normally derived wffs within SWM*, and *ext* identifies special wffs whose origin set was extended. A supported wff with *ext* origin tag has to be treated specially in order to avoid the introduction of irrelevancies (for a discussion on this issue see [Martins and Shapiro 1988]). The *set* indicates the dependencies of the supported wff on other wffs in the knowledge base. It is a set of hypotheses. The rules of inference of SWM* guarantee that the origin set of a supported wff contains *all and only* the hypotheses that were used in its derivation.

Some inference rules

The rules of inference of SWM* are grouped into two sets, pure logic rules and computational rules. *Pure logic rules* allow the introduction of new supported wffs into the knowledge base; *computational rules* update the information about sets known to be inconsistent.

The rules of inference make use of a function (Λ) to compute the origin tag of a supported wff resulting from the application of the rules of inference. The origin tag of a derived proposition will be *ext* if the origin tag of any of the propositions used in its derivation is *ext*, and will be *der* otherwise. The function Λ is defined as:

$$\Lambda(\tau_1, \tau_2) = \begin{cases} ext \text{ if } \tau_1 = ext \text{ or } \tau_2 = ext \\ der \text{ otherwise} \end{cases}$$

Pure logic rules

These rules correspond to traditional inference rules. They have the effect of adding new supported wffs to the KB. The addition of new supported wffs to the KB may be done in two different ways: a new supported wff is introduced from the outside (this is called a hypothesis) or a supported wff is derived from other supported wffs in the KB. Pure logic rules transform [[KB, KIS]] into [[KB′, KIS]] where KB $\subset$ KB′. The following are some of the pure logic rules:

Hypothesis (Hyp). From [[KB, KIS]] and any wff A$\in \mathcal{L}$, we may infer [[KB $\cup$ {<A, *hyp*, {A}>}, KIS]]. The wff A in <A, *hyp*, {A}> is called a *hypothesis*.

Negation Introduction ($\neg$I). This rule states that from the hypotheses underlying a contradiction we can conclude that the conjunction of any number of them must be false under the assumption of the others. From [[KB, KIS]], in which $<A\wedge\neg A, \tau, \alpha\cup\{H_1, ..., H_n\}>\in KB$, we may infer $[[KB\cup\{<\neg(H1 \wedge ... \wedge Hn), \Lambda(\tau, \tau), \alpha>\}, KIS]]$.

Implication Introduction ($\rightarrow$I).From [[KB, KIS]], in which $<C, der, \alpha\cup\{H\}>\in KB$, we may infer $[[KB\cup\{<H\rightarrow C, der, \alpha>\}, KIS]]$.

Modus Ponens - Implication Elimination (MP): From [[KB, KIS]], in which $<A,\tau_1, \alpha_1 \in>KB$ and $<A\rightarrow B, \tau_2, \alpha_2 \in>KB$, we may infer $[[KB\cup\{<B, \Lambda(\tau_1, \tau_2), \alpha_1\cup\alpha_2>\}, KIS]]$.

And Introduction (ΛI).From [[KB, KIS]] in which $<A, \tau_1, \alpha>\in KB$ and $<B, \tau_2, \alpha>\in KB$, we may infer $[[KB\cup\{<A\wedge B, \Lambda(\tau_1, \tau_2), \alpha>\}, KIS]]$; From [[KB, KIS]] in which $<A, \tau_1, \alpha_1>\in KB$, $<B, \tau_2, \alpha_2>\in KB$, and $\alpha_1\neq\alpha_2$, we may infer $[[KB\cup\{<A\wedge B, ext, \alpha_1\cup\alpha_2>\}, KIS]]$.

And Elimination (ΛE). From [[KB, KIS]] in which $<A\wedge B, \tau, \alpha>\in KB$, and $\tau\neq ext$, we may infer either $[[KB\cup\{<A, der, \alpha>\}, KIS]]$ or $[[KB\cup\{<B, der, \alpha>\}, KIS]]$.

Computational rules

These rules are triggered upon the discovery of inconsistent sets. They are obligatorily applied whenever a new inconsistent set is discovered. When this happens a new set is added to KIS. These rules transform [[KB, KIS]] into [[KB, KIS′]] in which $KIS \subset KIS'$.

Updating of Inconsistent Sets (UIS). This rule is obligatorily applied whenever a new contradiction is detected. From [[KB, KIS]] in which $<A\wedge\neg A, \tau, \alpha>\in KB$, and $(\forall s \in KIS)\ [s\not\subset\alpha]$,[3] we *must* generate the knowledge state $[[KB, KIS\cup\{\alpha\}]]$.

Derived Hypothesis (DH). This rule is obligatorily applied when a supported wff is derived such that there is already a hypothesis in the KB with the same wff and that hypothesis belongs to a known inconsistent set. Given [[KB, KIS]] in which $<H, hyp, \{H\}>\in KB$, $<H, \tau, \alpha>\in KB$, $\tau\neq hyp$, and $(\exists s \in KIS)$ [$(H \in s)$ and $(\forall r$

[3] This condition guarantes that the set α had not been discovered to be inconsistent.

$\in$ KIS) [r $\not\subset$ ((s - {H}) $\cup$ α)]],[4] then we *must* generate the knowledge state [[KB, KIS $\cup$ {σ: ($\exists$s $\in$ KIS) [(H $\in$ s *and* σ = (s - {H}) $\cup$ α) and ($\forall$r $\in$ KIS) [r $\not\subset$ σ]]}]].

Summary

Knowledge states are of the form [[KB, KIS]] in which:

1. KB is a set of supported wffs, a set whose elements are of the form <A, τ, α>, where A$\in \mathcal{L}$, $\tau \in$ {*hyp, der, ext*}, and $\alpha \subset \mathcal{L}$;

2. KIS is a set of sets of wffs, KIS $\subset 2^{\mathcal{L}}$.

The rules of inference of SWM* impose the following syntactic restrictions on the formation of knowledge states:

1. The origin set of every supported wff in the KB contains wffs that correspond to hypotheses existing in the KB:

$$(\forall < F, \tau, \alpha > \in \text{KB})\ (\forall H \in \alpha)\ [< H, hyp, \{H\}> \in \text{KB}].$$

2. For every wff appearing in a known inconsistent set, there is a corresponding hypothesis in the KB:

$$(\forall s \in \text{KIS})\ (\forall H \in s)[< H, hyp, \{H\}> \in \text{KB}].$$

We define derivability within SWM* ($\vdash_{SWM^*}$) as follows: Given [[KB, KIS]], we write

$$[[\text{KB, KIS}]] \vdash_{SWM^*} [[\text{KB}', \text{KIS}']]$$

if and only if there is a sequence of rules of inference of SWM* that transforms the knowledge state [[KB, KIS]] in the knowledge state [[KB$'$, KIS$'$]].

The rules of inference of SWM* guarantee the following results involving the derivability relation:

[4]This means that the set (s - {H}) $\cup$ α had not been discovered to be inconsistent.

1. Every supported wff in the KB can be derived from a subset of other supported wffs in the KB. Given [[KB, KIS]], $(\forall \mathcal{F} \in KB)\ (\exists \Delta \subset KB)$ such that:

$$[[\Delta, \{\}]] \vdash_{SWM^*} [[KB' \cup \{\mathcal{F}\}, KIS']].$$

2. The hypotheses in every known inconsistent set produce a contradiction. Given [[KB, KIS]], $\forall s \in$ KIS:[5]

$$[[\{<H, hyp, \{H\}>: H \in s\}, \{\}]] \vdash_{SWM^*} \{\{KB' \cup \{\bot\}, KIS']]\}].$$

Given a set of wffs $(\Delta \subset \mathcal{L})$ and a single wff $(C \in \mathcal{L})$, we say that the single wff is derivable from the set of wffs, written $\Delta \vdash C$, if and only if,

$$[[\{<H, hyp, \{H\}>: H \in \Delta\}, \{\}]] \vdash_{SWM^*} \{\{KB \cup \{< C, \tau, \alpha >\}, KIS]].$$

Belief spaces

As we said at the outset,among the propositions in the knowledge base, there are some in which theBRS believes and there may be some others in which the BRS does notbelieve.Inputs from the outside world or reasoning carried out by the BRS may lead to the detection of contradictions, in which case the BRS has to revise its beliefs in order to get rid of the contradiction and toaccommodate the new information.

Up to now, we have been concerned with the definition of the rules of reasoning of a BRS. In this section, we address the issues of defining the beliefs of a BRS based on SWM*. The BRS we define is called MBR, for Multiple Belief Reasoner.

We define a *context* to be a set of hypotheses. A context determines a *elief space*, which is the set of all hypotheses defining the context and all the wffs in KB that were derived exclusively from them. A belief space is represented by << [[KB, KIS]], C >>, where $(\forall H \in C)\ [< H, hyp, \{H\} > \in KB]$.

The belief space determined by a context is the subset of all the wffs existing in the KB that were derived (according to the rules of inference of SWM*) from the supported wffs corresponding to the hypotheses in the context. It contains those wffs that {\it have been derived} in the KB among all possible {\it derivable} wffs, which, again, stresses that we are

[5] The symbol $\bot$ denotes a contradiction.

not considering logical omniscience. The wffs in a belief space are characterized by the existence of a supported wff in KB with an origin set that is contained in the context, i.e.,

$$<< [[KB, KIS]], C >> = \{F: (\exists < F, \tau, \alpha > \in KB) \text{ and } (\alpha \subset C)\}.$$

Any operation performed by MBR (query, addition, etc.) is associated with a context. We refer to the context under consideration, i.e., the context associated with the operation currently being performed, as the *current context*. While the operation is being carried out, the only propositions that will be considered are the propositions in the belief space defined by the current context. This belief space will be called the *current belief space*. A proposition is said to be *believed* if it belongs to the current belief space.

Interaction with MBR

Gärdenfors [Gärdenfors 1988] defines epistemic inputs as "external forces" that are responsible for all changes in belief. In this section we define the epistemic inputs that are allowed in MBR. These epistemic inputs are functions from a belief space and a proposition into a belief space ($2^{\mathcal{L}} \times \mathcal{L} \Rightarrow 2^{\mathcal{L}}$). There are three different epistemic inputs:

1. *Assert hypothesis H*. The effect of this epistemic input is twofold, it adds the hypothesis $<H, hyp, \{H\}>$ to KB and also adds the hypothesis H to the current context. The effect of this input can be expressed as:
   Assert (<<[[KB, KIS]], C>>, H) =
   $$<<[[KB \cup \{<H, hyp, \{H\}>\}, KIS]], C \cup \{H\}>>.$$

2. *Deduce F*. This epistemic input originates inference in KB trying to deduce the wff F. The effect of this input depends on the contents of KB and on the wff F, but the following things can happen:

   (a) New supported wffs are added to the knowledge base. KB is transformed into KB′, where $KB \subset KB' \subset Cn(KB)$, where Cn(KB) is the set of all logical consequences of KB, it is defined as $Cn(KB) = \{\mathcal{F}: (\exists[[KB^*, KIS^*]])\ [\mathcal{F} \in KB^* \text{ and } [[KB, KIS]] \vdash_{SWM^*} [[KB^*, KIS^*]]]\}$. It may happen that $< F, \tau, \alpha > \in KB'$ and this is the desired result.

(b) During the inference originated by this input new contradictions may be discovered, and, in this case, KIS is updated.

(c) It may be discovered that the current context is inconsistent and that it should be revised (see next section).

The effect of this input can be expressed as:

$$\text{Deduce}\ (<<[[KB, KIS]], C>>, F) = << [[KB', KIS']], C'>>$$

where $KB \subset KB'$, $KIS \subset KIS'$, and $C' \subset C$.

3. *Add hypothesis H.* This epistemic input originates inference in KB trying to deduce consequences of the hypothesis H. The effect of this input depends on the contents of KB and on the hypothesis H, but the following things may happen:

   (a) New supported wffs are added to the knowledge base. KB is transformed into KB′, where $KB \subset KB' \subset Cn(KB \cup < H, hyp, \{H\} >)$. In this case $< H, hyp, \{H\} > \in KB'$.

   (b) During the inference originated by this input new contradictions may be discovered, and, in this case, KIS is updated.

   (c) It may be discovered that the current context is inconsistent and that it should be revised (see next section).

The effect of this input can be expressed as:

$$\text{Add}\ (<<[[KB, KIS]], C>>, H) = \\ <<[[KB' \cup \{<H, hyp, \{H\}>\}, KIS']], C' \cup \{H\}>>,$$

where $KB \subset KB'$, $KIS \subset KIS'$, and $C' \subset C$.

Detection of contradictions

When a contradiction is detected within MBR one of two things can happen, depending on whether the contradiction belongs to the current belief space or belongs to a belief space strictly containing the current belief space. The main difference between them is that the former may require changes in the current context and allows the deduction of new supported wffs, while the latter leaves this context unchanged and does not allow the addition of new wffs to the knowledge base.

Suppose that the current belief space is << [[KB, KIS]], C >> and that KB contains the supported wff $< A \wedge \neg A, \tau, \alpha >$. Suppose, furthermore, that α does not contain any member of KIS $((\forall s \in KIS)\ [s \not\subset \alpha])$, meaning that this contradiction had not been discovered yet. In this case, one of two things will happen:

1. *The contradictory wff does not belong to the current belief space*. This means that $\alpha \not\subset C$. In this case, the contradiction is recorded (through the application of UIS), but nothing more happens. The effect of doing so is to record that the set of hypotheses α is now known to be inconsistent.

2. *The contradictory wff belongs to the current belief space*. This means that $\alpha \subset C$. In this case, UIS is applied, resulting in the updating of the sets known to be inconsistent. The rule of ¬I can be applied (generating new supported wffs in the knowledge base) and a revision of beliefs should be performed if we want to work within a consistent belief space.

This revision of beliefs is accomplished by decreasing the current context. Since MBR only considers wffs in the current belief space, a decrease in the current context entails the removal of wffs from the current belief space. The resolution of a contradiction in the current belief space entails a *contraction* in Gärdenfors and Makinson's sense [Gädenfors and Makinson 1988]. This contraction is performed through a family of functions R_H^-, indexed by the wff, H, to be removed:

$$R_H^-(<< [[KB, KIS]], C >>) = << [[KB, KIS]], C - \{H\} >>.$$

From SWM*'s standpoint, after the discovery of the inconsistent set α ($\alpha \subset C$), the removal of *any one* of the hypotheses in α is *guaranteed* to remove this contradiction from the current belief space and restore unknown inconsistency to the current context if it was not known to be inconsistent before discovery of this contradiction.

Examples

Example 1: Flying horses

Suppose that we begin with the knowledge state [[{}, {}]], andthat we assert the following hypotheses.[6]

swff1: <White(Pegasus), hyp, {wff1}>
swff2: <Horse(Tornado), hyp, {wff2}>
swff3: <∀(x)[Horse(x) → ¬ Flies(x)], hyp, {wff3}>
swff4: <∀ (x)[WingedHorse(x) → Flies(x)], hyp, {wff4}>
swff5: <∀(x)[WingedHorse(x) → Horse(x)], hyp, {wff5}>
swff6: <∀(x)[WingedHorse(x) → HasWings(x)], hyp, {wff6}>

At this point, our knowledge state is:

[[{swff1, swff2, swff3, swff4, swff5, swff6}, {}]].

And the current belief space is:

<< [[{swff1, swff2, swff3, swff4, swff5, swff6}, {}]],
[[{swff1, swff2, swff3, swff4, swff5, swff6}>>.

Suppose, furthermore that we add the following hypothesis (Recall that this epistemic input originates inference, trying to deduce the consequences of the hypothesis *WingedHorse(Pegasus)*):

swff7: < *WingedHorse(Pegasus), hyp*, {*wff7*} >

In the current belief space, we can derive swff8, swff9, and swff10:

swff8: <¬ Flies(Pegasus), der, {wff3, wff5, wff7}>
swff9: <Flies(Pegasus), der, {wff4, wff7}>
swff10: <Flies(Pegasus) ∧¬ Flies(Pegasus), der,
{wff3, wff4, wff5, wff7}>

---

[6] We use the notation *swff1*: <*White (Pegasus) hyp*, {*wff1*}> to denote that <*White (Pegasus), hyp*, {*White (Pegasus)*}> is a supported *wff1* and that the wff *White (Pegasus)* is represented by *wff1*.

We thus discover that the set {wff3, wff4, wff5, wff7} is inconsistent. When this happens, the rule of UIS is applied, resulting in the following updated knowledge state:

[[{swff1, swff2, swff3, swff4, swff5, swff6, swff7, swff8, swff9, swff10\},
{{wff3, wff4, wff5, wff7}}]].

We should revise the system's beliefs by removing from the current context at least one hypothesis from the set {wff3, wff4, wff5, wff7}. The most natural decision would be to drop the hypothesis that $\forall (x)[\text{WingedHorse}(x) \rightarrow \text{Horse}(x)]$, and to consider the belief space:

<< [[{swff1, swff2, swff3, swff4, swff5, swff6, swff7, swff8,
swff9, swff10}, {{wff3, wff4, wff5, wff7}}]],
{wff1, wff2, wff3, wff4, wff6, wff7}>>.

Example 2: The Russell set

Suppose we have a knowledge state containing only one hypothesis, which states that there is a set, s, that contains all the sets that are not members of themselves:

$$[[\{<\exists(s)\forall(x)[\neg(x \mid x) \rightarrow x \mid s) \wedge (x \mid s \rightarrow \neg(x \mid x))], \textit{hyp}, \{\textit{wff1}\}\}>, \{\}]].$$

If we add the following hypothesis to the current belief space

$$\text{swff2: } < S \mid S, \textit{hyp}, \{\text{wff2}\}>$$

We generate the following supported wffs swff3 - using the rule of existential elimination - and swff4 - using the rule of universal elimination,[7] where "S" is *the* set containing precisely those sets that do not contain themselves):

swff3: $<\forall(x)[(\neg(x \mid x) \rightarrow x \mid S) \wedge (x \mid S \rightarrow \neg(x \mid x))]$, der, {wff1}>
swff4: $<(\neg(S \mid S) \rightarrow S \mid S) \wedge (S \mid S \rightarrow \neg(S \mid S))$, der, {wff1}>
swff5: $< S \mid S, \rightarrow \neg(S \mid S)$, der, {wff1}>
swff6: $<\neg(S \mid S)$, der, {wff1, wff2}>
swff7: $<(S \mid S) \wedge \neg(S \mid S)$, ext, {wff1, wff2}>
At this point, a contradiction is detected (swff7), triggering the application of UIS, which produces the knowledge state:

[7] These rules were not discussed in this paper, but their use is obvious (see [Martins and Shapiro 1988]).

[[{swff1, swff2, swff3, swff4, swff5, swff6, swff7}, {{wff1, wff2}}]]

We can apply the rule of $\neg$I to swff7 to infer swff8:

swff8: $<\neg (S \in S)$, ext, {wff1}$>$

We now revise the system's beliefs by applying the following contraction:

R^{-}_{wff2} (<< [[{swff1, swff2, swff3, swff4, swff5, swff6, swff7, swff8},
{wff1, wff2}}]], {wff1, wff2} >>) =
<< [[{swff1, swff2, swff3, swff4, swff5, swff6, swff7, swff8},
{wff1, wff2}}]], {wff1} >>

We can perform further reasoning, generating swff9 by $\wedge$E applied to swff3; swff10 by MP applied to swff8 and swff9; and swff11 by $\wedge$I applied to swff8 and swff10:

swff9: $<\neg (S \in S) \rightarrow S \in S$, der, {wff1}$>$
swff10: $<S \in S$, ext, {wff1}$>$
swff11: $<S \in S \wedge \neg (S \in S)$, ext, {wff1}$>$

Again, UIS is applied to swff11, resulting in the knowledge state:

[[{swff1, swff2, swff3, swff4, swff5, swff6, swff7, swff8,
swff9, swff10, swff11}, {{wff1, wff2}, {wff1}}]].

If further reasoning is to be performed in a consistent belief space, then wff1 (which is itself inconsistent) must be removed from the current context.

Summary

We discussed the structure and the rules that should underlie a computer program that is capable of revising its beliefs or opinions. The underlying model of this computer program is called MBR. MBR works with belief spaces (corresponding to Gärdenfors' epistemic states), sets of propositions that hold assuming some hypotheses (the context). We discussed the inferences allowed in MBR and the contradiction detection mechanisms. An implementation of MBR, is part of the SNePS system [Shapiro 1979], [Shapiro and Rapaport 1987], [Shapiro and Martins 1990], written in Common Lisp and running on Explorer and Symbolics Lisp Machines, Sun Stations, Macintoshes, and VAX systems at the Department of Computer Science, State University of New York at Buffalo, and at the Instituto Superior Técnico (School of Engineering of the Technical University of Lisbon, Portugal).

Acknowledgments

Stuart C. Shapiro contributed the Russell set example. Maria R. Cravo contributed the flying horses examples and many fruitful discussions. Many thanks also go to John Corcoran, Ernesto Morgado, Nuno J. Mamede, J. Terry Nutter, Carlos Pinto-Ferreira, William J. Rapaport, and members of the SNePS Research Group for their criticisms and suggestions.

This work was partially supported by Junta Nacional de Investigação Científica e Tecnológica (JNICT), under Grant 87-107 and by the Instituto Nacional de Investigação Científica.

References

Anderson A., Belnap N.: *Entailment: The Logic of Relevance and Necessity* Vol.1, Princeton, NJ: Princeton University Press, 1975.

Gärdenfors P.: *Knowledge in Flux: Modeling the Dynamics of Epistemic States*, Cambridge, MA: MIT Press, 1988.

Gärdenfors P., Makinson D.: Revisions of knowledge systems using epistemic entrenchment, *Proc. of the Second Conference on Theoretical Aspects of Reasoning about Knowledge*, Vardi (ed.), Los Altos, CA: Morgan Kaufmann, pp. 83–95, 1988.

Harman G.: *Change in View: Principles of Reasoning*, Cambridge, MA: The MIT Press, 1986.

Martins J.: The truth, the whole truth, and nothing but the truth: an indexed bibliography to the literature on truth maintenance systems, *AI Magazine 11*, 1990.

Martins J.P., Shapiro S.C.: Reasoning in multiple belief spaces, *Proc. of the Eight International Joint Conference on Artificial Intelligence*, pp. 370–373, Los Altos, CA: William Kaufmann, 1983.

Martins J., Shapiro S.C.: A model for belief revision, *Artificial Intelligence 35*, 1, pp. 25–79, 1988.

Shapiro S.C.: The SNePS semantic network processing system. In: *Associative Networks: Representation and Use of Knowledge by Computers*, N. Findler (ed.), New York: Academic Press, pp.179–203, 1979.

Shapiro S.C., Martins J.P.: Recent advances and developments: the SNePS 2.1 report, *Current Trends in SNePS - Semantic Network Processing System: Proc. of the First Annual Workshop*, Kumar (ed.), pp. 1–13, Lecture Notes in Artificial Intelligence 437, Springer-Verlag, 1990.

Shapiro S.C., Rapaport W.: SNePS considered as a fully intensional propositional semantic network. In: *The Knowledge Frontier: Essays in the Representation of Knowledge}*, McCalla, Cercone (eds.), New York: Springer-Verlag, pp. 262–315, 1987.

Shapiro S.C., Wand M.: The relevance of relevance, Technical Report No.46, Bloomington, IN: Computer Science Department, Indiana University, 1976.

Stalnaker R.: *Inquiry*, Cambridge, MA: MIT Press, 1984.

Building an Intelligent Second Language Tutoring System from Whatever Bits You Happen to Have Lying Around.

Yorick Wilks and David Farwell
Computing Research Laboratory, NMSU, Las Cruces, NM 88003.

Abstract: The Computing Research Laboratory (CRL) at New Mexico State University is currently engaged in the design of language teaching software, based on previously developed mature artificial intelligence and machine translation technologies within CRL. Our approach is unique because it uses the robustness of a natural language processing (NLP) system which incorporates both general world knowledge and task domain knowledge (Metallel), beliefs ascription (ViewGen), and semantic parsing techniques (PREMO) in the service of better student-system interaction.

Broadly stated, the central theoretical goal of our project is to investigate the uses of participant modeling through belief ascription in the development of an intelligent tutoring system (ITS) for second language learning, not only for the purpose of improved student-system interactions, but for the purpose of monitoring student performance and planning corrective intervention. We aim to produce a sophisticated, flexible, NLP-based tutoring system that will, on the one hand, help students acquire and maintain second language skills and, on the other, function as a workstation for investigating issues in second language acquisition and pedagogy.

Keywords: Belief Systems, Intelligent Tutoring System, Machine Translation.

Introduction

A rational way to begin research and development into such an ITS would be to start from first principles. The problem, then, lies in deciding which theories of language and pedagogy may prove useful to us. We shall begin with a brief survey of NLP techniques/theories that form the foundation of our system.

The following NLP technologies have been tested for a possible role in ITS. These specific NLP modules and techniques were all developed at CRL:

1) a machine translation (MT) system, ULTRA [6] a modular, five-language, interlingual MT system successfully working with vocabularies of approximately 10,000 words per language.

2) robust parsing techniques which use semantic structures and notions such as "preference" for extracting the most plausible interpretation from well or ill-formed linguistic utterances: the PREMO [2] and OSCON systems [8].

3) procedures for manipulating and generalizing large machine lexicons of the kind that will be needed for an adequate ITS package [29]: using technologies for extracting both symbolic frame-like structures and weighted network clusterings of word sense associations from learners' dictionaries like LDOCE and Cobuild.

4) an approach to belief modeling, based on the ViewGen System [2]: a default-based system for constructing plausible belief-set models of and about agents, to any level of nesting (of beliefs about beliefs) required by some given situation.

5) an approach to the pragmatics of cultural difference in solving the problem of translating documents (such as a business letter) from one language/culture to another (English or Spanish to Japanese, for instance), [4].

It is important to notice that, although they are all tools, these programs also imply AI theories of language and communication. In other words, although they have performance capabilities, they are more than mere peripherals, displays, windows and interfaces (the specifics of which will be discussed later). Understanding the underlying theory of these programs is crucial.

NLP tools for ITS

We are adopting a language teaching approach that assumes three commonly hypothesized levels of analysis, apart from simple grammatical knowledge: notional [25], functional [9] and situational [24]. The notional aspect of communicative competence is essentially semantic, i.e. a description of the speaker's intended message. It includes references to such notions as frequency of occurrence, motion, location, and so on, and is relevant to MT. The functional level concerns the speaker's goals, describing a situation, requesting information, agreeing with so-and-so's viewpoint, disagreeing, and so on, and is relevant to beliefs modeling. The situational aspect concerns the world context surrounding the communication, i.e. when the event concerns a business interaction, a travel interaction, a shopping interaction, etc., and is relevant to inter-cultural translations. We expect that all three must be taken into account in the construction of our ITS.

The following is a discussion of the theoretical and practical relevance of each of the five NLP modules mentioned above to ITS, in turn:

I) Translation: Since the object in learning a second language is not to translate back into one's first language, but learn to understand and generate wholly within the new language, and thereby achieve fluency (as one did in the learning of one's original language), we believe the development of a language-independent system for representing linguistic utterances would be central to an ITS.

The case for the relevance of MT is twofold: firstly, multilingual NLP is already available to us. Secondly, that form of MT makes the assumption that there is some underlying universal element in translation which makes the process possible by human or machine: virtually all theories of second language learning make this assumption, and this has also been the focus of CRL's multilingual ULTRA MT project [6], [28].

It follows that although to learn a second language is not necessarily to translate, the processes of second language learning and translation are parallel: we assume there to be a common world (physical or conceptual) that provides a cross-lingual, or interlingual element in both situations. In our own MT work, this hypothetical inter- lingual element is made explicit; in the ULTRA program, all translations pass through a common linguistic representation which is independent of both the source and target languages. In ViewGen, we assume a common world of beliefs which are also independent of language (see below).

II) Robust parsing: robust processing has been a focus of virtually all of the NLP projects at CRL. At the core of this effort is Preference Semantics [26], [27], an approach to natural language understanding that is based on the notion that language should be understood as a maximally coherent structure (in a defined sense), independent of syntax. The basic unit of analysis is therefore the utterance, rather than its syntactic counterpart, whether that be that a word, a phrase, a sentence or some larger textual unit. The framework for analysis is built upon both semantic/notional categories and structures, and discourse pragmatic/functional categories and structures.

A variety of parsers and generators have been developed within the preference semantics (PS) approach. They include the Semantic Definite Clause Grammars of English for the XTRA English-Chinese machine translation system [10] and Meta5 system, an implementation base for Collative Semantics [7]. Programs for parsing sentences when the input is ill-formed have also been developed within the PREMO paradigm [21].

These systems, while observing language-specific syntactic constraints through the use of feature unification, completely intergrate syntactic, semantic and pragmatic processing with the result that no syntactic level of representation can be identified. This is a crucial feature for

ITS, we believe, because that field has been limited, until now, by the unavailability of a computational parser for the ill-formed sentences learners may produce. This gap has usually been filled by slot-filling techniques in most available language teaching software (cf. critiques in [5] [22].

By using semantic parsing methods such as those embodied in PREMO, which are relatively insensitive to grammatical error in the source text, a pedagogical technique can be developed. Such a facility would yield a meaning-based, rather than a grammar-based, analysis:

(a) It would employ such a facility only when the syntactic parser (such as the ULTRA parser, see above) fails, on the assumption that that indicates a grammatical error by the student.

(b) It would then pass the structure derived by the semantic parser through a generator for the second language and print it, with some such rubric as: You should write (Corrected Second Language Sentence)

(c) and would perhaps pass the same representation through the MT system and generate a correct version in the student's native language adding: On the assumption that you mean (First Language Sentence).

III) Automated Dictionary Extraction: we are investigating, in particular, the use of dictionary-derived semantic networks and clusterings as possible aids to the student in vocabulary acquisition. We believe that the results of such empirical methods may prove superior to handcrafted lexicons on "psycholinguistic principles" such as WordNet [15].

For several years, CRL has been engaged in an NSF-supported project to extract semantic information from dictionaries such as LDOCE on a large scale, in order to increase the size and performance of NLP projects. An assumption of that work is that both explicit-symbolic and implicit-statistical information can be extracted from dictionaries and corpora, and that both forms of information can strengthen one other.

More importantly for our purposes here, since such dictionaries were not intended for computational linguists, but learners of English, it seems natural that the contents of such a dictionary (in this case, one with a basic two-thousand word vocabulary) be made available to a student of English for consultation at a screen, as well as in a book.

In combining our ULTRA MT work with methods of extracting information from LDOCE that include parsing the dictionary itself, as well as resolving the definition words to their appropriate senses, we have gone one step further: using the basic senses of LDOCE as an interlingual prototype for MT. Moreover, this interlingual translation method does not compromise the linguistic and cultural diversity of possible languages in any way.

We would like to extend this method, and use it to compensate for the temporary lack of such dictionaries in other languages. We will do this by tuning English-derived sense entries against foreign language texts like Japanese in order to adjust the semantic entries to the actual syntagms encountered in the second language texts, as in the case of actual (as opposed to predicted) classes of entities that function as verb objects. A similar procedure for hand-coded lexical entries is described by [1].

Another closely related form of dictionary research at CRL complements this: a group of colleagues [20] has been empirically building networks of words and word senses from dictionaries, corpora, and closeness information about concepts derived from native speaker informants, using a weighted network construction technique called PATHFINDER.

These techniques are relevant to ITS because they explore a range of clustering algorithms in search of the best concept clusters, and are in no way English-based. They could demonstrate that colocar-poner-meter is a group of closely associated Spanish verbs, as easily as that partisan-terrorist-guerilla is a set of closely associated English nouns. The crucial feature of this method is its ability to show relatedness, presented in a simple network form which is immediately comprehensible to a student, as well as a structure derived from the second language sources. In contrast, systems like WordNet [15] provide only relatedness without contrast, and do so by extension from English rather than from the corpora of the language being taught.

IV) ViewGen [2] is a program based on a default algorithm for constructing "environments" that represent the beliefs of others, down to any level of recursive nesting (e.g. "John's view of Joe's view of ...", and so on). Of particular importance is the ability to ascribe beliefs through this system. By constructing a complex model of individual belief spaces, the system can identify and respond to the mistaken or differing beliefs of others. This allows the tutoring system to construct a representation of the student's views of the task being performed, the overall goal of the task, the roles of the student and tutor in performing the task and, above all, the task domain knowledge.

On the assumption that a "common world" of shared beliefs is necessary for understanding and communication, ViewGen would be an appropriate tool for modeling beliefs and goals predicted by the system about the student user, possibly including (one level lower) the system's beliefs about the student's beliefs about the system itself.

In the big picture, ViewGen assumes a common world of knowledge (e.g. physical and technical) which all educated adults share. In any practical context of language learning, as in AI, it is axiomatic that shared representations of knowledge of the world indeed exist between agents and learners, contrary to skeptical theoretical models of communication [23]. Indeed, we could not communicate at all if we did not unconsciously make very large numbers of assumptions about what other people believe about the world (such as "the sun rises in the east", etc.). And modeling these belief environments explicitly could also aid us in teaching a second language.

From this simple principle, considerable complexity follows when any kind of expertise is introduced, and we can no longer assume a common world of shared knowledge by default. If, for instance, the speaker is a doctor and the listener is not, no shared expertise can be assumed, nor can one assume on a more mundane level that one's self-knowledge is necessarily shared by others.

In a similar way, for any subject being taught, the expertise of the teacher cannot be assumed by default. Hence, in the case of language teaching, the expert (computer or human) can only assume the student has that knowledge for which it has evidence, either because its retention is confirmed by questions, or because it follows by generalization from what has already been taught.

All this suggests a fairly rigid separation of knowledge of language from knowledge of the world in the system's model of the student. But in fact, such separation is not necessary, since it remains only to determine which belief sets are marked as expertise to be "run" or evaluated by accredited individuals (which may eventually include the user himself). Indeed, the system may simultaneously be teaching non-linguistic material (such as Japanese social customs as regards the sending and receiving of letters) and linguistic material.

We now turn to our main topic: a passive and active pair of modules that will provide the core of our system.

The Importance of Stick Man and Woman: The Passive Component

Anyone who has seen ITS demonstrations has encountered a stick man and woman who perform various tasks to provide a visual aid to language learning. As part of the linguistic theory that underlies our ITS design, their importance is more than historical.

To go back in time, language theory was influenced by Wittgenstein's "picture theory of truth" [30], a notion that contributed to a theory of situation semantics [3], both theories providing a notion of reference or meaning outside language. Another influential concept was that of languages as games, with different cultural standards of inference, proof, evidence, etc., games you had to know "from within" (like cricket) before you grasped their point. If that was the case, could you form a new game from a cross-section of words from a given language, as Ogden and Richards did by creating the notion of Basic English [16], a "mini-English" of a thousand words sufficient for all expression? And what of the visual equivalent of such a tool? One such tool was devised by Richards, who turned Wittgenstein's picture theory into a neat little volume called "English Through Pictures" [17] that has stood the test of time, and has been a bestseller ever since. As many theorists prefer, with this method, one learns a new language without referring to one's native language. Here is the beginning of French Through Pictures [18]:

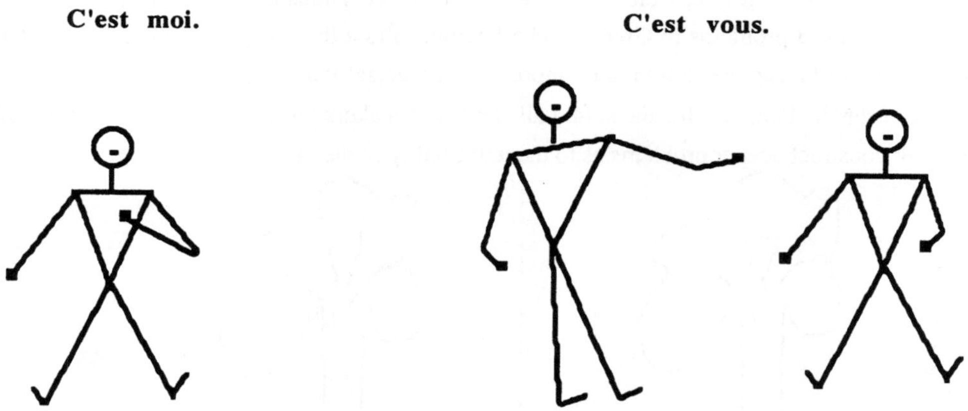

This is reminiscent of Wittgenstein's problem with the notion of a negative fact. Unlike most modern uses of stick people there is in fact a very complex structure underlying the sequence of pictures, based on binary contrasting of pairs. In the first pair above, the French sentences are apprehended as wholes, but the contrast is "moi" (me) versus "vous" (you), and so on for every pair. In a sophisticated philosophical analysis of this work Masterman [14] once argued (to an audience of astonished and largely uncomprehending philosophers) that there was a simple, primitive language of contrasts underlying the whole book, which formed a strictly hierarchical structure.

The purpose of this brief philosophical excursion is partly to remind readers where stick man and woman came from, and their long, honorable and lucrative role in second language teaching from what can seem a curiously modern set of assumptions about immersion in the second language. Their use was, for Richards, structured, not casual.

In a strange remark in the introduction to the French version, Richards complained about people all over the world who were stealing the book by pasting in strips of words from other language and creating a new version, and claimed, by contrast, that this French version was "by no means a mere translation of the English Pocket Book". I think he must have meant it was authentic, done with his blessing, because, what else could it be but a translation?

In some clear sense, the assumed universality and comprehensibility of the pictures across cultures, or at least close cultures, virtually defined a notion of translation: the stick pictures represent directly the meaning that the differing language strings have in common, and those strings could be said, by definition, to be translations of each other in virtue of that fact.

That does not require that every language book used the same pictures: only in the French version, for example, were there pictures of France. Indicating women by their skirts might have caused problems in Greece and Scotland. In fact there is good evidence [12] that schematic pictorial representation is no more truly universal than, say, onomatopeia (and the notorious French "Patatras" for the sound all English speakers know to be "Crash"). It would be easy to construct deeper problems as to the universality of the pictures:

The dog is behind the tree.
Mbwa ni mbele ya mimi.

The dog is in front of me.
Mbwa ni mbele ya mimi.

Here we have two pictures that could be used to teach the two English sentences The dog is behind the tree (from the speaker, since he is speaking) and The dog is in front of me. If the contrast of me and dog had already been introduced, this pair could be used to introduce the contrast pair in-front-of/behind.

Interestingly, the pair could not be used in Swahili Through Pictures to make such a contrast, since "mbele ya" (roughly corresponding to "in front of," appropriately inflected for noun class) would occur in both, given conceptualization of position in that language from the front of the speaker forward and not interrupted by intervening objects.

What follows from this is not the radical (and possibly destructive) conclusion that the pictures are language dependent, in a way that Richards' universality implicitly assumed was not the case, but that the contrasts made by given pairs will be language dependent in a small number of cases. Indeed, it may be that no real assumption of universality of concepts/pictures is required to explain how the system works as well as it does, and that would certainly suit its Wittegensteinian roots better. All that may be required is some universality of contrast (such as the pairs give) and that there is some functionally constructible set of such contrasts sufficient to establish, monlingually, how a term is used.

Why bring back all this old stuff; surely computer-based ITS must have killed the sales of these books. Probably not, in fact. Certainly, one motive is to say that the stick people have a longer and more structured history than many realize. Another is to seriously propose such courses as Richards' as prime candidates for automation, as we are doing, minus certain conventions that the possibility of screen movement makes redundant, e.g. the ghost figures who have left the room. However, the system also supports conventions quite strong enough to support the introduction of notions like belief structure, so as to underpin communication:

Such courses as Richards' are, in our view, prime candidates for automation. Such a system could support the introduction of notions like belief structure, as in the following example:

In this illustration, the dialogue can only be understood if one assumes certain beliefs of the man, about what the woman is doing.

Such a course is universalist and translation-based, even though the student is wholly passive (he only has to answer questions and tests every few pages as to the status of the stick people's situation: "Who left the room?", "Where is the hat now?", etc.). Since our central assumptions about language learning are basically those of the Communicative Language Teaching approaches [19], [13], [11], in particular that learning and maintenance of second languages is best achieved through meaningful language use, unlike such one-sided approaches to teaching, we expect our ITS to support a full range of activities. They will include passive activities (such as responding to commands, identifying important people on the basis of descriptions, and picking out or drawing pictures on the basis of descriptions), restricted active exercises (such as reponding to yes/no questions or WH-questions, filling out charts or forms, and using simple one word/phrasal descriptions or conversational formulae) and finally, fully active exercises (such as cooperative problem solving tasks, and role playing and open-ended discourse in which the learner is expected to contribute personal opinions, evaluations and information).

An Active Pragmatic Component for Writing

We propose to use an updated version of Richards' passive course, based on structured contrasts, and possibly allowing the student a translation as a last resort in a way the book could not. This aspect will be supplemented by a pragmatic and active program which will be based on an existing prototype at CRL, designed to teach writing in another language/culture, which uses stereotypes and templates to generate Japanese business letters for Americans who know no Japanese.

In its intended use as a letter generator, it teaches no Japanese whatever to the American, who would never see the final product. Instead, it displays a retranslation, through the ULTRA interlingual system (see above), turned back into English, possibly different from the original, but close enough. If it is deemed satisfactory, it can be mailed with confidence, even though the sender knows no Japanese at all! It is clear that the making explicit of such intermediate translation processes would be beneficial to any language tutoring system.

Implementation

How will our ITS be implemented, and what pedagogical techniques will it employ?

Initially, we are developing materials for adult learners who obtain an introduction to the fundamentals of the second language through the stick pictures and then go on to the active pragmatic component. The initial implementation of the prototype will focus on teaching, maintaining or improving standard English or Spanish. It will do this through the explicit task medium of writing business letters over a range of topics or occasions. As in our Japanese language prototype, the central content of the exercises will include the norms of business politeness and interaction in the second language culture, as well as the relevant linguistic expertise.

Long-term planning of activities and their internal sequencing will be based on the system's model of the student's second language knowledge, the system's second language knowledge, and the system's view of "natural sequencing", vis à vis notional and functional contexts of the task at hand. While initially such orderings will be programmed automatically, the system will eventually be able to infer the optimal order on the basis of general pedagogical principles. Although our focus will be on reading and writing, we believe these methods will be equally applicable to listening and speaking, and eventually hope to integrate both areas of language pedagogy.

Interface

The primary functions of the interface will be to provide a rich learning environment for the student, and a sophisticated channel of communication between student and system.More specifically:

- the system will employ user-friendly authoring tools develop CD-ROM audiovisual instructional materials, as well as to extend and modify both the second, and native language systems.

- the system will operate within a sophisticated, multimedia, hypermedia environment, and

- the linguistic and audio-visual channels of the interface will be optimally integrated.

The primary objective of adding graphics, sound, or video will be to create a fun, fanciful, and motivating learning environment. Thus far, we have developed a general interface prototype which allows us to gradually integrate multi-media techniques, and evaluate their utility in the context of actual student/instructor interactions. We have also explored the possible use of CD-ROM video display, sophisticated graphics, speech synthesis, speech analysis, the use of hypermedia techniques in learning activities, and the possibility of networking systems to allow for interaction with more than one student at a time.

Didactics

Given that the student and the tutorial system will be engaged in some sort of purposeful task, we believe the system should be careful when correcting the student, so as to be as unintrusive as possible. We feel that most correction should be masked in the form of clarifying and corrective dialog, such as "do you mean ...?", or, "don't you mean?"; "in other words ..."; "for example ...", and so on. Another tactic would be explanatory dialog, such as "wouldn't it be better if ...?", or, "but if ... then."; "since you think ..., then ...", etc. Such dialogue is a normal part of performing a cooperative task; to the student, it would appear to be no less than a natural response to an error from an agreeable partner.

Conclusion

A major benefit of such a pragmatic approach is its great capacity for adaptive, individualized instruction. Since the system will have broad conversational capabilities (over a number of limited task domains), and will be equipped with multilingual capabilities, its ability to communicate with the student will be quite rich. Furthermore, it will be able to perform a variety of tasks, which include monitoring the student's performance and modeling his second language knowledge, diagnosing errors in order to guide intervention, and tailoring instructional technique to the student's individual needs.

The strong foundation for our ITS in both natural language processing and pedagogical techniques, as well as its grounding in current research at CRL, makes this project a promising development in the field of translation and second language teaching.

References

1. Annick, P., and Pustejovsky, J.: Knowledge Acquisition from Corpora.In: Proceedings of the 13th International Conference on Computational Linguistics (COLING-90), Helsinki, Finland 1990.

2. Ballim, A., and Wilks, Y.: Artificial Believers. Hillsdale, NJ: Lawrence Erlbaum Associates 1991.

3. Barwise, J., and Perry, J.: Situations and Attitudes. Cambridge, MA.: MIT Press 1983.

4. Candelaria de Ram, S. and Yasuda, S.: Cultural Effects in the Machine Translation of Japanese Business Letters. Paper presented at the Western Conference of the Association for Asian Studies, Long Beach, CA.: 1989.

5. Cook, V., and Fass, D. Natural language processing by computer and language teaching. System, 14(2), pp. 163-170. 1986

6. Farwell, D. and Wilks, Y.: Ultra: a multilingual machine translator. Memoranda in Computer and Cognitive Science, MCCS-90-202, Computing Research Laboratory, New Mexico State University, Las Cruces, NM: 1990.

7. Fass, D.: Collative Semantics: a semantics for natural language processing. Memoranda in Computer and Cognitive Science, MCCS-88-118, New Mexico State University, Las Cruces, NM.: 1988.

8. Guthrie, L., McKevitt, P. and Wilks, Y.: OSCON: An operating system consultant. In: Proceedings of the 4th Annual Rocky Mountain Conference on Artificial Intelligence. pp. 103-113. Denver, CO: 1989.

9. Halliday, M: Learning how to mean: Explorations in the development of language. London: Edward Arnold 1975.

10. Huang, X-M: Semantic analysis in XTRA, an English-Chinese machine translation system. Computers and Translation, 3(2), pp. 101-120. 1988.

11. Johnson, K: Skill psychology and communicative methodology. Seminar at the Regional English Learning Centre, Singapore 1984.

12. Kennedy, J: Metaphor in Pictures. Perception, 11, 1982.

13. Littlewood, W: Foreign and second language learning: Language acquisition research and its implications for the classroom. Cambridge, UK: Cambridge University Press 1984.

14. Masterman, M: Translation. In: Proceedings of the Aristotelean Society. 1961.

15. Miller, G. and Fellbaum, C: WordNet and the Organization of Lexical Memory. This volume 1991.

16. Ogden, C., and Richards, I.: The Meaning of Meaning. London: Routledge & Kegan Paul 1936.

17. Richards, I.: The Pocket Book of Basic English (US Version of English Through Pictures). New York: Pocket Books 1945.

18. Richards, I.: French Through Pictures. New York: Pocket Books 1950.

19. Savignon, S.: Communicative competence: Theory and classroom practice. Reading, MA: Addison-Wesley 1983.

20. Schvaneveldt, R., (ed.). Pathfinder Associative Networks. Norwood, NJ: Ablex 1990.

21. Slator, B, and Wilks, Y: PREMO: Parsing by conspicuous lexical consumption. In: Advances in Parsing Technology, M. Tomita (Ed.). New York: Morgan Kaufman 1990.

22. Weischedel, R, Voge, W. and James, M: An Artificial Intelligence approach to language instruction. Artificial Intelligence, 10, pp. 225-240. 1978.

23. Whorf, B: Language, thought and reality: Selected writings of Benjamin Lee Whorf (J. Carroll, ed.). New York: Wiley 1956.

24. Widdowson, H.: Teaching language as communication. Oxford, UK: Oxford University Press 1978.

25. Wilkins, D: Notional syllabuses. Oxford, UK: Oxford University Press 1976.

26. Wilks, Y.: A preferential pattern-seeking semantics for natural language inference. Artificial Intelligence, 6, pp. 53-74. 1975.

27. Wilks, Y: Making Preferences More Active. Artificial Intelligence, 11, pp. 75-97. 1978.

28. Wilks, Y. and Farwell, D.: A white paper on research in pragmatics-based machine translation. Memoranda in Computer and Cognitive Science, MCCS-90-188, New Mexico State University, Las Cruces, NM.: 1989.

29. Wilks, Y., Fass, D., Guo, C-M., McDonald, J., Plate, T., and Slator, B: Machine tractable dictionaries as tools and resources for natural language processing. Journal of Machine Translation, 1990.

30. Wittgenstein, L: Tractatus Logico-Philosophicus. London: Routledge & Kegan Paul 1922.

5 INTERACTION AMONG AGENTS

Negotiating Goals in Intelligent Tutoring Dialogues

Michael J. Baker
Centre National de la Recherche Scientifique, Laboratoire IRPEACS, 93 chemin des Mouilles BP167 69131 Lyon-Ecully Cédex, France.

Abstract : This paper describes research towards developing a cognitive model for the generation of negotiation phases in educational interactions. We describe a first prototype model for generating tutorial interactions in Intelligent Tutoring Systems (the 'KANT' system [5,6,7]), and perform a preliminary assessment of the extent to which it models the required phenomena with respect to analyses of a set of computer-mediated tutorial dialogues for teaching the programming language PROLOG. KANT is based on viewing the ITS as a *dialogue participant,* rather than as a 'domain expert' or 'tool'. It incorporates mechanisms for determining which of a set of dialogue goals to negotiate in a tutorial interaction and for deciding whether to cooperate in negotiation, based on a model for dialogue focus. Our critique with respect to dialogue transcripts aims to specify an agenda for future work, and concentrates on variations in turn-taking mechanisms with the propositional attitudes of speakers, the range of negotiable phenomena to be modelled, and the logical representation of mental states in negotiation.

Keywords: Conflict, Cooperation, Motivation, Negotiation, Turn-taking, Tutorial dialogue, Tutorial goals.

The problem of modelling negotiation

In this paper we aim to describe research directions for developing a cognitive model of how phases of negotiation in tutorial dialogues may be generated in Intelligent Tutoring Systems (ITS). Our discussion concentrates on negotiation of *dialogue goals* rather than negotiating beliefs in the domain. We argue that such negotiation phases fulfill important functions in tutorial dialogues, and that there is therefore a strong case that future ITS should incorporate a model for their generation. If we look at previous work in ITS on modelling the teaching interaction [10,14,15,19,52], we find that negotiation as such is not addressed, which is not surprising given that none of this work aimed to include a model of "dialogue" in the sense where "... any agent must be regarded as both a producer and an understander, i.e. as a complete agent in interaction with some other complete agent(s)" [42]. We shall attempt to describe the function of negotiation in tutorial dialogues by describing a prototype model for intelligent teaching interactions, incorporated in the KANT system (Kritical Argument Negotiated Tutoring system) [5,6], and by critiquing the model with respect to analyses of a set of computer-mediated one-to-one teaching dialogues. We discuss a number of theoretical issues arising in the context of existing work on negotiation in dialogue, and future extensions to our model in order to incorporate new features identified in the analysis.

Viewpoints on the role of negotiation in education

The rôle of negotiation in dialogue has been considered from two main points of view in what may be broadly termed research in cognitive science and its application to education. The first point of view is the so-called "Standard Theory" [38], according to which "cognitive processes are caused by the execution of stored programs that operate on an internal symbolic representation of the world" (p. 563). The second point of view is that cognition is *situated* within communities of social relations, and 'embodied' in social action, rather than in some sense 'standing behind it'. This is what has become known as the 'situated learning' approach [29,30,47], according to which ""Cognition" observed in everyday practice is distributed - stretched over, not divided among - mind, body, activity and culturally organized settings ... " [29, p.1]. This view is sometimes presented as an extension of the first, and other times as a replacement paradigm. Somewhat surprisingly, both views have recently had something to say about the rôle of *negotiation and dialogue* in learning. Within the 'symbolic' view, researchers in conversation analysis [33], artificial intelligence [9], cognitive psychology and the hybrid enterprise of AI and Education [5,6,7] have aimed to specify the changes in mental states (beliefs, intentions, preferences,...) which underly generation of dialogue structures in negotiation. For example, in research on explanation generation, it is argued that explanation must take place within a negotiated dialogue, since it requires a reasonably extended interaction in order to negotiate (i) the knowledge assumed by dialogue participants, (ii) what will be accepted as an explanation, and (iii) mutual goals in the interaction [39,23]. Accordingly, researchers are turning increasingly towards the work of *conversation analysis* [45] in order to model coherence and complex features of turn-taking mechanisms [33], and approaches to discourse and dialogue based on the premises of *discourse analysis* [11]. Analysis of discourse units has generally been approached from the point of view of speech act theory [46]. For example, Levin and Moore [31] defined a set of "dialogue games" used in discourse comprehension, Power [43] showed how "conversational procedures" could be used in a cooperative planning program, and the early work of Allen and Perrault [1] formalised a number of illocutionary acts and described their rôle in simple dialogue planning systems. This early work included preconditions for speech actions which referred to the speakers' knowledge and beliefs, a line of research which has been continued to the development of logics for reasoning with belief [36,28] and with intentions [12]. The field of AI known as 'Distributed Artificial Intelligence' [9] includes an attempt to formalise the logical structure of the mental states of 'Rational Agents', and considers the problem of formalising negotiation from the point of view of distributed problem-solvers.

From the 'situated' viewpoint, negotiation is not something to be modelled by specifying dialogue units and patterns of mental states which generate and comprehend them; it is rather something to be studied as part of the social context in which the use of computers in education is situated. Thus, Seely-Brown [47] states that:

"Good learning situations and successful ITS are successful not because they enable a learner to ingest preformed knowledge in some optimal way, but because they provide initially underdetermined threadbare concepts to which, through conversation, *negotiation* and authentic activity, a learner adds texture." [47] (my italics).

As with all dichotomies, there are approaches which do not fit into these two viewpoints. Thus, for example, the neo-Piagetian approach of Doise, Mugny and colleagues [16], and Vygotskyan approaches to collaborative computer use, also stress the importance of cognitive and social factors in language use in the resolution of conflict in learning and development. Our own approach in this chapter is situated within the Standard Theory: our goals are to specify a theory of the changes in mental states which underlie conflict and cooperation and the generation of negotiation in dialogue, and to apply the theory to the generation of teaching interactions in ITS. In Ohlsson's [38] terms we retain the Standard Theory as one of dialogue *action* , and attempt to specify the abstract knowledge which underlies it. This is not, of course, an *a priori* argument for the validity of this approach in terms of a philosophy of action (see Clancey, this volume). In the context of AI and Education research, the two views are in fact most often compared using arguments which rely implicity on the perceived *prospects for practical solutions to current problems in the use of computers in education.* On these grounds, it may be argued that we will obtain most educational gains from putting current learning environments and educational expert systems into social settings *now* , and studying their situated use, rather than by expending research resources on theoretical pragmatics, cognitive science, agent theory ... what hope do we have that this research will help us to solve educational problems? In comment on this debate, we would simply want to stress that the philosophical and practical educational questions should be clearly separated.

Defining negotiation

From the point of view of social psychology, negotiation is defined as the process of "conferring with another for the purpose of securing agreement on some matter of common interest." [37]. Note that negotiation is not necessarily or exclusively concerned with the *resolution of conflict,* but rather with the *achievement of cooperation.* Galliers [22] gives a number of precise logical definitions of the mental states underlying negotiation and conflict, upon which our subsequent discussion in this paragraph is based. "Negotiation" is the name of a kind of interaction, and also of a process which takes place during that interaction, whereby the mental states of participants are altered so that they cooperate with respect to some proposition. She defines three "propositional postures" (attitudes of an agent with respect to some proposition): CONFLICT, COOPERATE and INDIFFERENT. In these terms, *negotiation is the process by which either of the propositional postures CONFLICT or INDIFFERENT are changed to COOPERATE.* These postures are defined with respect to beliefs, goals, preferences and commitments of agents, based on an extended version of the logic of Cohen and Levesque [12]. For example, CONFLICT can occur with respect to beliefs or goals; it can be individual (one agent is aware of conflict with respect to a proposition believed by another agent), or mutual (both agents possess individual conflict). For example, There is *individual goal conflict* between x and y concerning proposition p iff x has a goal for p to be true from now into the future, and x believes y to have the goal eventually not p, and x has a persistent goal for y to change his mind and to adopt the goal eventually p relative to q :

(G-CONFL-I x y p) = def (GOAL x (possibly p)) &
(BEL x (GOAL y (possibly (not p)))) & (P-R-GOAL x (GOAL y (possibly p)) q)

Individual COOPERATION is the recognition by x of y's goal that p be eventually true and x preferring p to (not p), resulting in the generation of a persistent goal for p, relative to y's possession of the goal:

(COOP-I x y p) = def (BEL x (GOAL y (possibly p)) & (PREFER x p (not p)) ->
(P-R-GOAL x p (GOAL y (possibly p)))

INDIFFERENCE is somewhat simpler. X is indifferent to y with respect to p iff x does not have a goal for y to believe or have a goal for p, or has not a goal for p which is relative to y's goal for p:

(INDIFFERENCE x y p) = def [(not (GOAL x (possibly (BEL y p))) &
(not (GOAL x (possibly (GOAL y p))))] OR
(not (P-R-GOAL x p (possibly (GOAL y p))))

In order, therefore, for agent x to negotiate the cooperation of another with respect to a proposition p, what is required is that x generates a belief in y that p or not-p is to be adopted as a goal, and that y has a preference for p, which leads to y adopting p as a goal. In general, what we observe is that change in belief takes place by supporting or contesting the reasons for holding a particular belief. Galliers' definitions give us some theoretical tools with which to approach the creation of a cognitive model for the processes underlying negotiation, with respect to analysis of dialogue transcripts. We adopt the following modified definition of negotiation :

Negotiation (definition)

'Negotiation' is the term for a sequence of dialogue exchanges during which the mental states of interlocutors are changed from the propositional postures of INDIFFERENCE (absence of cooperation or conflict) or CONFLICT with respect to one or more propositions, to one of COOPERATION with respect to one or more propositions, and where one or more interlocutor possesses the goal that this posture should be achieved.

Note the following with respect to this definition :

1 Negotiation is the name of a sequence of communicative actions defined with respect to changes in complex mental attitudes.

2 Initial attitudes do not have to be identical - one agent may be indifferent and the other in individual conflict.

3 The proposition(s) with respect to which do not have to be identical to those with which conflict existed initially - some other compromise may be achieved which leads to dropping the persistent goal that the other should adopt a speaker's belief. Where this is not the case, we view this as 'adversarial' negotiation, in analogy with argumentation [34].

4 We do not fix or define the range of utterance types which must occur in negotiated dialogue. Generally, in the case of goals, these will be some kind of OFFER / ACCEPTANCE / REJECTION, given the context of the persistent goal of achieving cooperation with respect to some proposition. In the case of beliefs, the speaker will generally ASSERT the proposition, which, according to Perrault [41] implies some intention that the proposition will be mutually believed - i.e. it is an offer of a candidate for mutual belief.

5 It is of course possible that negotiation takes place in which neither speaker has the goal that cooperation be achieved - such as 'arguing for the sake of it'. In tutorial dialogues with reasonably clear goals, we therefore make a minimal assumption of cooperativity.

As stated earlier, negotiated propositions may be goals or beliefs. In this paper we concentrate solely on negotiation of joint dialogue *goals*. Finally, we must emphasise that we use the term "dialogue" in the general sense of the *socio-cognitive processes which generate the structure of interaction at the level of propositions and the attitudes of agents towards them*. We are interested in the problems of how an interlocutor decides which proposition (goal or belief) to negotiate, how it is negotiated, and how an agent decides whether to cooperate or not with a proposition negotiated by another.

Negotiating dialogue goals : examples and analysis

Let us now consider some examples of the phenomena which we are trying to model. The following are examples of phases of negotiation between an adult human teacher and an adult learner in computer-mediated tutorial dialogues for teaching the programming language PROLOG. These dialogues will be used as examples throughout this paper. We use the following notation: "T = teacher", "L = learner", "<<...{comment}>> = omitted section from dialogue".The speakers adopted a number of idiosyncratic communication clichés, such as " ° " for ending a turn, and " ? " for an asynchronous interrupt, which we omit in the extracts for clarity. The dialogues were collected over a period of two years, and were conducted via electronic mail at a distance of over 400 miles. Due to space restrictions we shall discuss only short extracts from a single dialogue (the second of eight). The approach to dialogue analysis used depends on the questions we are seeking to answer. For example, Elsom-Cook [20] analyses this same set of dialogues in terms of a set of predicates for mentalistic concepts - beliefs, wants, commitments and preferences. In the long term, we aim to make similar analyses and to instantiate them within a cognitive architecture. There are of course a great many aspects of these dialogues which could be analysed : at the present stage in our research we are principally concerned with analysing: (1) the *turn-taking structures* associated with negotiation, and (2) the *range of propositions negotiated* in tutorial dialogues. The interest of 1, lies in the fact that since negotiation in dialogue can be viewed as one form of social interaction [45], conformity to and divergence from 'preferred' turn-taking structures gives evidence for *propositional attitudes* of agents [22] - CONFLICT, COOPERATION and INDIFFERENCE. Since there are probably no *a priori* limitations on what propositions can be negotiated in a dialogue, we aim to establish , some *empirical* limits on the range of such propositions for specific kinds of domains. In addition, we make some initial hypotheses which aim to explain *why negotiation occurs* in educational dialogues, *why negotiation succeeds or fails* and *why negotiation is implicit or explicit* . These questions can be viewed as preliminary to what is in a sense the hardest and most interesting problem : *through what dialogue actions and changes in mental states is conflict resolved by negotiation ?*

Negotiation Example 1 : INDIFFERENCE -> COOPERATION

T1: I would greatly enjoy doing some Prolog. Did you have something in mind?

L2: No, not really. Like I said I haven't really looked at your program with the idea of extending it yet. Could we do something simplish, just to make me feel good?!

T3: Certainly. You have a choice of something simple and interactive now, or something fairly simple with an interactive session later on today.

L4: Um. I'd like to do something now, cos I really should do the vp stuff later on ... is that ok?

T5: Fine. Ummm... How about writing a predicate called second_word, which takes as its argument a string, and instantiates its second argument to be the Atom corresponding to the second word of that string <<continues>>

In this extract the interaction structures are of the socially expected form, according to the Schegloff and Sacks [45] turn taking rules:

speaker1: negotiation
speaker2: response, negotiation
speaker1: response ....

This shows a high level of social cooperation in the definition of joint goals. Since the extract occurs at the beginning of the dialogue, there are no explicitly agreed joint goals (although there is certainly background common knowledge - [18,20]), so propositional attitudes (or "postures" [22]) are INDIFFERENCE, moving to COOPERATION. A wide range of phenomena are negotiated, all of which are *goals* for one or both speakers, rather than *beliefs*. This relates to the problem-solving domain discussed, and we would expect a greater degree of negotiation of belief in dialogues concerned with explanation. Propositions negotiated include: general and specific topics for problems to work on (prolog, strings, arguments, "write a predicate called second_word") and their level of difficulty, the interaction style of problem-solving, future planning of joint problem-solving goals, that the other speaker should negotiate a goal for a given topic (U2), and even 'time to think' (U12). Other remarks which may be made about this extract are that negotiation is exclusively *explicit* - presumably because at the beginning of the dialogue there is insufficient shared understanding of beliefs and goals to permit indirect and implicit utterances - negotiation of goals proceeds from general to specific in terms of the speaker, interaction style, and in terms of goals and subgoals in the domain, and *almost all negotiated goals succeed* (except for U3). We hypothesise that the gradual increase in specificity of goals negotiated is designed to minimise the probability of direct conflict. In this context, the cooperative turn-taking structure gives both conversants the chance to modify agreed goals successively.

Negotiation Example 2 : CONFLICT -> COOPERATION

T31: ? Can I say something?

L32: yes

T33: That's quite a lot wrong, I'm afraid. D'you want to tell me about it in English?

L34: Not really

T35: Ah. What do you want to do then?

L36: Stop?

T37: Oh. Really? I'd quite like to talk through this one, and it isn't exactly all that ego-boosting for your Prolog morale so far is it?

L38: What Prolog morale?

T39: Oh, come on. You can do it. It's just a lot of things to remember and you're out of practice. I suspect you've got the problem quite well sussed in English, but the difficulty is mapping it into prolog;

L40: No, the problem is that I haven't got it sussed in English. Um can I just talk about the first_word bit for now?

T41: Yes, that's fine. <<continues>>

In this extract, the interruption of the socially preferred or expected turn-taking structure is evidence for the propositional posture of CONFLICT, in which L responds negatively, and exchanges of negotiation and opposed counter-negotiation follow one after the other, for example :

T31: interrupts
negotiates
L32: responds
T33: utterance
U4: negotiates

and so on. The principal propositions negotiated are: that L explains and discusses their problem, that L negotiates another goal - a case of 'nested' negotiation - and that they stop or continue the dialogue. There are two cases of conflict : in the first, there is *individual then mutual goal conflict* with respect to the goal "T explains L's errors", and in the second with respect to the goal "continue the dialogue". *Why did conflict, and hence negotiation, occur at this point in the dialogue?* The teacher's initial negotiation succeeds in virtue of its non-specificity ("Can I say something?") thus making it less likely to directly conflict goals or beliefs, and in terms of its placement in the dialogue almost at the end of the student's (erroneous) problem-solving. We can imagine that an interruption in the middle of this process, and with greater specificity, would be less likely to be successful. The subsequent negotiations fail because the student is not *motivated* to continue to pursue the proposed goals because of their self-assessment of the likelihood of achieving agreed problem-solving goals (see the analysis in [20]). The first CONFLICT situation "T explains L's errors" is removed by the teacher succeeding in motivating the student sufficiently so that she agrees to choose a different and simpler sub-problem to work on. A prerequisite to this goal being pursued is that the second conflict with respect to "continue the dialogue" be resolved. In this case we may say that the teacher persuades or even *coerces* the student, by appealing to the reason why L wanted to stop.

In summary, we would make the following brief points with respect to these analyses, which will be relevant for assessing our current prototype model KANT :

1 At least for problem-solving dialogues, it seems clear that the range of propositions negotiated concern *the determination of joint problem solving goals, the temporal planning of actions to achieve them,* and *execution monitoring of their success*. An ITS which negotiates goals should therefore be potentially capable of negotiating almost any primitive of the domain and dialogue models.
2 Goals are negotiated with successive levels of specificity, and gradual assignment of speaker and negotiator roles , which we suggest is one strategy for avoiding potential conflict. Other strategies include indirect or implicit negotiation of goals (eg "Can I say something?", "I don't know what I'm doing") in cases of *interruption*.
3 Conflict is often resolved by criticising or supporting the reasons for adopting a particular goal. Successful negotiation of a goal from postures of CONFLICT is often closely related with attempting to *motivate* (or even *coerce*) the other to accept the goal by reference to affective factors ("I can't do it", etc.), and convincing the student that their metacognitive self-assessment of their problem-solving abilities is not correct. In terms of agent theory, the use of motivating moves in negotiation therefore requires a representation of *affective preferences and interests*.
4 Turn-taking structures and their conformity to expected forms vary with the propositional attitudes of speakers. Their attendant generation in a dialogue model therefore assumes the capacity to *recognise propositional attitudes* (CONFLICT, COOPERATION, INDIFFERENCE).

Now that we have introduced some of the phenomena which we aim to model, we describe and critique our current prototype model.

KANT: a model for high-level processes in tutorial interaction

The KANT system (Kritical Argument Negotiated Tutoring system, [5,6,7]) is a computational model for generation of structures associated with high-level tutorial interaction. A model of 'high-level' interaction [27,20] consists of the specification of a set of representations for cognitive states and processes which operate upon them, required to generate the abstract structure of dialogue, at the level of the *propositional content* of utterances. These representations include those which would be necessary for a model of an interlocutor in dialogue, such as their beliefs (concerning a domain of discourse, the beliefs of some other interlocutor, the previous dialogue which has occurred), their goals, intentions, preferences and other intensional representations. The model should be able to generate (at least) a subset of the phenomena which have been analysed in educational and other dialogues, including turn-taking, interruption, the goal-based dialogue units, and so on. The processes which are required include processes for modelling the intentions of interlocuteurs, how they represent coherence and relevance, how they choose how to respond, and so on. Despite its limitations, KANT was the first computationally tractable model for tutorial dialogue reported in the Intelligent Tutoring Systems literature to address the problems of managing negotiative dialogue, where each interlocutor (computer and human student) was given as great a degree of symmetrical freedom to pursue their goals as was possible at this stage of research. With respect to negotiation, KANT addressed two main questions :

1 how should a dialogue agent decide which goals to negotiate ?
2 how should a dialogue agent decide whether to cooperate or not in negotiation ?

In terms of symmetry in the interaction, each participant (ITS and student) is given approximately the same set of dialogue goals which may be negotiated, and each has the symmetrical ability to accept or reject the negotiated goals of the other. As stated earlier, *KANT is restricted to negotiating dialogue goals, and not beliefs in the domain.* In addition, as we shall discuss, it only models aspects of *one* form of negotiation : from INDIFFERENCE to COOPERATION. The crucial and difficult problem of resolving CONFLICT in negotiation is a major topic for future research. The preliminary solution adopted is that of simple *acquiescence* : the system is not *benevolent* in accepting everything proposed by the student, and in the case of rejection of a negotiated goal, each speaker is simply forced to accept this, the negotiated turn shifting to the rejecting speaker.

Our purpose in this chapter is to introduce an approach to modelling negotiation in tutorial dialogues, to argue for its educational importance, and to establish a future research agenda. We therefore do not have the space to discuss all aspects of the dialogue model incorporated in KANT (see [5,6,7]). After a general summary of the components of the system, we therefore illustrate how it functions with respect to an example interactive execution trace, and critique the model with respect to our dialogue analyses.

KANT: an outline of the program

The most fundamental representations upon which KANT is based, are *a set of dialogue moves* which represent the goals of a dialogue participant, and *a propositional network of justified beliefs* in the domain discussed. There is a close relationship between these two representations, in that the set of dialogue moves chosen are specifically adapted to communicating *justified beliefs* which characterise the knowledge domain which the dialogue model discusses (beliefs about musical structures in melodies [3,4]). KANT therefore generates dialogues moves corresponding to those which have been described for *critical arguments* [50,44], including structures for stating and illustrating beliefs and their justifications, and for critiquing the beliefs and justifications which have already been stated in the dialogue (by either dialogue participant). We shall give a brief outline of KANT by describing these data representations, then the processes which operate on them to generate high-level dialogue.

We followed existing research [13,31] in representing dialogue moves as planning operators, based on the general theory of language as rational action - "speech acts" [46]. Our dialogue moves had a similar structure, with the differences that extra kinds of preconditions were included for constraints on dialogue focus, the operators were parametrised (for speaker and negotiator rôles) in order to be adapted to interactive dialogue, and they included preconditions relating to negotiation of those goals. More importantly, the major differences between our model and previous ones lie in the procedural role which the goal operators play in dialogue generation : *the system does not construct plans* from these goal operators. Given the equal opportunity of each participant to influence the course of the dialogue by negotiation, we opted for a form of opportunistic dialogue, controlled by dialogue focus, and the relevance of sequences of hierarchical goals. In future work we may modify this situation to include a degree of *local planning*. Each dialogue move has

- a *header* (the goal name) ;
- *parameters* for the current negotiator, speaker, concept and instance discussed (n,s,c,i);
- *dialogue state preconditions* ;
- *negotiation preconditions* ;
- *submoves* ; and
- *dialogue actions* (if any).

Dialogue moves are represented in a *hierarchical and/or tree* with *levels of abstraction,* in terms of an increase in specificity of preconditions for relevance of the move descending in the tree. This relates to the fact that speech acts which "prepare the terrain" for others try to obtain "some of the conditions of appropriateness for the dominant act" [21], and to our analyses of general-to-specific negotiations in the dialogues discussed earlier in the chapter. The following is an example of an operator for the 'claim' dialogue move:

dialogue move: CLAIM
parameters: (c inst n s)
dialogue_state_preconditions:
((not (null c)) & ((null *dialogue_history*) OR ((in_focus? c (ltm_model s)) &

(not (known? c (ltm_model (dialogue_participant s)))) & (exists_ltm_trace? c (ltm_model s))))))

negotiation_preconditions: ((negotiate s (goal= 'CLAIM)) & (negotiate s c)))

subgoals: (OR ((concrete_claim (c inst s)) (abstract_claim (c inst s)))))

negotiation_effects:

((update_dialogue_history '((goal_name= 'CLAIM) (s= s) (c= c) (inst= inst)))))

action_effects: nil

actions: nil

At the highest level of the goal tree, a fundamental distinction is made between disjunctive 'claim' and 'challenge' goals. This corresponds generally to a distinction between stating something 'new' in the dialogue, related to the previous dialogue by local focus constraints, and a direct reference to a previously stated goal in the dialogue (eg critiquing a previous directly referred to claim). Within each branch, goals subdivide into abstract and concrete claims, and the making and justifying of the claim. On the 'challenge' branch, moves are included for essentially *critiquing* claims [14,35], such as disagreeing or agreeing with justifications, stating new justifications, and so on. The and/or goal tree is a fundamental representation used in decision-making in dialogue in KANT: it is searched during the process of trying to find a relevant goal to be discussed. When the student has a 'negotiated turn', the same set of goals is available, with the exception of making an 'abstract claim', or general explanation. This goal is excluded in view of our concentration on high-level decision making mechanisms: since the system does not generate utterances down to the sentence level, neither can it analyse the meaning of sentences input by the student. *Parameters* are values for speaker and negotiator rôles, and topic in terms of concept and instance to be discussed. These may have values inherited from higher in the dialogue goal tree, values which are proposed by the other speaker, or values may be derived 'actively' by procedures associated with satisfaction of dialogue state preconditions (such as 'finding a concept to discuss'). *Dialogue state preconditions* consist of a logical expression into which current parameter values are substituted, and evaluated with respect to a "dialogue state" [43], consisting of a representation of the beliefs of both interlocutors in semantic memory, and a restricted representation of their memories concerning the most recent instantiated dialogue moves negotiated and pursued in the dialogue so far. Other dialogue state preconditions refer to the dialogue history and the mental states of interlocutors. For example, a claim move is relevant if it is the beginning of the dialogue, and in order to make a claim, an interlocutor must have a memory representation for the concept to be communicated, and must believe that the other interlocutor does not "know" that concept. *Negotiation preconditions* simply state that for a *dialogue action* to be performed, the goal selected as relevant must be negotiated and accepted. *Submoves* are the subgoals in the dialogue goal tree, and *negotiation effects* are the set of procedures which update the speakers' belief representations as we describe next. *Dialogue actions* simply communicate the propositions agreed by negotiation, within the context of previous negotiations. For example, if a move "agree supports" is accepted, then the proposition communicated (belief/justifications) is interpreted as agreement with justifications for a stated belief.

Our model for memory encoding and retrieval during the course of dialogue is based on the ACT* model [2]. The beliefs and justifications of each participant are therefore represented as instances of concepts in a propositional network. We assume that if a concept is mentioned then both interlocutors encode a working memory trace for it, which has a probability of forming a long-term memory representation with repetition. We therefore make the simple assumption that encoded memory traces correspond to 'belief' in the way in which they are *used* in dialogue: beliefs are viewed as representations which when communicated in dialogue, have to be justified, whose justifications can be critiqued, and which can not serve as the basis of straightforward contradiction of a previously stated belief, i.e. belief is treated as a propositional representation upon which certain dialogue procedures may operate. The system distinguishes its own beliefs from those it attributes to the student according to this simple encoding hypothesis (a "student model"), and records a restricted set of propositions representing recent dialogue moves performed by both speakers. Retrieval from long-term memory is based on the phenomenon of *spreading activation* in semantic memory, from an input source. We have applied this feature of Anderson's theory to the definition of *focus* in dialogue [24,25]. From the point of view of the system, when it attempts to satisfy *relevance* [49] conditions for a negotiated dialogue move, it checks the current concept activation value with respect to its own working memory, being the traces with the highest activation level: if the concept is in working memory, then it is viewed as sufficiently in focus to satisfy this relevance condition in the dialogue state preconditions. If no concept is proposed, then it selects the concept with the highest activation level, in order to satisfy this precondition for a dialogue move. When it is the student's turn to negotiate a dialogue goal, the system therefore bases part of its decision as to whether to cooperate or not on checking its own representation of the activation level of that concept, thus judging its relative focus.

We have now discussed the basic data representations which need to be understood in order to describe the fundamental dialogue generation mechanisms of KANT. At the highest level, the dialogue consists of an alternation of *negotiated turns*. KANT incorporates simplified procedures for turn-taking which do not necessarily correspond to the full sophistication of the mechanisms described for natural human conversations [45]. They may be summarised as follows:

1 speaker1 negotiates a goal;
2 speaker2 responds with agreement or disagreement;

3 if speaker2 agrees, then speaker1 utters the agreed goal;

4 when the goal is uttered by speaker1, speaker1 may self-select, and attempt to negotiate subgoals of the first goal (step 1). These may succeed or fail.

5 depending on the degree to which speaker1 believes that speaker2 understands the subgoal to be negotiated, speaker1 may utter the subgoal, generate a preannouncement, or negotiate it as in step 1. Upon assent to a preannouncement, the subgoal is uttered.

6 if the speaker disagrees, then the negotiator role changes, and the disagreeing speaker takes a negotiated turn (goto step 1).

In step 4 above, we can see that the mechanism is in fact recursive - step 4 invokes step 1. We shall see this mechanism in operation when we present an example dialogue generation trace produced by KANT, later in this section. On a specific negotiated turn, the following are factors which are used in determining which goal to negotiate:

1 the structure of the and/or decision tree of dialogue moves, which defines mutually exclusive alternatives, and conjunctive possibilities ;

2 satisfaction of dialogue state preconditions for the relevance of a dialogue move, with respect to the dialogue state ;

3 choice of alternative mutually relevant dialogue moves according to a set of educational preferences.

When either speaker converses, the dialogue move tree is searched in order to find a set of terminal goals in the tree, which have attached dialogue actions (factor 1). For each goal encountered, its dialogue state preconditions are evaluated with respect to the dialogue state (factor 2). If alternative goals are both satisfied, then a set of educational preferences is applied in order to choose one (factor 3). If only one is satisfied, then search continues below that goal, and the conjunction of satisfied dialogue goals with attached dialogue actions will be uttered. If none are satisfied, then the speaker 'can think of nothing [relevant, preferred] to say', and the other speaker becomes the negotiator. The number of educational preferences required is related to the number of points where a choice may be made between goals, i.e. the number of disjunctive branches. In our prèsent simplified goal tree, there are only two: discriminating between claim and challenge goals, and between abstract and concrete claims (other preferences are required for preferred parameter instantiations of these goals, such as 'preferring the student to speak'). These preferences are derived from existing research in educational discourse. For example, the following preference relates to the stable 'initiate-response-feedback' pattern observed by Sinclair and Coulthard [48] in classroom educational dialogues, in effect preferring feedback to a response, thus making more connected dialogue : "Pref 1: Prefer to challenge an existing claim if relevant to do so, rather than making new claim [claim and challenge moves]".

Before considering some examples of dialogue traces generated by KANT, we finally need to say how a negotiator decides whether to *accept* a negotiated goal or not. The simple mechanism which we have adopted in the present version of KANT bases this decision on the same relevance preconditions which an interlocutor uses to decide which dialogue goal to pursue, i.e. *a speaker s1 agrees to accept a goal g instantiated with specific parameters negotiated by speaker s2 if and only if those parameters when substituted into the dialogue state preconditions of g evaluate as relevant.* Note that the restriction is not so strong as to demand that the goal be also *preferred* - in effect, one of the ways in which KANT side-steps the issue of resolving conflict. Clearly, this is a considerable simplification, resulting from the fact that the dialogue system does not incorporate a notion of longer-term and higher-level goals. Our negotiation mechanism is also simplified in that it could be modified to include further exchanges where the respondent does not accept a goal with some parameters, but then attempts to find values under which it would accept, which are then proposed in turn as a 'compromise'. We did not incorporate such further sophistications into KANT at this stage, preferring to reserve them for a phase of evaluating the model with respect to dialogue transcripts. Once a dialogue goal has been satisfied as relevant, discriminated according to preferences, and negotiated as accepted, dialogue actions (if any) may be performed, and effects propagated on the dialogue state. Since we concentrated on describing a model for high-level decision processes in dialogue, the performance of dialogue actions in KANT simply corresponds to *generating a text template* for communicating the concept and instance parameter values which have been satisfied as relevant and accepted for a goal, for a given speaker. When the student is the speaker, exactly the same dialogue generation mechanisms are used. The principal difference lies in the difference between input and output to the model. In the case of the student as speaker, the system generates summaries of the responses (yes and no) to negotiation, of the beliefs and instances chosen, and presents the set of dialogue moves available at a given point in the goal tree for the student to choose. In accordance with the model of dialogue focus based on spreading activation encorporated in KANT, subgoals which are negotiated as recursive continuation of dialogue actions are explored in order of highest activation level.

Example interaction trace generated by KANT

Finally, let us consider an example of a dialogue trace generated by KANT, describing the features of the model discussed so far. We do not have space to illustrate all features here, and so restrict ourselves to a single example which illustrates most features. In the example, typed input by the user is in *italics*, plain text is an output trace generated by KANT. The lines have been numbered (eg "9/") for reference in the commentary. This is an example taken from the middle of a 'dialogue' with KANT, i.e. an interactive trace. There are two negotiated turns, each of which consists of a negotiation phase, followed by a dialogue action, which is recursively continued in the second negotiated turn. In the first turn, the student is the negotiator and the speaker, in the second the system is the negotiator and speaker, and challenges the claim made by the student in the first. The domain discussed is that of a set of justifications for the existence of musical phrase boundaries in an example melody, integrated into a propositional network representation.

(KANT INTERACTION TRACE)

1/My turn over ... your move

2/Are you sure you want to continue the discussion? (y or n)

3/*y*

4/Please type who you want the SPEAKER to be ...(student or system)

5/*student*

6/Please type in the concept you want to talk about (if you want a full list of possibilities, type 'show')

7/*phrase_boundary*

8/Please type in the instance position you want to talk about

9/*p10*

10/I will tell you if I agree to cooperate ... Ok, I will cooperate

11/Please choose one but not both of the goals to pursue:

12/ CHALLENGE = make a challenge to a previous claim

13/ CLAIM = make a claim concerning a concept

14/*claim*

15/I will tell you if I agree to cooperate ... Ok, I will cooperate

16/Please choose one but not both of the goals to pursue:

17/ CONCRETE_CLAIM = make a specific claim about a concept instance

18/ ABSTRACT_CLAIM = make a general explanatory claim about a concept

19/*concrete_claim*

20/I will tell you if I agree to cooperate ... Ok, I will cooperate

21/Please choose a goal to pursue:

22/MAKE_INSTANCE_CLAIM = state a claim about an instance

23/SUPPORT_INSTANCE_CLAIM = state justifications for an instance claim

24/*make_instance_claim*

25/I will tell you if I agree to cooperate ... Ok, I will cooperate

26/You are pursuing the dialogue goal MAKE_INSTANCE_CLAIM, with

27/PHRASE_BOUNDARY as a concept, and P10 as its instance. Please confirm or disconfirm your intentions (y/n)

28/*y*

29/Ok, I'll remember that.

30/Please choose a goal to pursue:

31/SUPPORT_INSTANCE_CLAIM = state justifications for an instance claim

32/support_instance_claim

33/Please type in the justification(s) for the instance P10

34/(CONTRAST PARALLELISM)

35/I will tell you if I agree to cooperate ... Ok, I will cooperate

Lines 1-35: Negotiation phase (n= student, s= student, c= phrase_boundary, i= p10). At 1 the argument controller gives the negotiated turn to the student, the previous negotiator having been the system. At 2 we have a 'transition relevance point' [45], where speaker roles may shift and either participant may choose to terminate the dialogue. From 4 to 35 the dialogue goal tree is searched top-down, and at each point parameters which are unbound are presented to the student with the choices available, as well as the choices of dialogue move at that point. At the beginning, the 'DISCUSS' move is satisfied provided that the memory representations of both participants are not equal. For the student, the s, c and i parameters are presented for choice. The system now substitutes these chosen parameters into the preconditions of 'DISCUSS', which evaluate to 'true' and the system agrees to cooperate. The student now chooses the 'CLAIM' move, for which a summary explanation is given (lines 11-14). The system substitutes the parameters into preconditions, the concept 'PHRASE_BOUNDARY' is found to have a high enough focus level in the system's representation of the student's memory (and other preconditions are satisfied), so the system agrees to cooperate (line 15). A similar procedure takes place with respect to the proposed CONCRETE_CLAIM goal and its subgoals (conjunctive).

(KANT INTERACTION TRACE)

36/You are pursuing the dialogue goal SUPPORT_INSTANCE_CLAIM, with

37/PHRASE_BOUNDARY as a concept, P10 as its instance, and (CONTRAST PARALLELISM)

38/as the justifications. Please confirm or disconfirm your intentions (y/n)

39/y

Lines 36-39: Dialogue action. The student performs the dialogue action in the form of agreeing to a summary of the statement generated by the system. This is followed by a similar procedure for the conjunctive 'SUPPORT_INSTANCE_CLAIM' subgoal. After line 39 is generated, the system propagates negotiation and dialogue goal effects, which are to update the dialogue history and the memory models of each interlocutor. This involves 'PHRASE_BOUNDARY' becoming an input source of activation in both network representations, through which activation is spread, and increasing the appropriate node strength.

(KANT INTERACTION TRACE)

40/Are you sure you want to continue the discussion? (y or n)

41/y

42/My move ...

43/Do you accept that we pursue the dialogue goal CHALLENGE (== make a challenge to a previous claim) (y/n?)

44/y

45/ Do you accept that we discuss the concept PHRASE_BOUNDARY (y/n?)

46/y

47/ Do you accept that we discuss the concept instance P10 (y/n?)

48/y

49/ Do you accept that we pursue the dialogue goal CLAIM_SHARED (== agree with a previous claim) (y or n?)

50/y

51/I agree that P10 is an instance of the concept PHRASE_BOUNDARY

52/Do you accept that we pursue the dialogue goal AGREE_SUPPORTS (== agree with some previously stated justification types) (y or n?)

53/y

54/AGREE_SUPPORTS is the dialogue goal currently being pursued with the justification type(s) PARALLELISM.

Lines 40-54: Negotiation phase (n= system, s= system, c= phrase_boundary, i= p10). At 40 the argument controller passes a negotiated turn to the system. Both the claim and challenge moves are satisfied as relevant, but since a 'challengable' claim has been made, preference Pref1 operates to choose the challenge move. The concept parameter is now bound to the concept referred to in the previous dialogue move (i.e. PHRASE_BOUNDARY of CLAIM move), from the dialogue history, together with the instance p10 to be challenged. Examining its own memory representation and the supports claimed by the student in the previous turn, the system agrees with the previous support 'PARALLELISM', performing a dialogue action.

(KANT INTERACTION TRACE)

55/I want to try to explain what I mean by the justification(s) PARALLELISM. Is that ok? (y/n)

56/*n*

57/Ok, maybe we'll talk about PARALLELISM next time around...

58/Do you accept that we pursue the dialogue goal NEW_SUPPORTS (== state some justifications which we not mentioned for previous instance claim) (y or n?)

59/y

60/NEW_SUPPORTS is the dialogue goal currently being pursued with CHORD_PROGRESSION as the new support(s).

61/I want to try to explain what I mean by the justification(s) CHORD_PROGRESSION. Is that ok? (y/n)

62/n

63/Ok, maybe we'll talk about CHORD_PROGRESSION next time around...

64/Do you accept that we pursue the dialogue goal DISAGREE_SUPPORTS (== disagree with some previously stated justification types) (y/n?)

65/y

66/DISAGREE_SUPPORTS is the dialogue goal currently being pursued with CONTRAST as the disagreed support(s).

67/I want to try to explain what I mean by the justification(s) CONTRAST. Is that ok? (y/n)

68/n

69/Ok, maybe we'll talk about CONTRAST next time around...

70/My turn over ... your move

Lines 55-69: Dialogue action. At this point (line 55) the system decides that subconcepts of PARALLELISM are 'possibly known', and so generates a preannouncement in line 55. This is not accepted by the student, so the system continues to negotiate with other satisfiable subgoals of the CHALLENGE move. It states some NEW_SUPPORTS for the claim challenged which the student had not mentioned (line 60), then finally disagrees with the support CONTRAST for this claim (line 64). Again it attempts to pursue this dialogue action, which is refused by the student. After each of these actions, effects are propagated on the dialogue state as before. Finally, at line 69 the system has no futher satisfiable subgoals to negotiate, all subactions of dialogue actions have been refused, and its negotiated turn ends. At 70 the argument controller passes the negotiated turn to the student.

There are a number of features which we have not been able to show in this example such as the system refusing to cooperate with negotiation, the system negotiating that the student should speak, the student negotiating that the system should speak, and so on. Nevertheless, we have illustrated the major features of KANT, which would also apply in these other cases. We must emphasise that we are not claiming that the example which we have described would be suitable for 'real' use with students, and no effort has presently been made to develop an educationally suitable and robust interface. The example is *an interactive trace of the execution of a model for generation of tutorial dialogue*, incorporating a notion of dialogue focus and a negotiative style.

Future work: what was right and wrong with KANT?

There are a number of immediate criticisms which may be made. The negotiation phases are very lengthy: it would be possible to condense much of this into a single sentence, for example "Do you accept to tell me where you think there is an instance of a phrase boundary?". We did not adopt this approach initially because any such conjunction would require analysis into the 'finegrained' mechanism shown above in the case where this was *not* accepted - do they disagree with who speaks, with the topic, ... ? Furthermore, it is not clear that goals need *always* be negotiated, nor that they are always negotiated *explicitly*. The range of moves which can be performed with the present version of KANT is limited by the fact that there is no understanding of the student's utterances - propositions are simply compared and 'contrasted' - which is one effect of our initial hypothesis that dialogue mechanisms can be initially specified at a 'high' level. In general, the negotiation mechanism itself is too simple, and does not admit of interactive re-negotiation on a given negotiated turn.

Our analyses of computer-mediated dialogue transcripts have given us some analytical data with which to test the assumptions of the first protoype of KANT. Evidence that negotiation forms an important part of educational dialogues is clearly evident from these (and other) dialogues. As a rough measure, of the 83 exchanges in the example dialogue analysed here, approximately 46 are concerned with explicit or implicit negotiation. This dialogue was the second in a total series of 8, and so we would expect a greater degree of negotiation to be initially required in order to define general goals. In later dialogues, negotiation is much more implicit and compressed.

From our dialogue analyses we established that there are a number of cases in which goals are negotiated from general to specific, as a general conflict avoidance strategy. The general/specific dialogue move tree in KANT models this, together with successive satisfaction of parameters as goals become more specific. However, this kind of structure usually only occurs near the beginning of dialogues, and negotiation is much more compressed once speakers have more effectively modelled each other's goals and beliefs. This suggests that recognisable subgoals of an already agreed goal may be negotiated assuming the higher-level goal to still hold, even if they are not the current explicit focus. Our assumption was therefore too strong - KANT needs to incorporate negotiation at this general level of successive negotiation of parameters, and to subsequently be able to switch to a smaller 'grain-size', to negotiate completely instantiated goals in a single utterance.

The distinction between negotiation phases and performance of the negotiated goal in KANT, is generally supported by the transcripts - it relates basically to a difference between metacognitive and cognitive activities (and to dialogue/metadialogue). With respect to turn-taking structures, KANT can effectively modify structures occuring in the transition from INDIFFERENCE to COOPERATION, but does not of course model the change in structures in CONFLICT situations. A major part of future work is to study conflict resolution in dialogue, with its appropriate turn-taking and dialogue structures.

With respect to the range of propositions negotiated, KANT is severely limited by the *lack of a model for problem solving in the domain*, to which negotiation often refers. This is understandable given our research emphasis on dialogue rather than domain models. In future research we are exploring the close relationship between negotiation in dialogue and cooperative problem-solving in simple mechanics [8]. One issue which KANT could have dealt with concerns negotiating *termination* of the dialogue (as analysed earlier) : the system simply accepts if the student wishes to terminate the interaction. As Schegloff and Sacks [45] have argued, *closings* of conversations need to be *prepared* in order to be mutually acceptable, which includes the generation and careful timing of *preclosings*. Some aspects of conversation analysis applied to openings and closing of conversations have been incorporated as a 'grammar of adjacency pairs' in the advice system of Frohlich and Luff [33].

KANT includes mechanisms for recursive continuation of dialogue actions by further negotiation. Speakers do naturally extend their dialogue actions to subgoals which are strictly beyond the initially agreed goal, for example, in giving further information than is requested:

L12: ... If I did name("fish and chips", N). would I get N = [no, no, no, no, 32 no,no,no,32, no,no, etc]? **(negotiates (question"name predicate"))**

T13: No, actually, you'd get an error.
(dialogue action)

The first argument has to be atomic and the second list.
(extension of dialogue action)

Notice that the teacher remains the speaker, and that the extra information is still of a 'reasonable turn length'. It is clear that a simple 'yes or no' answer to such a question would appear 'unhelpful' and almost *conflictual*. We may therefore hypothesise that if the teacher wished to continue an extended discussion of some concept that this *would* be negotiated, or that if the continued extra information required the other to speak, then this would also be negotiated. The lessons which we draw are therefore that subgoals may be negotiated if they require an extension which is longer than the 'normal' length of a single turn, or require speaker change. Otherwise, a speaker may extend their negotiated and agreed dialogue action without explicit negotiation. We would require further empirical work in order to establish the precise extent to which turns may be extended by a speaker. The initial simplificiation in KANT of allowing a speaker to continue to negotiate subgoals of an action in a simple depth-first search manner must therefore also be modified. The question of how long a 'reasonable' turn is can probably be simply resolved by giving the student the possibility of *interrupting*. From the point of view of the system, however, we need further research before we could specify exactly *when* the system should interrupt the student. Given a certain educational philosophy which prefers the maximum of initiative to be taken by the student (see the educational preferences included in KANT), it is possible that this aspect should *not* be symmetrical for the system and student: we would want the student to be allowed to continue a turn as much as possible, provided the system recognises that their actions are relevant to achieving the agreed goal.

In the dialogues analysed we have not observed cases which can be straightforwardly interpreted as instances where a speaker refuses to cooperate with a negotiated goal because it is *not relevant* in the sense of being in focus. From the opposite point of view, all goals negotiated which *were* relevant to the previous goal were accepted, relevance being understood here in terms of focus on the goal and/or topic [25]. The model of relevance incorporated in KANT combines topic-based focus, with speaker roles and dialogue goals, in a complex set of preconditions with respect to the dialogue state. Conflicts arise mostly in the dialogues because the goals proposed concerned the form of the dialogue itself - such as its termination - rather than its topic. The extent to which a speaker accepts such negotiated goals must relate to higher level persistent goals, or commitments (again, in Cohen and Levesque's terms, [12]) - such as "that the student should complete the problem" - and the extent to which they are in direct conflict.

The simple encoding hypotheses used in KANT were consistent with the general theory of memory adopted [2], but are clearly only a first approximation of the features which need to be modelled. The hypothesis of encoding strength increasing with repetition, leading to a memory representation clearly does not address the problem of when a memory trace concerning another speaker's beliefs is genuinely *adopted by the hearer as their own*. This difficult problem will need to be addressed in the future in terms of recent AI theories of *belief revision* (see [26]).

In summary, we would claim that KANT succeeded in providing some initial answers to our two basic questions, as a basis for further research : what to negotiate, and whether to cooperate in tutorial dialogues. Our preliminary answers are based on a model for focus in semantic memory, and a hierarchical representation of dialogue moves. The system is essentially restricted to negotiating dialogue goals from a position where no joint interaction goals are currently established. An ITS which is able to negotiate learning goals, and which accords a larger degree of symmetrical autonomy to the student may be argued to provide a better basis for joint construction of knowledge *qua* justified belief rather than for its communication. Many hard problems for cognitive science remain, the most important of which concern the resolution of conflict in dialogue, and a theory of belief revision as a result of negotiation. KANT has provided us with a cognitive framework within which to situate this future research.

Conclusions

Negotiation plays an important rôle in tutorial dialogues, which argues strongly for its inclusion in interaction models in Intelligent Tutoring Systems. Given the different nature of the goals and beliefs of teachers (and ITS) and learners, it is clear that negotiation in educational discourse fulfills the important functions of securing cooperativity and genuine *engagement* in the educational process on the part of the student, and the possibility of a joint construction of meaning. As a phenomenon in interaction, it is closely linked with *metacognitive awareness* on the part of a speaker, as a prerequisite for negotiation of future cooperative control of joint dialogue goals. An important feature of metacognitive awareness is a speaker's assessment of their own capabilities and their *affective attitude* to towards the possibility of achieving their goals, in conditions of apparent failure. When we consider the problem of how one speaker can successfully negotiate their goals, therefore, the questions of affect and motivation are particularly important : in order to persuade a speaker to adopt a goal or belief we need to convince them to *prefer* that goal or belief, and it is clear that this is closely linked to motivation and other affective states. Progress for cognitive modelling in the area of affect [17], the emotions [40] and motivation [51] is now at the stage where we may have reasonable hope of including such aspects in models for dialogue in Intelligent Tutoring Systems. In future research we plan to validate and refine KANT by a combination of techniques. From the dialogues analysed we have already identified a number of modifications to be made. Modelling these additional phenomena requires the inclusion of additional *theoretical primitives* - to be derived principally from aspects of agent theory - for representing commitments, intentions, interests, preferences and affective states [22,12]. We aim to combine these theoretical primitives into a model which is situated within a *cognitive architecture* [2]. In order to model resolution of conflict by negotiation, we need to situate results from *belief revision* research in AI and agent theory within the cognitive architecture, in order to model the strategic dialogue action performed by human interlocutors. The dialogues which we have analysed are concerned with a *problem-solving domain*, and hence show strong emphasis on the negotiation of *goals* as opposed to *beliefs*. To explore the rôle of negotiation in the joint 'construction of meaning', we are currently analysing dialogue transcripts for students working in pairs, attempting to explain phenomena in physics (simple mechanics) [8]. Finally, in order to test an extended version of KANT with real users, we plan to develop a graphical interface to the system (which is implemented in LISP). This should enable us to test the extent to which students agree with the relevance decisions of the system, whether the dialogues are perceived to be coherent, and the extent to which conflicts which arise can be resolved.

Postscript

In the context of a collection of papers on "New Directions in ITS", we would like to propose a relatively new direction. Amongst current directions, we have a view of the ITS as 'guide', 'collaborator', 'tool', 'learning environment', 'domain expert', and so on. Each view has its own educational, philosophical, psychological and sociological theories, with its own answers concerning the most effective means for achieving its educational goals. All of these approaches do, however, have something in common : they assume that the student(s) will learn *during the interaction with the computer*. We would like to raise the question as to whether this needs to be the case - are one-to-one interactions of an hour or less duration between students and tutors in higher education and adult training principally concerned with *learning*, or are they rather concerned with assessing progress, negotiating new appropriate learning goals and motivating the student to achieve them outside that interaction ? An answer to such a question relies crucially on our assumptions concerning the social educational setting of computer use. Thus understood, we believe that the two viewpoints on negotiation discussed at the beginning of this chapter are in fact essentially complementary. We propose as a direction for ITS research that the computer may be viewed as a *negotiator of appropriate learning goals*, and *manager of the students' motivation to achieve those goals* in the wider educational context. Such a direction for ITS requires fundamental research on both the cognitive processes underlying negotiation in educational interactions and the wider social context within which educational goals may be achieved.

Acknowledgements

The research on the first prototype of KANT was conducted at the Open University, Centre for Information Technology in Education, under the supervision of Mark Elsom-Cook. Thanks to him for guidance and encouragement, and for providing the dialogues analysed. My ideas have greatly benefitted from discussions with Andrée Tiberghien at CNRS-IRPEACS (Lyon).

References

1. Allen, J. & Perrault, C.R.: Analyzing Intention in Utterances. Artificial Intelligence 15, 143-178, 1980.

2. Anderson, J.: The Architecture of Cognition. Harvard University Press, Cambridge, MA, 1983.

3. Baker, M.J.: An artificial intelligence approach to musical grouping analysis. Contemporary Music Review, 3(1), 43-68, Harwood Academic Publishers, 1989.

4. Baker, M.J.: A cognitive model for perception of musical grouping structures. Contemporary Music Review 3(2), Harwood Academic Publishers, 1989.

5. Baker, M.J.: A model for tutorial dialogues based on critical argument. Artificial Intelligence and Education, (eds. Bierman, D., Breuker, J. & Sandberg, J.), IOS Publishers, Amsterdam, 1989.

6. Baker, M.J.: Negotiated Tutoring: A Model for Interaction in Intelligent Tutoring Systems. PhD thesis in Cognitive Science, (Unpublished) Institute of Educational Technology, Centre for Information Technology in Education, The Open University, UK 1989.

7. Baker, M.J.: Arguing with the tutor: a model for tutorial dialogue in uncertain knowledge domains. Guided-Discovery Tutoring (ed. Elsom-Cook, M.), p. 141-170. Paul Chapman Publishing, London, 1990.

8. Baker, M.J.: Negotiated explanations in students' physics dialogues. Intelligent Learning Environments and Knowledge Acquisition in Physics. (eds. Tiberghien, A. & Mandl, H.), NATO ASI Series F, Vol. 86. Springer-Verlag, Berlin, 1992.

9. Bond, A.H. & Glaser, L.: Distributed Artificial Intelligence. Morgan Kaufmann, San Mateo, CA, 1988.

10. Brown, J.S. & Burton, R.R.: An investigation of computer coaching for informal learning activities. Intelligent Tutoring Systems (eds. Sleeman, D. & Brown, J.S.), Academic Press, 1982.

11. Brown, G. & Yule, G.: Discourse Analysis. Cambridge University Press, Cambridge, UK, 1983.

12. Cohen, P.R. & Levesque, H.J.: Intention is choice with committment. Artificial Intelligence 42(2-3), 13-261, 1990.

13. Cohen, P.R. & Perrault, R.: Elements of a plan-based theory of speech acts. Cognitive Science 3, 177-212, 1979.

14. Collins, A. & Stevens, A. L.: A cognitive theory of inquiry teaching. Instructional-Design Theories and Models: An Overview of Their Current Status (ed. Reigeluth, C. M.), Lawrence Erlbaum Associates, Hillsdale, NJ, 1983.

15. Clancey, W.: Knowledge-Based Tutoring: The GUIDON Program. MIT Press, Cambridge, MA, 1987.

16. Doise, W., Mugny, G. & Perret-Clermont, A.N.: Social interaction and cognitive development. European Journal of Social Psychology, 5, 367-83, 1975.

17. Donohew, L., Sypher, H.E. & Higgins, E.T.: Communication, Social Cognition and Affect. Lawrence Erlbaum Associates, Hillsdale, NJ, 1988.

18. Edwards, D. & Mercer, N.: Common Knowledge: The Development of Understanding in the Classroom. Methuen, London, 1987.

19. Elsom-Cook,M.: Design considerations of an intelligent tutoring system for programming languages. PhD thesis (unpublished), Warwick University, UK, 1984.

20. Elsom-Cook, M.: Analysis of a tutorial dialogue. Guided-Discovery Tutoring: A Framework for ICAI Research, (ed. Elsom-Cook, M.), Paul Chapman Publishing, London, pp. 113-131, 1990.

21. Ferrara, A.: Pragmatics. The Handbook of Discourse Analysis, Vol. 2 : Dimensions of Discourse (ed. van Dijk, T.), Academic Press, London, 1985.

22. Galliers, J.R.: A Theoretical Framework for Computer Models of Cooperative Dialogue, Acknowledging Multi-Agent Conflict. PhD thesis (unpublished), Human Cognition Research Laboratory, The Open University UK, 1989.

23. Gilbert, N.: Explanation as Process. Proceedings of 4th Alvey Workshop on Explanation, University of Manchester, UK, September 1988.

24. Grosz, B.J.: Focusing and description in natural language dialogues. Elements of discourse understanding, (eds. Joshi, A.K., Webber, B.L. & Sag, I.A.), 84-105, Cambridge University Press, Cambridge, UK, 1981.

25. Grosz, B.J. & Sidner, C.: Attention, Intentions and the structure of discourse. Computational Linguistics, 12 (3), 175-204, 1986.

26. Halpern, J. (ed.): Theoretical Aspects of Reasoning about Knowledge. Morgan Kaufmann, Los Altos, CA, 1986.

27. Kiss, G.: High-Level Dialogue in Man-Machine Interaction. A Survey Commissioned by the Alvey Directorate. Human Cognition Research Laboratory, The Open University, UK, 1986.

28. Konolige, K.: A Deduction Model of Belief. Pitman, London, 1986.

29. Lave, J.: Cognition in Practice. Cambridge University Press, Cambridge, UK, 1988.

30. Lave, J. & Wenger, E.: Situated Learning: Legitimate Peripheral Participation. Institute for Research on Learning, Report No. IRL 89-0013, December 1989.

31. Levin, J.A. & Moore, J.A.: Dialogue-Games: Metacommunication Structures for Natural Language Interaction. Cognitive Science 1, Part 4, 395-420, 1977.

32. Levinson, S.C.: Pragmatics. Cambridge University Press, UK, 1983.

33. Luff, P., Gilbert, N. & Frohlich, D.: Computers and Conversation. Academic Press, London, 1990.

34. McGuigan, S. & Black, J.B.: Creation and Comprehension of Arguments. Knowledge Structures, (eds. Galambos, J.A., Abelson,R.P. & Black,J.B.), Lawrence Erlbaum Associates, Hillsdale, NJ, 1986.

35. Miller, P.L.: A critiquing approach to expert computer advice: ATTENDING. Pitman Publishing, London, 1984.

36. Moore, R.C.: Reasoning about knowledge and action. SRI International AI Center Technical Report No. 191, 1980.

37. Morley, I. & Stephenson, G.: The Social Psychology of Bargaining. Allen & Unwin, London, 1977.

38. Ohlsson, S.: Cognitive Science and Instruction : Why the Revolution is Not Here (Yet). Learning and Instruction, (eds. Mandl, H., De Corte, E., Bennett, N. & Friedrich, H.F.), Pergamon Press, Oxford, 1990.

39. O'Malley, C.: Understanding Explanation. Cognitive Science Research Report No. CSRP-88, University of Sussex, UK, May 1987.

40. Ortony, A., Clore, G.L. & Collins, A.: The Cognitive Structure of Emotions. Cambridge University Press, Cambridge, UK, 1988.

41. Perrault, R.: An application of default logic to speech act theory. Intentions in Communication, (eds. Cohen, P.R., Morgan, J. & Pollack, M.E.), MIT Press, Cambridge A, 1990.

42. Petrie-Brown, A.: Intelligent Tutoring Dialogue: The structures of an interaction. Artificial Intelligence and Education (eds. Bierman, D., Breuker, J. & Sandberg, J.), IOS Publishers, Amsterdam, 1989.

43. Power, R.: The organisation of purposeful dialogues. Linguistics, 17, 107-152, 1979.

44. Reichman, R.: Getting Computers to Talk Like You and Me. MIT Press, Cambridge, MA 1985.

45. Schegloff, E.A. & Sacks, H.: Opening up Closings. Semiotica, 8 (4), 289-327, 1973.

46. Searle, J. : Speech Acts: An Essay in the Philosopy of Language. Cambridge University Press, UK, 1969.

47. Seely-Brown, J.S.: Toward a New Epistemology of Learning. Keynote Address to Montréal-ITS '88. Intelligent Tutoring Systems at the Crossroads of AI, (eds. Frasson, C. & Gauthiar, J.), Ablex Publishing, Norwood NJ, 1989.

48. Sinclair, J. & Coulthard, R.M.: Towards and Analysis of Discourse: The English Used by Teachers and Pupils. Oxford University Press, UK, 1975.

49. Sperber, D. & Wilson, D.: Relevance: Communication and Cognition. Basil Blackwell, Oxford, 1986.

50. Toulmin, S., Rieke,R. & Janik, A.: An Introduction to Reasoning. Macmillan , New York, 1979.

51. Weinhert, F.E. & Kluwe, R.H. (eds.): Metacognition, Motivation and Understanding. Lawrence Erlbaum, Hillsdale NJ, 1987.

52. Woolf, B.: Representing complex knowledge in an intelligent machine tutor. Artificial Intelligence and Human Learning, (ed. Self, J.), Chapman and Hall Computing, London, 1988.

Integration of Knowledge in Multi-Agent Environments

Pavel B. Brazdil
LIACC, Laboratory of AI and Computer Science, University of Porto, Rua Campo Alegre, 823, 4100 Porto, Portugal

Abstract. In this paper we discuss the technique of *knowledge integration* and which can be exploited in intelligent teaching systems (ITS) working in noisy domains. As several different formalizations can usually be found, it is difficult to determine which formalization is right and hence rely on an in-built formalization which enables it to identify students' errors. In our view this problem can be resolved by employing the method of knowledge integration. The method enables us to identify those parts of students' knowledge that would *improve* (or *impair*) overall performance. It is thus possible to avoid the usual trap that some systems fall into. They try to correct the student regardless whether their knowledge exceeds the tutor's!

Keywords: Formalization, Knowledge integration, Language differences, Learning concept definitions, Learning unknown concepts.

Introduction

In this paper we describe a method for merging several separate theories (knowledge bases). We believe that this technique can be exploited in intelligent teaching systems (ITS) oriented towards noisy domains. In these domains several different formalizations can normally be found. These often have a similar performance, and hence it is difficult to decide which formalization is right. It is difficult to rely on an in-built formalization of an ITS when correcting the student's errors. The method enables us to identify those parts of students' knowledge that would *impair* performance. The method can equally well identify the parts of students' knowledge that *improve* performance. It is thus possible to avoid the problem of correcting the student if this is not necessary.

This paper describes the technique of knowledge integration in some detail. It shows how different theories can be merged together. Our experiments in noisy medical domains have shown that the integrated theory usually had a much better performance than original theories.

Method of Knowledge Integration

In this section we will describe the method of knowledge integration in more detail. Basically, the process involves a preparatory phase in which a group of systems (agents) is selected and organized into a group that can function together. The group can include systems S_1-S_n that are capable of constructing theories from data, responding to external queries and communicating with one another. Here we shall assume that this has already been done and that the system organization is fixed[1].

Having defined the organization of the multi-agent system, it is necessary to determine the overall objectives. That is, for example, one can define which concepts are to be acquired and/or describe in some way the required performance. This is important if we want the multi-agent system to decide when to stop altering its theories. Here we will follow what has been done in the past and let the user control this issue. Consequently, here we will be concerned with, basically, the following three phases:

(1) Generation of independent theories (by consultation or inductive learning),
(2) Competitive characterization of system´s theories,
(3) Construction of the integrated theory.

In phase (1) the systems S_1-S_n work in an independent manner, and as a result produce theories T_1-T_n. Each system involved constructs its *own theory* on the basis of its own experience. Here S_i can represent either a human, or an inductive learning tool. In either case S_i will produce theory T_i.

In phase (2) the individual theories are *characterized* using tests. Without loss of generality let us assume that this is actually controlled by some agent SI. This agent poses a query to all the agents involved, waits for the answers and then proceeds with the next query. Any of the systems S_1-S_n could act as SI. The subsystem responsible for characterization of theories is referred to as INTEG3.1. Phase (3) is dedicated to the issue of constructing one integrated theory (TI) on the bases of the results obtained in phase (2). This task is also done by INTEG3.1.

The three phases mentioned could be followed by two additional ones:

(4) Adoption of integrated theory by one (or more) systems,
(5) Check whether the process should continue, and if so, go to (1).

---

[1] In general systems can be given the ability to reorganize themselves. These are some of the concerns of Distributed Artificial Intelligence (see e. g. [1]), but they are outside the scope of this paper.

In this paper we will be concerned mainly with the phases (1)-(3). The issue of how one could construct a 'closed loop system', capable of taking the integrated theory and using it input in further learning will be discussed in a future paper. The next section describes the phases (1)-(3) in more detail.

Generation of Individual Theories

Inductive Learning Subsystems

The decision concerning which system we should choose to generate individual theories is not really too important in the context of this work. Here we require only that the system(s) are capable of generating theories that perform reasonably well on tests. As we had earlier reimplemented AQ- and ID3- like systems, we decided to use these as the basic inductive engines in our set-up.

The inductive rule learning system *Irule1* is an incremental learning program that was partially inspired by CN2 [7]. This system updates the existing rules incrementally, using operations of generalization and/or specialization.

The reimplementation of ID3 based on earlier work (e.g. [13,5,6,7]) will be referred to as *Itree1* (Inductive Tree Learning System). So far this system does not incorporate pruning. The decision tree generated is automatically converted into a rule form which we find more amenable for further manipulation.

Different theories that are required by the knowledge integration system (INTEG3.1) are generated by the inductive learning systems in a series of *independent learning tasks*. In each task the inductive learning system generated a theory (consisting of a set of rules) on the basis of its own data.

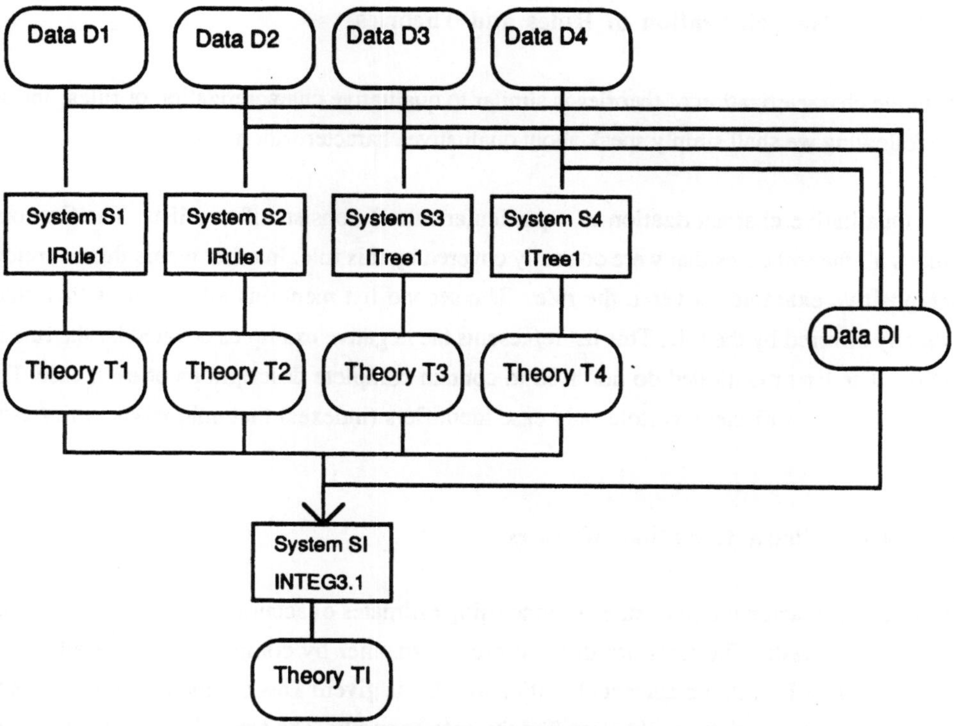

Fig. 1 Set-up for Knowledge Integration Experiments

Competitive Characterization of Theories

After the theories have been constructed by the individual systems they are characterized on the basis of integration tests for which we need some data. Let us refer to this data as the set DI. The easiest way to obtain this set is to take the union of the data sets D1 .. Dn. This is the approach we have actually adopted. In general, however, the set DI may consist of any other representative sample of data.

The results of tests are both qualitative and quantitative. The objective of qualitative characterization is to provide detailed information about relative benefits of individual rules or theories to the integration system. This information takes the form of lists of cases covered by a particular theory or rule. The objective of quantitative characterization is to estimate the overall accuracy of the individual theory (or rule).

Qualitative Characterization of Rules and Theories

Qualitative characterization of theories is similar to qualitative characterization of rules, and so in the following we shall simply speak about qualitative characterization of rules.

Qualitative characterization of a particular rule R consists of two lists. The first one mentions all the test cases that were correctly covered by this rule. In other words this list refers to the positive examples covered the rule. The second list mentions all the cases that were incorrectly covered by the rule. This list represents the negative examples covered by the rule in question. The lists mentioned do not need to contain complete descriptions of each case. For our purposes it is sufficient to store only case identifiers (indexes) that uniquely identify each case.

Quantitative Characterization of Rules

Quantitative characterization of rules is done using estimates of accuracy. These are calculated on the basis of tests. The tests are done in a usual manner by comparing the classification predicted by rule R with the correct classification that is given. This comparison enables us to decide whether the particular rule classified the case correctly. The classification errors caused by *misclassification* are sometimes referred to as errors of *commission*. Errors of *omission* arise whenever an expert or a system fails to classify some case, that is, when no classification is actually predicted.

Here we will use the notion of *rule quality* which depends on estimates of accuracy. In the following we shall describe one particular method of determining rule quality which has proved rather successful in practice.

In our system rule quality is calculated using the expression:

$$Q_R = AC_R * EST\_COV_{C,R} \qquad (1)$$

where AC_R represents an estimate of *accuracy* of rule *R* and $EST\_COV_{C,R}$ an estimate of coverage. The estimate of accuracy of rule *R* is calculated using the following formula:

$$AC_R = C_R / (C_R + ER_R) \qquad (2)$$

where C_R represents the number of correctly classified cases, and ER_R the number of misclassifications. As we can see AC_R represents a ratio of correctly classified cases to all relevant cases. The errors of errors of omission (EN_R) are not included in this expression. These play a role in $EST\_COV_{C,R}$ discussed below.

The expression $EST\_COV_{C,R}$ represents a function whose value depends on *coverage*.[2] When used, it forces the system to opt for rules with relatively high coverage of the corresponding class. The value lies between 1/e and 1. It is calculated as follows:

$$EST\_COV_{C,R} = \exp((C_R / N_C) - 1) \quad \text{where} \quad (3)$$

$$N_C = C_R + ER_R + EN_R \quad (4)$$

The antecedent of rule *R* determines with which class the rule is concerned (say C). Then N_C represents the total number of examples of this class. The expression C_R / N_C represents a ratio of correct classifications to the total number of examples of the class. The expression captures the notion of *relative coverage* of class C by rule R.
Let us consider an example. In our system, the assertion,

rule(1-5, metastase <-- earlyuptakein = *no* & defectinnode = *lac_central,* 15, 3).

for example, represents rule 1-5 (rule 5 of theory T_1). The numbers 15 and 3 represent number of correctly classified cases ($C_{1\text{-}5}$) and number of misclassifications ($ER_{1\text{-}5}$). The accuracy of this rule is thus

$$AC_{1\text{-}5} = C_{1\text{-}5} / (C_{1\text{-}5} + ER_{1\text{-}5}) = 15 / (15 + 3) = 0.833$$

Supposing we had 30 examples of *metastase* ($N_{metastase} = 30$) then $Q_{1\text{-}5}$ would be:

$$Q_{1\text{-}5} = 0.83 * \exp(15/30 - 1) = 0.833 * 0.61 = 0.506$$

Both qualitative and quantitative characterizations of theories are used in the construction of the integrated theory. More details about this method and about comparisons with other methods of estimating rule quality can be found in [3].

Generation of the Integrated Theory

The integrated theory TI is constructed on the basis of the candidate set TC. Initially set TC contains all the rules of the individual theories $T_1..T_n$. The objective is to select some rules from TC and transfer them into TI so as to achieve good performance (accuracy). The method relies on the qualitative and quantitative characterization of rules and includes the following steps:

---

2 This method was devised by Torgo (see [3] for more details).

(1) Order rules in the candidate set according to their estimates of quality.

(2) Select the rule R with the best quality and include it in TI.

(3) Mark the cases covered by R.

(5) Recalculate the quality estimates of rules excluding the marked cases.

(6) Go back to (1).

The process of adding new rules to TI terminates when the accuracy of the 'best rule' in TC falls below a certain threshold.

Results

The purpose of our experiments was to compare the performance of the integrated theory with the performance of the original theories.

The tests were performed on lymphography data obtained from JSI, Ljubljana. This data contains 148 cases which are characterized by 18 attributes and there are 4 possible classes.

Each theory was generated by an inductive system (*IRule1* or *ITree1*) on the basis of a given number of examples which were selected from a given pool by a random process. The numbers of training examples used were 5, 10 .. 50. In order to exclude the possibility of fortuitous results the experiments related to N training examples were repeated 20 times.

The performance of system S_1, obtained on the basis of, say, 15 training examples was assessed by calculating the mean performance of 20 similar theories generated by this system. The mean performance in this case was 57.0 %. The results of our experiments are shown in Table 1. The performance figures are shown in Table 1a. Standard deviations related to these measurements appear in Table 1b.

	5	10	15	20	25	30	35	40	45	50 examples
S_1	38.8	47.2	57.0	54.1	52.0	58.1	56.4	57.3	60.5	64.6 %
S_2	39.0	52.6	49.9	54.0	57.4	55.8	58.2	58.6	63.4	63.6
S_3	42.3	51.0	55.3	60.5	61.4	66.4	63.5	64.6	68.6	70.9
S_4	45.5	56.3	60.5	60.6	64.3	62.0	64.4	64.7	68.6	66.6
TI	55.1	66.5	70.0	73.1	74.2	73.4	73.8	74.4	75.9	76.5 %
Gain	13.7	14.7	14.3	15.8	15.4	12.9	13.2	13.1	10.6	10.0

Table 1a. Performance

The first four rows of the table show the performance figures of individual systems (S_1-S_4). Systems S_1,S_2 use IRule1 inductive learning method while systems S_3,S_4 use method ITree1. All the figures shown are *means* obtained on the basis of 20 independent experiments. The last row shows the gain calculated as a difference between TI and the mean (S_1+S_2+S_3+S_4) / 4. As can be seen the performance gains were around 15%.

	5	10	15	20	25	30	35	40	45	50 examples
S_1	14.6	8.8	7.7	9.0	7.7	9.7	10.7	6.9	6.5	9.6 %
S_2	16.1	12.7	13.0	9.2	9.9	7.2	8.1	9.3	9.0	11.0
S_3	17.9	15.3	12.7	10.6	11.3	8.1	9.2	9.7	6.0	7.0
S_4	23.0	14.0	14.3	11.5	11.1	10.0	7.6	7.4	9.9	10.1
TI	9.4	8.9	8.6	5.4	6.6	8.0	6.8	6.7	7.4	6.6 %

Table 1b. Standard Deviations of Performance

Table 1. Comparisons of the Integrated Theory TI and the Individual Systems (S_1-S_4).

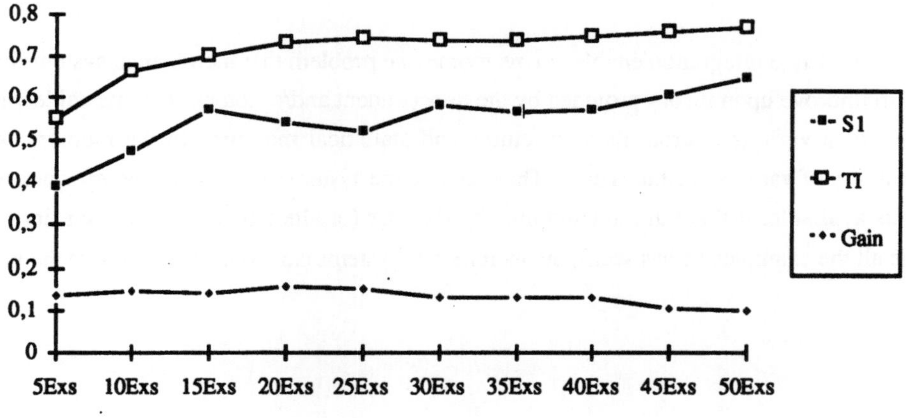

Fig. 2. Performance of the Integrated Theory TI and System S_1.

In this figure the performance of the integrated theory TI is contrasted with the performance of system S_1. Standard deviations are represented by vertical bars. The graph has been constructed on the basis of data shown in Table 1.

Fig.2 shows some of the performance results in a graphical form. The performance of the integrated theory TI exceeds the performance of the individual systems by about 15%. The integrated theory is also quite "stable", in the sense that its performance does not fluctuate as much as the performance of the individual systems (see Table 1b).

Discussion Concerning Knowledge Integration

Knowledge integration is concerned with issues that are related to those in incremental learning systems, such as ID4 [15], ID5 [17], AQ16 [9], for example. Both knowledge integration and incremental learning attempt to construct a theory that explains best the given data. There are some important differences between the two approaches, however.

When we talk about incremental learning, usually it is assumed that only one system is constructing theories by employing some incremental version of a given learning algorithm. In consequence all the data is actually analyzed by this system at one time or another. Knowledge integration, on the other hand, involves several systems all of which try to construct their own theories on the basis of their own experience. Although knowledge integration may require some common experience in the process of constructing an integrated theory, we are not in favour of simply transferring all the data to one system. People do not use only "raw data" when they communicate with others about certain world phenomena.

Knowledge integration enables to overcome one problem that incremental systems have - how to improve upon theory provided by the user (student and/or tutor). Incremental learning systems keep various internal data structures and statistical measures in the memory (e.g. informativity of various attributes etc.). These enable the system to update its theory when new data gets available. If these are not supplied by the user (or alternatively, if the user does not provide all the examples he has seen), the incremental systems can do little to improve the given theory.

Resolving Language Differences Between Agents

In the previous sections we have assumed that all agents use the same predicate vocabulary. The purpose of this part of the paper is to show what we can do if this assumption does not hold. That is, we will show how agents can overcome certain language differences automatically, without human intervention. As we shall see standard machine learning techniques can be used to acquire the meaning of other agents′ concepts.

The problem of language differences typically arises when knowledge is obtained from several different sources (human or not). As [16]have pointed out, that *same* term can have *different* meaning in different systems. They call this situation a *conflict*. *Different* terms may, however, have *identical* meanings. Shaw and Gaines call this situation a *correspondence*.

System INTEG3.1 which has been briefly reviewed earlier deals with the problem of *conflict*, but not of correspondence. The system uses empirical evidence to decide whose definition of a given concepts is 'best'. In this part we will be concerned with the problem of correspondence. Although, the meanings of *parent* and *father* are not identical, the system will establish how they are related.

Relation to Other Work

Murray and Porter [1989] have developed a system PROTOKI (a prototype of a larger system KI). The system is intended to provide support when new piece of information is integrated in the existing knowledge base. The process of integration involves three main steps: recognition, elaboration and adaptation. The third step is concerned with resolution of anomalies. These arise, for example, when conflicting solutions can be reached using different chains of reasoning. The prototype system inspects the explanation that lead to the anomaly and tries to determine the weakest premise. This premise is then modified.

On one hand Murray and Porter´s work goes further than ours. So far we have not tried to integrated knowledge consisting of rules that are chained. On the other hand PROTOKI requires a great deal of domain dependent knowledge, and besides, does not attempt to deal with the problem of *correspondence*. It does not try to establish relationships between similar concepts that may already exist within the system.

The remaining part of the paper is organized as follows. Section 5 is devoted to the description of how different agents can arrive at different (but overlapping) views of reality. Section 6 identifies some problems that can arise when agents try to integrate knowledge, but use different predicate vocabulary. A solution to this problem is described in Section 6.1.

Our Multi-Agent Scenario

The experiments described in later sections involve two agents (A, B) and the user. The user can be viewed as another agent. Our scenario also includes a micro-world of family relations. Actually, we will distinguish various views of this micro-world. All of these views are shown in Fig.3. Note that this figure shows how *we see* the domain. The agents′ representation of this domain will be shown later.

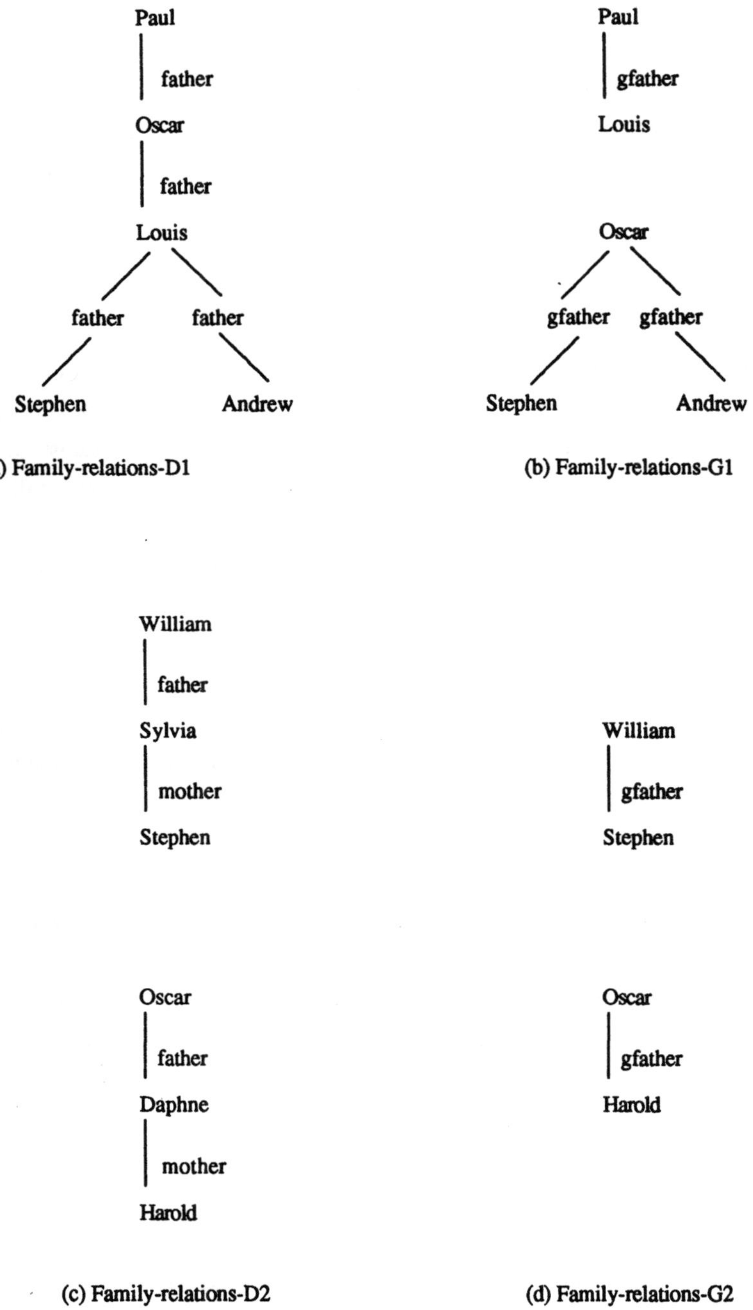

(a) Family-relations-D1 (b) Family-relations-G1

(c) Family-relations-D2 (d) Family-relations-G2

Fig.3 The given micro-world of family relations and its views.

The interpretation of this figure is rather obvious. The link between *Paul* and *Oscar*, for example, with the label *"father"* represents the fact that *"Paul is a father of Oscar"*. The term *gfather* is an abbreviation of *grandfather*.

The negative facts will be represented by the following assertions:

Oscar is not a grandfather of Sylvia.	Sylvia is not a grandfather Stephen.
Stephen is not a grandfather Oscar.	Louis is not a grandfather Sylvia.
Stephen is not a grandfather Stephen.	Paul is not a grandfather Andrew.

This micro-world will be referred to as *Family-relations-N1*. The microworld *Family-relations-N2* will be assumed to be identical to *Family-relations-N1*.

Agent´s Differing Views of Reality

Perceptive actions provide the agents with a *description* of the relevant part of the world. This description consists of a set of predicates that are part of A´s vocabulary. Here we will assume that A´s predicate vocabulary includes the following predicates:

father (X,Y), mother (X,Y), gfather (X,Y).

After agent A has executed a perceptive action, its knowledge base will include instances of the three predicates mentioned. If A´s perceptive action has been directed towards the micro-world of *Family-relations-D1*, its knowledge base will contain the assertions:

father ("Paul", "Oscar").	father ("Louis", "Stephen").	(D1A)
father ("Oscar", "Louis").	father ("Louis", "Andrew").	

Similarly, perception of *Family-relations-G1* will give:

gfather ("Oscar", "Stephen").	gfather ("Paul", "Louis").	(G1A)
gfather ("Oscar", "Andrew").		

The set G1A represents the "correct answer set" that we would like the agent to derive on the basis of its knowledge. Agent A´s view of the negative facts *(Family-relations-N1)* will be referred to as N1A.

In our scenario agent B has a somewhat different view of reality. First, let us assume that B´s predicate vocabulary includes:

parent (X,Y), male (X), female (X), gfather (X,Y),

but not *father(X,Y)* or *mother(X,Y)*. Second, let us assume that B´s attention is directed towards *Family-relations-D2*. B´s representation of the corresponding facts is:

parent ("William", "Sylvia").	parent ("Oscar", "Daphne").	(D2B)
parent ("Sylvia", "Stephen").	parent ("Daphne", "Harold").	
male ("William").	male ("Oscar").	
male ("Stephen").	male ("Harold").	
female ("Sylvia").	female ("Daphne").	

Agent B´s representation of *Family-relations-G2* will similarly be:

gfather ("William", "Stephen").	gfather ("Oscar", "Harold").	(G2B)

Agent B´s view of the negative facts *(Family-relations-N2)* will give assertions called N2B.

Construction of Different Theories of Reality

As we have mentioned earlier our agents are capable of inducing theories on the basis of given (observed) facts. The outcome of inductive process depends on a number of factors, such as:

- inductive method employed,
- the facts available,
- background knowledge,
- predicate vocabulary adopted,
- other "inductive biases".

Here we will assume that both agents use the same inductive method called GOLEM. The method is based on *Relative Least General Generalization* and is described in detail in [11].

The assumption concerning the agents´ inductive method simplifies somewhat our exposition here. However, the techniques described here are in no way based on (or limited by) this assumption.

The facts contained in the set (D1A) and the correct answer set (G1A) and the negative facts (N1A) enable agent A to generate the following definition of *´gfather´*:

gfather(X,Y) :- father(X,Z), father(Z,Y). (R1A)

Rule (R1A) covers all A´s positive examples of *'gfathèr'*, and so the correct answer set (G1A)
is no longer necessary for answering queries.

As B uses a different set of initial facts, and also, different predicate vocabulary, the rule generated by B is different from A´s:

gfather(X,Y) :- parent(X,Z), male(X), parent(Z,Y), female(Z). (R2B)

This rule covers B´s positive examples of *'gfather'* (set G2B).

We notice that A´s concept of *gfather(..)* is defined in terms of A´s vocabulary, that is, using the concept of *father(..)*. Similarly B´s concept is defined in terms of B´s vocabulary. In our case this vocabulary includes the concepts *parent(..)*, *male(..)* and *female(..)*. This is the reason why agent A fails to prove, for example,

gfather ("William", "Stephen")

using

gfather(X,Y) :- father(X,Z), father(Z,Y) (R1A)

and B´s data

parent ("William", "Sylvia").
parent ("Sylvia", "Stephen").
male ("William").

The reason for this failure is that A´s definition of *gfather(..)* contains the reference to *father(..)*, but B´s data uses the concepts *parent(..)*, *male(..)* and *female(..)*. As agents A and B use a somewhat different vocabulary, A´s definition cannot be applied to B´s data. In the next section we will see how this problem can be overcome.

Theory Integration

The aim of knowledge integration could be defined as follows. Consider all theories available and construct an integrated theory taking into account performance criteria of various constituents.

Suppose agent A has been designated to construct an integrated theory on the basis of the individual theories acquired earlier by agents A and B. As each theory consists of only one rule, the candidate rules set will contain the following two rules:

gfather(X,Y) :- father(X,Z), father(Z,Y). (R1A)
gfather(X,Y) :- parent(X,Z), male(X), parent(Z,Y), female(Z). (R2B)

The agent responsible for integration needs also to be supplied with available data (D1A, D2B) and required answers (G1A, G2B). The integration algorithm will test the given rules using the available data. Here we will skip the details. Both rules will be simply be included in the integrated theory. The resulting theory enables the agent to answer correctly any query selected from the set G1A or G2B. For example, the query

gfather ("William", "Stephen")

will succeed. Despite this apparent success, one important issue has remained unresolved. Agent A is unable to <u>perceive</u> <u>B´s</u> <u>micro-world</u> and <u>act</u> correctly. The perceptive action directed towards B´s micro-world *(Family-relations-D2)* will update A´s knowledge base with:

father ("William", "Sylvia"). father ("Oscar", "Daphne"). (D2A)
father ("Sylvia", "Stephèn"). father ("Daphne", "Harold").

It can be verified that the goal

gfather ("William", "Stephen")

will fail. The failure is due to the fact that A´s rules and data use *different vocabulary*. Rule R2B, for example, contains the predicates parent(X,Z), male(X), parent(Z,Y), female(Z)

For A these are unknown concepts. They do not figure among A´s primitive concepts, and moreover, agent A has no definitions showing what these concepts mean. In the next section we will show how these definitions can be acquired.

Acquiring the Meaning of Unknown Concepts

We have shown that rules acquired by communication can contain concepts that are simply unknown to the recipient agent. This can cause problems when these rules are used. In this section we will describe techniques that can overcome these problems. As we shall see standard machine learning techniques can be used to generate definitions of unknown concepts.

One crucial step in our method is the following. The agents should attempt to describe the "same situation" enabling them to formulate the required relationships. The technique used here seems to be quite common in human learning. Consider, for example, a mother and a child. The mother will often describe the situation the child can see. The child is able to learn the meaning of her mother´s concepts by relating the mother´s description to its own experience.

Let us apply this strategy to our scenario. Here we will use the micro-world of *Family-relations-D2* as our "common situation". As we have seen earlier, agent A´s view of this micro-world is:

father ("William", "Sylvia").	father ("Oscar", "Daphne").	(D2A)
mother ("Sylvia", "Stephen").	mother ("Daphne", "Harold").	

B´s view of this micro-world is:

parent ("William", "Sylvia").	parent ("Oscar", "Daphne").	(D2B)
parent ("Sylvia", "Stephen").	parent ("Daphne", "Harold").	
male ("William").	male ("Oscar").	
male ("Stephen").	male (" Harold").	
female ("Sylvia").	female ("Daphne").	

The concepts that are unknown to A and whose meaning is to be defined are:

parent(X,Z), male(X), female(Z).

These facts will enable the agent A to generate the required definitions.

Given these facts the inductive system will generate[3]:

```
parent (X,Z)  :- father (X,Z).      (RI1)
male (X)      :- father (X,_).      (RI2)
female (Z)    :- mother (Z,_).      (RI3)
```

The rules shown above relate B´s concepts (e.g. parent(..)) to A´s own concepts (i.e. father(..)). The new definitions enable the agent A to overcome the problem mentioned earlier. It can be verified that the goal

gfather ("William", "Stephen")

no longer fails. The solution of this goal requires rule R2B. Application of this rule generates the subgoals

parent("William",Z), male("William"), parent(Z,"Stephen"), female(Z),

all of which can be interpreted correctly thanks to the new definitions (RI1-RI3).

The application of rule RI1 to the subgoal *parent("William,Z)*, for example, will produce the subgoal *father("William",Z)*. In other words, B´s concept of *parent(..)* will be substituted by the concept of *father(..)* which is one of A´s primitive concepts.

Role of Interface Theory

Let us come back to our scenario and examine the constituents of the final theory obtained in the last section. Agent A´s theory consists of the following rules:

```
gfather(X,Y)  :- father(X,Z), father(Z,Y).                          (R1A)
gfather(X,Y)  :- parent(X,Z), male(X), parent(Z,Y), female(Z).      (R2B)
```

[3]The present version of GOLEM is unable to generate the definitions of male (X) and female (Z) shown here,

parent (X,Z) :- father (X,Z). (RI1)
male (X) :- father (X,_). (RI2)
female (Z) :- mother (Z,_). (RI3)

Rule R1A was generated by A's inductive subsystem on the basis of his own data. Rule R2B was obtained from agent B by communication. The rule was initially generated by B, and then supplied to A. Sometimes this type of learning is called "learning by being told". Agent A was spared the effort of generating the rule.

Discussion

In this paper we have described a technique of knowledge integration and the implemented system INTEG3.1. The practical results obtained with this system were rather good. The performance of the integrated theory significantly exceeded the performance of individual theories.

We believe that the technique of knowledge integration could be exploited in intelligent teaching systems (ITS) oriented towards noisy domains. In these domains several different formalizations can normally be found. These often have a similar performance and hence it is difficult to determine which formalization is right. The knowledge integration method described here enables us to overcome these problems.

The method enables us to identify those parts of student's knowledge that have attained a satisfactory level of performance. First an integrated theory is constructed on the basis of:

(1) rules in the student model,
2) in-built theory (ITS's knowledge of the domain).

If two rules have similar performance, preference is given to the rules in the student model. After the integrated theory has been obtained, one can simply see which of the student's rules have been included in the integrated theory. All the rules that have passed through may be considered "right". All the other rules (i.e. rules that have been left out) can be considered sub-optimal. As they have not been included, other rules exist (in the in-built theory) that are better.

The area of knowledge integration is relatively new and many problems are yet to be solved. Some of these issues have been addressed in the second part of this paper. It is shown that problems can arise when (a part of) agent's knowledge is transferred to another agent. The acquired definitions can simply contain concepts that are unknown to the recipient agent. These problems can, however, be overcome. We show that standard machine learning techniques can be used to generate required definitions.

Acknowledgements

This work was partly supported by Project *Ecoles* (Esprit 2 Project 3059). The author wishes to express his gratitude for this support.

The author acknowledges with gratitude the contribution of Luís Torgo in carrying out a part of the work reported here. Stephen Muggleton has collaborated with the author on the work oriented towards resolving language differences between agents and has also carried the experiments which involved GOLEM. Thanks also to Thomas Hoppe for carrying out some experiments with *ancestors* and *parents* at the Turing Institute, Glasgow, and also for a number of helpful comments.

References

1. Bond A.H. and Les Gasser (1988): Distributed Artificial Intelligence, Morgan Kaufmann.

2. Brazdil P. and Torgo L. (1990a): "Knowledge Acquisition via Knowledge Integration", in *Current Trends in Artificial Intelligence*, B. Wielinga et al. (eds.), IOS Press, Amsterdam, 1990.

3. Brazdil P. and Torgo L. (1990b): "Knowledge Integration and Learning", Working Paper, LIACC, University of Porto, 1990.

4. Brazdil, P. and Clark, P. (1990): "Learning from Imperfect Data", in *Machine Learning, Meta-Reasoning and Logics*, P. Brazdil and K.Konolige (eds.), Kluwer Academic Publishers.

5. Cestnik, B., Kononenko, I. and Bratko, I., (1987): "ASSISTANT 86 : A Knowledge-Elicitation Tool for Sophisticated Users", in *Progress in Machine Learning*, I.Bratko and N.Lavrac (eds.), Sigma Press, Wilmslow, England.

6. Clark, P. and Niblett, T. (1987): "Induction in Noisy Domains", in *Progress in Machine Learning*, I.Bratko and N.Lavrac (eds), Sigma Press, Wilmslow, England.

7. Clark, P. and Niblett, T. (1989): "The CN2 Induction Algorithm", *Machine Learning 3*, Kluwer Academic Publishers.

8. Durfee E., Lesser V.R. and Corkill D.D. (1989): "Cooperative Distributed Problem Solving", in *The Handbook of Artificial Intelligence, Volume IV*, Barr A., Cohen P.R. and Feigenbaum E.A. (eds.), Addison Wesley, 1989.

9. Janikow C.Z. (1989): "The AQ16 Inductive Learning Program: Some Experimental Results with AQ16 and Other Symbolic and Nonsymbolic Programs", Rep. of AI Center, George Mason University.

10. Morik K. (1989): "Sloppy Modeling", in *Knowledge Representation and Organization in Machine Learning*, K. Morik (ed.), Lecture Notes in AI, 347, pp. 107-134, Springer Verlag.

11. Muggleton S. and Feng C. (1990): "Efficient Induction of Logic Programs", in *Proceedings of the First Conference on Algorithmic Learning*, Tokyo, Japan, October 1990, Omsha Publ., Tokyo.

12. Murray K.S. and Porter B.W. (1989): "Controlling Search for the Consequences of New Information During Knowledge Integration", in *Proc. of 6th International Workshop on Machine Learning*, A.M. Segre (ed.), Ithaca, New York, Morgan Kaufmann.

13. Quinlan J.R. (1986): "The Effect of Noise in Concept Learning", *Machine Learning (vol. II)*, R.Michalski, J.Carbonell and T. Mitchell (eds.), Morgan Kaufmann.

14. Rada R. and Mili H. (1989): "A Knowledge Intensive Learning System for Document Retrieval", in *Knowledge Representation and Organization in Machine Learning*, K. Morik (ed.), Lecture Notes in AI, 347, pp. 65-88, Springer Verlag.

15. Schlimmer J.C. and Fisher D. (1986): "A Case Study of Incremental Concept Induction", in *Proceedings of the Fifth National Conference on Artificial Intelligence*, pp. 496-501, Morgan Kaufmann.

16. Shaw M. & Gaines B. (1989): Knowledge Acquisition: Some Foundations, Manual Methods and Future Trends, in *Proc. of Third European Workshop on Knowledge Acquisition for Knowledge-Based Systems*, J. Boose, B. Gaines and J.G. Ganascia (eds.), Paris, July 1989.

17. Utgoff P.E. (1988): "ID5: An Incremental ID3", in *Proc. of 5th International Workshop on Machine Learning*, J. Laird (ed.), Ann Arbor, Morgan Kaufmann.

18. Zhang J. and Michalski R. (1989): "Rule Optimization via SG-TRUNC Method", in *Proceedings of 4th European Working Session on Learning*, K. Morik (ed.), pp. 251-262, Pitman - Morgan Kaufmann.

Facing Hard Problems in Multi-Agent Interactions

Helder Coelho
Universidade Técnica de Lisboa, Instituto Superior de Economia e Gestão, Departamento de Matemática, 20, Rua Miguel Lupi, 2º, 1200 Lisboa and INESC, 9, Rua Alves Redol, 7º, 1000 Lisboa, Portugal

Abstract: The structure of intelligence is one of the concerns along the study of multiple agents, where their architectures may face the complexity of human-human dialogues. In fact, current advanced information systems face now major limitations, and one of them is the simple sequential question and answer structure of their interfaces. This topic concerns learning technology at large, where knowledge communication plays a key role to improve friendliness in studying environments. Along the present paper we discuss the themes concerned with governability of interactions, namely agent models, the formalism for the internal representation of the semantic content of communication acts, and the computational tractability associated with dialogue processing.

Keywords: Complexity issues, Hard problems, Knowledge communication, Multi-agents.

Introduction

What is an intelligence that it can perform the task of multiple agent interactions? What kind of theory is available for defining an intelligent agent? Recent advances in natural language interfaces (NLI) technology (e.g. speech recognition) have made it possible to build language systems that combine several desirable properties [13,16], such as user plasticity, multi-modality and response time. Despite these contributions, we know little about building a successful (true friendly) interface, and the technology is far behind the popular knowledge engineering, yet this application area is also having troubles after a first generation of systems found real problems in today´s workplace. Some believe that the lack of learnability (e.g. [20]) is one of the weak points, and others defend a joint effort in several connected subfields, such as knowledge representation, goal-driven activity, reasoning and belief maintenance. Such crossdisciplinary action is now necessary if a breakthrough towards the foundations of Artificial Intelligence (AI) is made, hoping to open a new theoretical alley around the human intellectual processes [15]. As a matter of fact, these topics can also be encountered when we focus on interactions among information and knowledge based systems (IKBS and KBS), for example (and in a smaller scale) between an Intelligent Tutoring System (ITS) and a student, and that is why we selected this particular arena as a testbed for our AI research. Ongoing work on multi-agent communication [5,6] has allowed us to identify features that are critical to the construction of microsocieties of intelligent agents, which may help to better understand how to push NLI and help the evolution of learning technologies. These societies are systems with distributed knowledge partitioned among multiple autonomous agents, each of them having the capability to interact and communicate with other autonomous entities. An agent of this sort has its own goals, capabilities, beliefs and knowledge, but no conscience at all. AI programs don´t know what they know and they are not aware of what they can do.

It is said that when progress is made difficult some search on the hard problems about thinking in AI (e.g. rationality, motivation, purpose and communication, see [8]) is necessary. Its understanding is often facilitated through the use of the proper metaphor. In the case of multiple agent situations, and even in man-machine ones [1], we believe that the metaphor is that of the interaction, covering three essential sorts, transaction, conversation and negotiation. Along the present paper, we select conversation to enlight two of its main properties: it constitutes an extended interaction over time which may involve continuity of topic and become non-linear, and it is a joint activity, with each agent contributing his share to the goal of making the interaction progress. We have identified four properties of interaction that support the conversational model of multi-agent systems, appropriate change, error correction, agent plasticity, and task structure. Some are not unique to this case and can be said to characterize other interaction modalities that can be found when, for example, we face negotiations (even in a conversation we may have negotiation of topic).

We also defend a paradigm, for building up societies of KBS within organizations, based on the process of communicating knowledge [21], which is relevant as a support of open systems architecture. But, structural definitions of KBS fail to account for the systems´ roles in enterprises, decreasing their impacts on users. To date, developing KBS has been almost described in terms of the implementation details. Such perspective is ill-suited to the analysis of organizational issues, namely those concerned with the open systems such as conflicts among and within organizations, yet these systems represent the communication, augmentation, or transfer of skills. It is interesting to observe that the same happens with ITS´s. Therefore, more research is required along this direction to clarify essential features of intelligence.

Multi-agent problems arise when several autonomous agents share a common environment (e.g. factory control, business organization, office of the future, learning and teaching in schools, building management) and they are closed associated to those AI hard problems. These problems are due to, say limited resources and shared competing goals, and can be tackled when modeling the agents and the worlds where they live and work. As a consequence, the agents have to deal with implicit and/or explicit interactions among themselves.

Finally, it is interesting to assert that those hard problems are shared with most of the mental and social disciplines of psychology, philosophy, linguistics, economics, politics, sociology and management. And, they are not isolated, depend heavily from outside AI and interact a lot among themselves.

Scope and Models

Multi-agent systems are just a case in the more general domain of Distributed Artificial Intelligence (DAI). Nowadays, AI has come of age and it is a matured scientific discipline where a computational perspective is imposed over the study of thinking. The characteristic method of mechanization is one of its constraints, and that means that some of those problems are intractable with respect to the accepted forms of mechanization. Can a view of what makes intelligence a coherent computational phenomenon be constructed? Or, the dream will consist of theory making?

The importance of most hard problems is out of discussion, because the state of the research in AI is framed by its real understanding, and this means capability to import knowledge from related fields and to proceed futher on with previous research. The parts of AI most directly affected by this absorption are the branches related with human psychology and linguistics. A good example is the work by [14] on vision. Another example is concerned with knowledge communication [21], and this implies to deal with organization theory and social sciences.

Let us consider communication in a broad sense. Natural language is not merely a vehicle for transmitting static information. Humans employ language and other modes for acting in their social environment. But, whether we speak of a human considering the effects of his words on a social setting or a machine evaluating the incremental effects of actions within a task environment, the evaluating agent must have a model to manipulate. For a system to communicate expertise, it must incorporate knowledge about the end user and how to communicate with him, as well as knowledge of the task domain. A simple solution (if feasible) would be to incorporate such user communication knowledge into the system during programming around a grammar of dialogues capable of handling nested exchanges. This trend corresponds only to extend the language ability by adding an extra and higher level of knowledge, but it is not very common nowadays as compared to the one around user models [12,24]. This approach (building a passive interface) necessitates an adequate conceptualization of the user's needs at the design stage which will not be easily modifiable. Otherwise, it would be desirable to provide agents with the capacity to dynamically profile individual users and tailor their behavior to each of them. This approach (the active interface) is characterized as providing an evolving subsystem whose task domain is managing the user dialogue based upon his model. In point of fact, there is a strong argument for pursuing interfaces that model users, in that an individual´s performance may vary significantly with characteristics of the information exchange. Such power is related with a learning machinery [4] during the transactions, in order to give a basis to evolving non-determinininistic dialogues.

Much of early work in natural language processing (NLP) was based on the presumption that the full expressiveness of a natural language could be modelled via grammar: syntax was of primary importance in communications among humans. Later on, it was discovered that communication was not limited to the surface form of a message. The senders and receivers in an exchange rely on more than grammar rules to transfer meaning. The conversants apply their knowledge (innate and acquired structures, say world models) in processing information. Conversational processes involve diverse acts, such as those of interpretation and those of inference, and depend on semantically interpreted structures (beliefs, intentions, goals and plans) and on precise contextual settings. Therefore, the success of an interaction (e.g. negotiation) is a function of the relative richness of the conversant model [3] and of the agent reasoning (via deduction, induction and abduction) power. These considerations apply directly to all communicating systems, say KBS, ITS´s, DSS´s and NSS´s, and are also important either in isolated settings or when we foresee them living in some sort of a society (real applications), such as in automated factories or high-tech buildings.

Yet, the efforts to improve the nature of artificial agents, by enhancing their architectures, are constrained by existing bounds on the modelling activity. As a matter of fact, a theoretical limitation on the prospects for true conversation settings derives from a paradox. The ability to model some agent implies a higher degree of complexity relative to the entity being modelled. This impasse introduces a dilemma for the architecture of each agent, both in terms of knowledge acquisition and interface design. In the first case, the modelling constraints a representation supporting the communication of knowledge. In the second case, the dilemma affects the act of communication itself, in what relates taking initiatives, controlling the conversation, and deciding the course of the task/problem solving process. Whether it be fixed (passive) or dynamic (active), the user model implicit in an agent determines the range of possible consultative conversation modes.

Settings

Multi-agent conversations can be studied in diverse settings with variable complexity, and where system flexibility is a key item. For example, let us consider an economic system as a collection of agents (enterprises and consumers) and a machinery for the allocation of goods to agents, which may take actions (e.g. messages to be sent to that machinery), such as:

action(agent,type, constraints)

Of course, the spectrum of these messages is limited to those allowed by the language of each agent. Also, we can represent these actions as facts and the system environment as an agent.

Consider now the case of a USA insurance agent, who must work on a variety of policies ranging from workers compensation to fire and property claims. Each of these policy types utilizes different knowledge resources. For workers compensation there are volumes of state regulations; for fire claims there are ISO rates; and for property claims there are flood zone specifications, Dunn & Bradstreet ratings, etc. Here, the bottleneck is upon the variety of required knowledge and data.

Finally, an office can be depicted as a collection of agents carrying out tasks (task-agent perspective) using a variety of means and communicating about these tasks in diverse media. Here, work is characterized as a structure of individual tasks, each one carried out in order to achieve specified results (to satisfy goals). An agent in the office can enter in dialogues with other people to help determine the tasks to be done, to assign tasks and coordinate between them, and to deal with problems that come up in executing them [26].

These three examples support the organizational viewpoint, so important to approach interactions in microsocieties, the confluence of multiple knowledge channels within an enterprise, and we may imagine KBS, ITS and DSS behind those agents to collect, analyze, interpret, and disseminate information and knowledge throughout the workforce, like a specific level of management. As IKBS penetrate all areas of an enterprise, there will rise a need to merge the various knowledge channels, or to let those agents behave as in society. The first alternative is one of the actual computing trends (the integration one), where the emphasis is on facilitation of individuals over facilitation of the group. The second alternative is toward computer-supported cooperative work, and it is based on the idea that intellectual effort is largely cooperative in nature [25].

The transition from isolated to cooperative work styles is difficult in real life, because it seems to contradict tacit conceptualizations of workers. Recently, experiments in innovative enterprises aimed to seize technology and gain a competitive edge proved that it is not always true that work teams develop notions of individual autonomy rather than intended cooperation preparatory to the social reorganization of work. Researchers have begun to examine how to facilitate cooperative work over electronic media using KBS, and therefore it is important to study organizational and societal aspects of automating complex mental labor using knowledge based technology. On account of this, it is urgent to face the hard problems in multi-agent interactions.

Communicating Knowledge

Knowledge is a commodity that can be traded, remembered, forgotten, discovered, exchanged, taken, or left. In this view it makes sense to speak of pieces of knowledge and to conceive of these pieces (structures) as being transferable, either among modules of an advanced information system or among systems themselves (say in the office of the future composed of integrated networks of independent agents, both humans and automated, or even in a school between a student and an ITS). The idea of control in communication is therefore associated to the organization of those elements (e.g. structures such as agenda, committee or society), and it became more important because KBS are no longer developed and inserted only into isolated functions.

Users of IT´s are increasing and demanding better usability in computer systems. The interface and human factors issues which affect conventional applications are also pertinent to KBS. Experience from pioneering work in USA indicates that development of the user interface can be expected to account for 50% of the system development time, but the kind of communication obtained has been less than satisfactory. Addressing such issues entails blending KBS with graphics, user-friendly interfaces, and distributed environments (multimedia contexts), but the final results lacked yet internal knowledge and self-awareness, say natural intelligence.

A human conversation involves a dynamic, non-linear and nested interplay (a kind of a dance according to Winograd), with talkers interrupting each other, correcting themselves, and making use of various speech effects. Turn-taking is controlled by a mutually-understood protocol, where contributions are well known, such as end his turn, give his conversation partner a chance to speak, ask for clarification from the partner, confirm what was said by the partner, and etc. But, unconstrained human-human interaction is not the most accurate model for human-computer or agent-agent interaction. Yet, other social models have been adopted, such as the commercial marketplace (where individuals negotiate with one another for the performance of services and the delivery of goods) and the scientific community. From the point of view of system's architecture, other ideas were put forward such as the committee (PSK: agenda plus blackboard) and the society, but no definite solutions have been met so far. Also, experiments in mixing approaches regarding communication methodologies, such as adopting shared global memory and message passing: shared memory communication for process working locally (or working as a team on one subproblem) plus memory passing for communications between processors or teams of agents. A compromise has been tested: one blackboard being implemented with object-oriented languages or several blackboards being integrated via message passing.

Some experiments with hypotheses about the nature of intelligence habe been pursued [6] in the quest of a better understanding of knowledge communicating systems, either in constrained settings like those involving ITS's or in more open situations (microsocieties) within the idea of an intelligent building. In the first direction, we may find research along the aim of modelling human users (students or civil servants), and consequently also other agents (systems). Along the second direction, it was designed and implemented a model of the belief system of an autonomous agent in a multi-agent environment, trying to formalize the connection between communication among the agents and the changes that take place on account of that. The analysis of the limitations of that implementation led to the definition of the model, as it was presented in [9].

These experiments have been conducted towards agent modelling, and not for defining the society from a global view. The research stressed the logics of knowledge/belief (limited reasoning ability, power to relate communication with beliefs), the definition of a model for an autonomous agent (classes of agents and inheritance forms, communication forms, and components of an agent and its relations), and the forms of conflict resolution (criteria, selection of cause axiom, and belief revision operation). Work already in progress is concerned with the suitable theory capable to embed that experimentation, but no coverage of intentions was taken into account till now. The research carried by [7], around a theory of rational interaction and communication by showing how agents can have interlocking commitments, is still in background.

Order on Problems

Complex task and problem solving systems differ not only in the degree to which they represent open or closed domains, but also in the interactional styles, ie. traditional modes (transactional, consultive, commentary and supervisory) versus human-like conversations. Complexity means different things, and we may endeavour descriptive complexity and computational complexity. A conversation may be quite complex in terms of the way its pieces are put together, and yet execute very slow, so that its computational complexity is high.

Anthropomorphic imagery has been for a while a kind of last frontier where we can find the limits of our ambitions, and in a way a support to describe the function and architecture of the intelligent programs (the project of an artificial creature has been a dream from the start of AI in 1956). Take the example of a society of human beings. Suppose you want to design an artificial creature able to behave natural. One of the first things you may pick up to define the creature as an intelligent entity is the capability to be communicated with. Such an aim is hard to tackle and involve serious problems, which are not separated and isolated in an ivory tower. For example, conversation maintenance activities invoke the need to understand the real features of an intelligent interlocutor and the conversational other. The interplay (temporal behavior) along any conversation changes from order (periodic and predictable) to chaos (random), and then it has a nature characterized by:

- time evolution with a complex pattern
- dynamic change of data
- number of possibilities to be ruled out
- quantity of effort to rule one possibility
- resemblant contingency

Consequently, the structure of the conversation can be complex with openings and closings to subdialogues and changes of topic by any agent in presence (namely, during the negotiation of the central topic), with shifts in tacking control of the flow, and with complex subdialogues to clarify or solve specific issues. Yet, dialogue government of major implemented systems is normally ruled out by the sequential search of the control rules.

How can an agent´s architecture face such complexity? Which hard problems can we expect in order to attain communication easiness or a resemblance of intelligence, ie. that ability to adapt appropriately in a situation even when the agent is ignorant of most of the information keen to the situation? How can a program embody descriptions (theories) about particular computations? In the quest for answers, suddenly, we reach the foundations of AI, where the big problems are not yet solved and no partial order is known on subject matters. From the group of ten (representation, decoding, inference, control of the combinatorial explosion, indexing, prediction and recovery, dynamic modification, generalization, curiosity, and creativity) put forward by [18], the seven ones (rationality, motivation, growth, perception, purpose, representation and communication) selected by [8] or the four ones (attention, self consciousness, control and intention) proposed once by Johnson-Laird, we can focus on the following ones because they are closely related and interwined:

```
                                  Big Problems:

         Rationality                 Growth                    Communication
              |                         |                             |
|-----------------------------| |-------------------------------------| |-------------------------------------|
Consistency Completness Adaptation Improvement Learning Coordination Control Consistency

          Purpose                                               Representation
             |                                                         |
    |-----------------------|                                   |---------------------
Meaning                 Design                              Imagination
```

Figure 1 - Big problems for big talk

What about the relations among these problems? Is there any order, hierarchy or heterarchy, to attack them? Are they structured? Can we stay happy by facing one of them, or are we forced to think simultaneously about all or some of them? Take the subproblem of control from the communication big problem. One of the standard and traditional approaches is the so-called blackboard, where a dialogue manager cohexist with the user modeling and the dialogue context experts, and the interaction among KBS must go through the dialogue manager. On the opposite side, the emergent and modern approach is supported on the rigorous distribution of knowledge among individual and autonomous agents. The interaction of those agents, in any of the approaches in reference, is governed by a specific dialogue capability (viewed as centralized or as distributed in all agents), and the communication between them adopts a common language to represent the various sets of semantics (the meaning of interaction). Compare now the big problem of communication to the one of rationality: here we can find difficulties around consistency and completeness, and where computational complexity is a factor of limited rationality.

These big problems have been envisaged by AI research almost in isolation, by adopting the cartesian methodology of dividing and conquering. Such an attitude, yet pragmatic, has several drawbacks, for example the avoidance of complexity by looking to local aspects in stead of global ones. This is the case of communication at large, where the aspects of rationality, growth, purpose and representation are interwined.

Need for (better) Solutions

We don´t think and converse linearly. So, any agent capable of multiple interactions requires a modelling framework that looks at dialogues as something more than discrete (and deterministic) question-answer pairs embedded in a cooperative process.

An interaction can be like a jigsaw puzzle where one has to assemble the parts of a structure in a particular way. Such point of view involve searching through a finite, but extremely large, structured set of possible patterns or arrangements, in order to find one that satisfies a stated set of conditions. Within this sort of puzzle there is the possibility of combinatorial explosion, and a massive amount of computation may be encountered unless some sublety is adopted in searching through the space of possible solutions. But, apart of combinatorics, when we study interactions we may face also complexity and randomness. And, that is why for a long time friendly and flexible interfaces have been so difficult to design and engineer.

The transition from systems that focus on syntactic-semantic phenomena to pragmatic-based systems [22] calls for 1) a theory of interactions, 2) a more flexible architecture rich in models, and even 3) a robust knowledge representation.

Complexity must be faced by a framework where we can plug in theories solving that complexity puzzle by assembling the pieces of the overall (global) theory. Such an effort pressuposes that theories need to communicate among them and to fit in. We envisage a theory of more or less satisfied expectations (Schank applied the idea of expectation to story understanding [19] by mixing a conceptual parser with a syntactical parser: prediction of a word, its meaning and place in the sentence) concerning how to organize and find the intentions and beliefs of each agent, based upon the fact that an interaction is attached to specific patterns (e.g. circular, elliptical, spiral, and so on), and according to possible interlocutor reactions. Within this theory, agents have the possibility to explore the n-dimensional space of their mental states, searching for dialogue deviations along the continuum from probability to surprise. These deviations arise from inconsistencies between communicating acts and the dialogue considered as a coherent plan, and involve at least three dimensions, the intentional, the attentional and the one concerned with the beliefs of each agent [11]. Agents expect communicative actions from other agents in the context of their interactions. Those unexpected reactions are inevitable in interactions where the participants are independent agents with their own goals and differing degrees of knowledge about each other and the subject under discussion. The intentions of each agent must be part of a structure that reflects the state of the plan of the interaction from the agent's point of view (beliefs). Expectations may be represented by attaching acts to intentions for each agent, and later on organized as a function of the attentional state.

A flexible agent architecture requires that all components be experts in some function and able to converse among themselves in order to cooperate in task solving, and to face conflicting goals and knowledge bases contradictory with others. The expectactions are managed by a planning module which drives the interaction and maintains a structure of the agent's intentions, while reacting to the other agent's intentions and depending on its beliefs. This means that different knowledge structures are necessary to reflect the state of an interaction, namely those attached to the dialogue controller, the context expert, the user modelling expert, the semantic expert, the interface expert, the domain expert, and obviously the interaction revision module. A variant of this architecture is being implemented in the Esprit II project 2474 (MMI2). Picking up, as an example, the dialogue controller, we can foresee the effect of interaction rules governing the pre-closing sequence: segmenting the dialogue into coherent units, where the interaction is related only with one topic. The rules create a global dialogue structure, yet they only act within the local context, by constraining the user (any other agent) to keep to the topic and avoid possibly confusing diversions.

Concerning the knowledge representation, the most suitable approach needs to be logic-based and object-oriented, allowing a strong communication environment and the visual examination of the agent's behaviour. Formalizing standard practices cover division of work, sharing and collaboration of information needed for tasks, and communicating about results, but they are impotent to take into account the unfolding of interactions, namely when deviations occur. Hence the representation of the state of interaction should reflect the structure of the whole interaction: keeping track of past history (chart of the dialogue) and anticipating the future forms that each agent expects from the other in the context of the current interaction. This means the adoption of knowledge structures able to cover not only the task plan, but also the interaction plan (enclosing the knowledge about the communication) and the pragmatic attachments (Grosz defends a triad of segments, purposes and focus space). Behind this line of research stands the theme of interaction microdynamics, capable to support the government of the global dialogue structure and the negotiations around the opportunity to shift topic that arises at junctions (openings and pre-closings à la Sacks and Schegloff [17]), where participants agree to cease the interaction or continue with a fresh topic. Another requirement of the representation formalism is the necessity that explanation be supported sufficiently to make it as natural as possible. This implies pragmatic reasoning and abduction machinery, which may be also used for conversation diagnosis and for repairing communication failures.

Conclusion

Knowledge communication, studied along the trend of multi-agent interactions, is relevant to enlight the architecture of the different parts of the interaction model of any advanced information system (e.g. ITS). However, its subject is at the interface among several disciplines, such as theoretical computer science, mathematics, computational linguistics and artificial intelligence, and this means a set of hard problems to tackle. Bringing more complexity to these problems is just a way to make them real, and that is the modern trend for AI.

Along this paper we defend the need to recapture the spirit of adventure, in order to understand the complexity of interactive communication, and to break down the current deterministic system organizations around separated models. In point of fact, exploratory learning done with ITS is heavily dependent on system´s flexibility, which is a function of more improvements. We believe this direction is now possible by separating the epistemological difficulties, on classifying and accessing the knowledge which users (students) may need, from the interactional problem of providing the means for those users explore fully the knowledge of the system, but by entangling this last problem with user modelling. The amalgamation between these two so-called components in determinant for a new generation of more advanced systems.

References

1. Coelho, H.: A Program Conversing in Portuguese Providing a Library Service. Ph. D. Thesis University of Edinburgh, 1979.

2. Coelho, H.: A Formalism for the Structural Analysis of Dialogues. Proceedings of the 9th International Conference on Computational Linguistics COLING82, Prague, July 5-10, 1982, Ján Horecky (ed.), North-Holland, 1983.

3. Coelho, H. and Lopes, G.P.: Planning, Natural Language Conversations and Logic. Proceedings of the International Conference on Artificial Intelligence Methodology, Systems and Applications, Varna, September, 1984.

4. Coelho, H., Lopes, G. P. and Viccari, R. M.: Models for Grammar Evolution. Proceedings of the 6th Brazilian Symposium on Artificial Intelligence, Rio de Janeiro, November 1989.

5. Coelho, H.: Zooming upon Microsocieties of Autonomous Agents. Proceedings of the 3rd School on AI Applications in Robotics (IFTR), Warsaw, April 1990, IFTR, 1990.

6. Coelho, H.: Understanding Multi-Agent Interactions, INESC Research and Development Journal, Vol.1, No.2, 1990.

7. Cohen, P. R. and Levesque, H.J.: Intention = Choice + Commitment. Proceedings of the Sixth American Conference on Artificial Intelligence (AAAI87), Seattle, June 1987.

8. Doyle, J.: Big Problems for Artificial Intelligence, AI Magazine, 9, 1, Spring, pp. , 1988.

9. Gaspar, G. and Coelho, H.: The Role of Self and World Consciousness During Dialogues in a Society of Agents. FCUL Working Report, 1989.

10. Gaspar, G.: Communication and Belief Changes in a Society of Agents. Proceedings of the Fifth Rocky Mountain Conference on Artificial Intelligence (RMCAI-90), Pragmatics in AI, Las Cruces, June 1990.

11. Gorsz, B.: Collaborative Planning for Discourse. Proceedings of the 9th European Conference on Artificial Intelligence (ECAI90), Stockholm, August 1990), Pitman, 1990.

12. Kobsa, A. and Wahlster, W. (eds.): User Models in Dialog Systems. Springer-Verlag, 1989.

13. Lee, K.-F.: Automatic Speech Recognition. The Development of the SPHINX. Kluwer Academic Publishers, 1989.

14. Marr, D.A.: A Computational Investigation into the Human Representation and Processing of Visual Information. MIT Press, 1982.

15. Partridge, D. and Wilks, Y.: The Foundations of Artificial Intelligence. Cambridge University Press, 1990.

16. Rudnicky, A.I. and Hauptmann, A.G.: Conversational Interaction with Speech Systems, Research Report CMU-CS-89-203, Carnegie Mellon University, 1989.

17. Sacks, H., Schegloff, E.A. and Jefferson, G.: A Simplest Semantics for the Organization of Turn-Taking for Conversation. Language 50 (4), pp. 696-736, 1974.

18. Schank, R.C.: Conceptual Information Processing. North-Holland, 1975.

19. Schank, R.C. and Riesbeck, C.K.: Inside Computer Understanding. Five Programs plus Miniatures. Lawrence Erlbaum, 1981.

20. Schank, R.C.: What is AI Anyway? AI Magazine, 8, 4, pp. 59-65, 1987.

21. Sernadas, C., Coelho, H. and Gaspar, G.: Communicating Knowledge Systems, Big Talk among Small Systems. Applied Artificial Intelligence, Vol.1, Nos. 3-4, 1987.

22. Viccari, R.M., Coelho, H. and Costa, E.: Pragmatic Attachments Devices for Conversation with Tutors. Applied Artificial Intelligence, Vol. 2, Nos. 3-4, 1988.

23. Viccari, R.M.: An Intelligent Tutor for Logic Programming - Idealization, Design, and Development (in Portuguese). Ph.D. Thesis University of Coimbra, 1989.

24. Wenger, E.: Artificial Intelligence and Tutoring Systems. Morgan Kaufman, 1987.

25. Winograd, T.: Where the Action is. Byte, December, 1988.

26. Winograd, T.: Can Office Technology Support Office Dialogues? Proceedings of the IFIP 11 World Computer Congress, Information Processing 89, San Francisco, August September 1989, G.X. Reiter (ed.), pp. 381-387, North-Holland, 1989.

List of Contributors

Michael Baker studied philosophy and psychology at Van Mildert College, University of Durham (UK), where he was awarded a first-class degree in 1983. He also studied musical composition and performance at Huddersfield Polytechnic (UK), Department of Music. In 1990, he was awarded a Ph.D. in Cognitive Science from the Open University (UK), where he conducted research in the Centre for Information Technology in Education, directed by Dr. Mark Elsom-Cook and Professor Tim O'Shea. His doctoral research concerned cognitive models for perception of musical structures, and models for generation of tutorial dialogues in Intelligent Tutoring Systems. He is currently a researcher in cognitive psychology at the Centre National de la Recherche Scientifique, working at the IRPEACS laboratory (Lyon, France). His research interests include cognitive models for generation and comprehension of dialogue, the relationships between reasoning, explanation and dialogue processes, and the role of negotiation and conflict in tutorial dialogues.

Pavel Brazdil is Associate Professor at the Faculty of Economics of the University of Oporto (Portugal). He received his Ph.D. from the Department of Artificial Intelligence, University of Edinburgh (UK), in 1981. His main research interests are in the domains of transfer of knowledge, knowledge integration and multi-agent learning, and evaluation of learning algorithms. That research is done in collaboration with other groups in the context of European projects. He had published several papers in books and conference proceedings and was co-editor of *Machine Learning, Meta-Reasoning and Logics* (Kluwer Academic Press, 1990). He was the Program Chair of the First Portuguese Conference on Artificial Intelligence (EPIA-86, Oporto) and of the Workshop on Machine Learning, Meta-Reasoning and Logics (Sesimbra, Portugal, 1988) and also Local Chair of the European Working Session on Learning (EWSL-90, Oporto). He was member of the Program Committee and referee of several international conferences.

Alison Cawsey is currently a research fellow at the Department of Artificial Intelligence, University of Edinburgh (UK) working on computational models of dialogue. Her Ph.D. (also completed at the University of Edindurgh) was concerned with the computer generation of interactive explanations.

Marta Cialdea graduated in Philosophy, with a curriculum in logic, at the University of Rome (Italy) later obtained a Ph.D. in Computer Science at the University Paul Sabatier of Toulouse (France), where she worked on automatic deduction procedures for modal logics. At present, she is involved in a project on Artificial Intelligence and Education, carried on by the Dipartimento di Informatica e Sistemistica, University of Rome. She has published various papers in international journals and conferences, both on modal proof procedures and on intelligent tutoring topics.

William Clancey is a Senior Research Scientist at the Institute for Research on Learning (California). He received a Ph.D. in Computer Science at Stanford University in 1979. He was involved in expert system research from the early days of the MYCIN Project in 1975, developing programs for explanation, the critiquing method of consultation tutorial discourse management, student modeling, and failure-driven learning. Currently he is Editor-in-Chief of The AAAI Press and a Senior Editor of Cognitive Science. Clancey also has considerable experience in the practical application of AI technology as a co-founder of Teknowledge, Inc. (1981) and recent founder and member of the Board of Directors of ModernSoft, Inc. (1989). Clancey holds a patent entitled "Knowledge-Based Tutor", a design for interactive, case-based probing relevant to both teaching and knowledge acquisition.

Helder Coelho graduated in Electrical Engineering at the Lisbon Institute of Technology (Portugal) in 1968 and obtained his Ph.D. in Artificial Intelligence at the University of Edinburgh (UK) in 1980. He was attached as a scientist to the National Laboratory for Civil Engineering for 16 years, where Portuguese AI was founded. His main interests are connected to natural language understanding and knowledge engineering within the logic programming paradigm. Since 1990 he has been a full professor for Artificial Intelligence at the Department of Mathematics in the Faculty of Economics and Management, Technical University of Lisbon, and leader of the AI project at INESC.

Ernesto Costa is Associate Professor at the Department of Electronic Engineering of the University of Coimbra (Portugal). He received a 3rd-cycle Thesis in Computing Science from the University Pierre et Marie Curie (Paris, France) in 1981. He also received a Ph.D. in Electronic Engineering (speciality Computing Science) from the University of Coimbra (Portugal) in 1985. Currently he is the Head of the Artificial Intelligence Group, Department of Electronic Engineering, University of Coimbra. His main research interests are in the areas of machine learning, real-time expert systems and applications of artificial intelligence to education. He has participate in several projects and published several papers in journals and in proceedings of conferences.

Pierre Dillenbourg is research assistant at TECFA, University of Geneva, Switzerland. His research activities focus on the impact of artificial intelligence on education. He was formerly research assistant at the universities of Mons (Belgium), Lancaster (UK), and Brussels (Belgium). He has conducted projects on self-improving tutoring systems and human-computer collaborative learning.

João Pavão Martins is Associate Professor of Computer Science at Instituto Superior Técnico (Technical University of Lisbon, Portugal). He received a Ph.D. in Artificial Intelligence from the State University of New York at Buffalo (USA) in 1983. His main research interests are in the area of Belief Systems. He participate in several ESPRIT projects. He published the book "Introduction to Computer Science Using Pascal" (Wadsworth Publishing Co.) and was co-editor of two others. He has published several papers in journals and proceedings of conferences.

Ramon López de Mántaras studied Artificial Intelligence at the University of California Berkeley (UCB), where he obtained a Master of Science degree, after a "Doctorat de 3ème Cycle" from the Université Paul Sabatier of Toulouse (France). He also holds a Doctorate in Computer Science from the Polytechnical University of Barcelona He was a researcher at the Electronics Research Laboratory at UCB working with Prof. Zadeh. Then he joined the Computer Science Department of the Polytechnical University of Barcelona where he became Associate Professor. In 1986 he was Visiting Full Professor at Université Pierre et Marie Curie of Paris. Currently he is Research Professor of the CSIC and Head of the AI Group of the Centre of Advanced Studies, Blanes, Spain, which he founded in 1985 and now has a staff of 18 researchers. The Group is engaged in fundamental research in expert systems and learning, participating in several ESPRIT projects as well as research projects sponsored by the Spanish government.

Gordon McCalla is a Professor of Computational Science at the University of Saskatchewan, Canada, and director of the Laboratory for Advanced Research in Intelligent Educational Systems (ARIES). He completed his B.Sc. degree with Honours in Mathematical-Statics in 1968 and his M.Sc. degree in Computing Science in 1970, both at the University of British Columbia, Canada, where his Ph.D. was awarded in 1977. His research for both his M.Sc. and Ph.D. degrees investigated knowledge representation issues for natural language understanding. Since 1977 his research interests have expanded to encompass work in dynamic planning, and since 1980 to include a growing involvement in the area of artificial intelligence and education.

Patrick Mendelsohn is professor at the University of Geneva (Switzerland). He is director of TECFA, the educational technology department. As experimental psychologist, he undertook intensive research on human memory in Grenoble (France). He is also author of several studies on the cognitive effects of programming with LOGO.

Jacobijn Sandberg majored in Psychology in 1982. Since then she has been working in Intelligent Teaching Systems, initially at the University of Utrecht, The Netherlands, where she was involved in the development of a program for teaching elementary mathematical problem solving. Presently she works at the University of Amsterdam where she is mainly participating in European research projects partly funded by the European Community (ESPRIT and DELTA). For ESPRIT she has collaborated with Joost Breuker and Radboud Winkels on EUROHELP (ESPRIT Project P280). The aim of EUROHELP was to develop a Help System Shell. For DELTA she worked on a project on learning system standardization (LEAST). She is working on a methodology project funded by the University of Amsterdam which focuses on the development of a methodology for Intelligent Tutoring Systems (MIOS).

John Self is a Reader in Computing at the University of Lancaster (UK). He has produced four books on artificial intelligence and education, most recently "Artificial Intelligence and Human Learning: Intelligent Computer-Aided Instruction" (Chapman and Hall, 1988). He is co-editor of the Journal of Artificial Intelligence in Education. At the moment he is involved in two projects funded by the European Economic Community under the DELTA programme, both concerned with learner modelling.

M. Felisa Verdejo is Professor at the Computer Science Department of the Technical University of Cataluña (LSI-UPC), Spain. She received a 3rd-cycle Thesis in Computer Science from the Université Pierre et Marie Curie (Paris, France) in 1976. She also received a Ph.D. in Sciences at the Complutense University, Madrid, Spain, in 1981. She has been the Head of the Artificial Intelligence Section at LSI-UPC since 1987. Her main research interests are in the areas of knowledge representation, computational linguistics, programming methodology and applications of artificial intelligence to education. She participates in national and European projects, and has published in different journals, conferences and books.

Martial Vivet is Professor of Computer Science at the University of Maine in Le Mans, France. He received a Ph.D. (French "State Thesis") in 1984 for his work on CAMELIA, a knowledge based problem solver for theorem proving and algebraic manipulations. Currently his research activity is centered around the applications of artificial intelligence to educational software. He leads a project that aims is to design an Intelligent Tutoring System shell by reusing the KEPLER shell. He is involved in several European projects (COMETT and DELTA). He was the Chairman of the 2nd European Seminar on ITSs, Le Mans, October 1988.

Yorick Wilks is Director of the Computing Research Laboratory at New Mexico State University, USA, a center of excellence for research in artificial intelligence and its applications. He received his doctorate from Cambridge University (UK) in 1968 for work in computer programs that understand written English in terms of a theory later called preference semantics: the claim that language is to be understood by means of a search for semantic "gists", combined with a coherence function over such structures that minimises effort in the analyser. This has continued as the focus of his work, and has applications in the areas of machine translation, the use of English as a "front end" for users of data bases, and the computation of belief structures. He was Professor of Computer Science and Linguistics at the University of Essex (UK) before moving to New Mexico. He has published five books in that area of artificial intelligence and numerous articles.

Radboud Winkels (1959) studied psychology at the University of Amsterdam in the Netherlands. In April 1987 he received his M.Sc. (cum laude) in Artificial Intelligence, and since then has worked in the Department of Social Science Informatics and the Department of Computer Science and Law of that university. His main interest is in the field of AI and education. Winkels expects to finish his Ph.D. thesis in the spring of 1991. Major projects he has been involved in are: the ESPRIT project EUROHELP, aimed at the construction of a shell for building Intelligent Help Systems for interactive computer programs, and the Intelligent Interactive Video project, a national project that resulted in an intelligent coaching system for physiotherapeutic diagnosis called the FysioDisc system.

Subject Index

NATO ASI Series F

Including Special Programmes on Sensory Systems for Robotic Control (ROB) and on Advanced Educational Technology (AET)

Vol. 64: Sensory Robotics for the Handling of Limp Materials. Edited by P. M. Taylor. IX, 343 pages. 1990. *(ROB)*

Vol. 65: Mapping and Spatial Modelling for Navigation. Edited by L. F. Pau. VIII, 357 pages. 1990. *(ROB)*

Vol. 66: Sensor-Based Robots: Algorithms and Architectures. Edited by C. S. G. Lee. X, 285 pages. 1991. *(ROB)*

Vol. 67: Designing Hypermedia for Learning. Edited by D. H. Jonassen and H. Mandl. XXV, 457 pages. 1990. *(AET)*

Vol. 68: Neurocomputing. Algorithms, Architectures and Applications. Edited by F. Fogelman Soulié and J. Hérault. XI, 455 pages. 1990.

Vol. 69: Real-Time Integration Methods for Mechanical System Simulation. Edited by E. J. Haug and R. C. Deyo. VIII, 352 pages. 1991.

Vol. 70: Numerical Linear Algebra, Digital Signal Processing and Parallel Algorithms. Edited by G. H. Golub and P. Van Dooren. XIII, 729 pages. 1991.

Vol. 71: Expert Systems and Robotics. Edited by T. Jordanides and B.Torby. XII, 744 pages. 1991.

Vol. 72: High-Capacity Local and Metropolitan Area Networks. Architecture and Performance Issues. Edited by G. Pujolle. X, 536 pages. 1991.

Vol. 73: Automation and Systems Issues in Air Traffic Control. Edited by J. A. Wise, V. D. Hopkin and M. L. Smith. XIX, 594 pages. 1991.

Vol. 74: Picture Archiving and Communication Systems (PACS) in Medicine. Edited by H. K. Huang, O. Ratib, A. R. Bakker and G. Witte. XI, 438 pages. 1991.

Vol. 75: Speech Recognition and Understanding. Recent Advances, Trends and Applications. Edited by P. Laface and Renato De Mori. XI, 559 pages. 1991.

Vol. 76: Multimedia Interface Design in Education. Edited by A. D. N. Edwards and S. Holland. XIV, 216 pages. 1992. *(AET)*

Vol. 77: Computer Algorithms for Solving Linear Algebraic Equations. The State of the Art. Edited by E. Spedicato. VIII, 352 pages. 1991.

Vol. 78: Integrating Advanced Technology into Technology Education. Edited by M. Hacker, A. Gordon and M. de Vries. VIII, 185 pages. 1991. *(AET)*

Vol. 79: Logic, Algebra, and Computation. Edited by F. L. Bauer. VII, 485 pages. 1991.

Vol. 80: Intelligent Tutoring Systems for Foreign Language Learning. Edited by M. L. Swartz and M. Yazdani. IX, 347 pages. 1992. *(AET)*

Vol. 81: Cognitive Tools for Learning. Edited by P. A. M. Kommers, D. H. Jonassen and J. T. Mayes. X, 278 pages. 1992. *(AET)*

Vol. 82: Combinatorial Optimization. New Frontiers in Theory and Practice. Edited by M. Akgül, H. W. Hamacher and S. Tüfekçi. XI, 334 pages. 1992.

Vol. 83: Active Perception and Robot Vision. Edited by A. K. Sood and H. Wechsler. IX, 756 pages. 1992.

NATO ASI Series F

Including Special Programmes on Sensory Systems for Robotic Control (ROB) and on Advanced Educational Technology (AET)

Vol. 84: Computer-Based Learning Environments and Problem Solving. Edited by E. De Corte, M. C. Linn, H. Mandl and L. Verschaffel. XVI, 488 pages. 1992. *(AET)*

Vol. 85: Adaptive Learning Environments. Foundations and Frontiers. Edited by M. Jones and P. H. Winne. VIII, 408 pages. 1992. *(AET)*

Vol. 86: Intelligent Learning Environments and Knowledge Acquisition in Physics. Edited by A. Tiberghien and H. Mandl. VIII, 285 pages. 1992. *(AET)*

Vol. 87: Cognitive Modelling and Interactive Environments. Edited by F. L. Engel, D. G. Bouwhuis, T. Bösser and G. d'Ydewalle. IX, 311 pages. 1992. *(AET)*

Vol. 88: Programming and Mathematical Method. Edited by M. Broy. VIII, 428 pages. 1992.

Vol. 89: Mathematical Problem Solving and New Information Technologies. Edited by J. P. Ponte, J. F. Matos, J. M. Matos and D. Fernandes. XV, 346 pages. 1992. *(AET)*

Vol. 90: Collaborative Learning Through Computer Conferencing. Edited by A. R. Kaye. X, 260 pages. 1992. *(AET)*

Vol. 91: New Directions for Intelligent Tutoring Systems. Edited by E. Costa. X, 296 pages. 1992. *(AET)*

MIX
Papier aus verantwortungsvollen Quellen
Paper from responsible sources
FSC® C105338
FSC
www.fsc.org

If you have any concerns about our products,
you can contact us on
ProductSafety@springernature.com

In case Publisher is established outside the EU,
the EU authorized representative is:
Springer Nature Customer Service Center GmbH
Europaplatz 3, 69115 Heidelberg, Germany

Printed by Libri Plureos GmbH
in Hamburg, Germany